A THEOLOGY (
BUILT ENVIRO

C000179804

Tim Gorringe's is the first book to reflect theologically on the built environment as a whole. Drawing on a wide range of both theological and social-scientific sources, Professor Gorringe explores Christianity in its urban settings, focusing on the use of space, design, architecture and town planning to make a theological critique. After considering the divine grounding of constructed space, he looks at the ownership of land, the issues of housing, town and country, and the city, and then considers the built environment in terms of community and art. The book concludes with two chapters that set the whole within the framework of the environmental crisis and asks what directions the Church should be looking for in building for the future. This unique book will challenge not only theologians, ethicists and sociologists of religion but also church teachers and professionals.

TIM GORRINGE is Professor of Theological Studies at Exeter University. He is the author of many books including *God's Just Vengeance* (Cambridge University Press, 1996), and *Karl Barth: Against Hegemony* (Oxford University Press, 1999).

A THEOLOGY OF THE BUILT ENVIRONMENT

Justice, Empowerment, Redemption

T. J. GORRINGE

PUBLISHED BY THE PRESS SYNDICATE OF THE UNIVERSITY OF CAMBRIDGE
The Pitt Building, Trumpington Street, Cambridge, United Kingdom

CAMBRIDGE UNIVERSITY PRESS
The Edinburgh Building, Cambridge CB2 2RU, UK
40 West 20th Street, New York, NY 10011-4211, USA
477 Williamstown Road, Port Melbourne, VIC 3207, Australia
Ruiz de Alarcón 13, 28014 Madrid, Spain
Dock House, The Waterfront, Cape Town 8001, South Africa

http://www.cambridge.org

First published 2002

Printed in the United Kingdom at the University Press, Cambridge

Typeface Baskerville Monotype 11 /12.5 pt   *System* LaTeX 2$_\varepsilon$ [TB]

A catalogue record for this book is available from the British Library

Library of Congress Cataloguing in Publication data

ISBN 0 521 81465 0 hardback
ISBN 0 521 89144 2 paperback

for
Ruth and Mo

Would that all the Lord's people were prophets
Numbers 11.29

Contents

Preface

For nearly a millennium and a half after Aristotle, economics was understood as a sub discipline of ethics. In the nineteenth century this connection was severed, with disastrous consequences for both people and planet from which we are only just beginning to retrieve ourselves. The case was not so bad for architecture and town planning, though even here brutalist and technocratic understandings of the human spread their poison almost everywhere. Wittingly or unwittingly every design for council estates, every barrio, every skyscraper, every out of town supermarket, expresses a view of the human, embodies an ethic. As I have noted in another context, ethics is the conversation of the human race about its common project, about where it is going and why it wants to go there. There are life affirming, but there have also been many life denying, ethical systems. Recognising this, the authors of Deuteronomy called their fellow countrymen to choose between two ways, a way of life and a way of death. We know only too well that there are ways of life and of death in the built environment.

Though they certainly did not get everything right, the authors of Deuteronomy took their stand on belief in the liberating power of the God of life. Five hundred years after they wrote Jesus of Nazareth endorsed that stand. Reflecting on what he stood for, John put into his mouth the words: 'I am come that they may have life, and have it in all its fullness.' Christianity, and therefore theology, has to be concerned with architecture and town planning because it seeks life in all its fullness.

No theology can dialogue solely with its own tradition, solely with other theologians. I have learned hugely from John Turner, Colin Ward, Nicholas Habraken, Christopher Day, David Harvey, whose class on Capital I was part of in Oxford, Richard Sennett, Peter Hall and Lewis Mumford. Mumford's contribution in particular calls for reassessment, for he wrote as a unique kind of ethicist, centrally concerned with the built environment and, as Rudolf Bahro noted, he was a genuinely prophetic figure. It is imperative Christians learn from him.

This book began with an invitation to address religious education teachers on the ethics of the built environment, and the material in it has been shared with clergy and laity in Britain, Germany, Norway and Canada. Whatever its inadequacies, I have found people eagerly engaged with the theme, and I am grateful for the many challenges these audiences provided. Iona Gorringe has been a constant companion in reflecting on the built environment on countless journeys in Scotland and England, and her enthusiasm for the project has always been profoundly encouraging. Readers will quickly become aware of my debt to Hugo Gorringe, and in particular his work on the constructed space of Dalit communities in South India. He has kept me supplied with a constant supply of relevant articles. I am grateful for Kevin Taylor's faith in the project at Cambridge, and also to Norman Shanks, for allowing me to offer this piece of work as my Mainland Project for membership of the Iona Community.

The book was begun in Dundee and finished in Exeter. Here Arthur Hannabuss and John Escott have exemplified the unpretentiousness and skill of vernacular building which I urge as, in part, an answer to our present discontents. No two people could make clearer both the limits of what conventionally we call 'education', and the profundity of a true education, the product of countless generations of skill, commonsense and craftsmanship. Without them the book could quite literally not have been written, as there would have been no roof under which to write it.

The book is dedicated with affection to an architect and a drama teacher and theologian who are a source of inspiration in this area as in others.

TIM GORRINGE
Exeter
Feast of St Benedict 2001

The theology of the built environment

> Keep these words that I am commanding you today in your heart... write them on the doorposts of your house and on your gates.
> (Deuteronomy 6.6–9)

To be human is to be placed: to be born in this house, hospital, stable (according to Luke), or even, as in the floods in Mozambique in 2000, in a tree. It is to live in this council house, semi-detached, tower block, farmhouse, mansion. It is to go to school through these streets or lanes, to play in this alley, park, garden; to shop in this market, that mall; to work in this factory, mine, office, farm. These facts are banal, but they form the fabric of our everyday lives, structuring our memories, determining our attitudes. How, as Christians, should we think of them? Are they a proper subject for theological reflection? Here and there great theologians, notably Aquinas and Calvin, have glanced in this direction, but the built environment forms no *locus* in theological ethics except insofar as it has dealt with land and property, and with the city as a metaphor for community, or our final destination.[1] It is in ethics that theology has engaged with the concrete – with war, economics, work, sexuality. Why not, then, with the built environment? We are invited to do that by the very terminology involved. Paul constantly urges his congregations to 'edify' one another. The word 'edify' comes from the Latin *aedificare*, to build.[2] The metaphorical use of the word points to a profound truth about the built environment. Form follows function; buildings serve a purpose. For good or ill buildings, from the humblest garden shed to the grandest cathedral, make moral statements.

Learning from Barth, I take it for granted that for the theologian ethics and dogmatics cannot be separated. They are continuous sections

---

[1] Land is the theme of the third chapter, and the city of the sixth.

[2] A point made by K. Harries, *The Ethical Function of Architecture* (Cambridge, Mass.: MIT, 1998), p. 11. The Greek word Paul uses, *oikodomeo*, has the same literal and metaphorical meaning.

on the theological railway, not a main line (dogmatics) and a branch line (ethics). In that case, what is called for is a theological reading of the built environment. This will differ from other ethical accounts in its reference to a primarily narrative frame. Like teleological ethics, it will raise the question of the purpose of our building and planning; it will always ask about context, and to this extent resemble situation ethics; in the ongoing debate which constitutes church life it will seek to discern the command of God in this area as in others; in all cases it will be concerned with the way in which the built environment furthers human virtue or destroys it. But in each case it will do so in reference to the narratives which give us our account of the Triune God: the stories of creation, reconciliation, redemption. To the question, 'Where do we find the measure of the validity of a given form of architecture or planning?' it will reply – precisely in these narratives and their explication.[3]

The point of this is not, of course, to teach planners and architects what to do. As Hans Urs von Balthasar has said, 'Christianity has no direct competence in the realm of worldly structures.' This has not prevented theologians from drawing up quite precise guidelines for economic structures, as in the theories of the 'just price' and the 'just wage' and in Catholic Social Teaching, or for armed combat, as in the so-called 'just war theory'. These theories follow, because, as von Balthasar goes on, the gospel 'sends Christians into the world with an image of the human whereby and according to which they are to organise its structures as responsibly as they can'.[4] Perhaps this is still to state the matter too ecclesiocentrically. In his work in Finnish cities Seppo Kjellberg has sought to understand theology as a science of reconciliation, promoting interdisciplinary dialogue, bringing all concerned with questions of the built environment together, but offering as its own perspective an understanding of the overall purpose of humankind within creation.[5] We can accept this if we understand 'reconciliation' in Barth's sense, as the vivifying and revolutionary action of God within human community seeking the realisation of life in all its fullness for all people. If 'reconciliation' meant the Church adopting a managerial role, 'mediating' between rich and poor, bosses and workers, oppressors and oppressed, pouring the oil of middle axioms on the troubled waters of social conflict, it would certainly be untrue to the gospel. Christianity brings to all debates about

[3] Ibid., p. 12.
[4] H. Urs von Balthasar, 'Liberation Theology in the Light of Salvation History' in J. V. Schall (ed.), *Liberation Theology in Latin America* (San Francisco: Ignatius Press, 1982) p. 144.
[5] S. Kjellberg, *Urban EcoTheology* (Utrecht: International Books, 2000), p. 26.

the structures of the world through which we reproduce ourselves – economics, social and criminal justice, but also town planning and building – its understanding of God become flesh, 'whereby and according to which', as von Balthasar says, they build. In view of the silence of the tradition it is essential to insist that Christian theology has at its core a vision of the human which is especially pertinent to the built environment. In his *Ten Books of Architecture*, written in the first century BC, the Roman architect and engineer Marcus Vitruvius Pollio gave a description of the geometry of the human body which formulated the principles of classical architecture, rediscovered and taken up again at the Renaissance.[6] For many centuries this perception provided the ground rules for an architectural practice which was by definition humanist, which sought and built according to human scale. For Vitruvius, in fact, we become human only *as* we build.[7] In the twentieth century another architect, Rudolph Schwartz, who regarded ethics as determinative for architecture, gave further expression to this principle.[8] Building, he said, is done with the whole body, so that it is the movements of the body which create living space.

What then comes into being is first and foremost circumscribed space – shelter, living space, ceremonial space, a space which replaces the space of the world. We could almost say, and indeed it is true, that building is based on the inner spaciousness of the body, on the knowledge of its extent and the form of its growth, on the knowledge of its articulation and of its power to expand. Indeed it is with the body that we experience building, with the outstretched arms and the pacing feet, with the roving glance and with the ear, and above all else in breathing. *Space is dancingly experienced.*[9]

[6] The passage runs: 'For if a man be placed flat on his back, with his hands and feet extended, and a pair of compasses centred at his navel, the fingers and toes of his two hands and feet will touch the circumference of a circle described therefrom. And just as the human body yields a circular outline, so too a square figure may be found from it. For if we measure the distance from the soles of the feet to the top of the head, and then apply that measure to the outstretched arms, the breadth will be found to be the same as the height, as in the case of plane surfaces which are perfectly square.' Vitruvius, *The Ten Books of Architecture*, tr. M. Morgan, (Cambridge, Mass.: Harvard University Press, 1914), p. 73. Leonardo produced a classical illustration of this claim. See on this the excellent discussion in M. J. Ostwald and R. John Moore, *Disjecta Membra: The Architect, The Serial Killer, His Victim and Her Medical Examiner* (Sydney: Arcadia Press, 1998).

[7] Vitruvius, *Ten Books*, Book 2, ch. 1, p. 38.

[8] Speaking in 1951 to architects concerned with rebuilding in Germany he told them: 'I am terribly sorry to say this, but you only get a house by marrying and by devoting yourself to that great law. That may well be much more demanding than designing a house with wonderfully large windows. But I don't think we can arrive at a house in any other way. And this should be the first step towards establishing a decent house, then a village, then a city.' Quoted in Harries, *Function*, p. 363.

[9] R. Schwartz, *The Church Incarnate* (Chicago: Chicago University Press, 1958), p. 27 (my italics).

This is a profound expression of the Vitruvian view, though the conclusion is more of an eschatological hope than a lived reality. In the twentieth century such humanist architecture was more the exception than the rule, as this kind of humanism was discarded in favour of a brutalist technocracy for which 'man' was a 'machine' and buildings, accordingly, 'machines for living in'.[10] At the same time, from Patrick Geddes onwards, sociologists have seen that if utopia cannot be produced by building better, at least the reverse is true, that there are environments which generate crime and physical and mental ill health.[11] Balthasar is right: in relation to the built environment the recovery of a new humanism is an urgent need, and in this Christian theology, as one dialogue partner amongst many, certainly has a role to play. Kjellberg, however, points out that the anthropocentrism of earlier Christian theology is inadequate. What is needed is what he calls a 'cosmological holism', which understands creation and incarnation, doctrine and ethics, together.[12] Balthasar is right that the church's involvement in the city was always based on the doctrine of the incarnation, the idea of the 'humanity of God'.[13] However, he seems to have forgotten what otherwise he has learned from Barth, that there is *no* theological assertion without its ethical correlate. It is not just Christian anthropology which determines our activity, but all the propositions of the creed. Christian faith *brings the whole Trinitarian economy of creation, reconciliation and redemption to its reflection on the world*. I shall, therefore, be attempting a Trinitarian reflection in what follows. A Trinitarian theological ethic will also, I shall argue, be a theology of grace, and for that very reason a theology of liberation.

Barth gave his entire *Dogmatics* a Trinitarian structure. He had, therefore, an ethics of creation, and planned an ethics of reconciliation and of

---

[10] The slogan of Le Corbusier. On these grounds Harries notes that it is possible to charge modernism with moral failure. *Function*, p. 9.

[11] See further on this the discussion in chapter 7.   [12] Kjellberg, *Urban EcoTheology*, p. 17.

[13] I cannot agree with Elaine Graham's criticism of the incarnational theology of *Faith in the City* as the perfect expression of 'the Church of England's position in a settled, harmonious social order' ('Theology in the City: Ten Years after *Faith in the City*', Bulletin of the John Rylands Library 78.1, 1996, p. 184). Incarnation can be an expression of the status quo, but for the Christian socialist tradition in which the Report stands it was always a reminder that God identified with the poor, and that justice demanded concrete, and more egalitarian, expression. Harvey notes that the socialist utopian literature of the nineteenth century contains a 'powerful and important critical element' (*Spaces of Hope* (Edinburgh: Edinburgh University Press, 2000), p. 195). The same applies to the views of the incarnation. To appeal to the incarnation as the ground of a humanist architecture is queried by both Schopenhauer, who criticised the Christian aspiration to verticality, as opposed to the horizontal which stays close to the earth, and by Bloch who contrasts Greek corporeal-humane proportions with Christian otherworldly ones (*The Principle of Hope* (Oxford: Blackwell, 1986), p. 716). But the incarnation, which begins with a story set in a cow shed, is precisely what announces a this worldly intention.

redemption. Different aspects of human life were grouped by him under these headings. For example, he dealt with the relations of women and men, with work, with respect for life, under 'creation'. As that which forms our 'third skin', however, I want to argue that the built environment relates to every area of Christian ethics, and that only a Trinitarian ethic, an ethic of creation, reconciliation, and redemption, is adequate to explore it. It is a fundamental principle of Trinitarian theology that *opera Trinitatis ad extra indivisa sunt*: the works of God cannot be divided. If it is God who acts, it is God who acts, not 'parts' of God, for God is indivisible. At the same time the Church has always spoken of 'appropriations', whereby we speak of some forms of divine activity more especially in terms of one person of the Trinity than another. In relation to the built environment we can say that God the Creator is the one who brings order out of chaos, and is therefore the source of all order and of the planning which gives form to our world. The perspective of creation points us away from the anthropocentric city to one in which the wider ecology is fundamentally respected. God the Reconciler is the one who 'breaks down the walls of partition' both between God and humans and between humans themselves. God is therefore the source of all attempts to realise community and of the justice without which community cannot survive. God the Redeemer is the author of all dreams and visions, the author of the imagination which seeks the new Jerusalem and anticipates it in structures here and now. One or other of these 'appropriations' lies behind my attempt to think through the question of the built environment theologically in each of the chapters that follow.

I speak here of God, the origin and end of good – which is to say, creative, reconciling, redeeming – human action. A major strand of theological reflection has wanted to confine truly good action within the sphere of the Church. We cannot say that the great pagans had true virtues, said Augustine. The best we can allow is that they did not depart from virtue very much.[14] I cannot share this view. God sustains in being all that is, works in and through all events, and elicits response in all created reality. It is, of course, foundational to Christian faith that God works through history, through the particularity of Israel, of Jesus of Nazareth, of the Church. In no way do I wish to reduce these historical particularities to myth or symbol. But the Christian scriptures are quite clear that God is not confined to Israel and Church, and they invite us,

---

[14] Augustine *Contra Julianum* 4.3.25. This conclusion follows because without faith it is impossible to please God, (Heb. 11.6). He wrestles with the issue from 3.18 on. This is probably the most intransigent of his Anti Pelagian treatises.

therefore, to move from the narrative of the particular to discern God at work in all things. Redemption was finished neither on Calvary, nor at the resurrection. The work of redemption is continued by the Holy Spirit. The Messianic writings, the narratives which speak of the life, death and resurrection of Jesus, together with all the texts which they presuppose, provide us with criteria to discern that work.[15] It is on these grounds that Aquinas, when turning his mind to the city, noted that there are two aspects of the work of God in the world, creation and governance, and invited rulers and planners to an analogous practice:

> One who is about to establish a city or a realm must, in the first place, choose a suitable site; healthy, to ensure the health of the inhabitants; fertile to provide for their sustenance; one which will delight the eye with its loveliness and give natural security against hostile attack . . . Having chosen the site, the next task which confronts the founder of a city or a kingdom is to plan the area to meet all the requirements of civic life . . . one must decide where to build towns and where to leave the countryside open, or to construct fortifications: centres of study, open places for military training, and markets, all have to be taken into consideration: otherwise neither city nor kingdom would long endure attack.[16]

This activity, the activity of establishing a city and setting up civic life, is not outwith the remit of theology and Church precisely because of God's activity in creation and providence. If God is active and not absent, then faith in the activity of that God informs our building and planning. Because God is the Creator, says Elaine Scarry, 'making' is set apart and honoured as the most morally authoritative of acts, creating divine resonances, amongst other places, at the doorway of the house and the gateway of the city. In imaging God as Creator the Hebrew bible conceives the whole cosmos as the proper territory for acts of artifice and intelligence.[17] These are not autonomous, but represent responses to the Creator Spirit.

There were, of course, very good reasons for the emergence of the divide between sacred and secular, specifically the desire to avoid the worst of all forms of government, theocracy.[18] Here above all we see how religion can lead us into the valley of the shadow of death. In this as in

---

[15] In his condemnation of liberal theology Graham Ward seems to me to miss this point. There is a difference between *reducing* incarnation, crucifixion, resurrection to metaphors, and learning from them how it is that God acts and seeking to discern God in the world in the light of them. *Cities of God* (London: Routledge, 2000), p. 43.
[16] Aquinas, 'On Princely Government', ch. 13 in *Selected Political Writings*, ed. A. D'Entreves (Oxford: Blackwell, 1948).
[17] E. Scarry, *The Body in Pain* (Oxford, Oxford University Press, 1985), p. 222.
[18] I read thus Marsiglio of Padua's *Defensor Pacis* which, in 1324, already argued for a properly secular realm. He had every reason for being sceptical of the claims of the Church.

other areas recognition of the Lordship of Christ over every aspect of life is a quite different matter from the tutelage of the Church over every area, or even the belief that piety is always what promotes true human integrity.[19] But this political need cannot blind us to the foundational impossibility of generalising the divide. A Trinitarian theology cannot allow a secular and sacred divide, in which 'secular' occupations are left to the non theologians, and theology confined to specialists. Rather, the rationale of such a theology will be a discernment of God active in God's world. This includes the built environment. This seems to be straightforward, but as I have noted, the written tradition is largely silent about this and amongst many Christians the secular/sacred prejudice is still strong. When you announce a lecture on the theology of the built environment people expect you to talk about churches, and are disappointed when you do not! This book is not about churches, but about supposedly 'secular' buildings and settlements. To answer the disappointment of those who look for a book on 'sacred' buildings and places I begin by considering the reasons for the silence of theology about the built environment, and ways we might go about such theological reflection.

GOD IN THE (EVERYDAY) BUILT ENVIRONMENT

Writing about the suburban house, John Archer remarks that eighteenth century European thought had articulated a number of fundamental polarities – subject/object, public/private, masculine/feminine – but that 'such distinctions had no more than putative existence until they could be realized in the material domain of everyday life'.[20] One may doubt both that Archer's polarities are the invention of the eighteenth century, and that they are exclusively European, but he is right that ideologies are only of consequence when they impinge on 'the material domain of everyday life' through legal and political codes, social practices, and the shaping of space. The built environment, which 'provides us with all the most direct, frequent and unavoidable images and experiences of everyday life', is never just happenstance.[21] It reflects conscious decisions which in

---

[19] As Blake puts it in *The Marriage of Heaven and Hell*: 'Let the Priests of the Raven of dawn, no longer in deadly black, with hoarse note curse the sons of joy. Nor his accepted brethren – whom, tyrant, he calls free – lay the bound or build the roof.... For every thing that lives is Holy.' *Complete Writings*, ed. G. Keynes (Oxford: Oxford University Press, 1969), p. 160.

[20] J. Archer, 'Colonial Suburbs in South Asia 1700–1850, and the Spaces of Modernity', in R. Silverstone (ed.), *Visions of Suburbia* (London: Routledge, 1997), p. 52.

[21] M. Smith, J. Whitelegg and N. Williams, *Greening the Built Environment* (London: Earthscan, 1998), p. 13.

turn reflect ideologies and class positions.[22] 'Grasped as an image', says Heinrich Rombach, 'the basic character of a farmhouse says a great deal more about the "spirit" of the country, and a style of building reveals more of the basic philosophy of a period, than the carefully smoothed-out texts of the school philosophy of that time.'[23] Not just farmhouses, we have to add, but council estates, tower blocks and out of town shopping centres; and not just philosophy, but theology. Theology, as one form of ideology, plays its part in the shaping of space, and not just in overtly religious buildings, nor just in pre secular societies.

I have insisted that a Trinitarian theology eliminates any fundamental distinction between sacred and secular. This seems to be a paradoxical claim the moment we look at the built environment, for humans have everywhere marked out sacred space from the secular. Karsten Harries suggests that the history of building forms an ellipse between the private and the public, domestic and 'pedigreed'. The archetypal version of the latter, in his view, is the church or temple (we must add, mosque).[24] There is, he insists, a necessary dialectic between these two forms, in that it is the whole point of 'architecture', by which he means the non domestic, to take leave of the everyday and then return to it with fresh eyes.[25] I think we cannot escape this ellipse, but it is not unproblematic from the perspective of the Christian tradition. Karl Barth noted that Christianity showed a certain preference for the oppressed, those falling short, for the immature and the sullen.[26] I would put it slightly differently and say that we find in Scripture, classically in the Magnificat, a prefer-ence for the everyday, the modest, humble and ordinary, and we cannot but take account of that in reflecting on the built environment. This leaves us with an embarrassment, because to be interested in 'architecture' is to be concerned almost solely with what I will call, following Redfield, 'the great tradition'.[27] Redfield distinguishes between the great tradition, the written and celebrated, the work of the philosophers, historians, the-ologians, the learned, and the little tradition, which for the most part comes to us only in scraps, in folk memories, songs, tales and ballads, in pamphlets crudely written. One of the remarkable things about the

[22] Cf S. Giedion: the main task facing contemporary architecture is 'the interpretation of a way of life valid for our period'. *Space, Time and Architecture*, 5th edn (Cambridge, Mass.: Harvard University Press, 1974), p. xxxii.
[23] Quoted in G. Pattison, *Art, Modernity and Faith* (London: SCM, 1998), p. 142.
[24] Harries, *Function*, p. 286.   [25] Ibid., p. 291.
[26] K. Barth, *The Epistle to the Romans*, tr. E. Hoskyns (London: Oxford University Press, 1933), p. 463.
[27] R. Redfield, *Peasant Society and Culture* (Chicago: University of Chicago Press, 1956) ch. 3.

New Testament is that it contains so many documents which bear the marks of the little tradition, written in a Greek which was an acute embarrassment to the first educated Christians. In the built environment the great tradition means the work of prestigious architects or planners, whilst the little tradition corresponds to the work of unknown craftsmen who have left their mark on every ancient village, town and city. Christianity, I shall claim, is wedded to the little tradition. This would not be contentious were it not for what seems to be the elective affinity between Christianity and the great tradition – in music, art, literature and, perhaps above all, building. Since one of my aims is to champion precisely the little tradition in the built environment, I will substantiate my claim about the Christian marriage, and by the same token ask about the reason for the deafening silence on the little tradition in architecture in Christian reflection.

Theology works between a triangle of text, tradition and experience. 'Tradition', here, almost invariably means the great tradition, from Origen to Barth or John Milbank. In this tradition, it is true, there have been many trends which have militated against a perception of God in our everyday built environment. There has been, in the first instance, a marked emphasis on the spiritual as opposed to the material, on the priority of the *civitas Dei* to the *civitas terrena*. We crave freedom from death, deception and distress, Augustine wrote, and we will never have that in this life. 'In our present state what human being can live the life he wishes, when the actual living is not in his control . . . life will only be truly happy when it is eternal.'[28]

The problem with this Platonising train of reflection is that it rules out true happiness in this life, and in so doing relativises the significance of what we do here. Even in the late twentieth century, with all its hedonism, activism and emphasis on the pleasures of the body, prominent representatives of this view could be found. Thus Edward Norman, in his 1978 Reith Lectures, claimed that the 'true Christ of history' directed people to 'turn away from the preoccupations of human society' and characterised Christianity as the 'evocation of the unearthly'.[29] No theological understanding of the built environment could emerge from this theology. Such a theology is interested only in church building, and in building which seeks to 'evoke the unearthly' at that. But such a theology shortchanges the world in which we live. As Nicholas Wolterstorff remarks:

[28] Augustine, *The City of God*, Book 14.25.
[29] E. Norman, *Christianity and the World Order* (Oxford: Oxford University Press, 1979), pp. 78–9.

The tragedy of modern urban life is not only that so many in our cities are oppressed and powerless, but also that so many have nothing surrounding them in which any human being could possibly take sensory delight. For this state of affairs we who are Christians are as guilty as any. We have adopted a pietistic-materialistic understanding of man, viewing human needs as the need for a saved soul plus the need for food, clothes and shelter. True shalom is vastly richer than that.[30]

On top of this relativising of the present has been an introspective tradition which began with Augustine's *Confessions* and which has concentrated on the inner life at the expense of the active. In medieval theology in particular there was a strong sense that communion with God required retreat, the cloister, cutting oneself off from the everyday. 'Unless a man has disentangled himself from all things created,' wrote Thomas à Kempis in the fifteenth century, 'he will not be free to make for the things of God', and this was a representative view.[31] Richard Sennett's marvellously rich meditation on the urban order, *The Conscience of the Eye*, begins with precisely this prioritisation of interiority. 'Nothing is more cursed in our culture', he writes, than the continuing separation between inner and outer. It makes the places we live in puzzling to us.'The street is a scene of outside life, and what is to be seen on the street are beggars, tourists, merchants, students, children playing, old people resting – a scene of human differences. What is the relation of these differences to inner life?' The Augustinian tradition, he says, deprives us of the ability to make sense of them.[32]

A further difficulty is symbolised by the medieval distinction, based on the Latin of 1 Corinthians 7.25, between precepts, binding on everyone, and counsels, taken up by those who sought to be perfect, which institutionalised a distinction between religious and everyday, sacred and secular.[33] Those who took monastic vows, and fulfilled the counsels, were the ones who led a truly Christian life. Politically, the division of powers between Pope and emperor corresponded to this distinction; socially, the division of realms between sacred and secular. The need to find God apart from the structures of everyday life found architectural expression in the theology of sacred space. To say that the eucharist can only be celebrated on 'consecrated' ground could be seen as denying the holiness

---

[30] N. Wolterstorff, *Art in Action* (Carlisle: Solway, 1997), p. 82.
[31] Thomas à Kempis, *The Imitation of Christ* (London: Burns & Oates, 1959), Book 1 ch. 20(a); Book III ch. 31.
[32] R. Sennett, *The Conscience of the Eye* (New York: Norton, 1990), pp. 9–10.
[33] Paul wrote: 'Concerning virgins I have no commandment (*praeceptum*) of the Lord, but I give my opinion (*consilium*) as one who by the Lord's mercy is trustworthy.'

of creation as a whole. To say one's prayers, to encounter the divine, one therefore went to special buildings, set apart, and within those buildings the chancel and altar area were in turn increasingly fenced off from the mundane world, accessible only to the clergy. In the middle ages, at least, sacred and secular architecture were distinguished in terms of vertical and horizontal axes, the one reaching to heaven, the other 'the temporal death-shadowed dwelling on earth'.[34] I shall return to this distinction in the following chapter.

The Reformation represented an attack on many of these distinctions, and the radical Reformation changed the idea of sacred space, so that the house once again became church.[35] Sacred space, however, would not be pushed away. In his famous essay, *The Sacred and the Profane*, Mircea Eliade argued that the distinction between sacred and profane was probably ineliminable, even in the most secularised of worlds. Human beings become aware of the sacred 'because it manifests itself, shows itself, as something wholly different from the profane', though in and through objects that are an integral part of our natural 'profane' world.[36] As a description of the sacramental I would regard this as unexceptionable. The sacramental precisely refuses any division of realms. It arises from a Trinitarian perception which sees God in all things, even in sin and death (the cross). Eliade, however, with much of the Christian tradition, goes on to talk of two fundamentally different orders of human experience so that we have sacred and profane space, sacred time and ordinary time, even sacred and profane love, the practical implication of Nygren's *Agape and Eros*. The effect of the distinction is, once again, to mark off only one small area of experience as the sphere of encounter with God. This is counter to any kind of Trinitarian perception but, as we know, the doctrine of the Trinity was, for most of the Christian centuries hitherto, virtually a dead letter.

In the nineteenth century the 'art for art's sake' movement represented another version of this separation of realms. There was art, and all the rest was not art. During this period, says Benevolo, 'Art took on the task of communicating emotion and organizing the language of the heart . . . the urban setting was cut off from this process. Art was stripped

[34] Harries, *Function*, p. 187.

[35] See, for example, Flora Thompson's account of the Methodist meeting in her hamlet in *Lark Rise to Candleford* (Oxford: Oxford University Press, 1954), ch. 14.

[36] M. Eliade, *The Sacred and the Profane* (New York: Harcourt & Brace, 1959), p. 11 He was drawing on Rudolf Otto's *Die Heilige* (*The Idea of The Holy*), published in 1917, which traced the root of religion to the 'numinous', which broke in on the believer and left her trembling in awe and fear. This experience was marked off as sharply as possible from the everyday.

from the city and became an experience specific to certain spaces, to be enjoyed during leisure time.'[37] When cities were ruthlessly rebuilt and only 'important' buildings preserved, quite apart from their original context, the separation of art and life and the transfer of beauty to the separate sphere of entertainment and free time was reinforced.[38] Harries remarks that religion and 'art for art's sake' have to be enemies because all religion claims integrative power.[39] I have put this differently, in terms of the claims of God upon the whole of our life, and the activity of God in the whole of life, but I agree.

A new cause for the division of sacred and secular appeared when existentialism, the philosophy which was to dominate the middle years of the twentieth century, privileged the extraordinary, 'boundary situations', and the experience of *angst*, over the everyday. When Paul Tillich fled to the United States in 1933 he took his existentialism with him, and was responsible for its dominance in Anglo Saxon theology until the end of the 1960s. For Tillich the refusal of the division of sacred and secular was part of what he referred to as 'the Protestant principle', and on a number of occasions he attempted short reflections on domestic building. His audiences, however, repeatedly brought him back to churches, and, whilst much theological reflection on art may stem from Tillich, no theology of the everyday built environment developed from his theology.[40] Although Tillich himself believed any situation or reality might be a vehicle of ultimate concern I suspect that the concern of existentialism with 'anxiety' or 'the boundary' is the reason for this.

Before existentialism had reached the zenith of its influence it was already Eric Auerbach, writing in Istanbul during the Second World War, who marked a reaction to these preoccupations. He began by comparing the Hebrew bible with Homer and noted how in the latter the representation of daily life remains in the peaceful realm of the idyllic, whereas in the Old Testament 'the sublime, tragic and problematic take shape *precisely in the domestic and commonplace* . . . The sublime influence of God here reaches so deeply into the everyday that the two realms of the sublime and the everyday are not only actually unseparated but basically inseparable.'[41] In the New Testament we do not, as is often suggested, enter a more spiritualised world. On the contrary, as Auerbach puts it,

[37] L. Benevolo, *The European City* (Oxford: Blackwell, 1993), p. 164.
[38] Ibid., p. 180.   [39] Harries, *Function*, p. 331.
[40] For his reflections on domestic architecture see ch. 8 in *On Art and Architecture* (New York: Crossroad, 1989) and for the way audiences drew him back to 'church' see ch. 17.
[41] E. Auerbach, *Mimesis* (Princeton: Princeton University Press, 1974), p. 22 (my italics).

the story of Christ embraces 'a ruthless mixture of everyday reality and the highest and most sublime tragedy'.[42] This fact, and the common language and style in which all this was recorded, set a problem for the early Church Fathers, who had to defend Christianity against the attacks of the educated, and in so doing discovered that Scripture had 'created an entirely new kind of sublimity, in which the everyday and the low were included, not excluded, so that, in style as in content, it directly connected the lowest with the highest'.[43] This, I suggest, will give us theological criteria for our understanding of the built environment. The same is true of the generalisation of vocation by Luther at the Reformation, which tacitly ennobles the calling of the ordinary craftsman, as against the exceptional genius, what we shall later call (in chapter 4) the vernacular against the pedigreed.

Others who helped to create the conditions for a theology of the everyday built environment include Paul Tillich's contemporary, Karl Barth. His second commentary on Romans, published in 1922, appropriated Otto's language of the *'ganz anders'* ('Wholly Other') in order to use it to attack the very view of religion it represented. Religion, for Barth, meant the domestication of grace – the defusing of the danger of God in our midst. On the edge of this attack was the sense that 'religion' became a privileged preserve which squeezed God out of ordinary life. This came into sharper focus in the course of resistance to Hitler, when Barth had to oppose the Lutheran 'two kingdoms' teaching. With increasing clarity Barth sought to put Christ at the centre of all human life – social and political as well as ecclesiastical, and by implication trivial, routine and humdrum as well as in the great events of war and revolution which he began by echoing in his work. The implications of this can be seen in his great ethics of Creation. Barth did not take up the theme of the built environment, but we have to ask, what are the implications of his attack on religion for this theme? What are the implications of the Lordship of Christ over all, as affirmed at Barmen in 1934, for the world we build?

Bonhoeffer famously developed Barth's attack on religion in his prison letters, going on to ask how it was possible to speak in a 'secular' way about 'God', in order to understand God as 'really the Lord of the world'.[44] The questions posed by this letter have rung down the decades since Bonhoeffer's correspondence was first published. They were taken up especially by the 'secular city' theologians of the 1960s. The concern with

[42] Ibid., p. 555.   [43] Ibid., p. 154.
[44] D. Bonhoeffer, *Letters and Papers from Prison*, 3rd edn (London: SCM, 1967), pp. 280–1.

secularisation began shortly after the Second World War, and the driving force was undoubtedly the massive fall off in church attendance, but there was also a more positive side to it. Led by Old Testament scholars like Von Rad, theologians pointed out that the roots of secularisation lay not in the Enlightenment but in Scripture. In Genesis, for example, sun, moon and stars are desacralised: they are there for street lighting, and not to be worshipped. The world is not an 'enchanted forest', but a garden to till and keep. The Exodus teaches us that no one rules by divine right and that all sacral politics can be challenged.[45] In the New Testament the idea of the holy is redefined, away from that which is set apart to a recognition of the common as itself holy – the point of Peter's vision in Acts 10.[46]

In *The Secular City* Harvey Cox argued that secularity was rooted in the Hebrew approach to history as a series of events beginning with Creation and heading towards a consummation. The impact of Hebrew faith on the Hellenistic world, mediated through the early Christians, was to 'temporalise' the dominant perceptions of reality so that the world became history – part of the priority of time over space which was assumed in most disciplines throughout the century. The effect of this was to negate any distinction between sacred and secular, for the secular or 'ordinary' was the true sphere of God's operation. Speaking about God in a secular fashion, in his view, requires placing ourselves at those points where the restoring, reconciling activity of God is occurring, where the proper relationship between people is appearing. [47]

Other theologians pointed out that the very etymology of the word 'profane' demonstrates that it is an unacceptable category for Christians to use. The word derives from the Latin *pro fano*, i.e. before or outside the temple. But according to Paul, 'We are the temple of the living God' (1 Cor. 3.16). For Paul the temple is not a building but the community living in the world. There cannot, therefore, be an idea of the profane as the sum total of common life outside the sphere of the holy.[48] From a very different standpoint, Teilhard de Chardin insisted that 'by virtue of the Creation, and still more, of the Incarnation, nothing here below is profane for those who know how to see it'.[49]

---

[45] H. Cox, *The Secular City* (Harmondsworth: Penguin, 1965), p. 46.

[46] So A. Hake, 'Theological Reflections on "Community" ', in A. Harvey (ed.), *Theology in the City* (London: SPCK, 1989), p. 57.

[47] Cox, *Secular City*, p. 265.   [48] J. G. Davies, *Everyday God* (London: SCM, 1972), p. 60.

[49] P. Teilhard de Chardin, *Le Milieu Divin* (Glasgow: Collins, 1967), p. 66.

If Eliade's two realms mean the de-sanctification of the everyday then the implications of secularisation, by contrast, as Richard Niebuhr rightly observed, is the sanctification of all things. What we learn from Scripture is that every day is the day that the Lord has made; every nation is a holy people called by him into existence in its place and time and to his glory; every person is sacred, made in his image and likeness.[50]

There is no doubt that the theology of the Secular City was wedded to the optimism of the early nineteen sixties, especially in its embrace of that acme of Enlightenment ideas, the notion that humankind had at last 'come of age'.[51] It was overly rationalistic and its critique of the city far too muted.[52] It succumbed to the danger, of which Barth had warned, of a loss of Christian distinctiveness following from (in this case, not so) secret respect for the fashion of the world, and secret respect for its glory. [53] Ten years after Cox's book appeared the Green Movement and 'Celtic Christianity' were urgently engaged in the re-enchantment of nature in face of its ongoing destruction, and sacral politics made a comeback with a vengeance. It was a classic example of Dean Inge's famous remark that any theology which marries the *Zeitgeist* quickly becomes a widower. What was right about it, however, was the celebration of a world in which God is continuously at work, not just in the 'nature' of the Romantic poets, but also in the environments human beings produce for themselves. As Seppo Kjellberg has remarked, Cox was correct to understand the city as a man- and God-made process 'resembling the kingdom of God, which is eschatologically forthcoming, but also already present'.[54] That the world is fallen does not mean that goodness, gratuity and divine creativity cannot be found in that world, or that God is not active there. What it calls for is discernment.

---

[50] H. R. Niebuhr, *Radical Monotheism and Western Culture* (London: Faber, 1961), p. 52.

[51] I nevertheless do not find that it is reducible without remainder to 'liberal correlationism' or a craven submission to the values of consumer capitalism, as Graham Ward maintains, which is to miss Cox's insistence on prophecy. Ward, *Cities of God*, p. 47. Although the coming of age theme is for the most part patently absurd it should give us pause for thought that it is the author of *The Cost of Discipleship* who introduced it into the debate, albeit unwittingly.

[52] So Jonathan Raban, *Soft City* (Glasgow: Collins, 1974). There is in this theology, he says, an 'overweening emphasis on the rationality of the city', especially in contrast with the countryside, and he insists by contrast that there is a great deal of superstition in the city and its tribalisms. The magic of the city, he says, 'is profoundly solipsistic, self-bound, and inward. Its very ignorance of plan or creation is its most obvious strength. One could not deduce the existence of God from the Portobello Road; but one might register from it the force of the amoral, the relative, the anarchistic' (p. 182).

[53] K. Barth, *Church Dogmatics* IV/2 (Edinburgh: T&T Clark, 1958), p. 668.

[54] S. Kjellberg, *Urban EcoTheology*, p. 109.

TRINITARIAN DISCERNMENT

To speak of God the Holy Spirit as God the Redeemer, a practice learned from Karl Barth, highlights the eschatological dimension of faith in God, its aspect as critical hope, in dialogue with all forms of secular utopia. 'Mere optimism about the future of human accomplishment and progress is never adequate for Christian witness,' writes Ben Sparks. 'There is an apocalyptic edge to the church's presence in the city, which requires us to be both prophets and builders for the well being of all citizens.'[55] Where Sparks uses 'apocalyptic' I would use 'eschatological', but the sentiment stands.[56]

Dreams, visions, and views of justice of course differ substantially, amongst Christians as amongst everyone else. Amongst liberation theologians there is a move away from 'a substantive theology' applied to diverse situations to 'a procedural theology where insight arises not from the application of timeless truths but from listening to the context in which God speaks'.[57] The problem is that contexts do not themselves speak. What we have to do is to discern God *in the context*. Any theology which wants to speak of God in the world is subject to a discipline of discernment. '[T]est the spirits to see whether they are from God' (1 John 4.1). In order to avoid bondage to some idolatry or other we need to measure our practices by revelation. For this reason theology is, as M. M. Thomas put it, 'a spiritual source of constructive and discriminating participation'. 'Certainly, we should not seek any new revelation of God in any historical event other than the Christ event, but faith in the divine revelation of Jesus Christ can be a key to understanding and discernment of God's creation, judgement and redemption in secular history.'[58] Here Thomas moves from the centrality of the Christ event to the Trinitarian economy. Nicholas Lash has argued that it is the task of the doctrine of the Trinity to obviate the danger of eliding God and the world, and therefore falling into idolatry, by insisting on *both* God's presence to the world, *and* God's difference. The doctrine gives us a grammar by which to speak of God. Thus, in the doctrine of the Spirit 'we learn to find God in all life, all freedom, all creativity and vitality . . . each

---

55 O. Ben Sparks III, 'From Eden to Jerusalem', *Interpretation* 54/1 (January 2000), p. 51.

56 Apocalyptic is an increasingly popular genre post Hiroshima and in the shadow of the environmental crisis. Its danger is luxuriating in hopes for an end for this wicked world. Eschatology, we have been taught by Moltmann, prioritises hope.

57 P. Hackwood and P. Shiner, 'New Role for the Church in Urban Policy?', in M. Northcote (ed.), *Urban Theology, A Reader* (London: Cassell, 1998), p. 74.

58 M. M. Thomas, *The Christian Response to the Asian Revolution* (London: SCM, 1966), p. 22.

unexpected attainment of relationship and community'.[59] The doctrine
of creation *ex nihilo*, on the other hand, insists on God's absolute difference from the world, whilst the doctrine of the incarnation points us to
the history of interpretative practice which teaches us to use the word
God, in the stories which take us from Exodus to Easter. The doctrine
of the Trinity, therefore, functions both 'to indicate where God is to be
found and – by denying, at each point, that what we find there is to
be simply identified with God – to prevent us from getting stuck in one
sidedness . . . The doctrine thus leads at every turn, to both affirmation
and denial.'[60] It offers us, in other words, rules for discernment in understanding where God is in the everyday world. This is not to say that
faith is a matter of 'mere' interpretation because, as Lash argues, the
interpretations we offer make a difference to our experience itself, just
as being in relation or being in community do, and that is the 'point' of
believing.[61]

Drawing on the theology of Gregory Nazianzus, Sigurd Bergmann
offers a liberation theology of the built environment with a Trinitarian
shape. The relationships of the Triune God point us to community; the
crucified God points us to the simultaneous presence of good and evil;
the Spirit works in each place for human freedom.[62] I shall be taking up
these suggestions in various ways in what follows.

GRACE AND THE BUILT ENVIRONMENT

I have tried to argue that Christian reflection on the built environment
will take the shape of a Trinitarian theological ethic, reflecting on God in
all reality, and thus refusing the pre Christian distinction between sacred
and secular. This articulates itself as a theology of grace. The word 'grace'
as part of Christian vocabulary we owe to Paul. He took over a word in
common parlance, *charis* (translated by the Latin *gratia*, and so by English
'grace'), which meant, amongst other things, charm, beauty, and spiritual
energy, and reinvented it in relation to his understanding of what had
happened in Christ. *Charis* means the fact that God works in weakness
rather than in power (2 Cor. 12.9) and signifies love in action (Rom. 6.1).
Christ inaugurates a new order *kata charin* (according to grace) rather than

[59] N. Lash, *Easter in Ordinary: Reflections on Human Experience and the Knowledge of God* (London: SCM, 1988), p. 267.
[60] Ibid., p. 267.   [61] Ibid., p. 248.
[62] S. Bergmann, *Geist, der Natur befreit. Die trintarische Kosmologie Gregors von Nazianz im Horizont einer ökologischen Theologie der Befreiung* (Mainz: Grünewald, 1995).

kata opheilema (according to what is due) (Rom. 4.4). Because it stands
for what God has done freely in Christ, with no conditions or strings
attached, it means radical giftedness, calling forth radical gift in return
(1 Cor. 12). By the same token, it is about our 'absolute dependence',
the fact that 'I am a debtor to all/to all I am bounden/Fellowman and
beast, season and solstice, darkness and light/And life and death', as
Edwin Muir put it in *The Debtor*. This great poem articulates what it
means to live in response to grace, namely in acknowledgement that I
am not my own, that I am bought with a price, that I am a debtor to all.

Augustine emphasised the need for grace to live the Christian life,
though what he meant by the term was fatally distorted by his contro-
versy with Pelagius, which forced him into extreme positions. Drawing
on his discussions, Aquinas defined grace as 'a kind of interior disposition
infused into us which inclines us to act rightly', 'something supernatural
issuing in human persons from God'.[63] He also thought of the sacraments as instrumental causes of grace, 'instruments of divine power'.[64]
Sacraments were, therefore, 'channels of grace'. Though these views
on grace can be interpreted freely they fail to do justice to the radical
quality of Paul's vision. First, in concentrating on the believing individual they underplay the sense in which creation is grace. The fact that
creation is grace, acknowledged every time we say 'grace' at meals, is
what illuminates the divine giftedness of everyday. The word 'grace' is
not a reference to a 'power' or 'influence' breaking through at certain key
moments but a way of saying that the God who loves in freedom sustains
the fabric of daily life, including our own. 'Sacraments' signify precisely
this.[65] What the eucharist signifies is not the existence of a sacred world
set over against the profane, requiring its own sacral space and time,
but rather the hallowing of the ordinary – of bread, wine, labour and
community. Because creation is grace, grace is concrete: it meets us in
what Padraic Pearse called 'the bulks of ordinary things' – and this of
course includes buildings and settlements, the places in which we live and
work. The theology of everyday life, therefore, is a theology of grace as
a theology of gratuity, of love 'for nothing', and of joy in the minutiae of
things.

Recognition that we 'live by grace' puts an end to all notions of
'building the kingdom'. The insistence that we do not and cannot do

[63] Aquinas, *Summa Theologiae* 1a2ae 108.1, 110.1.   [64] Ibid. 3a 62.1.

[65] Martin Buber recognised this in saying that the world becomes a sacrament through God's indwelling; 'everything wants to become a sacrament'. *The Origin and Meaning of Hasidism* (New York:
Horizon, 1960), pp. 96, 181.

this has been an obligatory caveat in all liberation theology from the beginning, and for good reason. 'Dear N.N.,' Karl Barth wrote to an enthusiastic theological student who used this language in 1967, 'in speaking thus you do not contradict merely one "insight" but the whole message of the whole Bible. If you persist in this idea I can only advise you to take up any other career than that of pastor.'[66] This seems to call in question Blake's famous verse:

> I will not cease from Mental Fight,
> Nor shall the Sword sleep in my hand
> Till we have built Jerusalem
> In England's green & pleasant Land.[67]

What is often not remarked is that Blake suffixes this poem with Numbers 11.29: 'Would to God that all the Lord's people were Prophets', a reference to the descent of the Spirit on elders who had not initially been 'ordained'. The poem is thus not Pelagian in intent at all, but an expression of confidence in God's Spirit to re-make human beings and therefore their world. I have taken this text as the superscription for the whole book precisely for this reason, and because it classically calls into question that reliance on either the state or technocratic expertise which has so disabled people in relation to the built environment. Building Jerusalem, the city of justice, peace and beauty, is a project which will never be completed this side of the kingdom, but it is a project to which we are called by the kingdom, by 'grace abounding in the lives of sinners'.

This was emphatically denied by the Calvinist sociologist and theologian Jacques Ellul, who attacked 'the Thomist heresy' that 'grace does not destroy nature but perfects it'. According to him the city is an attempt to prolong the momentary gift of Christ's healing during his life on earth. 'This is the tragedy of ideal cities, the terrible problem of modern urbanism, as of older utopianism; not believing that this meeting with Christ is unique, that it cannot be prolonged on earth, that it is only a sign of the hidden kingdom and an announcement of the kingdom to come.'[68] Cities represent the hubristic attempt to build an ideal place for full human development, equilibrium and virtue, the attempt to construct what God wants to construct, and to put humankind in the centre, in God's place.

[66] K. Barth, *Letters 1961–1968* (Edinburgh: T&T Clark, 1981), p. 283.
[67] W. Blake, *Milton, Complete Writings*, ed. G. Keynes (Oxford: Oxford University Press, 1969), p. 480.
[68] J. Ellul, *The Meaning of the City* (Grand Rapids, Eerdmans, 1970), p. 130.

However, whilst rejecting the Thomist doctrine of grace Ellul replaces it by a doctrine of pardon and acceptance which concretely amounts to the very same thing. We learn from the myth of the heavenly city, he says, that the golden age will be characterised by an acceptance of history, and not by its refusal.[69] Furthermore, because Christ is Saviour and Lord of both creation and humankind, he is also Saviour and Lord of human works. To the extent that in Christ, therefore, the city is not devilish, to the extent that it is destined to be transfigured, we must work along with others in the construction of the city.[70]

The city pardoned, or gracious building a sign of the liberative activity of God at work in the depths of creation? Whichever way we have it, what is essential is to recognise that, as Bonhoeffer put it, God is indeed and in truth Lord of the world, and therefore does not leave Godself without effect. 'Grace' is the word we use to talk about the way in which the liberating God works in the depth of the world. Because God's Word does not return to God void (Isa. 55.11) God's gracious activity has effects (what Aquinas called 'created grace') – what we can call 'gracious living'. This gracious living is, of course, the very opposite of what is usually designated by this phrase. It is, however, a fundamental reality in daily life, and not least in the built environment. Conversely, and equally importantly, the rejection of grace can also be seen writ large, and in concrete and glass, across our landscapes, the reality of sin. Sin calls for repentance, which in this context means learning new ways of building and planning which follow justice and do not have a hubristic approach to creation.

Because the older tradition of grace concentrates on the believer and the sacraments it misses the political sense of the doctrine, a sense on the whole not much remarked by the liberation theology of the late twentieth century.[71] The doctrine of grace, of the gratuitousness of all things, is, however, the most politically far reaching of all Christian doctrines. If creation is grace, if I am 'a debtor to all', then self evidently life is not there to appropriate the benefits for myself, to hoard things over against others. The only response to grace, as Barth always insisted, is gratitude, which politically means the struggle for social justice. It is precisely because he was a 'theologian of grace' that Barth was a political theologian. Grace, as a political doctrine, keeps the importance of the attempt to realise human equality on the agenda against the cynicism of 'realists' of all kinds, including theological realists. Because, as E. M. Wood puts it, 'a humane, "social", truly democratic and equitable capitalism is more

---

[69] Ibid., p. 162.   [70] Ibid., p. 180.
[71] An exception is the work of L. Boff, *Liberating Grace* (Maryknoll: Orbis, 1979).

unrealistically utopian than socialism' it will also involve a continuing commitment to alternative politics.[72]

To recognise grace as a political principle is important first because, as Luther used to say, grace is forgiveness. So if our demand for social justice issues from our experience of grace, then it is equally incompatible with hatred of the oppressor. I am a debtor to all – even my enemy. But grace has always retained in common parlance the sense of charm and beauty, and so to recognise grace as our political principle is at the same time to recognise the importance of the experiences of love, friendship, art and beauty to the political process. This is of the first importance when we recognise the built environment as part of that process.

LIBERATION THEOLOGY AND THE BUILT ENVIRONMENT

As a theology of human equality, of social justice, of forgiveness and of beauty the theology of grace is also a theology of liberation. Defining it thus needs care. Once the initial excitement of liberation theology had worn off by the end of the 1970s the problem with it was that it became just one option amongst others. Some have suggested that its usefulness is already passed, that it has nothing to say to the Network Society, and the world of Cyberspace.[73] By a theology of liberation, however, I mean a theology committed to its context, to the local as the key to the global, to the concrete, and to the necessity of praxis. It is also a theology which understands 'sin' in a structural way, as being spiritual precisely in economic, social and political dimensions. Because it does this it always follows Barth's advice and reads with the Bible in one hand and the newspaper – or various forms of social analysis – in the other. It is this method I follow in the present book, listening to what the geographers, planners and architects have to say in order to bring this material to theological reflection. Neither sin nor redemption can be understood either individualistically or abstractly. Here I want to try and understand them in relation to the built environment.

Characterising liberation theology thus I would borrow a distinction from Anselm and say that there are two kinds of theology: that which names the God of cross and resurrection, the God who is radical gift in

---

[72] E. M. Woods, *Democracy against capitalism: Renewing historical materialism* (Cambridge: Cambridge University Press, 1995), p. 293.

[73] So Graham Ward in *Cities of God*, pp. 28, 51. On my definition what he sets out is a form of liberation theology. The problem is, however, that the focus is exclusively on community, and does not take into account the environmental dimension which is crucial to any contemporary reflection.

Godself, the theology of liberation, on the one hand, and the theology
of bats and owls disputing about the midday sun on the other. Christian
theology is concerned, in Paul Lehmann's phrase, with what it takes to
make and to keep human life human. It is concerned with what God
does (if anything) to free us from all those things which de-humanise us,
which Scripture and tradition name variously as sin or the 'principalities
and powers'. Because we are earth and not angels these things are
essentially bound up with the physical and historical material, with
bodies and buildings and structures and institutions. The process of
liberation goes on there and not just in our minds and souls. And the
claim of the gospel is that, appearances to the contrary, this process of
liberation does go on here and now – it is not something we simply have
to sigh for in the next life.

In understanding redemption as liberation in relation to the built
environment I take Walter Wink's work on the Powers as a fundamental
clue.[74] The New Testament language of 'the Powers', he argues, refers
to 'the actual spirituality at the center of . . . political, economic, and
cultural institutions':

> The spiritual aspect of the Powers is not simply a 'personification' of institutional
> qualities that would exist whether they were personified or not. On the contrary,
> the spirituality of an institution exists as a real aspect of the institution even when
> it is not perceived as such. Institutions have an actual spiritual ethos, and we
> neglect this aspect of institutional life to our peril.[75]

Places, as well as churches and nations, have what is sometimes an almost
tangible inner spirituality, which marks them off from every other place,
and puts its impress on its citizens. Architecture can be an especially
eloquent expression of this inner spirituality. Wink gives the example of
being in a church in Peru which was 'dead'. 'What could the priest say that
could counteract the thunderous statement made by a building erected
on the site of a razed Inca temple, by virtual slave labour, adorned with
gold leaf stolen from a high civilization by a group of Spanish thugs, and
whose chapel had been converted into a curio shop?'[76] *Mutatis mutandis*
this question is raised in virtually every human settlement, from the

[74] W. Wink, *Naming the Powers, Unmasking the Powers, Engaging the Powers,* all Minneapolis: Fortress,
1984, 1986, 1992 respectively.
[75] Wink, *Engaging the Powers,* p. 6. Harries cites a dispute between Ernst Gombrich and Hans
Sedlmayr as to whether style teaches us that spiritual collectives are independent realities.
Gombrich thought such talk weakened resistance to totalitarian habits of thought (Harries,
Function, p. 64). Wink demonstrates precisely the contrary.
[76] Wink, *Unmasking the Powers,* p. 74.

smallest village to the greatest city, and in relation to all of our buildings. Stephen Sykes has warned that the use of the term 'spirituality' requires care, but in Wink's sense it provides us with a crucial theological tool for understanding the built environment, and equally spells out the Church's task in seeking a world made conform to Christ, a specifically Christian reading of 'Vitruvian man'.[77]

At the turn of the new millennium the material for Christian rumination is particularly densely related and intractable. We have to come to terms with a world population which has doubled in fifty years to top 6 billion, and which has to be not just fed, but housed. We have to come to terms with a change in the balance of human settlements which has profound psychic and spiritual consequences for us. Deep into the twentieth century villages have been home to most of the human race, but in the last decade of that century the proportion of people in cities finally exceeded fifty per cent, and the trend towards urbanisation continues, despite what is called 'counter urbanisation' in some parts of the First World. I shall argue that a liberation theology of the environment seeks to call the world 'home', but these changes call the homeliness of the world in question. The impact of these changes is intensified by the pattern of transport use which became general by the end of the twentieth century. The twentieth century refined and generalised, but did not make substantial advances on, the modes of transport invented at the end of the nineteenth century. These modes of transport, available to a greater and greater share of the world's population, have put tremendous pressure on both resources and environment, and led to the construction of vast highways and, to use Jane Jacob's phrase, the sacking of cities. Many environmentalists claim, I shall argue, rightly, that either new inventions and new technologies, or the taming of the aeroplane and the motor car are necessary both to urban and planetary survival. By the end of the twentieth century the environment had become a vital dimension of any liberation theology. The changes brought about both by urbanisation and by new technologies also pose profound problems for human consciousness. To be human, we said, is to be placed. But, as Manuel Castells has argued, the sense of place, of historical, regional and cultural

[77] S. Sykes, 'Spirituality and Mental Sickness', in M. Nation and S. Wells (eds.), *Faithfulness and Fortitude* (Edinburgh: T&T Clark, 2000). He writes: 'To define "spirituality" as "the human propensity to find meaning in life" is not merely to retreat from the concrete specificity of Christian spirituality. It is a transformation from a God centred account to one focused on humanity, which, if offered as a substitute for a Christian understanding, would be simply in massive contradiction to the main strands of the Christian tradition' (pp. 71–2). This does not apply to Wink's understanding.

memory, is increasingly dissolved in what he calls the 'space of flows' –
the dominance of the world by finance capital, and by great corporations
operating through information technology, whose true home often seems
to be 'cyberspace'. But in this situation the alienation which Marx was
analysing in the 1840s, in the context of the first industrial revolution, is
greatly intensified, and human beings lose the sense of being at home in
the world. Another dimension of this alienation is the loss of charm in all
forms of the built environment. The built environment reflects not just
ideologies but, in Wink's terms, spiritualities. Profound, creative, grace
filled spiritualities produce grace filled environments; banal, impoverished, alienated spiritualities produce alienating environments. If that
is the case, and I believe it is undeniable, then theology is anything but
incidental to the debate about the built environment which is such a vital
dimension of the human future. Christians in the city 'have the opportunity to lead and advocate for neglected understandings of the city and
of civil government', but in order to do this they need serious biblical
and theological reflection.[78] Where Ben Sparks speaks of 'the city' here I
have placed the built environment as a whole. Nearly half of humankind
live in villages and suburbs, and exactly the same goes for them. What I
am attempting is not an essay in urban theology, or theology of the city,
although some chapters deal primarily with the city, but a theological
reflection on the living environment we make for ourselves.

I begin with an exploration of the most basic dimension of thinking
about the built environment, the divine grounding of our experience of
space, and I set out a Trinitarian mapping of that space. In the third
chapter I go on to a major theme of the Hebrew bible, explored at
length in the Christian tradition, and of fundamental significance in
an unjust world, the ownership of land. The human dwelling is the
theme of the next chapter, an area where renewal of imagination is of
key importance as, in the West, we seem to have built ourselves into a
dead end. I then attempt a theological reflection on the ancient theme of
town and country, before turning to the meaning of the city. In chapters 7
and 8 I examine the built environment as shaper of community and as
work of art before, in the final two chapters, asking what is required of
us as builders, planners and place dwellers in the opening decades of
the new millennium, foregrounding here the question of eschatology,
what we can hope for. The Trinitarian appropriations, the attempt to
understand the world as it is as created, and in the process of redemption

[78] Sparks, 'From Eden to Jerusalem', p. 49.

and reconciliation, are fundamental to each chapter. I assume, in my treatment of supposedly secular, non theological material, that God the Creator calls all things into being, that God the Reconciler works even now for justice and peace, both through the Church and outwith it, and that God the Redeemer offers us grounds of hope where otherwise that seems more than fragile. In all this I am not attempting to show that, in this or that particular instance, religion, whether Christian or otherwise, lay behind this or that settlement or building. Sometimes this is obvious, at other times it is not. Rather, I take it for granted that theology's major part in the ideologies of all human cultures, not excluding the present, always functions to shape our world. 'The faith and trust of the heart make both God and idol,' said Luther. The question is not really about interesting aspects of cultural history. It is much more about what we are doing with our present. Christians are, as Stanley Hauerwas puts it, following Augustine, 'resident *aliens*', which is to say, called to live counter culturally (Mark 10.43) but to do so as *residents*, as those totally committed to their locality and to the earth (Jer. 29.5). As such they need both to be informed about their world and to reflect on it in the light of their tradition of unsettlement. It is the task of theology to help them to do that, and this book is one small part of that process. Theology is always primarily addressed to the Church, but it is addressed to the Church at a particular time, seeking to understand itself and what, in faith, it has to contribute to the world of which it is an indissoluble part. What happens when we bring together the Bible and the writings of town planners, urban theorists and architects? This book is one tentative attempt to find out.

CHAPTER 2

Constructed space and the presence of God

> ... you have made the Lord your refuge,
> the Most High your dwelling place ...
>   (Psalm 91.9)

After my insistence on beginning with the concrete, I now take a slight
step backwards to discuss the conditions of possibility for the built environment, space in general. Does God have space in Godself? If God is
a-spatial can our spaces – which are always both literally and metaphori-
cally constructed – be redeemed? In asking about the grounding of space
in God, we are asking about the possibility of ultimate redemption for
what we have made of the world. In exploring the issue I shall seek
to bring into conversation Christian and non Christian ideologies, or
theology and secular theory. Picking up the theme of the first chapter I
shall end with an attempt at a Trinitarian mapping of space.

THE IDEOLOGY OF SPACE

In the broadest sense the built environment is a political question – it
concerns the constitution of the *polis*, the shape of the human community. 'Shape' here is not a metaphor. At levels of complexity greater than
hunter gatherer societies, all human communities are class, caste, gender,
and sometimes racially divided. We need only think of the contrast between palace and slum, caste village and outcaste *cheri*, the white suburbs
of Johannesburg and the townships, the gender division implicit in most
Western housing.[1] Christian theology has quite often taken issue with
these distinctions, in the attack on caste, or on apartheid, for example,
but the question of space has only been addressed in the most general
terms. This is doubtless partly because, as argued in the previous chapter,

[1] For example, writing of India P. Sainath notes: 'The cultural geography of the Indian village
is carefully laid out to assign to Dalit dwellings the lowliest and least desirable areas'; quoted by
V. Devi, 'A Cry for Justice', *Frontline* 17/13 (24 June–7 July 2000) p. 50.

theology has often been drawn to abstraction, nourished by a Platonic conviction of the superiority of the spiritual to the material. More recently it shared with other disciplines a conviction of the priority of time over space, cast theologically in the ideas of the 'great acts of God' and 'Hebrew dynamism'. All this has meant that theology has overlooked the fact that politics is about *possession*. This is extraordinary given founding narratives about conquest and promised land, and I shall be exploring the issues that arise from this in the following chapter.

The demonstration that all space is *constructed* was a central concern of Henri Lefebvre, who argued that all societies 'produce' their own versions of space. The arrangement of cities, the forms of the built environment, the relation of town and country, he showed, in an argument now fundamental to most geographical and sociological theory, all express a particular vision of the world, an ideology. The ideology of space is inescapable: we encounter it the moment we emerge from our front door, drive to the out of town shopping centre or visit the local post office. In the built environment social relations are inscribed concretely in space. All ideologies 'project themselves into a space, becoming inscribed there, and in the process producing that space itself'.[2] It is sometimes enough to enter the space of a factory, a state, or a community, comments David Harvey, to conform to its supposed requirements in ways that are both predictable and unthinking. 'Thus does the symbolic order of a city's spaces impose upon us ways of thinking and doing which reinforce existing patterns of social life.'[3] Not just the city either, for the physical plan of Indian villages was designed to reinforce deference and submission, as was the relation of great house and labourer's cottage in Europe. The relation between space and ideology is dialectical: ideology is dependent on space, but our use of space both expresses and affects our ideology. An ideology requires 'a space which it describes, whose vocabulary and links it makes use of, and whose code it embodies'. Indeed, Lefebvre suggests that 'what we call ideology only achieves consistency by intervening in social space and in its production, and thus taking on body therein. Ideology per se might well be said to consist primarily in a discourse on social space.'[4] To instantiate this claim he turns, perhaps oddly, to the Church. 'What would remain of the church if there were no churches? The Christian ideology ... has created the spaces which guarantee that it endures.'[5]

[2] H. Lefebvre, *The Production of Space* (Oxford: Blackwell, 1991), p. 129.
[3] D. Harvey, *The Urban Experience* (Oxford: Blackwell, 1989), p. 250.
[4] Lefebvre, *Production*, p. 44. [5] Ibid. He makes the same point about capitalism.

Lefebvre has an obvious point, though rather than 'ideology' in the singular, we have to insist on the plurality of Christian ideologies.[6] By and large Lefebvre is right that 'monumental buildings mask the will to power and the arbitrariness of power beneath signs and surfaces which claim to express collective will and collective thought'.[7] It is very doubtful, though, that, as he claims, '[t]he use of the cathedral's monumental space necessarily entails its supplying answers to all the questions that assail anyone who crosses the threshold'. On the contrary, though these buildings make claims, they can also be understood primarily as celebration, a sort of carnival in stone, or as an invitation to faith, rather than as an attempt to compel assent. This certainly seems to have been Huizinga's view. 'Of no great truth was the medieval mind more conscious', he wrote, 'than of St Paul's phrase: Videmus nunc per speculum in aenigmate, tunc autem facies ad faciem.'

> The Middle Ages never forgot that all things would be absurd, if their meaning were exhausted in their function and their place in the phenomenal world, if by their essence they did not reach into a world beyond this . . . About the figures of the Divinity a majestic system of correlated figures crystallizes, which all have reference to Him, because all things derive their meaning from Him. The world unfolds itself like a vast whole of symbols, like a cathedral of ideas. It is the most richly rhythmical conception of the world, a polyphonous expression of eternal harmony.[8]

Of course figures like Constantine or William of Normandy, or even the wealthy merchants who paid for the Suffolk wool churches, built churches with a very obvious ideological intent. But in the case of many anonymous religious buildings (whether mosques, temples or churches), which were not part of the self justification or self glorification of rulers or the rich, it is open to argument that they preserve almost uniquely a genuinely democratic space, as the product of a deeply felt piety shared by the workers who put them up, and often enough paid for by the alms of the poor. I shall return to the significance of religious buildings in chapter 8.

---

[6] We only have to think of the different theologies implicit in Hagia Sophia in Constantinople (Istanbul), in early Norman, Romanesque and Perpendicular cathedrals, in Wren's churches, and in Baptist chapels to see that. The exclusive mystery invoked by Cyril of Jerusalem, the power of Byzantine emperors and Angevin kings, the romance of the Virgin Queen, the deism of mercantile capitalism, the work ethic of seventeenth and eighteenth century Protestantism – all these have found expression in church buildings. So survival through time is one thing, but meaning is another.

[7] Lefebvre, *Production*, p. 143.

[8] J. Huizinga, *The Waning of the Middle Ages* (Harmondsworth: Penguin, 1965), p. 203.

To instantiate the ideological power of buildings by pointing to the Church is of course highly ironic given the proud boast of the second century apologists that they had no shrines or altars. The missionary bishop Lesslie Newbigin used to advise villagers in South India not to put up buildings but to meet in private houses, and in the 1970s regarded it as the great strength of the church in Nepal that it had no special buildings, but met in clearings and under trees. He was disappointed that in his first diocese, Madurai in South India, every village congregation sooner or later wanted to put up a 'church'. To him this detracted from the truth that it was the congregation which was the church. But is the dream of doing without buildings impossibly idealist – the product of a theology too purely committed to the Word to the exclusion of structures? And does it imply some failure to take account of the implications of the incarnation for embodiment? Newbigin would have agreed with Barth that the misuse of the category of the incarnation 'cried to high heaven'. But is it sound theology to restrict talk of the incarnation solely to the Christ event, and does it not in fact have profound implications for our social and political practice, as Christian socialists have always claimed?

All ideologies rest on a view of the human, and if the built environment is a concrete form of ideology we naturally look to its implicit meanings. We have already seen some of these instantiated in the different theologies which lie behind the various forms of church architecture. In a version of Foucault's now celebrated 'heterotopias' Lefebvre instances spaces dedicated to voluptuousness (the Alhambra of Granada), to contemplation and wisdom (cloisters), to power (castles and chateaux) or to heightened perception (Japanese gardens).[9] He could have gone on to domesticity (kitchens, Delft courtyards), production of very various kinds (mills, factories, mines), terror (prisons, torture cells, Gulags), debate (agora, parliamentary buildings), buying and selling (market places, malls), the dead (the Taj Mahal!) and the oldest and most obvious of all dedicated spaces, the sacred. All of these have significance for the liberative theology I wish to develop, and some of them I shall return to in due course. Power and the sacred are, however, fundamental to the whole project, and I shall therefore pursue them a little further here.

Power is one of the most obvious meanings of space, and not just in castles and chateaux. As Foucault put it: 'A whole history remains to

[9] Lefebvre, *Production*, p. 137.

be written of spaces – which would at the same time be the history of powers . . . from the great strategies of geopolitics to the little tactics of the habitat.'[10] The built environment as a whole is the orthography of power and class. This was true when William of Normandy ordered a detailed record taken of his whole newly conquered realm, detailing every mill and homestead – centres of production and domestic space – and placing fortresses at strategic points throughout the kingdom. Then, in the greatest of his building programmes, he covered the land with churches, abbeys and cathedrals, claims in stone to ideological legitimacy.

This strategy did not end with the Norman builders. 'Today more than ever', wrote Lefebvre in 1974, 'the class struggle is inscribed in space.' Whether that 'more than ever' was really justified is a question. Perhaps 'still' would be a better way of putting it. As an instance we could follow Sudipta Kaviraj's brilliant exploration of the changing dynamics of space as power in Calcutta.[11] First there was the colonial city, where whole areas were proscribed to Indians, and which centred around a beautiful central park, the Maidan, designed to remind the rulers of the great London parks. Like them the Maidan was 'public', which meant an expression of civic pride rather than something created for the exclusive pleasure of a ruler or some member of the nobility. After Independence the Indian administration continued to lay out parks, which beautified the city and emphasised the contrast between nature and culture. Cricket was played in them, a slow and rather expensive game, suited to the middle class. The parks were ringed with railings, as the colonial parks had been, to mark the boundary between the workaday world and recreation. At some point, however, someone erected a makeshift shop against the railings of one of these parks. Soon, the entire park was ringed by shops, and the railings became invisible. In the earlier regime, the parks were there for middle class constitutionals and family picnics. Of course, they were there for everyone, they were 'public', but the poor only came into them apologetically, aware that they were there on sufferance. Now, however, the poor took over the park. Football took over from cricket and the centre of the park became a mass of dry mud. The grass died out, filth accumulated, the poor moved in more or less permanently, and the parks became a form of urban slum. 'Ironically, the English term *public* would be used in the discourse of this crucial détournement of space. If asked,

[10] M. Foucault, *Power/Knowledge* (London: Harvester Wheatsheaf, 1980), p. 149.
[11] S. Kaviraj, 'Filth and the Public Sphere: Concepts and Practices about Space in Calcutta', *Public Culture* 10/1 (1997), pp. 83–113.

the people would reply that they settled there precisely because this space was *pablik*, not owned by individual property owners, and as poor people they had a quasi-claim to settle in such state or municipal property.'[12] The poor now in the park were far more tolerant of garbage than the middle class. Its accumulation was their way of keeping the former occupants out.

Kaviraj's 'détournement' might seem a version of the Magnificat. The poor end up as possessors, and the rich are sent empty away. But in some respects this is a hollow victory. Possession may be nine tenths of the law, but it is by no means the equivalent of liberation, as D. H. Lawrence indicated in castigating the ugliness of nineteenth century industrial housing, and insisting that the human soul needed beauty more than it needed bread.[13] The story forms an interesting contrast with that of the success of another group of poor people, this time from Liverpool, in Britain. British municipal housing ('council housing' or 'corporation housing') was a response to the many damning reports on slum housing produced in the nineteenth century, and in particular an attempt to provide 'homes fit for heroes' after World War I. As it actually materialised, however, it was often far from that. First, municipal budgets meant that this housing was sometimes put up as cheaply as possible, on the meanest lines.[14] Second, in an effort to see that houses did not deteriorate residents were forbidden from doing their own decoration, but 'the council' saw that it was done every three or four years. The net result was a potent affirmation of the class divide, between owner-occupiers and those who were 'a burden on the rates'. Thus, when the citizens of Liverpool were involved in designing new housing in the 1980s they were adamant that the new housing should not look 'corpy'. Peter Hall quotes the bricklayer chair of one housing corporation involved in the 1980s re-build: 'Council housing is the worst housing ever... It's boring, pathetic, inhuman – like someone went into the architect's department and said, "I want 400 houses – get the drawings in by half-three". They're not houses for *people*.'[15] Liberative détournement, this story makes clear,

---

[12] Ibid., p. 108.

[13] Cited in M. Drabble, *A Writer's Britain: Landscape in Literature* (London: Thames & Hudson, 1979), p. 224.

[14] So Jeremy Seabrook wrote: 'The estates have been constructed with the greatest parsimony of compassion and amenity. They are sketchy, spare and denuded... They invite violence and negation: and the best to be hoped for from the people who are compelled to live here is a sullen and passive indifference' (*City Close-Up* (Harmondsworth: Penguin, 1971), p. 14). This echoes my own experience of growing up in council housing in the previous two decades.

[15] P. Hall, *Cities of Tomorrow* (Oxford: Blackwell, 1988), p. 271.

requires both empowerment and something more, the possibility of beauty, precisely what was lost in Calcutta. I shall return to this question in the eighth chapter.

Today feminist geographers make the point that the power implicit in the arrangement of space is also gendered. Patriarchy has a crucial spatial dimension, a point which is obvious as soon as it is made, but which most of the time, like all good ideologies, is invisible. In the haut bourgeois house women were often allowed into the library only with male permission: the drawing room was their preserve, an arrangement which emphasised that rationality and real power lay with the men. In working class houses until very recently kitchens, where women were expected to spend much of their time, were often cramped and ill lit.[16] In the workplace, studies of North American offices have shown that women work significantly more in shared open space than men.[17] Dolores Hayden argues that the separation of dwelling and workplace has militated against women's empowerment, and functioned to keep them in the domestic world.[18] A liberative theology, which will automatically be a feminist theology, shares with these geographers a concern for re-thinking gendered space.

A crucial aspect of power which finds expression in the built environment is *propaganda*, something which rulers have known from Hellenistic, if not Egyptian and Mesopotamian, times. 'Political space is not established solely by actions,' says Lefebvre. 'The genesis of space of this kind also presupposes a practice, images, symbols and the construction of buildings, of towns and of localized social relationships.'[19] The twentieth century was rich in the perception of this truth: consider the different forms of Fascist and Stalinist monumentality, and the authoritarian visions of Le Corbusier, measured against the utopian socialism of Unwin's Letchworth, which was inspired by a romantic vision of the middle ages.[20] In Wink's terms the Powers express themselves in many forms in the built environment. Wink speaks of the Powers being created, fallen and redeemed. We know what 'fallen' buildings look like. Do we know what they look like redeemed? The very question makes the point

---

[16] It was, however, a point of principle with Raymond Unwin to see that the kitchen should get some sunshine during the day.

[17] D. Spain, *Gendered Spaces* (Chapel Hill: University of North Carolina Press, 1992), p. 206.

[18] D. Hayden, 'What would a non sexist city be like?', *Signs* 5/3 (Supplement) (1980), pp. 170–87.

[19] Lefebvre, *Production*, p. 245.

[20] As Graham Ward correctly notes, the attempt to recall the middle ages in built form took no account of the fact that this form expressed a world view which was now irrecoverable. *Cities of God* (London: Routledge, 2000), p. 39.

that humane and non imperialist cultures are essential before we learn to build like this.

Over against spaces dedicated to power Lefebvre set *spaces for pleasure* and voluptuousness but believed that while such spaces have existed, they are few and far between. 'An architecture of pleasure and joy, of community in the use of the gifts of the earth, has yet to be invented.'[21] The reader of Scripture will at once think of the 'city' of the Song of Songs, but perhaps that is any environment seen in the light of romantic love. Lefebvre thought that in and through the space of leisure a pedagogy of space and time was beginning to take shape. That was in 1974. Was he thinking of the tourist beaches already well established by that time? Of the erosion of every popular mountain trail and indeed every climbing route? What would he have made, I wonder, of Disneyland Paris and the ever larger out of town shopping centres? The pedagogy of places dedicated to leisure seems only too imbricated in the pedagogy of power.

Lefebvre distinguished *spatial practice* – the particular use of space of a given culture; *representations of space*, which the relations of production impose; and *representational spaces*. In medieval Europe, for example, spatial practice embraced the network of local roads close to peasant communities, monasteries and castles, and also the many roads between towns and the great pilgrim and crusader ways. Representations of space, on the other hand, were borrowed from Aristotelian and Ptolemaic conceptions, as modified by Christianity: the so called 'three tier universe' of heaven and hell, with the earth at the centre. Representational spaces, for their part, 'determined the foci of a vicinity: the village church, graveyard, hall and fields, or the square and the belfry. Such spaces were interpretations, sometimes marvellously successful ones, of cosmological representations.'[22]

If we map this scheme onto the present then surely we end up with a situation where representations of space are concerned above all with leisure and consumption, and where such pedagogy of space and time as there is, is wedded to the market. For those in the West representational spaces include spaces dedicated to consumption (shopping malls), to keeping the need for reflection at bay (amusement arcades), and to the fetishisation of the body (sex shops, body piercing studios). Equally in our own day the lyrical spaces of mountains, lakes and forests, celebrated the moment industrial capitalism began to emerge, have been first defended

[21] Lefebvre, *Production*, p. 379.   [22] Ibid., p. 45.

and then problematised as reserves and national parks. For they too are reinscribed with the fundamental meaning of leisure, and the problem of over use becomes ever more serious.

The representation of space in our society is in turn something like an account of 'real estate'. The development of map making, David Harvey argues, meant that space came to be represented, like time and value, as abstract, objective, homogeneous and universal in its values. Space was bought and sold as a commodity and the effect was to bring all space under the single measuring rod of money value.[23] Once money becomes a mediator of commodity exchange this radically transforms and fixes the meanings of space and time in social life. It is not only time but space which 'is' money, a process compounded by the growth of casino capitalism where property is bought and sold as an investment in the same way as stocks and shares.

The contrast between these two spatial mappings, the medieval and the modern, speaks volumes, for what has disappeared is the transcendent reference, and what has taken its place is Mammon. In chapter 9 I will take up the environmental implications of this fact. The social implications are examined by Castells in terms of a contrast between the 'space of places' and the 'space of flows'.[24] By the latter he means the social reality of the world in the information society, where money is made and information accessed in seconds by the world wide informational network. Just as the pack horse defined space in medieval times, and the railway for the industrial revolution, so information technology does now. In the network, 'no place exists by itself, since the positions are defined by flows'. The key points in this space of flows are the 'nodes' and 'hubs' which are the key movers in the global economy, and in high technology manufacturing. Information is managed by a global elite who constitute 'symbolically secluded communities, retrenched behind the very material barrier of real estate pricing', a sort of super class.[25] World wide they create a uniform lifestyle which supersedes historical specificity, a uniformity reflected in the architecture of postmodernity. Everyone, of course, still lives in a territorially defined place, but because power lies with the space of flows the meaning and dynamic of places is altered. He sees a schizophrenic tension arising between flows and place:

[23] Harvey, *Urban Experience*, p. 177.
[24] M. Castells, *The Rise of the Network Society* (Oxford: Blackwell, 1996), pp. 410ff.
[25] Ibid., p. 416.

The dominant tendency is toward a horizon of networked, ahistorical space of flows, aiming at imposing its logic over scattered, segmented places, increasingly unrelated to each other, less and less able to share cultural codes. Unless cultural *and physical* bridges are deliberately built between these two forms of space, we may be heading toward life in parallel universes whose times cannot meet because they are warped into different dimensions of a social hyperspace.[26]

Perhaps this schizophrenia is not as new as he thinks it is, but the problems he raises are real and call into question especially the possibility of fashioning community, the theme of the seventh chapter.[27] Public space is essential for this task, a fact recognised from the creation of the Greek agora onwards.[28] We have many public spaces of course, but fewer and fewer with resonance for civic society, and those we have are increasingly threatened by municipal neglect and vandalism.[29] In the North, over all classes, the privatisation of space is a symptom of the problem. Space has become a dominant metaphor in contemporary Western culture, expressing its ruling individualism. Everyone wants their own 'space' and housing needs change accordingly.[30] In Engels' Manchester, as in the Third World today, many families crowded into a single room and one toilet served and serves perhaps twenty or thirty families: now middle class families require a separate room for each member and some North American homes have more latrines than Third World houses have rooms. For the contemporary Westerner, says Brueggemann, '"Space" means an arena of freedom without coercion or accountability, free of pressures and void of authority. Space may be imaged as week-end, holiday, avocation, and is characterized by a kind of

---

[26] Ibid., p. 428.

[27] As Harvey remarks, the importance of the information revolution can easily be exaggerated (*Spaces of Hope* (Edinburgh: Edinburgh University Press 2000), p. 62). Castells' space of flows and space of places call to mind earlier versions of local and global, universal and particular. Is it really the case, as Graham Ward assumes in *Cities of God*, that we are living in a radically new age, as far as cities are concerned, in which the older theologies of the city no longer have any relevance?

[28] Kaviraj argues that the idea of 'the public' emerged in Europe in the eighteenth century (*Filth*, p. 86). The delimitation of public and private is much older, however, written into the Norman forest laws, the laws of common land and, in churches, into the distinction between nave, chancel and altar. We know that the naves of medieval churches were 'public space' in the fullest possible sense, used for a wide variety of 'secular' purposes.

[29] A clear example of this is what happened to Tompkins Park in New York, as detailed in chapter 7. In Britain the increasing neglect of public parks, and the elimination of 'park keepers' from municipal budgets, mark a change in perceptions about the importance of public space.

[30] Harries is more sympathetic to the need for private space in which we dwell 'at least for a time with our own dreams and thoughts'. For that reason there is something inhuman about glass architecture. K. Harries, *The Ethical Function of Architecture* (Cambridge, Mass.: MIT, 1998), p. 196.

neutrality or emptiness waiting to be filled out by choosing.'[31] Compare
the Yagua of the Amazon who live in large open houses and who achieve
'privacy' through a convention whereby they become 'invisible' by turning away from the centre of the house.[32] Empty space can be a positive
asset, as Peter Brook has shown, putting it at the heart of theatre,[33] but
the emptiness Brueggemann speaks of arises from the absolutisation of
'choice'. It is not humankind faced with 'two ways', as Deuteronomy
suggested, but facing the rows of supermarket shelves. It is an absence
of any transcendent referent.

The priority of space in the North is bound up, as David Harvey points
out, with the ideology of private property, which secures our exclusive
rights to dominate a parcel of space. The reason that car and home ownership make such an attractive combination, he adds, is that it ensures an
individualised ability to command and protect space simultaneously.[34]
The same ideology accords purpose to all the individual buildings of
an area – houses, factories, shops, schools and churches – without their
serving together the total life of the community. The recovery of new and
more creative forms of social space, therefore, hangs on the emergence
of a different kind of ideology, a new vision of the human. 'All theology is
anthropology.' Does its failure to impinge on the space of our everyday
world rest, as suggested in the previous chapter, on the presumption of
a fundamental difference between sacred and secular space?

SACRED SPACE AND SECULAR SPACE?

'The earth is the Lord's and all that is in it' (Ps. 24.1). The implication of
this affirmation seems to be that, as argued in the previous chapter, there
can be no division between secular and sacred space, no territories which
can be carved up between God and Caesar – an implication crucial to
Jesus' famous answer to the Pharisees (Mark 12.13f.). God as Creator,
Redeemer and Sustainer is to be found in all space and all space is
grounded and has its origin in God. And yet most, if not all, cultures have
sacred spaces – springs, wells, groves, mountains, churches, mosques,
temples. Can we in fact dispense with an account of sacred space?

In his defence of sacred space Mircea Eliade appeals to the story of
the burning bush: 'Come no closer! Remove the sandals from your feet,
for the place on which you are standing is holy ground' (Exod. 3.5).

---

[31] W. Brueggemann, *The Land* (Philadelphia: Fortress, 1977), p. 5.
[32] A. Rapoport, *House, Form and Culture* (New Jersey: Prentice Hall, 1969), p. 66.
[33] P. Brook, *The Empty Space* (Harmondsworth: Penguin, 1972).
[34] Harvey, *Urban Experience*, p. 197.

Anthropologists find stories like this in every culture. As opposed to such sanctified spaces 'there are other spaces that are not sacred and so are without structure or consistency, amorphous . . . For religious man, this spatial nonhomogeneity finds expression in the experience of an opposition between space that is sacred – the only real and real-ly existing space – and all other space, the formless expanse surrounding it'.[35]

This experience of the non homogeneity of space, Eliade claims, is primordial, and it is this alone which allows the constitution of a world, revealing the central axis for all future orientation. 'When the sacred manifests itself in any hierophany . . . there is also revelation of an absolute reality . . . The manifestation of the sacred ontologically founds the world.'[36] The claim is, then, that we cannot do without Eliot's 'still point of the turning world'. The chaos of the homogeneity and relativity of profane space cannot sustain a world. A profane world is therefore, for Eliade, a contradiction in terms: it lacks the form imposed on chaos to make a world. Hegel agrees. For him '[t]he task of architecture is to build a bridge between humanity and divinity, to provide both individual and community with an integrating centre'.[37]

Now it is quite clear that space is not all on a level. Eliade instances the familiar image of a church. You step off the street and you are in a 'different world', a difference which can be accentuated by stained glass, candles and incense. Here in these 'sacred' precincts the profane world is transcended. But we have to ask whether 'sacred' space can be as precisely physically located as Eliade claims. In addition to space which is overtly religious there is other space which has religious or pseudo religious significance. If sport is an *ersatz* religion, is a football stadium sacred or profane? What was going on when Anfield Road, in Liverpool, was filled with flowers after the Hillsborough disaster? Did Kensington Gardens become a sacred place when the same thing happened after the death of Princess Diana?

Further, Eliade's categorisation of sacred space seems too formalised for the sacred space we actually experience. In the first place, *memory* plays a crucial part. People often feel that ancient churches are 'sacred' because they are places where 'prayer has been valid' – they represent a tradition

---

35 M. Eliade, *The Sacred and the Profane* (New York: Harcourt & Brace, 1959), p. 20. According to Eliade four features mark all sacred space: first, a break in the homogeneity of space which is, secondly, symbolised by an opening by which a passage from one cosmic region to another is made possible (this may mean nothing more than the opening of a church door off the street); thirdly, communication with heaven is expressed by one or another of certain images, all of which refer to the axis mundi: pillar, ladder, mountain, tree, vine and so on; and finally, around this cosmic axis lies the world, hence this axis is located 'in the middle' at the navel of the earth (p. 37).

36 Ibid., p. 21.   37 Harries, *Function*, p. 140, referring to Hegel's *Lectures on Aesthetics*.

of engagement with the transcendent which engages us in turn. It is this, I would argue, which we cannot do without rather than Eliade's sacrality. In 1966 the architect Denys Lasdun noted that 'the important thing about buildings of the past is the character that they give a place . . . without a sense of place there can be no sense of belonging'.[38] This *sense of place* has been at the centre of much of the discussion of space in the past thirty years. Walter Brueggemann makes a fundamental distinction between space, which we use as a category, and 'place'.

Place is space which has historical meanings, in which important words have been spoken which have established identity, defined vocation, envisioned destiny . . . Place is indeed a protest against the unpromising pursuit of space. It is a declaration that our humanness cannot be found in escape, detachment, absence of commitment and undefined freedom.[39]

In Scripture 'there is no timeless space but there also is no spaceless time. There is rather storied place, that is a place which has meaning because of the history lodged there. There are stories which have authority because they are located in a place.'[40] It is not a profane world which is a contradiction in terms but a world which has lost its memory. Without memory, 'chaos is come again'.

Quite independently, Christian Norberg-Schultz mounted a similar argument, appealing to Heidegger. For him the purpose of architecture is to create 'dwelling'. Human beings 'dwell' when they experience the environment as meaningful, and this happens when spaces become places. A place is a space which has a distinct character. Sacred places orientate us and help us find identity. 'In man's understanding of nature we thus recognize the origin of a concept of space as a system of places. Only a system of meaningful places makes a truly human life possible.'[41] Of course these grand statements only have any significance when we try and translate them to apply to council estates, tower blocks, favellas and so forth. Stripped of the fancy rhetoric what all this means is that people en-story and en-soul their places and then, in the course of the dialectic of material life, their places en-soul them.

Because this is the case, new sacred places emerge, and some sacred places lose their aura, as stories lose their power to move. It is doubtful if anyone today experiences a theophany in the remains of the temple of Capitoline Venus, for example. And turning a shrine into a museum is

---

[38] Quoted in F. W. Dillistone, *Traditional Symbols and the Contemporary World* (London: Epworth, 1973), p. 85.
[39] Brueggemann, *The Land*, p. 185.   [40] Ibid.
[41] C. Norberg-Schultz, *Genius Loci* (New York: Rizzoli, 1980), p. 28.

as good a way as any of 'de-sanctifying' it – a key problem currently for congregations who need to appeal to English Heritage for funds to restore their churches. There are also, it seems, spaces which are properly sacred to individuals, but not to society as a whole – one thinks, for example, of Thomas Hardy's *After a Journey*, one of his poignant laments for his first wife. The transcendent dimension here is, as it is paradigmatically in Scripture, bound up with relationship, and it is memory which marks the place out as 'sacred'.[42] Because space is a social and ideological reality, and not simply, as it was believed for centuries to be, either a container for all possible objects, or a category of our thinking, it has a *history*, both individual and corporate, in which the secular and the sacred are deeply intertwined.

Fundamental to a Christian understanding of sacred space has to be the puzzling verse in John 4:

Jesus said to her, 'Woman, believe me, the hour is coming when you will worship the Father neither on this mountain nor in Jerusalem . . . [t]he hour is coming, and is now here, when the true worshippers will worship the Father in spirit and truth . . . (4.21, 23)

This passage does not mean, as it has sometimes been taken to do, that henceforward there is worship of an undifferentiated God undifferentiatedly omnipresent. Karl Barth insisted that it had to be read Christologically: 'The opposite of Jerusalem and Gerizim and all temples made with hands . . . is not the universe at large . . . but Jesus.' This does not mean, however, that space ceases to be important, to be replaced, in Calvinist fashion, only by the 'word of the Cross'.

On the contrary, we have only to glance at the way in which the terms 'spirit' and 'truth' are used elsewhere in St John's gospel and we shall see that it is worship of God mediated through Jesus as the One who makes everything known to us . . . God does not cease to dwell in the world in definite and distinct ways . . . He does not cease to be in special places.[43]

These 'special places' are those of individual and community encounter, as I have argued.

There is also the question whether what Eliade identifies as sacred space is as crucial as he maintains. 'The manifestation of the sacred

---

[42] Calling attention to relationship as the true locus of transcendence may seem obvious, but we should think of Kant's 'starry heavens' and the Romantic approach to the sublime, as in Wordsworth's *Prelude*. Human relationships play no part here.

[43] K. Barth, *Church Dogmatics* II/1 (Edinburgh: T&T Clark, 1957), p. 481.

ontologically founds a world...The chaos of the homogeneity and relativity of profane space cannot sustain a world.' This could be read as a way of *defining* what is to count as sacred. Laurie Lee's evocation of the village of Sladd, for example (in *Cider with Rosie*) or Alison Uttley's account of the Derbyshire farmhouse of her childhood (in *The Country Child*) both undeniably constitute a 'world' in the fullest sense Eliade could require but overtly sacred space (i.e. the local church) is entirely peripheral to both. There is nothing amorphous or lacking in structure about these spaces. In both cases the domestic kitchen is the true focus of shared life. Sennett suggests that it was the industrial revolution which made the home the secular version of spiritual refuge, shifting the notion of sanctuary from church to domestic interior.[44] But is the sanctity of 'secular' space not implicit in ancient notions of hospitality, carried over and raised to a higher power in the upper room and the house churches of the first and second centuries? Is this not what was signified in the *lares* and *penates* of Roman religion, and the significance of the domestic shrines of contemporary Hinduism?

I would say, rather, that all space is *potentially* sacred, waiting for the moment of encounter in which it mediates God. We can understand it through the same analogy by which Barth understands Scripture. Scripture is not *per se* the Word of God, he said, but it *becomes* it, as the water of the pool of Bethesda healed when the angel stirred it. If that is the case, then *sacred space is bound up with event, with community, and with memory.* What we conventionally understand as sacred spaces have a sacramental significance with regard to all other space: they are a reminder of the potential for epiphany of all other spaces.

THE DIVINE GROUNDING OF OUR EXPERIENCE OF SPACE

For much of Christian history John's claim that 'God is Spirit' has been taken to mean that whilst God may have created space God in Godself must be 'above' it – space-less – in the same way that God is 'above' time. But this leaves our spatiality without theological grounding and by implication a matter of secondary or penultimate significance. If God does not possess time in a pre-eminent sense, Karl Barth argued, then the reality of our own time is threatened. Similarly, to fully appreciate our own spatiality we need a theology of the 'eminent spatiality' of God.

[44] R. Sennett, *The Conscience of the Eye* (New York: Norton, 1990), p. 21.

Talk of divine 'space' seemed nonsense not just in the classical tradition of Christian theology, but to the theologians of secularisation, who argued that space and time stand necessarily in tension. Thus Harvey Cox argued that in the Hebrew bible YHWH was divested of spatiality and this meant that he could not be localised at any given geographic spot. Rather, God travelled with God's people.[45] Opposing divine spatiality was part of the struggle with the nature religions of Canaan which, in investing the divine with spatiality, sanctioned royal power and the status quo. Christianity originally maintained the hostility to divine spatiality of the Hebrew bible, but part of the Constantinian 'fall' was 'a fatal respatialization' of Christianity. Its 'non spatial genius' was not rediscovered even at the Reformation. For that it had to wait for the twentieth century and the secular city.

Of course Cox had a point. Ideologies of space can be used to sanction the status quo, and indeed if we want a classical example of the way that happens we need look no further than 1 Kings chapter 8, Solomon's invocation of God at the dedication of the temple. But Cox misses Lefebvre's insight that if space is *produced*, then in dealing with space we are dealing with history. 'Space' is neither the container of all reality, as in the Platonic tradition, nor the sum of the dimensions and relations of objects, as it is for Kant, but a way of understanding *political* reality. The Conquest traditions of the Hebrew Scriptures, as well as the history books, ought to have made that clear. The idea that 'Hebrew thought' privileges time over space, a commonplace of the mid twentieth century, can be seen now for what it was, a product of an essentially historicist or existentialist reading of the texts which missed half of what there was to hear.

A hint that there might be a divine spatiality is given by the frequent use of the preposition 'in' in Scripture. 'In God', said St Paul on the Areopagus, 'we live and move and have our being' (Acts 17). Here he is echoing, if not directly quoting, Stoic views and this highlights the problem which Christianity has always had with the divine spatiality. For Stoicism was pantheistic, and pantheism ultimately identifies the universe and God. Both Christianity and Judaism, however, have insisted that God is not a member of this or any universe. They have, then, on the one hand affirmed God's omnipresence, but at the same time been chary of discussing the implications this has for space. So for Aquinas God's omnipresence in the first instance follows from the fact that God is the cause of all existence. 'Since it is God's nature to exist, he it must

---

[45] H. Cox, *The Secular City* (Harmondsworth: Penguin, 1968), p. 69.

be who properly causes existence in creatures, just as it is fire itself sets other things on fire . . . Now existence is more intimately and profoundly interior to things than anything else . . . So God must exist and exist intimately in everything.'[46] So God fills all places by giving existence to everything occupying those places. Thomas appeals to the analogy of the soul and the body: as the soul exists wholly everywhere in the body, so God exists wholly in each and every thing. We can say that 'God exists in everything by power (*per potentiam*) inasmuch as everything is subject to his power (*eius potestati subduntur*), by presence inasmuch as everything is naked and open to his gaze, and by substance inasmuch as he exists in everything causing their existence'.[47] Divine spatiality, on this account, is primarily a matter of God's *esse*, which sustains in being all that is, and of the creative power that implies. It is not actually about *place*.

Drawing on the biblical language which talks of God's own place Karl Barth outlined a theology of divine spatiality which offers a theological grounding for all forms of created space, and therefore for the built environment. In his discussion of time, Barth talks of God's 'eminent temporality', God's preceding, accompanying and coming after time, and it is this divine temporality, according to him, which grounds our own temporality. In the same way it is God's 'eminent spatiality' which grounds our own created spatiality. Space, in other words, is not something contingent, something which will one day be annihilated and 'be no more', because it has its true and intrinsic ground in God. God is present to other things, and is able to create and give them space, because God in Godself possesses space apart from everything else.[48] What truth, Barth asks, could correspond to phrases like 'in Christ', 'in God' and 'in the Spirit' if God were not genuinely and primordially spatial? 'If it is not an incidental or superfluous belief that we can obtain space from God and find space in him, but a truth which is decisive for the actuality of creation, reconciliation and redemption and the trustworthiness of the Word of God, we cannot evade the recognition that God himself is spatial.'[49] Here, if I am not mistaken, Barth has gone beyond any of his predecessors.

The spatiality of God, and therefore the spatiality of creation, is not monochrome. God is present 'to everything with a presence which is not uniform but distinct and differentiated'.[50] What the tradition calls 'omnipresence' 'is not a shroud which is itself unmoved . . . On the contrary, it is itself that which moves and is moved, which is the real mover

---

[46] Aquinas, *Summa Theologiae* 1a 8.1.   [47] Ibid. 1a 8.3.
[48] Barth, *Church Dogmatics* II/1, p. 474.   [49] Ibid., p. 475.   [50] Ibid., p. 473.

and object of movement in this totality.'[51] In relation to the previous discussion of sacred space this both means that God is free to be present in some places in a way which God is not in others, but precisely because this is a matter of the divine freedom it rules out the possibility of this being a matter of manipulation.

Barth's account of the divine spatiality is explicitly Trinitarian. The origin of all space, according to him, is to be found in the Trinitarian relations. It is the fact that God is present to Godself, that there is a divine proximity and remoteness, which is the basis and presupposition of created proximity and remoteness.[52] God's omnipresence is to be understood primarily as a determination of God's love, in so far as God is not only one, unique and simple, but as such is present to Godself and therefore present to everything which by God is outside God.[53]

> God's omnipresence is the perfection in which he is present, and in which he, the One, who is distinct from and preeminent over anything else, possesses a place, his own place, which is distinct from all other places and also preeminent over them all ... God's presence necessarily means that he possesses a place, his own place, or ... his own space ... If God does not possess space, he can certainly be conceived as that which is one in itself and in all. But he cannot be conceived as the One who is triune, as the One who as such is the Lord of everything else.[54]

Unlike Aquinas, therefore, Barth has understood omnipresence primarily through relationality, and not through God's creative and sustaining power. As triune, God possesses space. God in turn gifts space and time to us. Space is the form of creation in virtue of which, as a reality distinct from God, it can be the object of God's love.[55]

Following and developing Barth's ideas Jürgen Moltmann appeals to the kabbalistic notion of the *tsimtsum*, the space God makes within Godself for any other reality. God is therefore 'the dwelling place of the world created by him'.[56] If God is omnipresent, then creation cannot be 'outside' God. Later Moltmann gave this a more explicitly Trinitarian cast, appealing to the Trinitarian *'inexistentia'*, the indwelling of the Persons in each other. God, therefore, creates a space which 'corresponds to his inner indwellings'.[57] Space is not identical with God, as in pantheism,

---

[51] Ibid., p. 477.
[52] Ibid., p. 463. Tillich also thought of space in terms of relations (*On Art and Architecture* (New York: Crossroad, 1989), p. 84), as does a secular thinker like Doreen Massey (*Space, Place and Gender* (Cambridge: Polity, 1994), pp. 264–5).
[53] Barth, *Church Dogmatics* II/1, p. 464.   [54] Ibid., p. 468.   [55] Ibid., p. 465.
[56] J. Moltmann, *God in Creation*, tr. M. Kohl (London: SCM, 1985), p. 149.
[57] J. Moltmann, *The Coming of God*, tr. M. Kohl (London: SCM, 1996), p. 299.

but the dimension of God's omnipresence. 'Absolute space' means the direct presence of God in the whole material world and in every individual thing within it.[58] Here he is not far from Aquinas. But he goes further in arguing that a space for the created world comes into being which is neither the uncreated omnipresence of God nor the relative space of objects. The created world does not exist in the 'absolute space' of the divine being but in the 'ceded space' of God's world presence.[59] This account makes clearer than does Aquinas that the space we occupy is grace, a gift. As I have argued, grace has a radical political dimension: if something is gift it cannot be possessed, owned, hung on to, counted as 'mine' as opposed to 'yours', and when it comes to territory this proves to be a vital principle.

According to Ecclesiastes, everything has its time, and Moltmann extends this to the recognition that everything has its space also. Instead of beginning with God's freedom, like Barth, Moltmann proposes an ecological concept of space, in which every created reality has its own proper environment. Creatures too, however, have their own *'inexistentia'* and so '[e]very human person exists in community with other people, and is also for them a living space. Every living thing is as the subject of its own life the object for other life as well.'[60]

SPACE: THEOLOGICAL AND SECULAR ONTOLOGIES

These accounts of created space bring theology into dialogue with those geographers, such as David Harvey and Edward Soja, who are led to an ontology of space from their concern with its social production. Readers allergic to metaphysics may want to go straight on to the next section (page 48), but since theology is concerned with the ground of all reality it cannot avoid it, and the work of these geographers invites us in this direction.

Harvey appeals to Leibniz and Whitehead for a metaphysic which will lead towards a relational theory of space, place and environment. In Leibniz' theory of internal relations he finds four suggestive possibilities. Leibniz argues that space and time are mutually coordinate and that neither is more fundamental than the other. This allows a plurality of distinct spaces as opposed to a single all-comprehending superspace, and also allows space and time to be viewed as ordering systems inherent within social practices that are 'chosen' rather than given. As

---

[58] Moltmann, *God in Creation*, p. 154.   [59] Ibid., p. 156.   [60] Moltmann, *Coming of God*, p. 301.

such it provides a framework through which we can understand the relations of production, consumption, exchange and distribution within capitalism.[61]

For Whitehead, who wrote, of course, after the discovery of relativity, space and time are relations derived from processes and events. What this means is that spatio-temporality cannot be examined independently of processes. Spatial science cannot be divorced from the environment because 'space-time, place and environment are all embedded in substantial processes whose attributes cannot be examined independently of the diverse spatio-temporalities such processes contain'.[62]

Soja goes not to Leibniz, but to existentialism and phenomenology, interestingly beginning with Buber. For Buber spatiality was the beginning of human consciousness, in that humans were unique in objectifying the world and setting themselves apart. 'This process of objectification defines the human situation and predicates it upon spatiality, on the capacity for detachment made possible by distancing, by being spatial to begin with.'[63] All social theory, Soja suggests, springs from a chicken and egg dilemma between consciousness and the place which determines consciousness.

Marxist geographers are unlikely to turn to Barth and Moltmann for an ontological grounding to their work, but both offer much which is pertinent to this discussion.[64] The problem, then, is to find an ontology which will ground an understanding of space as relationality, and allow us to understand it as at once produced, in process, and given. These theologians provide such an ontology.

First, event and relation are Barth's two fundamental categories in speaking of God. With regard to the being of God, Barth insisted, 'the word "event" (*Ereignis*) or "act" (*Akt*) is final, and cannot be surpassed or compromised. To its very deepest depths God's Godhead consists in the fact that it is an event . . . the event of his action, in which we have a share in God's revelation.'[65] This event is an event of relation:

As and before God seeks and creates fellowship with us, he wills and completes this fellowship in himself. In himself he is Father, Son and Holy Spirit, and therefore alive in his unique being with and for and in another . . . He does not

---

[61] D. Harvey, *Justice, Nature and the Geography of Difference* (Oxford: Blackwell, 1996), pp. 74, 250–5.

[62] Ibid., pp. 263–4.

[63] E. Soja, *Postmodern Geographies* (London: Verso, 1989), p. 132. The work of Buber's to which he refers is 'Distance and Relation', an article published in *Psychiatry* 20 (1957).

[64] For Barth as a political and historical materialist thinker see my *Karl Barth: Against Hegemony* (Oxford: Oxford University Press, 1999).

[65] Barth, *Church Dogmatics* II/1, p. 263.

exist in solitude but in fellowship. Therefore what he seeks and creates between himself and us is in fact nothing else but what he wills and completes and therefore is in himself.[66]

Like Buber, though earlier and independently, Barth grounds spatiality in 'togetherness at a distance'. 'Presence as togetherness . . . includes distance. But where there is distance, there is necessarily one place and another place. To this extent God's presence necessarily means that he possesses a place . . . his own space.'[67] As we have seen, space has its origin in this pattern of relations.

Leibniz' metaphysic of space thinks of a world of internal relations in which each monad mirrors and reproduces all the relations there are. Harvey identifies three problems with this position, all of which are addressed by Barth. First, if everything is about flows, how are we to speak of individuals or particulars? Where Harvey has 'flows' here, Barth has 'relations'. His ontology is one of the event of relationship, in which relationship and event are mutually defined. This means that individuals or particulars are a necessary part of the dialectic of reality. 'Space' is what makes individual existence possible: 'Space is the form of creation in virtue of which, as a reality distinct from God, it can be the object of his love.'[68] Moltmann, for his part, proposes a perichoretic space of reciprocal in-existence, so that community is the social space of reciprocal self development.[69]

Secondly, Whitehead pointed out that in the case of internal relations everything depends on everything else and therefore we cannot know about anything until we know about everything. But Barth, on the basis of revelation, posits an ontology in which everything is indeed related, but on the basis of freedom and choice ('election'). Relationality is affirmed as ultimate, in that God is relation, but this does not mean that everything depends on everything else. Everything is related, in Barth's view, in its dependence on the source of all reality, God, which is the truth the old doctrine of omnipresence sought to capture. 'God's omnipresence is bound up with the special nature of his presence in his revealing and reconciling work ontologically (in its reality) . . . It is only the One who is present in this special manner and place who is also the God present in the world as a whole' of all act and event.[70] This particular problem does not, therefore, arise for Barth.

---

[66] Ibid., p. 275.   [67] Ibid., p. 468.   [68] Ibid., p. 465.

[69] Moltmann, *Coming of God*, p. 301. *Perichoresis* is the Greek term for the mutual indwelling of the three persons of the Trinity, which Moltmann has already referred to as *inexistentia*.

[70] Barth, *Church Dogmatics* II/1, p. 478.

Thirdly, if all monads internalise all there is, then they can only change under their own volition. How are we to account for change except by a series of unique and non related acts? Leibniz's account is self contradictory. Barth is freed from this internal contradiction because he does not presuppose Leibnizian monads but creatures made in the image of the One who loves in freedom, between whom there is a ceaseless interaction of 'secondary causation'. 'Providence' is the account of God's overruling of all events as an *accompanying*, the ceaseless re-weaving of all created acts of volition.[71]

To illustrate the practical significance of the Leibnizian doctrine Harvey instances the relations of consumption, exchange and distribution which are separate moments of a process in which each moment internalises the others. These moments, Harvey suggests, must be understood in their own right if an idealist view of internal relations is to be avoided.[72] But this is precisely how Barth does understand relations. And because 'God', that is, the fundamental nature of reality and the being in whom space is grounded and takes its origin, is the one who loves *in freedom* then the space which is created is precisely one in which ordering systems are chosen rather than given (as they are with Leibniz). Again, as the one who *loves* in freedom the issue of power, which Foucault above all recognised as bound up with space, is directly addressed.

Of course we have no need of the hypothesis. In the world we experience the distinction and relationship between the limited and that which limits it.

If we find the essence of God in the non spatiality and timelessness of the basis of the world, this means neither more nor less than that God is drawn into the dialectic of the world's antithesis. But this leaves the way open for Feuerbach's question whether God might not be man rather than man in God, and to this question there is no decisive answer. If the only thing which exists is this antithesis which comprehends God, the relativity of the two spheres cannot prevent us from ascribing now to the one and now the other the dignity and function of deity. And this necessarily is what has happened and will always happen apart from the knowledge of revelation and faith.[73]

The Triune God is not to be understood simply as the negative of our experience of space and time, but as its creative origin and ground, and therefore as the possibility of its eschatological redemption. We are invited to understand our experience therefore in and through the narrative

---

[71] K. Barth, *Church Dogmatics* III/3 (Edinburgh: T&T Clark, 1961), pp. 90–154.
[72] Harvey, *Justice*, pp. 73–4.   [73] Barth, *Church Dogmatics* II/1, p. 467.

of this God's creative engagement in creation, incarnation and at
Pentecost.

A TRINITARIAN MAPPING OF SPATIALITY

If we propose a theological, as opposed to a purely sociological or philosophical, reading of space this will be in virtue of the compelling power
of the whole story. But the explanatory power of a Trinitarian understanding of God as a way of understanding space is far from negligible.
Developing the suggestions outlined at the end of the previous chapter I
suggest that the following represents a Trinitarian mapping of spatiality
which might ground the kind of revolutionary practice which Lefebvre,
Harvey and Soja all seek.

God the Redeemer (more traditionally, God the Holy Spirit) is the
author of all hopeful visions and of all human creativity. 'God', then, is
the inspirer of all those visions of a better human environment, whether
in the utopian vision of Ebenezer Howard or that of one of his sharpest
critics, Jane Jacobs. Because 'God' is relational event there cannot be any
divine blueprint (Ezekiel 40–8 notwithstanding) but rather a constant negotiation of those spatial forms in which life, justice and joy are nurtured.
If 'event' is the final word when it comes to God, then 'imagination' is
for the built environment, as Marx reminds us in the famous passage in
Capital.[74] The built environment is a product of vision, and the fact that
so much of it is palpably bad and life denying is due to what theologians
call 'sin', which is to say the denial of relationship, justice and integrity.
All necrophilic building emerges from views where power has corrupted,
and sometimes corrupted absolutely. The command to 'discern the spirits, whether they are of God' is therefore as vital in the built environment
as in any other area of political theology.

God the Creator is the one who brings order out of chaos, the structuring of space by form which we shall consider in detail in chapter 6.
Because God has often not been understood as the One who loves in
freedom, but rather as 'sole ruler of the universe', this activity has been
thought of as a form of Stalinist central planning. Not by accident has
the reaction to modernity alleged that human beings have wanted to
'play God', and not least in the built environment. But the order which
emerges from the God who loves in freedom is much more akin to the
consultative process which generated the Liverpool re-build mentioned

[74] 'What distinguishes the worst architect from the best of bees is this, that the architect raises his
structure in imagination before he erects it in reality' (*Capital* Pt I ch. 7).

above, which was fully consultative from the start. 'Would that all the Lord's people were prophets' (Num. 11.29) is the decisive text for the ordering process in the light of the Trinitarian revelation, as Blake saw.

God the Reconciler takes flesh in order to teach peace to the nations. Alienation, domination and reconciliation can all be and are expressed in the built environment. In the 'Christian' middle ages Jews were herded into ghettoes; in corporate housing in much of the twentieth century domestic architecture underlined the fact that there were second class citizens; many traditional societies had male and female 'sides' or social space and, as Dolores Hayden and Daphne Spain have illustrated, this remains an issue. If reconciliation is to go beyond pious talk it needs to take shape in the built environment where social justice is, quite literally, made concrete. But peace, as Richard Sennett has helped us to see, is not about the absence of difference and even conflict, but rather about what we do with it, how we live with it and harness it creatively.

Imagination, order, and justice are, then, the keywords of a Trinitarian theology of space and the built environment in which the relational event which grounds all reality, God, seeks correspondence. In the remainder of the book I want to see if it is possible to make sense of that claim in relation to the land in which we dwell, the dwellings we live in and the settlements we create.

CHAPTER 3

The land

The land shall not be sold in perpetuity, for the land is mine; with me you are but aliens and tenants.

(Leviticus 25.23)

Space is constructed, but land, property, territory, is *possessed*. After an ontology of space the most fundamental presupposition of any theology of the built environment – and potentially the most politically explosive – is a theology of the land. Without land we cannot live, but how is it to be allocated and husbanded? Hilaire Belloc described human beings as 'land animals' because '[t]he very first condition of all, viz, mere space in which to extend his being, involves the occupation of land'.[1] The problem is that, even before pressures of population became serious, land for some has, at least since the agricultural revolution in Neolithic times, meant dispossession for others as it does today in the Balkans and in Palestine. And conquest has left the world littered with struggles for autonomy – in Chechnya and Tibet, in Sri Lanka, in Kurdistan, in Sudan. Always and everywhere land is both vital for sustenance and for all the goods of identity, but at the same time one of the most obvious foci of aggression.

Even in relatively peaceful and stable democracies land is problematic. In the early part of the twentieth century the right to roam over mountain and moorland was only established in Britain through mass campaigns, imprisonment, and the need to face much violence on the part of landowners' agents, and even today it leaves much to be desired. 'For the visitor', wrote Marion Shoard about Britain in 1997, 'the countryside remains largely inaccessible.'[2] Everywhere inequality is inscribed in space, though perhaps rarely as dramatically as in England

---

[1] H. Belloc in *The Catholic Encyclopaedia* (New York: Universal Knowledge Foundation, 1913), vol. VIII, p. 775.

[2] M. Shoard, *This Land is Our Land* (London: Gaia, 1997), p. 474.

and Scotland, a situation which can still be traced largely to the impact of the Norman invasion of 1066! Half of Scotland's 19 million acres is owned by 608 land owners, and 10 per cent by 18.[3] In England the top 1 per cent of the population own nearly two thirds of the land.[4] Details of ownership are shrouded in secrecy. 'If we based our knowledge on information offered by landowners or by Government', comments Richard Norton-Taylor, 'we would have little idea about who, and how many, owns the land today.'[5] Many ideologies, theological and otherwise, have been framed to justify this situation, for inequality in land ownership is not self evident. According to social anthropologists human beings have existed as hunter gatherers for the vast majority of their history.[6] Hunter gatherers live, where they still exist, in egalitarian, non patriarchal and non property owning communities and archaeological evidence suggests that ancient communities were the same. Was it a memory of this situation which led to the myth of the golden age when, as Virgil put it, 'no peasants subdued the fields; it was not lawful even to assign or divide the ground with landmarks: men sought the common gain, and the earth itself bore everything more generously at no one's bidding' (Georgics I)? This Eden, like hunter gatherer society, knows no agriculture. The problem with it is that hunting and food gathering sustain less than ten people per acre. The agricultural revolution was necessary for human development and expansion, for real growth in the quality of life, but it is this revolution which begets the 'Fall' into inequality: on this fact all are agreed. The puzzle is to know how to interpret it. Why was the emergence of stratification necessary? Two current suggestions are that 'aggrandising' individuals subordinated others, which we can call the 'fatal flaw' theory, or that some families slowly grew worse off by a combination of factors, the 'hard luck' theory.[7] On the first view, competition occurs where abundant resources can be converted into scarcer, desirable goods or services. In the context of competitive feasting excess subsistence resources are converted into desirable resources and, as research amongst existing hunter gatherers has indicated, 'ambitious

---

3 A. Wightman, *Who Owns Scotland* (Edinburgh: Canongate, 1996); R. Callander, *How Scotland is Owned* (Edinburgh: Canongate, 1998).

4 Royal Commission on the Distribution of Income and Wealth, report No. 7, 1979. The Commission was abolished three months into the Thatcher government.

5 R. Norton-Taylor, *Whose Land is it Anyway?* (Wellingborough: Turnstone, 1982), p. 28.

6 K. Sale, *Human Scale* (London: Secker & Warburg, 1980), p. 182, citing a lecture by René Dubos.

7 Brian Hayden represents the first theory: 'Competition, Labor, and Complex Hunter Gatherers', in E. Burch and L. Ellanna Berg (eds.), *Key Issues in Hunter Gatherer Research* (Oxford: Oxford University Press, 1994), pp. 223–43; Peter Bogucki represents the second: *The Origins of Human Society* (Oxford: Blackwell, 1999).

individuals vie with one another for control over excess resources, labor, and the wealth and power that such control confers'.[8] On the second view, settled communities were organised around households whose relative position was constantly changing. Illness, failure to capitalise on new developments such as animal traction, or sheer bad luck, could lead to downward mobility in which households would sink below existing norms of accumulation of property and prestige. In what are called 'transegalitarian societies', in which full equality is no longer in place, but there is no developed social stratification either, asymmetries of power would slowly consolidate. 'Wise decision making and good luck would have played a critical role.'[9] If the 'hard luck' theory is right, then it was not violence, envy, cupidity or any other vice which was responsible for the 'Fall', no sinister bias in human nature. It happened imperceptibly, perhaps over millennia. As social complexity and the level of surplus increased, however, so did inequality. Significantly, societies which did not generate significant surpluses did not generate the same kind of inequality. Visiting Norway at the end of the eighteenth century, Mary Wollstonecraft discovered that '[t]he Norwegians appear to me the most free community I have ever observed'.[10] The foundation of this freedom, as it had been in tribal Israel and large parts of Europe, was security of tenure for the peasant farmers who formed the bulk of the population. There was a (small) class divide in this society, and there was poverty and hardship, but not the vastly unequal pattern of land ownership which Norwegian ancestors foisted on much of the rest of Europe. The result is that class is to this day in Norway not the issue it is in a country like Britain.[11] The absence of large fertile plains for farming probably has much to do with this, as it has with the observation that that there are no caste societies above 6,000 feet, as the local economy is too impoverished to sustain them.[12]

Neither of these theories calls in question Marx's response to something like the 'hard luck' theory: that 'primitive accumulation', which he

[8] Hayden, 'Competition', p. 239.   [9] Bogucki, *Origins*, p. 214.

[10] M. Wollstonecraft, *Letters written during a Short Residence in Sweden, Norway and Denmark* (London, 1889), p. 63.

[11] There is a debate about how real equality is in Norway. In a celebrated book, *The Distant Democracy* (London: Wiley, 1977), Willy Martinussen argued that Norway was in fact characterised by widespread apathy, alienation and social inequality. These findings were challenged by W. Lafferty, *Participation and Democracy in Norway* (Oslo: Oslo University Press, 1981). Significantly, Norway exploited its oil resources as a government, without using the big oil companies, and the revenues have gone into social welfare and national infrastructure. The result is one of the few compelling examples of a rising tide lifting all boats.

[12] D. Quigley, 'Is a theory of caste still possible?', in M. Searle-Chatterjee and U. Sharma (eds.), *Contextualising Caste* (Oxford: Blackwell, 1995), pp. 38–9; H. Alavi, 'The two biraderis: kinship in rural West Punjab', in T. N. Madan (ed.), *Muslim Societies in South Asia* (New Delhi: Vikas, 1994).

read as the reality of original sin, quickly supervened. 'In actual history it is notorious that conquest, enslavement, robbery, murder, briefly force, play the great part.'[13] John Ball and Gerrard Winstanley had already suggested much the same thing.[14] Lewis Mumford argued that the rise of inequality was greatly exacerbated by the rise of the city. Consequent upon the discovery of agriculture human beings lived for millennia primarily in villages, the mother of the human race, the place where ethics were first formed.

But at some point a great elevation of the ruler and the priest took place: apparently after 3000B.C., when there was a similar expansion of human powers in many other departments. With this came vocational differentiation and specialization in every field. The early city, as distinct from the village community, is a caste-managed society, organized for the satisfaction of a dominant minority: no longer a community of humble families living by mutual aid.[15]

I shall return to this rather romanticised view of the village in the fifth chapter.

The development of agriculture not only led to inequality, it also raised the question of land use, illustrated by the story of Cain and Abel. There pastoralists and agriculturalists have to allocate land between them, and murder is the result. With the coming of kings, land is set apart for royal use, and we have land which exists purely for pleasure. The Norman conquerors of Britain appropriated huge areas of forest for hunting, dispossessing existing communities and criminalising access. The story

---

[13] 'This primitive accumulation plays in Political Economy about the same part as original sin in theology. Adam bit the apple, and thereupon sin fell on the human race. Its origin is supposed to be explained when it is told as an anecdote of the past. In times long gone by there were two sorts of people; one, the diligent, intelligent, and, above all, frugal elite; the other, lazy rascals, spending their substance, and more, in riotous living. The legend of theological original sin tells us certainly how man came to be condemned to eat his bread in the sweat of his brow; but the history of economic original sin reveals to us that there are people to whom this is by no means essential... Thus it came to pass that the former sort accumulated wealth, and the latter sort had at last nothing to sell except their own skins. And from this original sin dates the poverty of the great majority that, despite all its labour, has up to now nothing to sell but itself, and the wealth of the few that increases constantly although they have long ceased to work. Such insipid childishness is every day preached to us in the defence of property.' K. Marx, *Capital*, vol. 1, Pt 8, ch. 26.

[14] Walsingham, a hostile witness, said that John Ball 'tried to prove... that from the beginning all men were created equal by nature and that servitude had been introduced by the unjust and evil oppression of men against the will of God...'. Froissart, *Chronicles*, ed. G. Brereton (Harmondsworth: Penguin, 1968), p. 212. Winstanley argued that buying and selling land 'was brought in by war'; 'For the power of inclosing Land, and owning Property, was brought into Creation by your Ancestors by the Sword; which first did murther their fellow creatures, Men, and after plunder or steal away their land.' A Declaration from the Poor Oppressed people of England, in Gerrard Winstanley, *Selected Writings* (London: Aporia, 1989), p. 26.

[15] L. Mumford, *The City in History* (Harmondsworth: Penguin, 1991), p. 50.

of Solomon illustrates the need to allocate land for 'defence capability' (1 Kgs 9.19), another continuing theme throughout human history.

However land inequalities arose, the question today is how to deal with them. In areas such as North and South America, Australia and New Zealand, and Zimbabwe, where primitive accumulation happened relatively recently, and indigenous peoples were dispossessed by white settlers, there has been since the 1970s a global movement to reverse the injustices by which land was taken from them. 'At the heart of this movement', Leonie Sandercock notes, 'there are land claims that are profoundly or potentially destabilizing of established practices of land-use planning, land management, and laws of private property.'[16] The same might be said of challenges to ownership in the North, which is why access to land was criminalised in Britain in 1994.

Urgent questions of another sort are raised by current practices of land use, especially in the North. Increasingly there is the question of whether there will be enough land to feed the world's burgeoning population. Cities, in which slightly more than half the world's population now live, are parasitic on the countryside which supplies their food. But as they grow, so some of the most fertile of the earth's land disappears under concrete, whilst naturally dry land is used by exploiting precious, and effectively non renewable, aquifer resources. Should derelict areas in cities be developed as high intensity housing, or turned into urban farms to improve the environment? Should forests be felled to enable ranching, as is still happening in Brazil? How can we arrive at a proper valuation of these resources? If they are truly global, will the global community fund them?

The theological importance of these questions is illustrated by the fact that the issue of land is central to the Hebrew bible. 'In the whole of the Hexateuch', wrote von Rad in 1943, 'there is probably no more important idea than that expressed in terms of the land promised and later granted by Yahweh.'[17] Walter Brueggemann agrees with von Rad's assessment. Land is, he says, 'a central, if not *the central* theme of biblical faith'.[18] What, then, does it have to say to our condition?

[16] L. Sandercock, *Towards Cosmopolis* (Chichester: John Wiley, 1998), p. 17.

[17] G. von Rad, *The Problem of the Hexateuch and other Essays* (Edinburgh: Oliver & Boyd, 1966), p. 79. A very different understanding of the significance of land, though one I shall not explore here, is proposed by Elaine Scarry. What makes 'the land' such a resonant category, she says, is that it is almost God's body, a separate form of substantiation. God confirms God's existence by the gift of the land. *The Body in Pain* (Oxford: Oxford University Press, 1985), p. 195. Put like this land is almost an anticipation of the incarnation. It functions as gift in an even stronger sense than Brueggemann argues for.

[18] W. Brueggemann, *The Land* (Philadelphia: Fortress, 1977), p. 3.

IDEOLOGIES OF THE LAND IN THE HEBREW BIBLE

Redactor is Rabbenu: the fundamental rule for reading Scripture, which anticipates the 'canonical criticism' of the past thirty years. Scripture, as it is read in the church, is read as an interconnected whole, and not, as scholars have taught us to read it, as a collage of documents, heavily edited, from many different periods. In contemporary reading, however, these results cannot be ignored, and we return to the whole only in the light of the various modes of critical study.

Gerhard von Rad discerned a twofold theology of the land. The first he derived from cultic circles, and this views the land as God's property. We find this view in Leviticus, though it certainly has earlier roots: '[T]he land is mine; with me you are but aliens and tenants' (Lev. 25.23). According to this theology, earth and soil were not tribal property but were the gift of YHWH, and held in fief by Israel. The laws regarding harvest – firstlings (Exod. 23.19), tenths (Exod. 22.28), the leaving of gleanings (Lev. 19.9ff.) all emphasise this same understanding – they constitute a recognition of YHWH's right to ownership. In line with this tradition is the view that Israel too is God's property or inheritance (Deut. 9.26).

The second tradition he called 'historical'. This is the view that the land is Israel's heritage, promised by God to the patriarchs. Since it belongs to God, God's commandments must be observed if Israel is to live in the land. According to the Deuteronomists it was the wickedness of the earlier inhabitants which led to their expulsion and if Israel was not obedient it would suffer the same fate (Deut. 9.4; 4.40).

Fifty years on from this study, Norman Habel has offered a still more complex analysis of six ideologies of the land which he finds in the Hebrew bible, which come from different milieux and offer significantly different insights.[19] Common to many of them is the description of land as *nahalah*, usually translated as 'inheritance'. Habel defines the term thus: 'A *nahalah*, in its primary meaning, is not something simply handed down from generation to generation, but the entitlement or rightful property of a party that is legitimated by a recognized social custom, legal process, or divine charter.' The terms he prefers to use to translate it are 'portion', 'share', 'entitlement', 'allotment', and 'rightful property'.[20] In the light of current discussions of a 'stakeholder economy' we could also use the phrase 'stake in the land'.

The first of Habel's categories is a royal ideology, justifying the rights to power of David's successors in Jerusalem. Here land is the source

[19] N. Habel, *The Land is Mine: Six Biblical Ideologies* (Minneapolis: Fortress, 1995).
[20] Ibid., p. 35.

of wealth for the royal family. In a piece of hyperbole which echoes the claims of the victory stelae of Assyrian and Babylonian kings the psalmist envisages the king of Israel as a world ruler:

> May he have dominion from sea to sea,
> and from the River to the ends of the earth.
> (Ps. 72.8)

Habel comments, 'The people, as a whole, have a right to the land as their entitlement from God. The monarch has a higher entitlement, which extends to the whole earth. The rights of the ancestral families of the land are subsumed under the rights of the monarch to appropriate land needed to increase the wealth of the court.'[21]

The second is the theocratic ideology of Deuteronomy, according to which the land, specifically Canaan, of which YHWH is 'the owner', is an unearned gift. This gift, however, is conditional on good behaviour, and can be revoked. Land itself can form a temptation if it becomes a source of sufficiency other than God (Deut. 8.11–20). Peasant land-holders have an entitlement, a *nahalah*, as their stake in YHWH's gift but '[a]ny Canaanites who happen to survive the wars of YHWH are destined to survive as slave labour with no obvious rights to power or property (Dt 21.10–11)'.[22] Within the community the Levites have special status as a landless elite claiming power over the landed, evoking echoes of Plato's guardians, who have power but no property.

Third, Habel picks out what he calls the 'ancestral household ide-ology' of Joshua, according to which land is a cluster of family lots in Canaan promised by YHWH. The similarity to the peasant hold-ings of Deuteronomy is obvious. 'Each entitlement, given by divine lot according to the command of Moses, apparently becomes the inheri-tance of its ancestral family and household in subsequent generations. Thus the ideology of the book of Joshua provides a charter for ancestral households to claim these inherited lands as territory given by divine decree, regardless of what may have happened to the ownership of these lands over time.'[23] Deuteronomy constantly urges that the Canaanites – considered the source of Israel's idolatry and downfall – should be driven out. That is bad enough, but here, says Habel, 'the terror ideology is relentless'.[24]

In Jeremiah the land appears as YHWH's own *nahalah*, which Israel has abused.

---

[21] Ibid., p. 32.　　[22] Ibid., p. 51.　　[23] Ibid., p. 57.　　[24] Ibid., p. 61.

> ... when you entered you defiled my land,
> and made my *nahalah* an abomination.
>
> (Jer. 2.7)

As a consequence the land suffers, and YHWH suffers with it.

> How long will the land mourn,
> and the grass of every field wither?
> For the wickedness of those who live in it
> the animals and birds are swept away ...
> I have forsaken my house,
> I have abandoned my *nahalah,*
> I have given the beloved of my heart
>   into the hands of her enemies.
>
> (Jer. 12.4, 7)

Jeremiah believes the land will be restored to Israel. At that time, though a reformed monarchy will be restored, power will not lie with the Levites nor with the king, but will be shared by the whole people as promised in the famous vision of the new covenant.

In Leviticus 25–7 Habel finds an agrarian ideology in which, as in Deuteronomy, YHWH is the ultimate land owner, but where the land itself must keep the sabbath. 'By returning the land to its divine owner, the Israelites acknowledge their absolute dependency on the goodness and authority of the landowner.'[25] YHWH's ownership means that no land can ever be sold in perpetuity. This is the foundation of the famous Jubilee legislation according to which land which has been lost because of debt slavery has to be restored every fiftieth year. This ideology assumes a town and country division, envisaging a situation in which peasant farmers will be completely free from domination by the urban elite. Leviticus makes a distinction between 'the land', which may not be sold in perpetuity (Lev. 25.23), and property within a walled city. This can be redeemed within a year of sale, but not thereafter.

If it is not redeemed before a full year has elapsed, a house that is in a walled city shall pass in perpetuity to the purchaser, throughout the generations; it shall not be released in the jubilee. But houses in villages that have no walls around them shall be classed as open country; they may be redeemed, and they shall be released in the jubilee. (Lev. 25.30–1)

Finally, in the Abrahamic stories we have an 'immigrant ideology' where 'land is a host country where immigrant ancestors find God at

---

[25] Ibid., p. 102.

sacred sites, discern promises of future land, and establish peaceful relations with the indigenous peoples of the land'.[26] Abraham fosters a way
of life which mediates blessing and creates peaceful relations with the
owners of the land, the Canaanites.

Curiously, both von Rad and Habel miss the point that the discussion
of land in the Hebrew bible does not begin in Genesis 12, but with the
creation narratives. According to the second creation story humankind
(*Adam*) is taken from the dust (*adamah*) – rooted, therefore, in the soil
(Gen. 2.7). 'Adam' serves the *adamah*. Humankind has a special and
absolutely necessary relationship to the soil: its vocation is defined in
terms of tilling and caring for it (Gen. 2.15). This common rooting in
the earth is the ground of human solidarity. But in the Genesis narrative
this solidarity is at once challenged by the first murder. Abel's blood
cries to God 'from the earth' (*erez*) – the word which is usually used for
the territory of a group, as in '*erez Israel*', the land of Israel (Gen. 4.10).
Cain has to flee this *erez*, becomes a wanderer, and establishes cities.
But the memory of human solidarity remains rooted in the earth, which
cries out for justice. Human solidarity is literally 'grounded', part of
the earth we all tread and which sustains us all. How is this cry from
the earth to be dealt with? The answer of the Hebrew bible is: through
observing Torah, God's directions for everyday life. In doing this we fulfil
our vocation, we serve the *adamah*, and then blood no longer cries out.[27]
Redactor is Rabbenu means that we begin with Genesis, and not with
Exodus, with human solidarity in the soil, and the witness of the earth
against dispossession. Humankind is rooted originally in the soil and not
a particular *land*. 'Being bound to the earth is to be distinguished from
being bound to a homeland. To be bound to the earth relates not to
a place in which I am born and in which my children will be brought
up ... but to life according to Torah.'[28]

What can we take as common between these various ideologies? The
first thing is the claim that the earth belongs to God and is therefore
gift. As such it is a concrete form of what Protestantism spoke of as
justification by faith, as Deuteronomy above all makes clear. According
to the Deuteronomist Israel is given a land 'with fine, large cities that
you did not build, filled with all sorts of goods houses that you did not
fill, hewn cisterns that you did not hew, vineyards and olive groves that
you did not plant' (Deut. 6.10–11). This is true not just of Canaan but of

[26] Ibid., p. 135.
[27] So K. P. Lehmann, 'Die Gerechten erben das Land', in *Texte und Kontexte* 80 4/98, p. 20.
[28] A. Wolf-Steger, 'Gegen den Ausverkauf des Landes', in *Texte und Kontexte* 80 4/98, p. 6.

every 'promised land'. We do not live from our own righteousness but on the basis of God's free gift of grace. Land is not possession but gift. This constitutes 'the sign of a concrete grace . . . not abstract, but a historically real grace, which leads to the formulation of very precise directions for everyday life and to the offer of grace for all peoples'.[29] Though Israel is gifted the land, it dwells in it as a guest and not as a possessor. The inner relationship between promise, Torah and land constitutes the 'concrete Utopia' of the Bible, according to Klaus-Peter Lehmann. This triangular relationship 'demythologises the relation of human beings to the land and constitutes it in terms of relations of righteousness, or more precisely, in terms of relationship to God'.[30]

Secondly, we have seen that *nahalah* occurs in most of the ideologies Habel identifies. The principle of *nahalah* is that every family has its own, roughly equal, stake in the land. The history of primitive accumulation, recorded, amongst other places, in the history of Solomon and his successors, is the history of the end of this situation. What the prophets call 'doing justice' means finding a way to restore it. This is an absolutely concrete political imperative in almost every country on earth (China perhaps being an exception, if we exclude the occupation of Tibet).

Implied in these ideas of gift and stakeholding is the Deuteronomic point that justice is required for Israel to dwell in the land in peace. What is primary is not possession and enjoyment, but obeying Torah, God's concrete guidelines for everyday life. To set those aside, every strand of the Hebrew bible emphasises, is to court disaster. Failure to obey Torah means they will be uprooted and cast into another land (Deut. 29.29) and the land itself will be cursed (Deut. 29.23).

Finally, we live in a world awash with refugees, and many strands of the scriptural narrative speak directly to their condition. We see from the creation narrative that whilst borders may be needed for expediency, they cannot be absolute. *Adamah* comes before *erez* and has prior claim. Abraham, the founder of Israel, spends his life as a stateless person, trying to buy safety for himself even by compromising the integrity of his wife (Gen. 20). And the theme of the exile in Egypt constituted a fundamental ethical guideline for Israel in many directions, but not least in relation to the refugee: 'When an alien resides with you in your land, you shall not oppress the alien. The alien who resides with you shall be to you as the citizen among you; you shall love the alien as yourself, for you were aliens in the land of Egypt' (Lev. 19.34).

---

[29] Lehmann, 'Die Gerechten', p. 18.   [30] Ibid., p. 23.

But how is it possible to understand the gift of land as *justificatio impii* in the light of what Habel correctly identifies as texts of terror? A number of responses to this question may be made. The first, which has effectively been the strategy of liberation theology, is to adopt the thesis of Norman Gottwald that there never was a conquest, but that a small group of escaped slaves joined up with marauding bands coming down from the north and the peasantry of the Canaanite city states to overthrow the petty rulers of Canaan, and establish an egalitarian tribal federation, which lasted for something like two hundred years. Not conquest, then, but a people's revolution.[31] Even if one is disposed to accept this reading of what actually happened, however, it does not change the way historically Scripture has been understood and acted upon, nor the way the text as it stands seems to ask to be read. However, if we follow the basic hermeneutic rule and read the part in the light of the whole, two things have to be said. First, it is obvious that the narrative as a whole, from the Abraham stories to the books of Nehemiah and Ezra, is framed by landlessness and dispossession. We are not reading a text written by conquerors, but by losers. At the beginning of the patriarchal narrative Abram leaves his father's house and native land to go to a land YHWH will show him. He becomes a wanderer without a stake in any land. Having acquired such a stake his descendants lose it due to famine, and are reduced to slavery in Egypt. This is reacquired at the conquest, but only in the context of an ongoing struggle with the Philistines. When this is over Israel survives uneasily in the midst of super power rivalry until the monarchy collapses and the leaders are taken into exile. Though the exiles returned Israel never enjoyed full autonomy again. It is in the period of exile and return that most of the texts in the Hebrew bible were redacted, if not written, and this has an important bearing on the preoccupation with the land, and on ideologies like those of Deuteronomy. The idea of driving out the Canaanites is a fantasy of the powerless. As Nietzsche saw, such fantasies may be poisonous, and have in fact been so at many points in Christian history when used as justification for mass slaughter and conquest. But of course they are only one strand in the text, and need to be read against the Servant Songs of Isaiah and the promises of universal reconciliation which likewise emerge at this time. There is a debate going on in Scripture which we need to listen to, and sometimes to take sides about.

As an illustration of that fact we know that reading Scripture as a whole has in fact often legitimated quite different practices than those

[31] N. Gottwald, *The Tribes of Yahweh* (London: SCM, 1979).

of conquest and dispossession. Here is Thomas Bewick's description of a shepherd, Anthony Liddell, early in the nineteenth century:

The whole cast of his character was formed by the Bible, which he had read with attention, through and through. Acts of Parliament which appeared to him to clash with the laws laid down in it, as the Word of God, he treated with contempt. He maintained that the fowls of the air and the fish of the sea were free for all men; consequently, game laws, or laws to protect the fisheries, had no weight with him.[32]

This use of Scripture as a guide to our approach to the land has, I would argue, been at least as important, if not more so, than that of the justification of possession.

SPIRITUALISING THE LAND?

Appeal to what Christians still call the 'Old Testament' is one thing. But is not everything different in the New? 'My kingdom is not from this world,' said Jesus (John 18.36). Does this not apply to land ownership? Is it perhaps the case that everything we learn in the Hebrew bible is relativised or even set at nought by the New Testament?

Under conditions of alienation it is hardly surprising that the land might become a transcendental symbol. This is what W. D. Davies argues occurs in the New Testament period, and especially after the sack of Jerusalem in AD 70. In Mishnah Sanhedrin 10.1, for example, 'inheriting the land' is equivalent to having a share in the world to come, whilst the Testament of Job clearly contrasts the present perishable world, including the land of Israel, with 'the glory that is imperishable'.[33] After AD 70, Davies argues, Pharisaism was 'prepared to adjust to the absence of the land' and effectively placed Torah above political power and the control of the land.[34] But here too no one ideology held sway. There was, says Davies, 'no one doctrine of the land, clearly defined and normative, but . . . a multiplicity of ideas and expectations variously and unsystematically entertained'. Some Jews continued to believe that land and promise were indissoluble, but not all. Nevertheless the connection between land and promise 'is not always to be "spiritualized", but accorded its full terrestial or physical and historical actuality'.[35]

On the whole Davies does not find evidence for this multiplicity of views in the New Testament. The terminology of promised land plays

[32] Cited in R. Williams, *The Country and the City* (London: Hogarth, 1985), p. 100.
[33] W. D. Davies, *The Gospel and the Land* (Berkeley: University of California Press, 1974), p. 125.
[34] Ibid., pp. 127–8.   [35] Ibid., p. 157.

little part there, nor does *erez Israel*. Only in Stephen's speech in Acts 7 is 'land' a major theme. This speech is at first sight a curious rendering of Israel's history which concentrates on the patriarchs, and then moves very swiftly over the occupation and the reigns of David and Solomon before coming to a sudden conclusion. And what it takes from the Solomonic history is the reminder that God 'does not dwell in houses made with human hands'. Davies reads the speech as insisting that Israel has been too transfixed with historical and earthly securities, with the Temple and Jerusalem. Instead 'the extra territorial dimension of God's challenge and presence' have to be recognised.[36] Jankowski, more convincingly, draws attention to the role the promise to the patriarchs plays in the speech. Despite the promise of land Stephen points out that they never settled, and their situation is that of Luke's addressees, post 70 – once more forced into diaspora. The message of the speech, then, picks up the theme of the risen Christ, that the gospel must be preached 'to the ends of the earth'. It makes the point that it is '*the earth freed through the Messiah* which is the promised land'.[37] This is not a spiritualisation, but a radicalisation, an inclusion of the entire world in the promise to Abraham.

Davies recognises that the Gospel of John is not to be read through Platonising spectacles and that it has a concern for earthly realities. According to him, however, John has reached a position where Christology comprehensively takes the place of any concern with the land. Geography is of no fundamental interest to him, but rather 'the personal confrontation with the One from above, whose Spirit bloweth where it listeth and is not subject to geographical dimensions that had been dear to Judaism'.[38] Both in John and in Hebrews we have the emergence of a sacramental reading in which physical realities are important, but only as the means whereby the infinite God and spiritual realities are made imaginable. 'Such "sacramentalism" could find holy space everywhere, but especially where Jesus had been: this sacramentalism was later on to inform the devotion to the Holy Place among many Christians throughout the ages.'[39] This interpretation confirms what we saw in the last chapter in our reflections on sacred space. Sacramentalism, of course, is certainly not spiritualisation, but rather a way of teaching us to see the spiritual in the material.

Paul appeals to Abraham, the person to whom above all the promise of the land was made. But in Davies' view 'Paul ignores completely the

---

[36] Ibid., p. 272.
[37] G. Jankowski, 'Dieses Land', in *Texte und Kontexte* 80 4/98, p. 57 (my italics).
[38] Davies, *Gospel*, p. 335.   [39] Ibid., p. 367.

territorial aspect of the promise.' 'In Galatians we can be fairly certain that Paul did not merely ignore the territorial aspect of the promise for political reasons: his silence points not merely to the absence of a conscious concern with it, but to his deliberate rejection of it.'[40] Paul universalises salvation by locating it in Christ rather than tying it to a particular land. This does not mean, however, that Paul spiritualises the promise. Rather, as Gerhard Jankowski argues, 'Paul does not have the land, but the whole world order before his eyes . . . Jews and non Jews together, as descendants of Abraham, inherit the world order.'[41] Paul does indeed have a political perspective, but it is not the autonomy of Israel in 'their own' land, but the freedom of all people in the whole earth.

Davies concludes his discussion as follows:

The witness of the New Testament is . . . twofold: it transcends the land . . . Yes: but its History and Theology demand a concern with these realities also. Is there a reconciling principle behind these apparently contradictory attitudes? There is . . . The New Testament . . . personalizes 'holy space' in Christ, who, as a figure of History, is rooted in the land . . . but, as Living Lord . . . is also free to move wherever he wills.[42]

The attitude of the New Testament to the land can therefore, according to Davies, be summed up in the themes of rejection, spiritualisation, historical concern and sacramental concentration. This is a straightforward statement of the attitude of the great tradition in Christian theology towards the question of land. But Jankowski suggests what I believe is a more accurate way of putting it, namely that in the New Testament we have a universalisation of the promise, and of a concern with land which moves beyond Palestine to 'the whole inhabited earth' of Pentecost.

That this is the case can be argued from the famous passage from the *Epistle to Diognetus*, which dates probably from the end of the first century:

For Christians are distinguished from the rest of men neither by country nor by language nor by customs. For nowhere do they dwell in cities of their own; they do not use any strange form of speech . . . But while they dwell in both Greek and barbarian cities, each as his lot was cast, and follow the customs of the land in dress and food and other matters of living, they shew forth the remarkable and admittedly strange order of their own citizenship. They live in fatherlands of their own, but as aliens. They share all things as citizens, and suffer all things as strangers. Every foreign land is their fatherland, and every fatherland a foreign land . . . They pass their days on earth, but they have their citizenship in heaven.[43]

[40] Ibid., pp. 178–9. [41] Jankowski, 'Dieses Land', p. 55. [42] Davies, *Gospel*, p. 367.
[43] Tr. from H. G. Meecham, *The Epistle of Diognetus* (Manchester: Manchester University Press, 1935).

A more radical relativisation of attachment to land and place is hard to imagine, but this is not the same as spiritualisation. This can be seen by comparing it with the attitude of the marginal groups Leonie Sandercock finds operating on what she calls 'the borderlands'. These groups, she says, 'redefine "home" as a state of being in the world, rather than standing in one place, murmuring about our roots'.

Home is the struggle for communities of resistance. And home is that place, wherever, which encourages varied and ever changing perspectives, a place where one discovers new ways of seeing reality. They describe a new consciousness, a consciousness of the borderlands, shaped by cultural collision, forged out of emotional states of perplexity and confusion, open to 'foreign' ways of seeing and thinking.[44]

This is actually not at all a bad way of describing the post resurrection community.

Also in favour of a less spiritualised reading of the New Testament we can note, first, that it derives from the period of the Roman occupation of Palestine, and deliberately distances itself from the Zealot struggle for freedom, which was judged to be either impractical or insufficiently radical. 'Land' in this period might spell 'chauvinist struggle', which can never be liberating. Secondly, Paul is a city dweller, a citizen of the empire, moving freely round the whole of the Mediterranean, and this is his remit. It is this in part which accounts for the universalisation of the promise of which we have already spoken. Thirdly, Davies, like so many New Testament scholars, fails to see that the New Testament presupposes the Old at every point. So we cannot read the Beatitudes, or Jesus' parables, or his first sermon at Nazareth, without the Jubilee year or Deuteronomic theologies of the land in mind. Davies' reading is driven by the assumption that the New Testament is only continuing what was the trend in important strands of inter testamental Judaism, but in some respects Jesus was clearly appealing back past that to 'scripture'. Furthermore, as Brueggemann points out, the theme of kingdom, which is the heart of Jesus' proclamation, includes among its nuances the idea of a historical, political, physical realm, i.e. land, and Jesus tells his followers to pray for this to come 'on earth'. Brueggemann finds a continuance in the Jesus movement of the theology he finds in Torah, namely that the way to land is by loss, whilst the way to lose land is to grasp it. Similarly in Paul, the law and gospel theme can be understood in terms of grasping land and receiving it freely. 'The assertions of Paul are about

[44] Sandercock, *Towards Cosmopolis*, p. 120 (my italics).

living faithfully in history, about being secure in a world which promises no security, about having a place in a displacing world.'[45] To argue, then, that land is or is not a New Testament concern, literally or spiritually, misses the point. 'It is rather the history of a gift and grasp which concerns the church. It is a radical affirmation in the New Testament, based on the Hebrew bible, that to grasp is to lose, whilst to risk is to be given.'[46]

There is no doubt that, as Brueggemann puts it, '[S]piritual Christianity, by refusing to face the land question, has served to sanction existing inequities'.[47] Richard Sennett makes essentially the same point in his claim that Christianity drove a wedge between inner and outer, thereby disenfranchising us from the city. These attitudes cannot appeal to the Christian Scriptures as a whole where 'the voice of the dispossessed' demands a share of the land. That other parts of the Christian tradition have understood this becomes obvious when we turn to the questions of possession and identity.

POSSESSION

The theology of common ownership

'In the beginning of Time', wrote Gerrard Winstanley, in his great manifesto of 1649, 'the great Creator Reason, made the earth to be a Common Treasury, to preserve Beasts, Birds, Fishes and Man . . . not one word was spoken in the beginning that one branch of mankind should rule over another.' [48] The recreation of the situation of the book of Judges was his goal. There can be no freedom, he wrote, 'unless the Land of England be freely set at liberty from proprietors, and become a common Treasury to all her children, as every portion of the Land of Canaan was the common livelihood of such and such a Tribe, and of every member in that Tribe, without exception, neither hedging in any, nor hedging out'.[49] That the land was originally held in common was taken for granted by nineteenth century anthropology.[50] Today we are more discriminating.

---

[45] Brueggemann, *The Land*, p. 178.   [46] Ibid., p. 183.   [47] Ibid., p. 193.

[48] Winstanley, 'The Levellers Standard Advanced', in *Selected Writings*, p. 10.

[49] Winstanley, 'A Declaration . . .', in *Selected Writings*, p. 31.

[50] So, for example, Sir George Campbell in J. W. Probyn (ed.), *Systems of Land Tenure in Various Countries* (London: Cassell, Petter & Galpin, 1881), p. 215: 'We are too apt to forget that property in land, as a transferable mercantile commodity absolutely owned and passing from hand to hand like any chattel, is not an ancient institution, but a modern development, reached only in a very few advanced[!] countries. In the greater part of the world the right of cultivating particular portions of the earth is rather a privilege than a property; a privilege first of a whole people, then of a particular tribe or a particular village community, and, finally, of particular

Many societies were organised in this way, Marion Shoard affirms, but
not all. The Ojibwa Indians in Canada, for example, were organised on
a 'fiercely individual basis' and land was parcelled out on the assumption
of absolute ownership. Trespassers were not just prosecuted but shot. In
fact, in relation to land, a huge variety of possibilities have been tried,
but one thing seems certain, and that is that sooner or later inequitable
systems of land ownership are challenged.[51]

The idea of the Great Society that '[a]ll things under heaven ought
to be common' has functioned as 'a memory which could be used as
an aspiration'.[52] Political theorists have wrestled with the question since
at least the time of Plato, who believed the Guardians should have all
things in common, and recognised the divisiveness of private property.[53]
Aristotle reviewed three possibilities: that land might be privately owned,
but the produce stored for common consumption; that ownership and
cultivation should be common but the produce parcelled out for private
use; and that land and its produce should be held in common. The first
was his preferred option. He noted that some partiality for such things
as oneself, one's property, and so forth is almost universal. But property
cannot be a goal in life. As far as he is concerned the only property which
is necessary 'is such as is necessary for life, capable of being stored, and
useful for the community of the household and city'.[54]

Stoic arguments about self sufficiency, and about all sharing in the
rights of creation, were particularly important for the early Church
Fathers. Here is John Chrysostom on property:

Mark the wise dispensation of God! That he might put mankind to shame, he
has made certain things common, as the sun, air, earth and water . . . whose
benefits are dispensed equally to all as brethren . . . observe that concerning
things that are common there is no contention, but all is peaceable. But when
one attempts to possess himself of anything . . . then contention is introduced,
as if nature herself were indignant, that when God brings us together in every
way, we are eager to divide and separate ourselves by appropriating things, and

individuals of the community. In this last stage the land is partitioned off to these individuals as
a matter of mutual convenience, but not in unconditional property; it long remains subject to
certain conditions and to reversionary interests of the community, which prevent its uncontrolled
alienation, and attach to it certain common rights and burdens. Cf. the Belgian anthropologist
Emile de Laveleye: "In all primitive societies, the soil was the joint property of the tribes and was
subject to periodical distribution among all the families, so that all might live by their labour as
nature has ordained. The comfort of each was thus proportioned to his energy and intelligence;
no one, at any rate, was destitute of the means of subsistence, and inequality increasing from
generation to generation was provided against."' Cited in H. George, *Progress and Poverty* (London:
Dent, 1911), p. 370.
[51] Shoard, *This Land*, p. 3.   [52] Williams, *Country*, pp. 42–3.
[53] Plato, *Republic*, Book V.   [54] Aristotle *Politics*, 1256b29–30.

by using those cold words 'mine' and 'thine'. Then there is contention and uneasiness. But where this is not, no strife or contention is bred.[55]

Signally anticipating Marx's view that accumulation was usually through violence and fraud, Basil of Caesarea writes:

'Whom do I injure' [the rich person] says, 'when I retain and conserve my own?' Which things, tell me, are yours? Whence have you brought them into being? You are like one occupying a place in a theatre, who should prohibit others from entering, treating that as one's own which was designed for the common use of all.

Such are the rich. Because they were the first to occupy common goods, they take these goods as their own. If each one would take that which is sufficient for one's needs, leaving what is in excess to those in distress, no one would be rich, no one poor.[56]

This tradition, says Charles Avila,

has remained the well kept secret of the very Churches that have revered [the Church Fathers] as saints . . . Nothing, in fact, could be more striking than the extent to which the Roman law theory and practice of ownership, which the fathers attacked and sought to replace, has retained the ascendancy all through the Christian centuries that have elapsed since their thundering critical voices fell silent.[57]

In fact the tradition of common ownership never did fall entirely silent. The Great Society appealed to it in the middle ages, as Williams reminds us. The Diggers took up the theme in the seventeenth century. According to Winstanley: 'All the Prophecies, Visions, and Revelations of Scriptures, of Prophets, and Apostles . . . doth all seat themselves in this work of making the earth a Common Treasury.'[58] The right to share the land on a communal basis was implied in the creation narratives in Genesis, according to him. He looked forward to a new order:

But when the earth becomes a common treasury as it was in the beginning, and the king of Righteousness comes to rule in every ones heart, then he kills the first Adam; for covetousnesse thereby is killed. A man shall have meat, and drinke and clothes by his labour in freedom, and what can be desired more in earth. Pride and envy likewise is killed thereby, for every one shall look upon each other as equall in the Creation; every man indeed being a perfect Creation of himself.[59]

55 Homily XII on 1 Timothy 4, NPNF, ed. P. Schaff, 26 vols. (Grand Rapids: Eerdmans, 1886), vol. XII.
56 Text in C. Avila, *Ownership: Early Christian Teaching* (Maryknoll: Orbis, 1983), p. 49.
57 Ibid., p. 11.
58 G. Sabine (ed.), *The Works of Gerrard Winstanley* (New York: Russell & Russell, 1965), pp. 259–60.
59 Quoted in A. Bradstock, *Faith in the Revolution: The Political Theologies of Muntzer and Winstanley* (London: SPCK, 1997), p. 99.

For him communal ownership and the resurrection of Christ were inter-changeable concepts:

[W]hen he hath spread himself abroad amongst his Sons and daughters, the members of his mystical body, then this community of love and righteousness, making all to use the blessings of the earth as a common Treasurie amongst them, shall break forth again in his glory, and fill the earth, and shal be no more supprest: And none shal say, this is mine, but every one shal preserve each other in love.[60]

These ideas re-appeared in secular form in the following two centuries in the writings of Rousseau and Proudhon, and Henry George made of them a whole programme, appealing explicitly to a theology of creation:

If we are all here by the equal permission of the Creator, we are all here with an equal title to the enjoyment of his bounty – with an equal right to the use of all that nature so impartially offers. This is a right which is natural and inalienable; it is a right which vests in every human being as he enters the world, and which during his continuance in the world, can be limited only by the equal right of others. There is on earth no power which can rightfully make grant of exclusive ownership in land. If all existing men were to grant away their equal rights, they could not grant away the right of those who follow them. For what are we but tenants for a day? . . . The masses of men, who in the midst of abundance suffer want; who, clothed with political freedom, are condemned to the wages of slavery . . . instinctively feel that 'there is something wrong'. And they are right.[61]

Common ownership of land was what he proposed as a remedy, a proposal taken up by the early British Labour Party, which wanted the nationalisation of land. That proposal was quietly dropped, and even the 1945 Labour government did not moot it. The challenge posed by such a theology is, however, far from a dead letter. It re-emerged in late twentieth century Scotland, when Alister McIntosh challenged the Scottish Landowners' association on exactly the same set of principles. McIntosh appealed to the fact that in Scottish law God remains the absolute sovereign. He therefore appealed to Leviticus 25:23 – 'The land shall not be sold in perpetuity, for the land is mine.' Like George, he proposes a land tax which would bring down capital values and generate revenue. These funds would then be used to restore the land to the community as has already happened on the Isle of Eigg.[62] James Robertson is one of a number of economists who favour re-pristinating George's proposals, advocating site-value taxation as 'the most neutral and most efficient of all taxes, inducing no distortions and generating no loss of welfare'.[63]

[60] Ibid., p. 117.   [61] George, *Progress and Poverty*, p. 241.   [62] *Guardian*, 6.8.98.
[63] J. Robertson, *Transforming Economic Life* (Totnes: Green Books, 1998), p. 44.

The right to private property

As we have seen, according to a number of the scriptural ideologies tribal Israel had a 'stakeholder economy' in which every family was assured of approximately equal access to resources by organisation into extended families, clans and tribes. All but the royal ideology were designed to see that land could not be cornered and become the possession of the few. But of course this is exactly what did happen. Isaiah of Jerusalem curses 'those who covet fields and seize them, houses and take them' (Isa. 5.8; cf. Mic. 2.2). The king came to be the biggest land owner – his estates managed by stewards (1 Chron. 27:25–31) and worked by slaves or a levy (1 Sam. 8.12). The wealthy looked for 'investment opportunities' which slowly but surely encroached on tribal institutions and ways of life. By the eighth century, as we know from prophetic protests, many formerly free Israelites had ended up as debt slaves or landless labourers.[64] The story of Naboth's vineyard is the most famous example of the way in which this fundamental condition of Israel's existence could be set aside. Ahab wanted to rationalise his property – to take over Naboth's land, which adjoined his palace, and re-locate him – give him another vineyard somewhere else. But Naboth refused: 'I will not give you my ancestral inheritance (*nahalah*).' His wife Jezebel was Sidonian, and used to kings getting their own way. She promptly had Naboth murdered, and presented Ahab with the vineyard. At this point Elijah, representative of the old traditions of Israel, intervenes:

Then the word of the Lord came to Elijah the Tishbite, saying, Go down to meet King Ahab . . . You shall say to him, 'Thus says the LORD: Have you killed, and also taken possession? . . . In the place where dogs licked up the blood of Naboth, dogs will also lick up your blood.' (1 Kgs 21.17–19)

Walter Brueggemann again attempts to understand the question raised here in terms of a theology of grace. He argues that there is a pattern throughout this history, namely that 'gifted land gives life but managed land does not'.[65] The regulations of the Torah are there, he argues, to protect Israel's understanding of the land as gifted, and to protect the poor.

Many states illustrate the pattern of Israel's history, beginning with a stakeholder economy, and ending up with a huge gulf between rich and poor. Rome seems to have begun with the allocation of small and approximately equal lots, and the patrician class emerged through primitive accumulation. When Roman law was formulated, much later, it

[64] Following N. Gottwald, *The Hebrew Bible: A Socio-Literary Introduction* (Philadelphia: Fortress, 1985), p. 324.
[65] Brueggemann, *The Land*, p. 35.

accorded absolute rights of ownership, *dominium*, 'to have, to hold, to use, to enjoy, to do as one pleases'. The rediscovery of Roman law in Padua in the tenth century led to the adoption of this idea of ownership in much of Europe.

In England free ceorls seem to have constituted the majority of land holders in the early Saxon period, but following that there was a steady regression. According to the feudal law of the eleventh century ownership was still not absolute. The King was only lord paramount of every acre, and the royal demesne, the *terra regis*, always remained the treasure of the realm.[66] Feudal landright was local, varying according to the custom of the manor. With the transfer of power to the King in Parliament, and the establishment of statute law, 'landownership passed from an empirical order of things to a realm of permanent definition' and as this happened 'doctrine hardened against the villeins'.

The median of the Middle Ages was the darkest hour for servile tenants. The thirteenth century had settled the law: all villein property, land and goods, is held *nomine alieno* – it is the lord's. About this doctrine was woven an ever increasing restrictive practice. A villein had no right to dispose of his goods or land save as the lord should let him. Force of circumstance mitigated the rule . . . but the harsh doctrine was logically pursued in many other directions.[67]

The rise of the middle class in the fifteenth to eighteenth centuries led to that change in the approach to property which Sir George Campbell noted, according to which property in land became 'a transferable mercantile commodity absolutely owned and passing from hand to hand like any chattel'. Various ideologies arose to meet the new situation, the most important of which was Locke's idea that it is the work which we put into land which makes it ours, and Hegel's view that we can only find self realisation through property: 'If emphasis is placed on my needs, then the possession of property appears as a means to their satisfaction, but the true position is that, from the standpoint of freedom, property is the first embodiment of freedom, and so is in itself a substantive end.'[68] In fact, as M. Longfield noted briskly in 1881, these justifications are specious. Ownership in land and labour cannot be compared, he argues, because 'land is the gift of the Creator of the world to mankind'. 'Every argument

[66] D. R. Denman, *Origins of Ownership* (London: Allen & Unwin, 1958), p. 80. Homage is what is distinctively characteristic of feudalism. 'Feudum', at the Norman conquest, 'denotes the concrete, tangible lands of a feudal tenant and the abstract idea of an interest held of a superior in exchange for services rendered.'

[67] Ibid., p. 121.

[68] G. W. F. Hegel, *Philosophy of Right* (Oxford: Oxford University Press, 1967), p. 42.

used to give an ethical foundation for the exclusive right of property in land has a latent fallacy. It omits a portion of the value which ought not to be left out of consideration.'

The foundation of the right to property in land is not ethical, but political. Its origin is expediency. In order that it may be cultivated to the most advantage, it is necessary that the cultivator should be secured in the enjoyment of the fruits of his intended industry. For this purpose it is necessary that the person who is permitted to use the land should be permitted to enjoy it for a certain length of time, to make it his interest to cultivate it in the most productive manner. This period varies with the increase of foresight and agricultural knowledge.[69]

Again, it is only convenience which leads to the permission of absolute ownership, 'subject to such taxes and regulations as the State shall from time to time think it reasonable to impose'.

A little earlier Marx pointed out that '[a]n isolated individual could no more have property in land and soil than he could speak'.

He could, of course, live off it as substance, as do the animals. The relation to the earth as property is always mediated through the occupation of the land and soil . . . by the tribe, the commune, (or some other social formation) in some more or less naturally arisen or already historically developed form. The individual can never appear here in the dot-like isolation in which he appears as mere free worker.[70]

What Marx looked to was 'individual property based on the acquisitions of the Capital era: i.e. on cooperation and the possession in common of the land and of the means of production'.[71] What we have at present, however, is the absolutisation of the 'right to property'. Samuel Whitbread told Marion Shoard in 1982:

Possession is nine-tenths of the law. I am in possession here. I control what I have got here. In fact, in my case it happens to be 11,000 acres of farmland, and forestry, and in your case, if I may say so, it may be a flat in South London. The actual ethics of possession are the same. I think one should be at liberty to do what one likes with one's own.[72]

Of course 'the ethics of possession' are not the same at all. In Marion Shoard's case it is that of one among millions of stakeholders. This property is very rarely a source of wealth, and not often inherited over generations. In Whitbread's it is that of a tiny number who, usually by

[69] M. Longfield, 'Land Tenure in Ireland', in Probyn, *Systems*, p. 71.
[70] Marx, *Grundrisse*, ed. D. McClellan (Harmondsworth: Penguin, 1973), p. 491.
[71] K. Marx, *Capital* (Moscow: Progress, 1954), vol. 1 p. 715.
[72] Shoard, *This Land*, p. 394.

inheritance but sometimes by the amassing of large fortunes, have cornered the bulk of the land and use it for their own pleasure, profit and advantage. It is this use, or abuse, of the land which is the real ethical problem in the light of what Torah has to say.

IDENTITY

The command against amassing land is clear enough, but this does not settle the issue. For on the one hand, land is one of the major foci of inequity and injustice on many levels, but on the other human beings seem to need attachments to places – roots – to thrive. This has traditionally been a theme of right wing thinkers, as it is today in the debates about the Common European currency, but, as David Harvey has signally demonstrated, it is equally a concern of the left in the attempt to find a space of protection from rootless capital.

'We are plants which, whether we like it or not – must with our roots rise out of the earth in order to bloom in the ether and bear fruit.'[73] This is Heidegger, who earlier cast a deep shadow on his ideas of land and place by his enthusiastic support for the Nazi party. But place is also central, for example, to Raymond Williams' novels, and a theme he turns to elsewhere. 'A new theory of socialism', he wrote,' must now centrally involve *place*.'

Remember the argument was that the proletariat had no country, the factor which differentiated it from the property owning classes. But place has been shown to be a crucial element in the bonding process – more so perhaps for the working class than the capital owning classes – by the explosion of the international economy and the destructive effects of deindustrialization upon old communities. When capital has moved on, the importance of place is more clearly revealed.[74]

Like spaces, places are *constructed*, a product, of institutionalised social, political and economic power. 'The creation of symbolic places', says Harvey,

is not given in the stars but painstakingly nurtured and fought over precisely because of the hold that place can have over the imaginary . . . If places are the locus of collective memory, then social identity and the capacity to mobilize that identity into configurations of political solidarity are highly dependent upon

[73] M. Heidegger, *Discourse on Thinking* (New York: Harper & Row) 1966 pp. 47–8, cited in Harvey, *Justice*, p. 301.
[74] R Williams, *Resources of Hope* (London: Verso, 1989), p. 242. The same is true for groups like the Palestinians. Yasser Arafat argues that their deepest need is identity, and that that requires land.

processes of place construction and sustenance . . . Materiality, representation and imagination are not separate worlds.[75]

The vision of the unity of the world wide proletariat, now replaced in some feminist rhetoric by that of a world wide solidarity between women, drew on earlier visions of universal brotherhood, Christian and Muslim, instantiated by the earlier quotation from the Epistle to Diognetus. It has an obvious significance in a world of ethnic cleansing and of the mass movement of refugees and 'ethnic minorities'. On the other hand, the significance of attachment to place cannot be denied, and its significance finds powerful biblical expression. In an article written in 1933, the year the Nazis came to power in Germany, von Rad reflected on 'rest' in the Old Testament. 'Rest' is about security. Thus the narrative of Joshua concludes with it: 'Thus the LORD gave to Israel all the land that he swore to their ancestors that he would give them; and having taken possession of it, they settled there. And the LORD gave them rest on every side just as he had sworn to their ancestors'(Josh. 21.43–4). 'Rest' and possession of the land are bound up with each other. As von Rad puts it:

It is emphasised that redemption is a present reality and that all Israel is the chosen people; and it is evident that this notion of the land which Israel is to inhabit . . . is a theological concept of the highest order . . . *We must not spiritualise any of this: this 'rest' is not peace of mind, but the altogether tangible peace granted to a nation plagued by enemies and weary of wandering. It is altogether a direct gift from the hand of God.*[76]

This is well said, and it highlights the importance of the possession. On the one hand it is clear that we must not lose ourselves in abstraction, and retreat into merely spiritual realities. People need security and the opportunity to put down roots to flourish. That flourishing is evidenced by the emergence of thousands of different cultures world wide, with their own languages, cuisines, arts, religions and ways of doing things. Such diversity is unthinkable without 'rest' and possession. 'It is land that fully permits Israel to be Israel,' says Brueggemann. 'It is land that fully permits Yahweh to be known as Yahweh. It is land that permits Yahweh and Israel to have history together.'[77] The loss of the land means 'the collapse of all public institutions and all symbolic expressions of well being and coherence'.[78] The 'all' here is too strong. Jeremiah, whom

---

[75] Harvey, *Justice*, p. 322. From a rather different perspective Harries argues that it is the function of buildings to turn space into place. K. Harries, *The Ethical Function of Architecture* (Cambridge, Mass.: MIT, 1998), pp. 154, 213.
[76] Von Rad, *Hexateuch*, p. 95 (my italics).   [77] Brueggemann, *The Land*, p. 142.
[78] Ibid., p. 114.

Brueggemann calls 'the poet of the land *par excellence*', is also the poet of the exile and refugee and urges his compatriots to settle down in Babylon, 'build houses and dwell in them', and work for the good of their conquerors (Jer. 29). Even without land, some expressions of well being and coherence remained. YHWH was 'with' Israel for two thousand years of its history, as it found itself 'scattered amongst the nations'. 'Place' remained in the promise, rehearsed each year at Passover, in the sabbath meal, and in the local synagogue community. The same might be said of the mosque for today's European Muslims.

The dissolution of place, Harvey suggests, amounts to a loss of identity. 'It suggests a fundamental spiritual alienation from environment and self that demands remedial measures.'[79] The history of Israel from Abraham suggests that that is only very partially true. The ideologies in both Joshua and in Deuteronomy emphasise that Canaan is gift. Israel inherits cities, cisterns, vineyards and olive trees which it did not build, hew or plant. For Brueggemann this implies a theology of radical grace, but this is hardly how it can have seemed to those who built the cities, dug the cisterns and established the vineyards which were occupied. Since the biblical promises are regularly invoked by the religious right in Israel, with the results for the Palestinians of which we are all aware, it does not seem possible to characterise these passages solely in terms of 'grace'. W. D. Davies is perhaps nearer the mark in finding evidence of a bad conscience which Israel then has to justify. He cites, for example, a very late text, 1 Maccabees 15:33, in which Israel seems to protest too much: 'We have neither taken other men's lands, nor have we possession of that which appertains to others, but of the inheritance of our fathers.' It is the promise, the 'inheritance of our fathers', which is used here to justify the occupation. Hence the repeated refrain, 'the land which I promised . . .'. Israel has to convince itself of the legitimacy of the original act of dispossession through which it came into the land. According to this ideology conquest and grace are one and the same thing. This makes it impossible to read the story of the land purely in terms of grace, for the twin ideologies of the chosen people and the promised land, appropriated by various 'peoples of the book', have been some of the most noxious in human history, as we can see from the effects in North America, South Africa and the Balkans. Historically, promised land for some has always meant dispossession and death for others.

Dispossessed themselves, by Rome, Jews were harried amongst the nations, forced into ghettoes, the victims of pogroms, for nearly two

[79] Harvey, *Justice*, p. 308.

thousand years. The Holocaust was the culmination of this whole process. But with the land restored again another people is dispossessed, and Israel has the land at the cost of constant wars and the non stop threat of terror, quite apart from what conquest and aggression do to one's own culture. The ambiguities of possession and place seem to be inescapable.

The need for settled place is also raised by the operations of global capital, able to move its plant at will, and frequently leaving whole economies and large workforces high and dry. 'The bourgeoisie', said Marx and Engels in a famous passage in the *Communist Manifesto*, 'historically, has played a most revolutionary part':

[W]herever it has got the upper hand [it] has put an end to all feudal, patriarchal, idyllic relations . . . All fixed, fast frozen relations, with their train of ancient and venerable prejudices and opinions, are swept away, all new formed ones become antiquated before they can ossify. All that is solid melts into air, all that is holy is profaned, and man is at last compelled to face with sober senses his real conditions of life, and his relations with his kind.

This applies also to land, as they go on to note, in the destruction of national industries and the globalisation of industry. International capital changes our understanding of place, as David Harvey argues, through uneven capital investment, the geographical division of labour, the compression of space–time relations which abolish the frictions of distance, and setting places in competition with each other in an attempt to lure capital investment. 'The cathedral city becomes a heritage centre, the mining community becomes a ghost town, the old industrial centre is deindustrialized, speculative boom towns or gentrified neighbourhoods arise on the frontiers of capitalist development or out of the ashes of deindustrialized communities. The history of capitalism is . . . punctuated by intense phases of spatial reorganization.'[80]

In reaction to this Kirkpatrick Sale invokes the sacrality of place. 'The only political vision that offers any hope of salvation is one based on an understanding of, a rootedness in, a deep commitment to, and a resacralization of, *place*.'[81] In the light of the Balkan conflict, however, with its pseudo mystical belief in 'greater Serbia', that looks a rather dismal prospect. And any sacralisation of place seems to be bad news for the refugee, who has no part in the memory which makes place. These difficulties suggest that what we need is not a resacralisation of place, but something like the theology of Jeremiah, peculiarly appropriate to our own day, but applicable to most of human history as well. Jeremiah was certainly committed to *erez Israel* – he bought a field in Anathoth

<hr />

[80] Ibid., p. 296.   [81] Cited in ibid., p. 302.

and went through all the rigmaroles of legal purchase to prove the point
(Jer. 32). But he did not imagine that the people of Israel would be without
God in Babylon either, and announced as a 'word from the Lord' that
the exiles should work for the good of the city. What this suggests, as
does the New Testament idea of the universalisation of the promise, and
the Epistle to Diognetus' insistence that 'every foreign land is a father
land', is that place is not an absolute but a relative good. Rootedness
is essential for the flourishing of difference, and the world would be a
very boring place without it. On these grounds the cultural imperialism
of McDonalds, Coca-Cola and the rest needs to be resisted whenever
possible. But the need to cater for very large numbers of refugees, caused
now not just by wars and economic displacement but by climate change,
is likewise an absolute priority. Local identities have never been static, in
any case, and large influxes of refugees simply mean a speeding up of the
pace of change for a while in the course of which the understanding of
place will change. Whether or not this is for the good can be decided by
all that happens to the arts of human flourishing. At the same time the
emergence of what Webber called the 'non place urban realm', where
high mobility leads to the dissolution of localised senses of community
and their replacement with more functional communities, needs to be
resisted.[82] Somehow we need to create for ourselves both *open* place, at
the same time as open *place*.

Trinitarian ethics and the stewardship of land

At the end of her account of land ownership in Britain Marion Shoard
writes: 'For the first thousand years after the birth of Christ the land of
Britain was effectively in the hands of its people. The last thousand years
have been a kind of dark age in which the people have been shunted
into a landless wilderness while the few have lorded it over their space.'[83]
Mutatis mutandis the words could have been written about the transition
from pre monarchical to monarchical Israel. There are countries where
the pattern of ownership is not as unequal as in Britain, but by and
large the story is the same the world over.[84] Whenever it occurs it is
justified by ideologies, sometimes drawn straight from the royal ideology
of scripture. Opposed to this are the insistence on land as gift, and on

---

[82] M. M. Webber, 'The urban place and the non-place urban realm', in *Explorations into Urban Structure* (Pennsylvania: University of Pennsylvania Press, 1964).

[83] Shoard, *This Land*, p. 483.

[84] As noted at the start of the chapter, Norway, which never had feudalism, is a case in point. Far from having trespass laws, it has the right to roam enshrined in its constitution.

stakeholding. The two imply each other: a roughly equal allocation is the practical outworking of gift to 'Adam'. What would this mean, however, to a post industrial society in which increasing numbers live in mega cities? What would it mean, concretely, to honour the scriptural injunctions about land as gift and land as *nahalah*? How could these principles be enshrined in law, and written into the social fabric so that they made a real difference to the lives of the vast majority of ordinary people? Are they condemned to be a dead letter? What steps need to be taken to alter the barbarous disproportion of ownership which prevails? David Harvey properly insists on the impossibility of beginning with a tabula rasa, on the need to work within the limits of the possible.[85] Small steps towards change might, then, include the following.

In the first place law needs to be altered to make clear that *possession can never be absolute*, in the sense that Whitbread and his fellow land owners think it is. There is indeed a place for stewardship, another argument often advanced by the land owning classes, but stewardship is on behalf of all. *Adamah* comes first. We are debtors to all, as Muir rightly said. There may well be a case, as the Indian constitution believed in 1947, for setting a ceiling on ownership, but in principle there is nothing wrong with some disparity so long as it is not a warrant for exclusion and abuse of power as it currently is. In the late middle ages, comments Marion Shoard, land owners accepted that they must share their rights over their land with the rest of the community. 'That principle was forgotten in the eighteenth century. Now we need to return to it.'[86] She advocates the extension of town planning legislation to the whole countryside as a way of giving the community a say in the fate of the land. This raises the question of the democratic deficit, for land use is under constant discussion, but in a situation where the rich and powerful, and especially the Corporations, can sway politicians and planning authorities as the poor cannot. Put theologically, setting limits to absolute possession, and bringing it under proper democratic control, is a political realisation of belief in God as *Creator*, as Winstanley, John Ball and the Great Society clearly saw.

Secondly, if we seriously accept that land is gift this has implications for *access* to land and *land use*. Enjoyment of rural beauty long antedates the industrial revolution, but escape or retreat to 'the countryside' is now a major source of enjoyment for huge numbers of people: 20 million – a third of the population – were engaged in leisure cycling in Britain

---

[85] D. Harvey, *Spaces of Hope* (Edinburgh: Edinburgh University Press, 2000), pp. 206ff.
[86] Shoard, *This Land*, p. 432.

---

in 1995, and 18 million people head for the countryside on summer Sundays! Because *adamah* comes first, access has to be understood as a right, rather than be criminalised, as it was in Britain in 1994. At the same time, agricultural land, 'the countryside', cannot be construed exclusively or even primarily in terms of leisure, as a resource for the towns. Following the Foot and Mouth epidemic in Britain in 2001 the old 'Ministry of Agriculture, Fisheries and Food' has been abandoned and replaced by a 'Department of Environment, Food and Rural Affairs'. This move follows a series of crises, including a 'crisis of overproduction' within Europe, but is also a recognition of the fact that tourism is now far more lucrative than farming. That fact represents both the growth in leisure and disposable income for a large section of society, but also the assumption, constantly proclaimed by European politicians, that 'the issue of food security is a thing of the past'. Memories are short, and it is imperative to heed the warnings of the Worldwatch Institute that feeding 8 billion, or whatever the plateau figure of the earth's population turns out to be, will not be easy, and in any event cannot be done at present Northern levels.[87] Land use, at least in Britain, has often been irresponsible in this respect. The larger and more centralised the housing system, argues John Turner, the more wasteful the use of land. Alice Coleman's land-use surveys show that huge areas of farming land have been needlessly built over, often in the interests of the public housing estate.[88] I return to this issue in chapter 9. Theologically, the question of land use is an expression of God the *Redeemer*, who seeks and commands fullness of life for all people.

Thirdly, we live in a world where the majority are effectively excluded from their *nahalah*. These people, the homeless and the refugee, those who live in wretched apartments and flats in sink estates, are owed their own stake in the land *as of right*, in virtue of the solidarity they share with the rest of us. What is lamely called 're-housing' is an imperative of what Paul calls the law of grace. Theologically, this is a political realisation of God the *Reconciler*, who seeks justice for the oppressed and commands hospitality for the refugee. It raises the question of housing for six or eight billion, and it is to this question I now turn.

---

[87] A. T. Durning, *How Much is Enough?* (London: Earthscan, 1992), pp. 65ff.

[88] J. F. C. Turner, 'Issues in Self-Help and Self Managed Housing', in P. Ward (ed.), *Self-Help Housing: A Critique* (London: Mansell, 1982), p. 108. Mark Shucksmith, on the other hand, believes that the prevention of rural housing since World War II in Britain has been socially regressive and socially exclusive: *Housebuilding in Britain's Countryside* (London: Routledge, 1990), p. 202. He is not, however, in favour of carte blanche.

CHAPTER 4

The human dwelling

Build houses and live in them; plant gardens and eat what they
produce.

(Jeremiah 29.5)

The house comes before the city: as the most vulnerable of mammals
human beings need shelter. Even the homeless must find shelter somehow, in doorways, in cardboard cities, in subways. And from the earliest
period human beings have turned raw shelter into something else,
something richer, so that the built environment has become perhaps the
most important lived dimension of art and culture. As Lewis Mumford
reminds us, human beings were symbol making animals before they were
tool making animals, and reached specialisation in myth, religion and
ritual before they did in material aspects of culture.[1] These ideological
factors found expression especially in the dwelling. Amos Rapoport in
particular has shown that house design cannot be understood just as
a response to climate and local building potentials. These have their
place, but they do not seem to be decisive. Rapoport found 'extreme'
differences in urban pattern and house types within quite small geographical areas, which he argued showed that culture is much more
decisive a factor in building than climate.[2] His conclusion is that
'Nonutilitarian factors seem of primary importance' in the construction of ordinary dwellings. These include religious beliefs, family and
clan structure, and social organisation.[3] Today we are used to the
idea of Feng shui and Sthapatya veda, which discern different spiritual

---

[1] L. Mumford, *Art and Technics* (New York: Columbia University Press, 1952), quoted in A. Rapoport,
House, Form and Culture (New Jersey: Prentice Hall, 1969), p. 42.
[2] For example, the ancient Egyptians knew the vault but rarely used it because it was at odds with
their image or idea of building. In prehistoric Crete the tightly clustered settlements must be
attributed to the gregarious instincts of the people rather than to defence. In seventeenth and
eighteenth century Europe fashions for building in wood or stone overrode the convenience of
local materials. Rapoport, *House*, pp. 25, 31.
[3] Ibid., pp. 41, 47.

79

energies in different parts of the house and claim to improve health and rest.[4]

At the other end of the scale Palladio, writing during the Renaissance, gave the ordering of the house an explicitly theological rationale. Buildings, he says, should appear like a well finished body. 'Our blessed Creator has ordered the parts of our body, so that the most beautiful should be in places which are exposed to sight, and the less decent in hidden places.'[5] By the less decent he meant kitchens. We can disagree with his Christology and argue that on the proper understanding of the gospels the kitchen should have pride of place, but the theologico-architectural principle is absolutely sound.

The symbolic function of the house continues into modern times. Papworth, writing during the Regency, attributed to the Englishman's character the desire to 'congregate about him in his dwelling and domain all the means of domestic comfort ... and there lay up his chief resources against the cares of life', so that his home was not so much a castle as 'the depository of his most interesting pleasures, the anticipated enjoyment of which gives energy to his mind and cheers his exertion towards the accomplishment of his undertakings'.[6] In truth this seems not to be an English, but a middle class, characteristic. Certainly these remarks are true of middle class America where a study found the word 'house' had nine meanings, including relationships with others, social networks, statement of self identity, a place of privacy, a locus of everyday behaviour and base of activity, a childhood home and a place of upbringing and shelter and physical structure.[7] Rather on the lines which Papworth indicates, North American developers never build houses but 'homes', a word which, as John Steinbeck observed, reduces Americans to tears. And yet this is far more dream than reality. 'The dream home is surrounded by trees and grass in either country or suburb, and must be owned, yet Americans rarely stay in it more than five years. It is not a real need but a symbol.'[8] Some have argued that the idea of 'home' only developed with the growth of demands for comfort and privacy after the

[4] For Sthapatya veda see Kathleen Cox, *Vastu Living: Creating a Home for the Soul* (New York: Marlowe & Co., 2000). Victor Papanek speaks of architecture, including the buildings of Christopher Day, which 'awakens our innermost mythic responses'. *The Green Imperative* (London: Thames & Hudson, 1995), p. 99. He is, as we shall see, an advocate of some form of vernacular architecture. He is also of the view that in large parts of the Far East the importance of Feng shui and the whole cosmological approach to architecture 'can hardly be overstated' (p. 131).

[5] A. Palladio, *The Four Books of Architecture* (New York: Dover, 1965), Bk II, ch. 2.

[6] A. Edwards, *The Design of Suburbia* (London: Pembridge, 1981), pp. 27–8.

[7] A. Rapoport, *The Meaning of the Built Environment* (Tucson: University of Arizona Press, 1982), p. 25.

[8] Rapoport, *House*, p. 132.

sixteenth century, whilst others argue that it only arises when people's work is separated from their place of residence, when it becomes the antithesis to work, a place of leisure and of affective rather than exploitative relationships.[9] Clichés about 'home sweet home', 'no place like home' and so on seem to date from the rise of industrial society.[10] Hugh Stretton points out that, in affluent societies, a third of our capital is invested in the home, a third of our life spent there, three quarters of our social life is spent there and that 'above all, people are produced there and endowed there with the values and capacities which will determine most of the quality of their social life and government away from home'.[11] This is recognised by the workers Peter Saunders cites who speak of 'home' in terms of the building where happiness was enjoyed, 'the love that's in it'.[12] On the other hand there is Leonie Sandercock's account of home discussed in the previous chapter, where 'home' is the struggle for communities of resistance, and Doreen Massey cites Toni Morrison's *Beloved* as undermining 'for ever any notion that everyone once had a place called home which they could look back on ... and where they could afford to locate their identities'.[13] Other feminist critics point out that the idea of home, and the housing policy driven by it, affirms and reproduces the traditional nuclear family and the woman's role within it.[14]

[9] W. Rybczynski, *Home* (London: Heinemann, 1988); D. Hayward, 'Home as an environmental and psychological concept', *Landscape* 20 (1975), pp. 2–9. This seems to me doubtful in the light of what we learn in ancient literature. The *Odyssey*, for example, is really a huge poem about homecoming, where 'home' is both the 'high roofed house', flocks and herds, Ithaca, but also the loyal wife, and a marital bed carved out of an olive tree. Caught with Calypso, Odysseus still sits day by day on a promontory and weeps for home. Homer even includes that corniest of Hollywood clichés, the faithful hound, and does what no Hollywood director would dare do, has the dog die the moment his master returns home and he has recognised him. Recall also Leonie Sandercock's account of home discussed in the previous chapter, where 'home' is the struggle for communities of resistance, that place, wherever, where one discovers new ways of seeing reality.

[10] Rybczynski (*Home*, p. 24) cites Ariès's argument that 'home' did not exist for the poor until the twentieth century, but music hall ballads seem to contradict this, at least for Britain. Interestingly, the idealisation of the cottage with roses around the door as the image of 'home' is found in Dickens from 1840 on. This was part of his loathing of industrialisation, but it also calls into question the idea that 'home' for the poor had to wait for the twentieth century, as does Miss Mitford's even earlier *Our Village*.

[11] H. Stretton, *Capitalism, Socialism and the Environment* (Cambridge: Cambridge University Press, 1976), p. 183.

[12] P. Saunders, *A Nation of Homeowners* (London: Unwin Hyman, 1990), pp. 271–2.

[13] D. Massey, *Space, Place and Gender* (Cambridge: Polity, 1994), p. 166. bell hooks agrees with Sandercock. For her, 'home is that place which enables and promotes varied and ever changing perspectives, a place where one discovers new ways of seeing reality'. Cited in ibid., p. 171.

[14] S. Watson and H. Austerberry, *Housing and Homelessness: A Feminist Perspective* (London: Routledge, 1986).

The process by which a house becomes a 'home' signifies, then, not only the difference between shelter and dwelling, but the difference between colonial and imperial experience, sometimes the difference between rich and poor. Karsten Harries has argued that the old sense of dwelling was part of a situation where place meant destiny, and that it is a good thing to be free of it.[15] 'To be genuinely at home in this world, we have to affirm our essential homelessness . . . every attempt to step into the true centre, to come home in this sense . . . denies the essential ec-centricity of human dwelling – an ec-centricity that needs to be thought in relation to a centre, but a centre that withdraws whenever we seek to seize it.'[16] On a practical level this is to some extent recognised by those who choose to live in mobile homes, which provide 'shelter at modest cost', though here too the trappings of permanence quickly become apparent.[17] The mobile home owner could appeal to Abraham, and the notion of essential homelessness can obviously appeal both to the biblical tradition (Heb. 11.8–10) and to the Augustinian tradition of the restless heart. What we have to set it against is the logic of incarnation to which Palladio appeals. The old rootedness of place, in which 'home' is first and foremost village and town, rather than street and house, still survives not only in the South, but in many places in the North as well, and in both 'home' may apply to a particularly significant or loved house. There is a sense in which this bondage is perfect freedom, teaching one a depth of knowledge and respect for one's immediate world impossible for the footloose to obtain.[18]

The meanings attached to the houses we live in are important because, as Christopher Day puts it, we do not *look at* buildings, but rather *breathe them in*. Architecture can be used to manipulate, as with Nazi stadiums, intending to overawe, or shopping malls, persuading us to buy, but most of the time we do not notice buildings and then they work on us without any conscious resistance. Buildings, and especially the houses we live in, form, as Day puts it, the third human skin.[19] Houses express, and are intended to express, a moral order: Jane Austen's novels spell this out in detail, and *Mansfield Park* turns on it. The plan books which became popular from the third decade of the nineteenth century onwards quite explicitly distributed domestic space so as to reinforce patriarchal values:

---

[15] K. Harries, *The Ethical Function of Architecture* (Cambridge, Mass.: MIT, 1998), pp. 162, 168.
[16] Ibid., p. 200.   [17] Ibid., pp. 144, 147.
[18] I shall return to this question in chapter 7. My own experience suggests that extreme mobility is far from universal and that even in the North there are still many people (one could not put a percentage on it) who lead traditionally rooted lives.
[19] C. Day, *Places of the Soul* (London: Thorsons (an imprint of HarperCollins), 1990), pp. 10, 42.

the library for men, the parlour for women, and the dining room for the meeting of the sexes. Twentieth century domestic architecture in Europe and the United States is a mapping of changing ways of understanding family and gender relationships.[20] The oldest, and still enduring, ideology of the domestic dwelling is as sacred site, and this is where we can begin a consideration of its theological significance.

THE HOUSE AS SACRED SITE

'Even in the crudest neolithic village', says Mumford, 'the house was always more than mere shelter for the physical body: it was the meeting place of a household; its hearth was a centre of religious ceremony as well as an aid to cooking; it was the home of the household god and the locus of the family's being, a repository of moral values not measurable in money.'[21] The central site of 'secular' life was also the site of the sacred. This is one of the themes in the great story of the three angelic visitors in Genesis 18 which, in bringing together both eager hospitality and the presence of God, identifies the practice of hospitality as a typical locus of the sacred, as do many ancient cultures. For the early Christians, confined to domestic space by Roman proscription, the house was the centre of fellowship, the site of the eucharistic celebration, and 'the extension of hospitality through the meal setting was the central act that served to define the worshipping community'.[22] For these communities, for perhaps two hundred years, the house was 'sacred space'. In the 1960s the Abbé Depuyst observed that the main problem of modern church building was to find the type of real house which today offers the deepest and most human kind of hospitality, and to think how best to adapt it for the purpose of church architecture.[23] This is a challenge which has not been taken up on any level, perhaps because, in a highly individualised society, such profound hospitality is difficult to find.[24]

According to Mircea Eliade the house is 'the universe that man constructs for himself by imitating the paradigmatic creation of the gods, the

---

[20] D. Spain, *Gendered Spaces* (Chapel Hill: University of North Carolina Press, 1992), pp. 127–135.
[21] L. Mumford, *The City in History* (Harmondsworth: Penguin, 1991), p. 256.
[22] L. Michael White, *Building God's House in the Roman World: Architectural Adaptation among Pagans, Jews and Christians* (Baltimore, Johns Hopkins University Press, 1990), p. 109.
[23] *Modern Architecture and Christian Celebration*. Cited in F. W. Dillistone, *Traditional Symbols and the Contemporary World* (London: Epworth, 1973), p. 102.
[24] It invites reflection in that the poor are often, though not necessarily, the most profoundly hospitable. How could you generalise that for public architecture? If it indicated a return to the ordinary house for the eucharist, what would be the implications for the suburban community, with its own traditions of hospitality (dinner parties)?

cosmogony'.[25] On his view the longing of homo religiosus to inhabit a divine world creates a desire that his house should be 'like the house of the gods'.[26] Eliade does not support his case with examples, though he could have referred to the Koran, which lays down precise instructions for the placement of doors and windows.[27]

In another sweeping statement Eliade claims: 'The symbolism of the centre is the formative principle not only of countries, cities, temples and palaces but also of the humblest human dwelling, be it the tent of a nomad hunter, the shepherd's yurt, or the house of the sedentary cultivator.'[28] However that might be, Rapoport's anthropological studies showed that religion affects the form, plan, spatial arrangements and orientation of the house, and may be the influence which leads to the existence of round and rectangular houses. The reason for a culture never having had a round house, for example, may well be due to the needs of cosmic orientation, as a round house cannot easily be oriented.[29] The impact of such orientation can be seen not only in Pawnee villages, which are a replica of stars in the sky, or those of the Hottentot, for whom the circle is the perfect form, but also in no nonsense Yorkshire, where streets follow the ancient Scandinavian pattern laid out according to the daily movement of the sun.[30]

In a celebrated lecture in 1951 Heidegger picked up on the religious significance of the dwelling house in describing a Black Forest farmhouse in which 'the self sufficiency of the power to let earth and heaven, divinities and mortals enter in simple oneness into things, ordered the house'.

It places the farm on the wind sheltered mountain slope looking south, among the meadows close to the spring. It gave it the wide overhanging shingle roof whose proper slope bears up under the burden of snow, and which, reaching deep down, shields the chamber against the storms of the long winter nights. It did not forget the altar corner behind the community table; it made room in its chamber for the hallowed places of childbed and the 'tree of the dead' – for that is what they called a coffin there . . . A craft which, itself sprung from dwelling, still uses tools and frames as things, built the farmhouse.[31]

Heidegger mentions the 'altar corner', and other traditional cultures also had sacred, or privileged, areas within the house. The pious Hindu still has a place for the household god or gods, where *puja* (worship) is offered daily. At the turn of the second millennium in the West

[25] M. Eliade *The Sacred and the Profane* (New York: Harcourt & Brace, 1959), p. 56.
[26] Ibid., p. 65.   [27] R. Sennett, *Flesh and Stone* (London: Faber, 1994), pp. 192–3.
[28] Eliade, *The Sacred*, p. 65.   [29] Rapoport, *House*, p. 41.   [30] Ibid., p. 51.
[31] M. Heidegger, *Poetry, language, thought* (New York: Harper & Row, 1971), p. 160.

Christopher Day tries to design rooms which are congenial places for silence and meditation. 'My office as a room', he says, 'is a silent office, even though we talk there. It is not oppressively empty when it is empty, but peacefully at rest. It is an office more like a church than a factory . . . if we think of work as the raising of matter, as provision of food for the human spirit, then places of work *need* this sort of atmosphere.'[32] Design is a key factor for, as Day remarks, in smooth plastered, gloss painted rooms, you *need* a radio, hi-fi or television for company, to fill the empty space.[33]

Eliade's unsubstantiated assertions about the intentions of 'religious man' seem far too sweeping, and yet a secular philosopher like Gaston Bachelard agrees with him: 'Our house is our corner of the world . . . our first universe a real cosmos in every sense of the word.'[34] Not only our memories, says Bachelard, but the things we have forgotten are 'housed'. Our soul is an abode. And by remembering 'house' and 'rooms' we learn to 'abide' within ourselves.[35] For him 'the house is one of the greatest powers of integration for the thoughts, memories and dreams of mankind . . . Without it man would be a dispersed being. It maintains him through the storms of the heavens and through those of life. It is body and soul. It is the human being's first world.'[36]

We have to measure these claims against the harsh realities of living for the vast majority of people. Are they true in Easterhouse? In the tower blocks to be found everywhere from Moscow to Chandigarh to Hong Kong? In the slums of Rio or downtown Edinburgh or Paris? In the vast suburban sprawl of London? In refugee camps in Palestine or the Balkans? What about the nine and a half million people in contemporary Britain who cannot afford to keep their homes heated and free from damp? Human experience in these places shows that it is possible to 'abide' without ever knowing the kind of house which Bachelard recalls. And what about the sense of the sacred? Architecture can only flourish if dwellings are in harmony with the people who live in them, with nature and culture, says Victor Papanek.[37] In turn those people need to be in harmony with a larger scheme of things. If human beings are, as Marx argued, alienated, made strangers to their world, by the structures of industrial society, it is hardly surprising that poor buildings result. In nineteenth century Britain it was still the hearth, a symbol of the family, which was the focus of the sacred, if Dickens is to be believed. The kitchen table could remain such a symbol, but the habit of individual 'snacking' destroys some of that resonance. Has the semi

[32] Day, *Places*, p. 147.   [33] Ibid., p. 142.
[34] G. Bachelard, *The Poetics of Space* (Boston: Beacon, 1969), p. 5.
[35] Ibid., p., xxvii.   [36] Ibid., pp. 6–7.   [37] Papanek, *Green Imperative*, p. 104.

circle around the television replaced – or destroyed – the sacred? Has the cult of sexuality replaced it with the bedroom? 'It may be that the modern house orients itself to the view, beach, sun and sky, and that this orientation, and the picture window, replace the religious, symbolic orientation of the past. Therefore, a new symbol takes over – health, sun, and sport as an idea ... in the United States the ideal of health becomes a new religion.'[38] In reflecting theologically on these questions there appears to be a twofold tradition, both in scripture, and in the architectural literature on housing, which I shall attempt to follow.

TWO HOUSES: PEOPLE AND STRUCTURE

Gaston Bachelard's idea of a 'place of abiding' is sharply questioned, in the first place, by the biblical use of the term 'house'. The Hebrew word for house, *beit*, is a key word in the Hebrew bible. Like the Greek *oikos*, which translates it in the Septuagint, it originally means the structure but, because there is no separate word for the small family unit, comes to do service for both house and family, and then for a whole people. At the beginning of the monarchy a stark contrast is set up between true and false 'houses'. David announces his intention to build a 'house' (i.e. a temple) for YHWH, but the prophet Nathan intervenes, punning on the word '*beit*':

Thus says the Lord: are you the one to build me a house to live in? I have not lived in a house since the day I brought up the people of Israel from Egypt to this day ... Then King David went in and sat before the LORD, and said, 'Who am I, O Lord GOD, and what is my house, that you have brought me thus far?' (2 Sam. 7.5–6, 18)

According to this theology YHWH never dwelt in a house, but lived in a tent, and moved with the people. The very idea of a 'house' implies much too static a picture of one who is a 'wayfaring God'. Judaeo Christian culture, comments Richard Sennett, is at its very roots about spiritual dislocation and homelessness. 'Our faith began at odds with place, because our gods themselves were disposed to wander.'[39] This is to put it too strongly, as we shall see, but there is, to say the least, an ambivalence about settlement in Judaism and Christianity which there may not be in cosmically oriented cultures.

---

[38] Rapoport, *House*, p. 132.
[39] R. Sennett, *The Conscience of the Eye* (New York: Norton, 1990), p. 6.

The promise of a 'house', meaning a temple, is interpolated into the story in 2 Samuel, and its fulfilment recorded in that very subtle piece of counter propaganda disguised as propaganda, 1 Kings 1–11.[40] The narrator tells us that Solomon spent seven years building the Temple and thirteen on his own palace, a stone built structure which, he emphasises, was extremely costly (1 Kgs 7.9–11). A judgement is clearly passed on this conspicuous consumption. Immediately after Solomon's death the kingdom disintegrates. Throughout the writings of the great prophets luxury housing is the target of some of the fiercest invective.[41] Three or four centuries later we hear this comment from one of the occupants of some Old Testament Canary Wharf:

I made great works; I built houses and planted vineyards for myself; I made myself gardens and parks, and planted in them all kinds of fruit trees. I made myself pools from which to water the forest of growing trees . . . I bought male and female slaves, and had slaves who were born in my house. (Eccles. 2.4–7)

All of this, he sees, is nothing but 'vanity' – and indeed it is, because premised on injustice.

There is little to support Bachelard's sense of 'abode' in the Hebrew bible, therefore. There is far more resonance with the ideas of bell hooks, Leonie Sandercock, or Toni Morrison. We saw in the last chapter the importance of *nahalah*, which implies a house, everyone dwelling under their vine and fig tree. But when we look to what is actually said about dwellings, there is little but a fierce critique of luxury housing, and an insistence on the absolute priority of political process, the people who constitute a 'house' over the buildings themselves.

In the New Testament this relativisation of the importance of the house is radicalised. Jesus, according to Luke, was born in an outhouse and, according to Matthew, became a refugee immediately after his birth. The nineteenth century artists liked to depict Jesus 'at home' learning the carpenter's trade, but Jesus seems to have aligned himself with the rootless and homeless: 'Foxes have holes, and birds of the air have nests, but the Son of Man has nowhere to lay his head' (Luke 9.58). When this tradition is interpreted through the Christian idea of incarnation it means that God takes God's place alongside those who have no home, who lack, perhaps, even shelter. The apocryphal *Acts of Thomas* contains a nice story about Thomas landing in India and extracting huge sums

---

[40] For this aspect of the narrative see above all, Stefan Heym, *The King David Report* (London: Sphere, 1984).

[41] For example, Amos 3.15, 5.11; Isa. 3.14–15, 5.7ff.; Jer. 22.13ff.

of money from the king on the promise of building him a house. No
house materialises. When he is arrested for fraud he reveals that all the
money has been given to the poor in order to build the king a 'house in
heaven'.[42] Like Nathan, Thomas directs attention to the needs of the
poor, and away from pharonic building projects. This is not to deny the
need for shelter. On the contrary, God is the one who 'shelters you under
his wings' (Ps. 61.4), who provides shelter and water for Hagar, cast out
into the desert, or for Jonah overlooking Nineveh. The editor of the book
of Hosea includes an oracle which promises that they shall 'again live
beneath my shadow (*tsel*), they shall flourish as a garden' (Hos. 14.7).
The biblical tradition, whilst critical of the housing of the rich, is not
hostile to the establishing of homes as such. Rather, it offers a vision for
the refugee:

> They shall build houses and inhabit them;
>   they shall plant vineyards and eat their fruit.
> They shall not build and another inhabit;
>   they shall not plant and another eat;
>   for like the days of a tree shall the days of my people be,
>   and my chosen shall long enjoy the work of their hands.
>   (Isa. 65.21–2)

Likewise in the gospels there is no radical condemnation of the security
of the house. In Mark, for example, the house is a 'safe' site for the discipleship community. 'There Jesus dines with the outcast (2.15; 14.3) and
attends to the crowds (1.32; 3.20); it is the locus for private instruction
(7.17; 9.33; 10.10) and healing. Only once is the house a site of conflict
(3.20ff.), and this is explained by the fact that this episode narrates the
rejection of Jesus by his own family.'[43] This helps us to understand why
the house becomes the centre for early Christian worship after the resurrection. What is challenged, however, is possession and exclusive use.
In the story commonly known as the 'rich young ruler' we find a vision
of a radical re-distribution of property. The story of the rich young man
turns, Ched Myers argues, on the fact that he possesses many *ktemata* –
lands. These are the properties he has acquired through the debt default
of others, against the prophetic injunctions and the clear commands of
Torah.[44] Jesus points out that if Torah is followed there will be plenty for
everyone:

[42] *The Apocryphal New Testament*, tr. M. R. James (Oxford: Oxford University Press, 1923), p. 364ff.
    The story is a neat inversion of the usual burden of 'pie in the sky when you die'.
[43] C. Myers, *Binding the Strong Man* (Maryknoll: Orbis, 1988), p. 151.
[44] C. Myers, *Who Will Roll Away the Stone?* (Maryknoll: Orbis, 1994).

Jesus said, 'Truly I tell you, there is no one who has left house or brothers or sisters or mother or father or children or fields, for my sake and for the sake of the good news, who will not receive a hundredfold now in this age – houses, brothers and sisters, mothers and children, and fields, with persecutions . . . (Mark 10:29–30)

In attempting a theological reflection on the house it is essential to keep this perspective on the twofold tradition in mind. It is true that evidence of imagination and beauty is to be found in the meanest slums and shanty towns. Lefebvre writes: 'The vast shanty towns of Latin America manifest a social life far more intense than the bourgeois districts of the cities . . . these districts sometimes so effectively order their space – houses, walls, public spaces – as to elicit a nervous admiration.'[45] And even the crudest shelter quickly takes on some aspect of a 'home', through the placing of a paper image of a deity, for example, something to mark this space as special, as somewhere to come home to. In this sense there is something to be said for Bachelard's remark that, '[i]f we look at it intimately, the humblest dwelling has beauty'.[46] From the outside, says Janice Perlman, favellas and barrios may seem filthy and congested, with open sewers and dust and dirt flying everywhere.

Things look very different from inside, however. Houses are built with a keen eye to comfort and efficiency, given the climate and available materials. Much care is evident in the arrangement of furniture and the neat cleanliness of each room. Houses often boast colourfully painted doors and shutters, and flowers or plants on the window sill. Cherished objects are displayed with love and pride.[47]

This is undoubtedly true, but at the same time it is essential not to romanticise poverty.[48] The slum clearers were and are right that there are

[45] H. Lefebvre, *The Production of Space* (Oxford: Blackwell, 1991), pp. 373–4.

[46] Bachelard, *Poetics*, p. 4.

[47] J. Perlman, *The Myth of Marginality: Urban Poverty and Politics in Rio de Janeiro* (Berkeley: University of California Press, 1976), pp. 242–3.

[48] Cf. this description of nineteenth century London from Engels' *Condition of the Working Class in England* (1845), a description which recalls many Third World slums today: 'The houses are occupied from cellar to garret, filthy within and without, and their appearance is such that no human being could possibly wish to live in them. But all this is nothing in comparison with the dwellings in the narrow courts and alleys between the streets, entered by covered passages between the houses, in which the filth and tottering ruin surpass all description. Scarcely a whole window pane can be found, the walls are crumbling, door posts and window frames loose and broken, doors of old boards nailed together, or altogether wanting . . . Heaps of garbage and ash lie in all directions, and the foul liquids emptied before the doors gather in stinking pools. Here live the poorest of the poor' (Marx/Engels *Collected Works* 50 vols. (Moscow: Progress, 1975), vol. IV, p. 332). In Britain in 2001 there were also an estimated 3 million people who experienced homelessness, some caused by re-possession – the dark side of Peter Saunders' vision of a nation of homeowners, as he himself admits in his final chapter.

conditions in which human beings ought not to be expected to live, and this housing is found not only in the South but in the so called 'developed' countries. Against this background Bachelard's *'Poetics of Space'* can seem a trivial irrelevance. And yet it is true that human beings have found, and continue to find, great significance in the houses in which they live and invest them with meaning.

TWO HOUSES: VERNACULAR AND MONUMENTAL

Just as we have two traditions in speaking of 'the house' so, argues Christopher Day, we have two traditions of architecture, high and low.

One concerns itself with cosmic rules – proportion, geometry and classically-differentiated elements representing material principles: relation to the earth, to the vault of the heavens, to the vertical boundaries of free stretching space ... this is the stream of great architecture – temples, cathedrals, sometimes palaces and civic buildings. In scale and commitment to a singular idea such buildings often dominate the surroundings.

The other stream is the vernacular. Its keynote is response to climate, materials, social form and tradition. It concerns itself very much with textures, meetings of materials and tends to be rich for the senses. Almost without fail, the resulting landscape or townscape warms the soul ... The high architecture stream is inspired by cosmic ideas, the vernacular stream is rooted in daily reality – one is learnt by prolonged esoteric study, the other by making, doing and building, by mud, dirt and wood shavings. Both are artistic but neither is complete or balanced without the other: they need to be brought into conversation.[49]

Day's twofold distinction corresponds to the Sri Lankan theologian Aloysius Pieris' distinction between cosmic and metacosmic religions: high and literate traditions on the one hand, with their great scriptures, buildings, works of art and great music, and folk religion on the other, with its small local shrines, folk dances and folk music.[50] Like Day he believes neither tradition can be dispensed with. The American architectural critic J. B. Jackson likewise speaks of a twofold tradition, between houses built to last and those with a life expectancy of a generation or less, 'mansions' and 'dwellings'. A dwelling, he argues, is a makeshift place, more or less thrown together, often moveable and not of much consequence if destroyed. The words 'manor' and 'mansion' however come from a root meaning lasting, enduring. In the sixteenth and

---

[49] Day, *Places*, p. 28. As noted in chapter 1, Harries likewise contrasts vernacular and 'pedigreed' architecture, and believes they form an ellipse. *Function*, p. 272.
[50] A. Pieris, *An Asian Theology of Liberation* (Edinburgh: T&T Clark, 1988), pp. 69–85.

seventeenth centuries in Europe there was, he argues, an architectural revolution in which wood and mud were replaced by stone.[51]

The opening of Francis Bacon's famous essay, 'Of Building', could well apply to vernacular architecture: 'Houses are built to live in, and not to look on; therefore let use be preferred before uniformity, except where both may be had. Leave the goodly fabrics of houses, for beauty only, to the enchanted palaces of the poets, who build them at small cost.' The vernacular is by and large a tradition of great simplicity. The word 'vernacular' comes from the Latin *verna*, meaning a slave born in the household, and by extension the life of one confined to a village or estate. Thus a vernacular culture implies 'a way of life ruled by tradition and custom, entirely remote from the larger world of politics and law; a way of life where identity derived not from permanent possession of land but from membership in a group or super-family'.[52] This dominance of tradition means that vernacular building 'displays very few devices not found in primitive buildings'.[53] Lefebvre remarks of a peasant dwelling that it is 'an object intermediate between work and product, between nature and labour, between the realm of symbols and the realm of signs'.[54] The German word for peasant, *Bauer*, points up the connection between the peasant and building.[55] Adolf Loos puts this epigrammatically in remarking that '[t]he houses of peasants are shaped by the hand of God'.[56] What he means by this is the way in which vernacular architecture responds so subtly to its region that it seems to be a 'natural' creation. Think of the igloo, with its L shaped tunnel, to trap the wind, its raised sleeping platform, its ventilation louvres, its rounded shape to deflect fierce winds. It is a masterpiece of engineering. Rapoport speaks of the 'amazing skill' shown by primitive and peasant builders in dealing with climatic problems and their ability to use minimum resources for maximum

---

[51] J. B. Jackson, *Discovering the Vernacular Landscape* (New Haven and London: Yale University Press, 1984) pp. 91 ff.

[52] Ibid., p. 149.   [53] Rapoport, *House*, p. 121.   [54] Lefebvre, *Production*, p. 83.

[55] Talking of Chipping Camden, in Gloucestershire, Branford and Geddes remark: 'You ask who planned and erected these buildings and ordered their layout and their proportions, so that the whole, from great church to cottage, unites into a single harmony. You are told it was the work of local masons, who built without architects and, as it were, like bees, by tradition, not by book learning.' V. Branford and P. Geddes, *The Coming Polity* (London: Williams & Norgate, 1919), p. 132.

[56] 'May I take you to the shores of a mountain lake? The sky is blue, the water is green and everything is at peace. The mountains and clouds are reflected in the lake, as are the houses, farms and chapels. They do not seem man made, but more like the product of God's workshop, like the mountains and trees, the clouds and the blue sky. And everything breathes beauty and tranquillity.' 'Architecture, 1910' in *The Architecture of Adolf Loos*, an Arts Council exhibition (London: Arts Council, 1985).

comfort. 'The Eskimo has only snow and ice, fur and bone, and some driftwood; the Sudanese have mud, reeds and some palm logs ... the marsh dwellers of Iraq have only reeds. While this scarcity does not determine form, it does make some solutions impossible and reduces the choice to an extent, depending on the severity of the limitations.'[57] 'It is perhaps symptomatic of professional blindness', says Jeffrey Cook, 'that the often amazing comfort and environmental performances of vernacular architecture continue to be largely ignored by professional designers of the built environment.'[58] The vernacular has been defined as 'a common sense approach built out of necessity'. Ecologically there are many advantages in making a virtue out of necessity.

Traditionally we built according to our limits. Today, however, there are no apparent limits. Building form is defined by our technology, by global markets and by consumer taste. Traditionally, resources had to be used wisely, because their scarcity and the effort needed to manufacture them were automatically understood. We now use more and more of them, and bring them from further and further away.[59]

The vernacular tradition responded to local climate conditions, and also embodied a deep knowledge of, and respect for, its materials: it understood the difference between beech, oak and pine, the capacities and limitations of granite or limestone, of slate or marl, and it adapted design accordingly.[60] The vernacular, however, represents response not just to climate and materials, but to social form and tradition. 'The folk tradition', says Rapoport, 'is the direct and unselfconscious translation into physical form of a culture, its needs and values – as well as the desires, dreams and passions of a people.'[61] Vernacular architecture manifested no '*libido dominandi*', none of the desire to dominate which Augustine believed characterised the earthly city.[62]

---

[57] Rapoport, *House*, p. 105.

[58] J. Cook, 'Environmentally benign architecture', in R. Samuels and D. Prasad (eds.), *Global Warming and the Built Environment* (London: Spon, 1994), p. 143.

[59] M. Smith, J. Whiteleg and N. Williams, *Greening the Built Environment* (London: Earthscan, 1998), p. 63.

[60] At the Seminary at which I worked for seven years in Southern India, eleven degrees above the equator, the choice on construction was between vernacular houses or houses designed by a leading British architect. The latter were chosen, partly on grounds of cost, and incorporated large glass walls. As everyone who lived in them noted, the architect was rightly called 'Baker'. A short step away in the centre of the city vernacular houses allowed a passage of air, and deep shade, which offered relief and made life bearable, even in the very height of summer.

[61] Rapoport, *House*, p. 2; cf. Vance: 'Self conscious architecture withers without public adulation, so only the vernacular form can live in the crowded area of organic growth.' J. E. Vance, *The Continuing City* (Baltimore: Johns Hopkins University Press, 1990), p. 50.

[62] B. Rudofsky, cited by Harries, *Function*, p. 271.

Thomas Sharp argued that all houses should harmonise with their landscape. Of course, in Manhattan that might mean building a skyscraper, but in the towns and villages of which he was thinking he thought rootedness was essential to good housing – and this is part of the vernacular tradition, as houses were all built from local materials, as we have seen. In modern housing, by contrast, everything may be imported.[63] In addition to the need for harmony Simon Fairlie suggests that 'irrectitude' – a lack of straightness – is desirable, on the grounds that 'Nature abhors a straight line'. The lines of vernacular buildings are 'soft, blurred, gently inclined or wavering; they are distinct from the landscape, yet remain at home within their setting of rolling hills or burgeoning foliage'.[64]

The modern brick built villa, whatever stylistic concessions it may make to the local vernacular, imposes an artificial geometry upon the landscape. Its rigid outline, its mechanical tiling, its machined window frames, its telephone wires and TV aerial . . . all speak of another world. Distinctiveness has turned into intrusion, aspiration has become arrogance, and Nature has been relegated to the status of backdrop – a 'view'.[65]

The Viennese painter Hundertwasser found modernist architecture 'morally unendurable' and preferred the 'material uninhabitability of the slums' to the 'moral uninhabitability of functional, utilitarian architecture'.[66] 'These days houses in many places look as if they are ready to leave,' commented Ernst Bloch, with special reference to Bauhaus functionalism. 'In fact, the sensitivity of western architecture goes so far that it sensed Hitler's war quite a long time in advance, in a roundabout way, and prepared for it.' It exhibited, he said, a complete bankruptcy of ideas.[67]

This critique of the architecture of much of the twentieth century, both modern and postmodern, is well taken. At the same time we must not romanticise the buildings of the past which, where they survive, are now often sold as 'dream houses'.[68] In a country where most vernacular

---

[63] T. Sharp, *Town and Countryside* (Oxford: Oxford University Press, 1932), p. 69.

[64] S. Fairlie, *Low Impact Development* (Charlbury: Jon Carpenter, 1996), p. 4. Harries likewise speaks of the 'war against straight lines' waged by the Viennese painter Hundertwasser. *Function*, p. 241.

[65] Fairlie, *Low Impact Development*, p. 4. [66] Harries, *Function*, p. 240.

[67] E. Bloch, *The Principle of Hope* (Oxford: Blackwell, 1986), p. 733.

[68] The radical priest John Ball, in 1380, complained that 'in the Eastern counties dwell men in four walls of wattled reeds and mud, and the north east wind from off the Fen whistles through them'. Cobbett, at the beginning of the nineteenth century, commented on thatched cottages: '[Near Cricklade] the labourers seem miserably poor. Their dwellings are little better than pig beds, and their looks indicate that their food is not nearly equal to that of a pig. Their wretched hovels

94 *A Theology of the Built Environment*

architecture has disappeared, like Britain, what survives are the houses
of the better off artisans. Much vernacular building was undoubtedly
wretched and often condemned in the early twentieth century as rural
slums.[69] On the other hand, as we have seen, it also had great virtues.
Unselfconsciousness, lack of pretension or desire to impress, direct response to a way of life, climate and technology, use of the 'model and vari-
ations' method of building, the attitude towards nature and landscape,
all play a part in the beauty, simplicity and effectiveness of vernacular
architecture.[70]

Fairlie's remarks on the vernacular raise the question whether it is
not essentially rural, and whether it has any place in a world which is
now more than half urban. Could a new vernacular meet the needs of
sustainability? In one sense it certainly could, for '[v]ernacular buildings
waste nothing: they hate to destroy a structure, and will adapt the most
unlikely buildings for new purposes'.[71] By 'vernacular' here I do not
mean the neo vernacular of contemporary architect designed houses,
'*volks* vernacular', but the emergence of a genuine vernacular, which
is to say, that of the people of a distinct region. In Britain it seems
extraordinary that between a third and a half of the world's population
still build their own homes, and that self help accounts for 40 per cent
of domestic building in Belgium, West Germany, Austria, Italy, France,
Norway, Finland, and Ireland. In Britain it is well under 10 per cent.[72]
Colin Ward and Simon Fairlie have recorded the difficulties people
encounter when they set out to build for themselves. Whereas speculators
and the rich can do what they like, the poor are obstructed by planning
regulations at every turn. This is due in part to the professionalisation
of knowledge which, as Ivan Illich argued, 'makes people dependent
on having their knowledge produced for them' and leads to 'a paralysis
of the moral and political imagination'.[73] Not just of the moral and
political, but of the *practical* imagination. Creativity is supposed to be for
the gifted few and the rest of us are compelled to live in environments
constructed by them. Building upon this lie, says Simon Nicholson,

are stuck upon bits of ground on the road side . . . It seems as if they had been swept off the fields
by a hurricane, and found shelter under the banks on the road side!' Cited in R. Williams, *The
Country and the City* (London: Hogarth, 1985), p. 109.

[69] G. Mingay, 'The rural slum', in S. M. Gaskell (ed.), *Slums* (Leicester: Leicester University Press,
1990), pp. 92–143.

[70] Rapoport, *House*, p. 77.   [71] C. Ward, *Talking to Architects* (London: Freedom, 1996), p. 13.

[72] It is still, however, 12,000 homes a year. Fairlie, *Low Impact Development*, p. 94. This difference
between Britain and continental Europe is one of many which follow from the fact that Britain
was the first country to industrialise, and eradicated its peasantry more effectively, and earlier,
than any other. Saunders, *Nation*, p. 13.

[73] Cited in Ward, *Talking to Architects*, p. 20.

the dominant cultural elite tell us that the planning, design and building of any part of the environment is so difficult and so special that only . . . those with degrees and certificates in planning, engineering, architecture, art, education, behavioural psychology and so on – can properly solve environmental problems. The result is that the vast majority of people are not allowed (and worse – feel that they are incompetent) to experiment with the components of building.

The majority of the community has been deprived of a crucial part of their lives and lifestyle.[74]

Until 'all the Lord's people are prophets' we cannot have a new vernacular. But if we apply the criteria developed in the first chapter, which follow from the manifestation of God in and through the humble and modest, surely there is a strong theological case for its re-discovery?

At the opposite end of the scale to vernacular building is the monumental, buildings designed either to overawe the populace, or to impress the owner's peer group by their demonstration of wealth and good taste. Though Bacon began his essay on building with a caution about building to impress, it is of course monumental building he has in mind: The servants' dining area, he warns, should be at the top of the stairs, 'For otherwise you shall have the servants' dinner after your own: for the steam of it will come up as in a tunnel.' And that is all he has to offer for the labouring classes.

As we see from the stories about Solomon, the great house represents an ancient tradition. In imperial Rome, where the patrician houses were spacious, equipped with bathrooms, heated in winter by hypocausts which carried hot air through chambers in the floor, they constituted, in Mumford's view, 'perhaps the most commodious and comfortable houses built for a temperate climate anywhere until the twentieth century'.[75]

From the European Renaissance on, this tradition has littered the countryside with its products, aspiring, as Henry Crawford puts it in Jane Austen's *Mansfield Park*, to turn 'a house' into 'a place'. Today such 'places' constitute the bulk of our 'heritage'. Raymond Williams offers a trenchant and necessary comment on this tradition:

People still pass from village to village, guidebook in hand, to see the next and yet the next example, to look at the stones and the furniture. But stand at any point and look at the land. Look at what those fields, those streams, those woods even today produce. Think it through as labour and see how long and systematic the exploitation and seizure must have been, to rear that many houses, on that scale. See, by contrast, what any ancient isolated farm, in uncounted generations of labour, has managed to become, by the efforts of any single real family . . . And then turn and look at what these other 'families', these

[74] Cited in ibid., p. 23.   [75] Mumford, *City*, p. 256.

systematic owners, have accumulated and arrogantly declared. It isn't only that you know, looking at the land and then at the house, how much robbery and fraud there must have been, for so long, to produce that degree of disparity, that barbarous disproportion of scale. The working farms and cottages are so small beside them . . . What these 'great' houses do is to break the scale, by an act of will corresponding to their real and systematic exploitation of others.

To stand in that shadow, even today, is to know what many generations of countrymen bitterly learned and were consciously taught: that these were the families, this the shape of society. And will you then think of community?[76]

Williams echoes the scathing critiques of Isaiah or Jeremiah and raises for us the question of historical memory. If 'heritage' is largely the great house does this serve to glorify or perpetuate the social relationships which produced it? But would we be better off without this aspect of our culture? He also raises the question of class. The British Conservative administration of the 1980s encouraged the building of new mansions on the grounds that they were a legacy for the future, but for whom? Do we need this kind of 'high art' tradition? Would we be better off entirely without it? Is it sufficient to wander around the great houses remembering, with Walter Benjamin, that every monument of culture is at the same time a monument of barbarism? These are questions which ought to be discussed by the community of faith, but on which there has never been consensus, as we could see by comparing, say, Eusebius of Caesarea, the panegyrist of Constantine and his building programme, and John Chrysostom, the scourge of the rich in fourth century Constantinople.

MASS HOUSING

Mass housing was not the invention of the nineteenth century. In imperial Rome the proletariat lived in some forty-six thousand tenements containing around two hundred people each.[77] After the decline of Rome, however, we have to wait for the late middle ages, at least in Europe, before we find multi storey tenement blocks, and the conditions of ancient Rome were not equalled until the industrial revolution which was

---

[76] Williams, *Country*, pp. 105–6.

[77] In stark contrast to the patrician residences these tenements, says Mumford, 'easily take the prize for being the most crowded and insanitary buildings produced in Western Europe until the sixteenth century . . . not only were these buildings unheated, unprovided with waste pipes or water closets, unadapted to cooking; not merely did they contain an undue number of airless rooms, indecently overcrowded . . . they were in addition so badly built and so high that they offered no means of safe exit from the frequent fires that occurred' (*City*, p. 256).

in various ways responsible for the decline of vernacular building. Partly because it was coincident with a great increase in population, and the growth of great cities at the same time, it usually led to the 'throwing up' of thousands of houses on the cheap. Partly it signalled the advent of mass production, which was antithetical to the local trades and traditions which had produced the vernacular. 'Man is regressing to the cave dwelling', wrote Marx in 1845, 'but in an alienated malignant form.'

> The savage in his cave (a natural element which is freely offered for his use and protection) does not feel himself a stranger; on the contrary he feels as much at home as a fish in water. But the cellar dwelling of the poor man is a hostile dwelling, 'an alien, constricting power which only surrenders itself to him in exchange for blood and sweat'. He cannot regard it as his home, as a place where he might at last say, 'here I am at home'. Instead, he finds himself in another person's house, the house of a stranger who lies in wait for him every day and evicts him if he does not pay the rent.[78]

Here what Marx has in mind is not so much the actual physical conditions of the house, but the fact that the poor had no control over it and could be evicted at will. More than a century later John Turner agreed with him, finding the 'hideousness of characteristic modern housing' to be but a reflection of 'the defilement of personal relations and the desecration of life, as well as the dirtying of the environment'.[79] Mumford applied the same verdict to all industrial housing, where he found, in 'block after block':

> the same dreary streets; the same shadowed, rubbish filled alleys, the same absence of open spaces for children's play and gardens; the same lack of coherence and individuality to the local neighbourhoods . . . no effort is made to orient the street pattern with respect to sunlight and winds . . . The age of invention and mass production scarcely touched the worker's house or its utilities until the end of the nineteenth century.[80]

If this was a *belle epoque*, he comments, it belonged to the bourgeoisie. For the working class what was provided was minimal living space, the lowest possible threshold of tolerability.[81] This was true even of buildings which set out to remedy the slum problem, such as the Peabody buildings in London which had a slum density of 300 to 450 people per acre.

By the 1880s some of the working class, at least, could afford to move out to new row housing. 'As in housing for the privileged, these modest

[78] K. Marx, *Economic and Political manuscripts* (Moscow: Progress, 1974), p. 118.
[79] J. F. C. Turner, *Housing by People* (London: Marion Boyars, 1976), p. 35.
[80] Mumford, *City*, p. 530.   [81] Ibid., p. 316.

row houses consisted of uniform blocks, with individual small yards and outhouses in the back.' Though middle class critics thought the architectural quality was appalling, '[b]y working class standards ... the house was an immense achievement. People slept on a different floor than they ate; the smell of urine and faeces no longer pervaded the interior.'[82] In continental Europe and North America the apartment block offered a mediating form between mass housing and suburbia, providing, chiefly for the middle class, accommodation which was popular and often elegant, as well as being built according to human scale and avoiding urban sprawl.

Great efforts were made to clear the slums and, in both the socialist bloc and in countries like Britain, national or local government stepped in to build houses on a large scale. The principle behind this building programme was excellent: the provision of decent, affordable, and secure housing for all. To vest it in local government or the state also meant that it was not subject to the 'discipline of the market', where poorer tenants could be priced out, but that standards and rents were democratically accountable.[83] These principles remain important, but there was a crucial factor missing in the provision of mass housing, namely, the involvement of the people who had to live in the houses. The key issues raised by mass housing are those of ownership, design, and empowerment.

Alice Coleman, in a famous study, laid the blame for the perceived failure of planned housing on what she calls a 'quasi religious' belief in the perfectibility of human nature, by which she meant ideals about public ownership as opposed to private.[84] She found that ownership was a key factor. Litter, graffiti, excrement, and so on were, she found, twice as common in council owned blocks of flats as in owner occupied.[85] In his survey of three British towns, Peter Saunders found that tenants are much less inclined to develop attachments to their houses than are

---

[82] Sennett, *Flesh and Stone*, p. 334. So also Saunders, *Nation*, p. 149, pointing out the huge fall in numbers of people sharing a room between 1951 and 1976, and citing the view that '[t]he poor live in what would have been thought of in the pre-capitalist period as ill-maintained castles'.

[83] In Britain at the beginning of the third millennium Government favours replacing council housing with housing associations. It is, however, much easier to evict housing association tenants. There are seventeen grounds for eviction, some automatic. Rents are higher, and there is no democratic control through the election of local councillors.

[84] A. Coleman, *Utopia on Trial: Vision and Reality in Planned Housing* (London: Shipman, 1985), p. 3, citing Philip Johnson with approval. She herself is accused of having a biologically deterministic view of human nature which played into the hands of right wing councils eager to shed their responsibilities to care for the poor. J. Morris and M. Winn, *Housing and Social Inequality* (London: Shipman, 1990), pp. 169ff.

[85] Coleman, *Utopia*, p. 23ff.

owners.[86] In Britain much of the problem, as noted in chapter 2, was a prohibition on doing any improvements to the property whatever, a sure fire recipe for alienation.[87] Bureaucratic rigidity and racial and gender inequalities and discrimination have also played their part.[88]

Alongside the question of ownership, design is also a key factor. Why is it that the estates of Raymond Unwin remain attractive today, where tower blocks, by and large, are not? An answer may lie in the contrast of the Guild socialism of Unwin, which was romantic, intimate and humanist, and the technocratic and authoritarian vision of Le Corbusier. He divided the residential area of his radiant city into two types: six storey luxury apartments for the elite with 85 per cent of the ground left free, on the one hand, and accommodation for the workers, built around courts, on the other, with 49 per cent of the ground left free. The architecture which this authoritarian and classist ideology led to were the tower blocks of the second half of the twentieth century. In Britain they formed a major part of the massive public building programme – four million homes – between 1945 and 1969. Tower blocks stood for modernity, sunlight and glass as opposed to soot, damp and narrow back to backs. They also addressed the problem of suburban sprawl. In the view of many, however, they failed. They 'were built for community. They worked for solitude.'[89] The Pruitt Igoe scheme in the United States is symbolic of them as a whole. Completed in 1955–6 they were dynamited in 1972, having proved unlettable and a focus for vandalism and street crime. The post mortem on the scheme emphasised that the architect had designed like a sculptor, seeing the grounds of the project as nothing more than a surface on which he was endeavouring to arrange a whole series of vertical elements into a compositionally pleasing whole. The social dynamics of these buildings, remarks Peter Hall, had not been thought through. They were put up without regard to people's preferences. 'The cold brutality of the architecture made the blocks feel bleak and comfortless, and alienation, loneliness, and stress became common experiences.'[90]

---

[86] Saunders, *Nation*, p. 294.
[87] Saunders gives many examples: 'We wanted to combine the bathroom and the outside toilet but they wouldn't agree. We wanted to rip a fireplace out and they wouldn't agree. We ripped a hedge out to make a driveway without asking because it's a waste of time – the answer's always "no"' (ibid., p. 91). Colin Ward records someone evicted for painting his house cream, when all the rest were red. *Housing: An Anarchist Approach* (London: Freedom, 1983), p. 40.
[88] I. Cole and R. Furbey, *The Eclipse of Council Housing* (London: Routledge, 1994), chs. 5 and 6. At the same time they note that 61% of council house users expressed satisfaction with their accommodation (ibid., p. 164).
[89] Andrew O'Hagan, 'Higher Hopes', *Guardian Weekend*, 13 March 1999.
[90] P. Hall, *Cities of Tomorrow* (Oxford: Blackwell, 1988), p. 238.

Studies conducted in Britain found that psychoneurotic illnesses were three times higher in multi storey buildings than in low level detached buildings.[91] Even here, away from the tower blocks, mass housing is often characterised by what Jane Jacobs calls a 'great blight of dullness'. It is well known, says the Dutch architect Nicholas Habraken, that all the products of mass housing are marked by an appearance of uniformity. 'The only way to ensure uniformity is the rigorous exclusion of individual man ... Nature knows no uniformity, but seeks ever greater variety.'[92] Mass housing represents an institutionalised, regimented, view of human nature.

Aside from uniformity Coleman found fifteen design faults, including the number of dwellings per block, spatial organisation, the use of overhead walkways, the number of storeys, and the use of corridors, all of which made 'an iniquitous imposition upon people who cannot cope with them'.[93] Her recommendations included a strong affirmation of Robert Frost's dictum, 'Good fences make good neighbours.' Contemplating twentieth century mass housing, Bachelard's verdict is severe: 'In Paris there are no houses, and the inhabitants of the big city live in superimposed boxes.'[94] This verdict might call into question Bachelard's whole romantic and oneiric account of 'the house'; on the other hand we could say that all such housing reflects a devastatingly inadequate account of what it means for human beings to be made in the image of God and housed accordingly.

On top of ownership and design, however, is the question of involvement. One of the key differences of mass building from the vernacular, apart from the question of scale, is that it is conceived and executed 'top down', the crux of Alice Coleman's case. Tower blocks were not created by people in the community, for themselves, but either by 'experts' or by councils looking for cheap housing solutions. 'Rarely were people asked whether they wanted to move into a box in the sky,' comments Herbert Girardet.[95] The need for consultation has been a central contention of Nicholas Habraken, John Turner and Colin Ward, who find the key to the problem in people being able to control their own environment. 'The inhabitants of a Mass Housing town cannot possess their town,' wrote Habraken. 'They remain lodged in an environment which is no part of themselves ... what happens to day is nothing but the production

[91] H. Girardet, *The Gaia Atlas of Cities*, rev. edn (London: Gaia, 1996), p. 82.
[92] N. Habraken, *Housing Supports: An Alternative to Mass Housing* (London: The Architectural Press, 1972), p. 21.
[93] Coleman, *Utopia*, p. 3.   [94] Bachelard, *Poetics*, p. 26.   [95] Girardet, *Gaia Atlas*, p. 80.

of perfected barracks.'[96] Talking of the housing of the poor, the barrios and favellas of Latin America, John Turner remarks that never before did so many do so much with so little. By contrast, 'when we contemplate the projects intended to house or rehouse the masses through corporate agencies, public or private, capitalist or communist, our only possible conclusion is that never before was so little done for so many with so much'.[97] Turner argues that when dwellers control the major decisions and are free to make their own contribution to the design both the process and the environment produced stimulate individual and social well being. When they have no control the opposite is the case.[98] A decade before Turner Hundertwasser was arguing in Vienna that '[e]veryone ought to be able and compelled to build, so that he bears real responsibility for the four walls within which he lives'.[99] Following the Habitat Conference of 1976 social regeneration budgets came to require community consultation for their awarding, but we are still light years away from Turner's 'building by people'.

The same points about control apply to interiors, as we saw in relation to council housing in the second chapter. The distrust of the ability of ordinary people to think and act for themselves which this exemplifies found paradigmatic expression in Le Corbusier, who notoriously had no time for individual idiosyncracy. 'We must never lose sight of the perfect human "Cell"', he wrote, 'the cell which corresponds most perfectly to our physiological and sentimental needs. We must arrive at the "house machine" which must be both practical and emotionally satisfying and designed for a succession of tenants.' This anti humanist philosophy was shared by 'experts' in child rearing, education and others at the time, all obsessed by what Mumford called the 'myth of the machine'.[100] In all these areas it has proved equally damaging and has had to be abandoned.

SUBURBAN HOUSING

In the nineteenth century a new mode of housing made its appearance, neither elite nor vernacular – suburban. Suburbs in themselves were not new, but the rise of a new middle class brought with it the demand for a new type of housing. The very first of these houses, in the 1820s, were

[96] Habraken, *Housing Supports*, p. 13.
[97] C. Ward, *When We Build Again* (London: Pluto, 1985), p. 70.
[98] Quoted in ibid., p. 64.   [99] Cited in Harries, *Function*, p. 240.
[100] Habraken believes that Le Corbusier's '*machine à habiter*' was meant 'poetically' and that it was functionalism which turned it into a slogan. *Housing Supports*, p. 17.

a continuation of elite building, but the process of cultural seepage had already produced pattern books for the salaried classes by 1835. This housing was architect designed, and from the start the emphasis was on *difference*. An estate like that in North Oxford is a good example of what could be achieved for the upper middle class in the second half of the nineteenth century. Built for tradesmen, clergy, and a few of the dons who were newly allowed to marry, the houses are all different, with a wealth of individual detail.[101] Dislike of monotony was a predominant and recurring feature of Victorian criticism. 'The freedom of each architect, each householder to express himself as he saw fit had moral and political as well as aesthetic significance. The facade was to represent the special creative vision of the designer, just as the house represented the independence and identity of the family it contained.'[102] Some are quite heavily 'gothicised', with fairy tale windows and turrets, but most are content with varied roof lines and individual porches. A stone's throw away are the cottages which provided houses for the servants who worked here, and for the University, providing altogether humbler dwellings.

As cultural seepage continued so the element of difference became more and more attenuated. In Britain nearly three million suburban homes were designed by unqualified assistants or from pattern books between the wars.[103] In the United States the Levitts built 17,000 homes for 82,000 people using prefabricated materials and standardised designs. In Peter Hall's judgement, 'Levittown is dull. The residential streets are slightly too long, wide and straight. It lacks imagination or visual delight.'[104] Mumford's verdict is still more severe, describing the suburbs as 'a multitude of uniform, unidentifiable houses, lined up inflexibly, at uniform distances, on uniform roads, in a treeless communal waste, inhabited by people of the same class, the same income, the same age group ... Thus the ultimate effect of the suburban escape in our time is, ironically, a low grade uniform environment from which escape is impossible.'[105] Herbert Gans, who conducted his field work by living in Levittown, replied to this that it represented a thinly veiled attack on the culture of working and lower middle class people, implying that mass produced housing leads to mass produced lives. Only the rich can afford custom built housing, he pointed out, and these charges were not levelled against the upper class terraces of the eighteenth and nineteenth

---

[101] T. Hinchcliffe, *North Oxford* (New Haven: Yale University Press, 1992), p. 49.
[102] Edwards, *Design*, p. 22.   [103] Hall, *Cities of Tomorrow*, p. 76.
[104] Ibid., p. 296.   [105] Mumford, *City*, p. 553.

centuries.[106] Others point out that even Levittown has softened over the years, and because suburban dwellers continually make little changes to both house and garden there is a great deal of difference on the micro scale. Gans insisted that it was a good place to live, and its popularity has held.[107] James Richards, who somewhat implausibly celebrated the anarchic spirit of suburbia, thought that the fact that the modern subur- ban style can produce similar effects to English picturesque casually and as if by instinct constituted a proof that it is a form of the vernacular.[108] These defenders of suburbia are justified to the extent that the suburbs remain a popular destination. Colin Ward contrasts the success of the suburban house with the failure of the municipal estate. The difference, he points out, was not in the quality of building, but that in one people had control and in the other they did not.[109]

THE NEED FOR A NEW VERNACULAR

At the millennium world population stands at more than six billion, the last billion added in just twelve years. Current estimates are 9 billion by 2050, but this may well be an underestimate. We are familiar with the question of how they are to be fed and watered, but the question of how they are to be housed is also urgent, given the fact that the majority of the world's population live in poverty. Rapoport argues that four objectives need to be borne in mind for successful housing: it should have social and cultural validity; it should be sufficiently economical to ensure that the greatest number can afford it;[110] it should ensure the maintenance of the health of the occupants;[111] and finally, there should be a minimum of maintenance over the life of a building.[112]

The need for social and cultural validity raises the obvious question of what constitutes validity. Colin Ward points out that in the new city of Milton Keynes the houses that are most disliked are those designed by the most prestigious architects, whilst the most sought after are those

---

[106] H. Gans, *The Levittowners* (London: Allen Lane, 1967).

[107] H. Gans, *People, Plans and Policies: Essays on Poverty, Racism and Other National Urban Problems* (New York: Columbia University Press: 1991), p. 140.

[108] J. M. Richards, *Castles on the Ground: The Anatomy of Suburbia* (London: John Murray, 1973) (1st edn 1946), p. 30.

[109] Ward, *When We Build Again*, p. 18.

[110] In primitive and vernacular contexts, Rapoport notes, most, if not all, people have houses, as opposed to the situation under any form of capitalism.

[111] In relation to climate, he says, traditional housing succeeds, in relation to sanitation and parasites it usually fails.

[112] Rapoport, *House*, p. 129.

which most resemble the traditional image of house-and-home, with a pitched roof and a chimney on top, and a front porch with roses round the door.[113] Part of the reason for this is, of course, lay disenchantment with contemporary art in general. It is also, however, to do with a pattern of alienation in the built environment which echoes the analysis of the early Marx. The architect, says Papanek, is commissioned by a speculator, himself acting for an investor. The person who lives in the house stands in no direct relationship to the chain of talent, speculation, greed, know how and craft which produces the house. 'The end user's only contribution seems to lie in passively adapting to land rights, market forces, existing structures and decisions made for and about him or her.'[114] For this reason Habraken calls for individual involvement 'to break the bonds of Mass Housing'. Mass Housing, he argues, was an emergency measure which became generalised, and which we need to abandon.[115] His solution is for 'supports' – concrete frameworks, with mains services connected, which people can then fashion to their own design.[116] For many years John Turner and Colin Ward have argued a similar position.[117] What Rapoport calls cultural validity Turner speaks of in terms of dweller control:

When dwellers control the major decisions and are free to make their own contributions in the design, construction, or management of their housing, both this process and the environment produced stimulate individual and social well-being. When people have no control over nor responsibility for key decisions in the housing process, on the other hand, dwelling environments may instead become a barrier to personal fulfilment and a burden on the economy.[118]

It is dweller control which is the key. Saunders argues that ownership contributes to our sense of self and identity, and this would a fortiori be the case with self build.[119] Although Turner insists that self build can produce good housing on any criteria over a period of years, he does not want a situation where people are compelled to build their own houses, nor does he reject all high technology. Rather, he argues that planning should be proscriptive, warding off bad practice, rather than prescriptive,

---

[113] Ward, *When We Build Again*, p. 88.   [114] Papanek, *Green Imperative*, p. 127.

[115] Habraken, *Housing Supports*, p. 24.

[116] Habraken described supports as 'constructions which are not in themselves dwellings ... but which contain individual dwellings as a bookcase contains books ... a construction which allows the provision of dwellings which can be built, altered and taken down, independently of others' ibid., pp. 59–60.

[117] Turner, *Housing by People*; J. F. C. Turner and R. Fichter, *Freedom to Build: Dweller Control of the Housing Process* (London: Macmillan, 1972); Ward, *Housing*.

[118] Turner and Fichter, *Freedom to Build*, p. 241.   [119] Saunders, *Nation*, p. 80.

and that central government's major role is in providing infrastructure. His experience in the United States, the Lewisham example cited earlier, and Hans Harms' history of self build in Germany show that this is not an option only for the Third World, but that it can make perfect sense in the North too.[120]

The houses Turner speaks of are often energy efficient, and thus sustainable, a key feature of any contemporary building, but we also need to note William Morris' demand that housing for ordinary people should be beautiful. Every person should be ensured, said Morris, 'first, Honourable and fitting work; Second, A healthy and beautiful house; Third, Full leisure for rest of mind and body'.[121] Despite the lack of comment on the house in the Christian Scriptures I believe these demands follow squarely from what they have to say about what it means to be human. Morris loathed in particular the utilitarianism of the nineteenth century. The word expressed, he thought, 'a quality pretty nearly the opposite of useful, and means something which is useful for nothing save squeezing money out of other people's necessities'.[122] If we ask why mass housing has so often been a disaster then the utilitarian ethos which inspired it is very often to blame. For Morris, '[a] house, a knife, a cup, a steam engine ... anything that is made by man and has form, must either be a work of art or destructive to art'.[123] He insisted that people should have nothing in their houses which was not either useful or beautiful.[124] Morris was famous for his rages, and what he would have made of the twentieth century house one can only imagine. 'It has remained for our own generation', the Goodmans commented acidly in 1947, 'to perfect the worst possible community arrangement – the home of the average American.'

This home is liberally supplied with furniture and the comforts of private life, but these private things are neither made nor chosen by personal creation or idiosyncratic taste, but are made in a distant factory and distributed by unresisted

[120] J. F. C. Turner, 'Issues in Self-Help and Self-Managed Housing'; H. Harms, 'Historical Perspectives on the Practice and Purpose of Self-Help Housing'. Both in P. Ward (ed.), *Self-Help Housing: A Critique* (London: Mansell, 1982).

[121] W. Morris, 'Art and Socialism', in *The Collected Works of William Morris* (London: Longmans, 1910–15), vol. XXII, p. 210.

[122] W. Morris 'Makeshift', in M. Morris (ed.), *William Morris, Artist, Writer, Socialist*, vol. II (Oxford: Blackwell, 1936), p. 474.

[123] W. Morris, 'The Socialist Idea in Art', in *Works*, vol. XXIII, p. 255.

[124] W. Morris, 'The Beauty of Life', in *Works*, vol. XXII, p. 76. Ernst Bloch likewise speaks of the 'intense (*heftige*) will towards colour, form and ornament', which pervades the world and which resists mechanisation. It 'demonstrates that the light which has shone throughout history until the intrusion of the man-made commodity, and fills all our museums, has not been extinguished in the Bauhaus and similar hollow cheering' (*Principle*, p. 387).

advertising. At home they exhaust by their presence – a bare cell would give more peace or arouse less restlessness. They print private life with public meaning. But if we turn to read this public meaning, we find that the only moral aim of society is to provide private satisfactions called the 'standard of living'. This is remarkable. The private places have public faces, as Auden said, but the public faces are supposed to imitate private faces.[125]

An artefact is better if it is aesthetically pleasing, says Wolterstorff, echoing Morris.

Perhaps the ugly concrete-block flats in lower-class housing developments serve rather effectively the housing needs of those who live in them. Yet they are not good houses – not as good as they could be. Something is missing, something of the joy that rightfully belongs to human life, something of the satisfaction that aesthetically good housing would produce in those who dwell there.[126]

These aims demand, as some Green thinkers have argued, and as Turner and Ward imply, a search for a new vernacular. The vernacular is the language of ordinary people. According to Rapoport it is the sharing of a world view, and other image and value systems, which makes possible the process of vernacular building.[127] In many cases traditional buildings, which used wood or stone, are now too costly to build, but also the common shared value system and image of the world which they expressed has been lost.[128] Victor Papanek has shown that there is no need for contemporary vernacular building to take the form of a nostalgic throw back to the past. New materials can be used, new functions designed for, but the principles of the vernacular can still be honoured.[129] In the older industrialised world, however, it is the loss of shared value systems which is the key problem. This is the reason that, as Gillian Darley points out, the 'neo vernacular' of postmodernism is as alienated in its way as the modernism it succeeds.[130] A new vernacular must be precisely that: genuinely of the people. It is this which Turner

[125] P. Goodman and P. Goodman, *Communitas: Means of Livelihood and Ways of Life* (New York: Random House, 1960 (1st edn 1947), p. 184.
[126] N. Wolterstorff, *Art in Action* (Carlisle: Solway, 1997), p. 170.
[127] Rapoport, *House*, p. 48.   [128] Ibid., p. 6.
[129] Papanek, *Green Imperative*, p. 137. He remarks that the Hopi Indians are building motels with souvenir shops 'without sacrificing their own vernacular approach to space and place'.
[130] G. Darley, 'Local Distinctiveness: An Architectural Conundrum', in *Local Distinctiveness: Place, Particularity and Identity* (London: Common Ground, 1993). She writes: 'Superficial neo-traditionalism has gone a long way towards destroying and devaluing precisely the traditional qualities that professionals and the lay public alike believe that they are safeguarding.' Harries likewise talks of re-building in post war Germany which borrowed certain aspects of the vernacular 'without preserving the former's life'. *Function*, p. 272.

was asking for in his three principles of self government in local affairs
and the freedom to build; the use of the least necessary power, weight and
size of tools for the job; and the confinement of planning to an essentially
legislative role, and separating it clearly from design.[131] A quarter of a
century after his plea state housing is far less in evidence, but the building
of speculators is often little less heteronomous. Building by people is still
not a policy option.

Put theologically these demands for new housing can be translated into
a threefold, or trinitarian, form. In virtue of the theology of creation the
theologian is concerned for an ecologically sustainable mode of building;
in virtue of the concern for justice we need to affirm, with the post Second
World War US government, the *right* of everyone 'to a decent house in a
suitable living environment';[132] in virtue of belief in the Spirit at work in
all that makes for life, we are concerned with houses which speak to the
human soul.

(I) CREATION: HOUSING FOR SIX BILLION HAS TO BE ENVIRONMENTALLY SUSTAINABLE

At present, as Ian Lowe puts it, 'Many buildings in cities combine so
many features of bad design that they might have been sponsored by the
electricity industry to boost flagging sales.'[133] Sustainability has to be a
key feature of building in the future. How is this to be achieved? Much
can be done with existing housing stock, as the Wise group has shown
in Glasgow, where thousands of otherwise rather poor homes have been
insulated and draught proofed by a scheme using unemployed people.[134]
When new building is involved, the autonomous house, which meets all
its energy and recycling needs, has justifiably attracted a great deal of
attention. Autonomous houses have been built in Freiburg and Southall,
by Robert and Brenda Vale, which store and filter rainwater, have com-
posting toilets and so on. Perhaps more radically, earth sheltered houses
have been developed at Hockerton in Nottinghamshire, and Newark
Council have agreed to build more of these to accommodate council
tenants. These houses provide all their own energy, collect their own

---

[131] Turner, *Housing by People*, p. 155.
[132] D. Harvey, *Justice, Nature and the Geography of Difference* (Oxford: Blackwell, 1996), p. 394.
[133] I. Lowe, 'The greenhouse effect and future urban development', in Samuels and Prasad (eds.), *Global Warming*, p. 61.
[134] A. Sinclair, 'Social Integration and Creation of new Urban Activities', in J. Miller and V. Mega (eds.), *The Improvement of the Built Environment and Social Integration in Cities* (Luxembourg: Office for Official Publications of the European Communities 1992), pp. 223ff.

water, and treat their own sewage. They are much cheaper to build than conventional houses, and make a minimal impact on the environment. At Hockerton every adult member of the community is required to undertake some work in growing vegetables and tending the garden.[135] Depending upon how the environmental crisis develops such ideas could prove a crucial part of the future. At present the problem is precisely with generalisation. It is partly that Hockerton seems to demand a lifestyle commitment which most people would not find attractive, but also that Hockerton is land hungry, and this precludes it being adopted on a very large scale. There is also a problem with design. At Milton Keynes the energy efficient houses were unpopular because they looked strange. In pursuit of sustainability 'an imagery was projected which most people found incomprehensible'.[136] For this reason Peter Smith, the Chair of the RIBA Sustainable Futures Committee, has designed houses which go a long way to reducing energy needs, but which look far more conventional. As Smith puts it, 'ultra-low energy homes do not have to wear their environmental credentials on their sleeve' and may cost little more than, if as much as, a conventional house.[137]

One of the questions they present is that of density. Can this form of development become a form of mass housing? David Harvey argues that high density urbanised living and 'inspired forms of urban design' are the only paths to a more ecologically sensitive form of living in the twenty-first century. For Harvey, in agreement with Castells, the urban and everything that goes into it is as much a part of the solution as it is a contributing factor to ecological difficulties. Cities, he argues, 'have always been fundamentally about innovation, wealth creation and wealth consumption and getting things right in cities is the only real path towards technological and economic improvement for the mass of the population'.[138] Habraken was arguing forty years ago that 'the great problem of society' was 'to find a formula for a housing process which allows comfort and human dignity to exist hand-in-hand, while maintaining the town as conglomerates of compact building'.[139] His proposal for 'supports' was his suggested answer, a proposal which has not, so far as I know, been tried in any extensive way.

[135] Hockerton Housing Project Information Pack, Newark, Notts, 1998.
[136] J. Ballinger and D. Cassell, 'Principles of energy efficient residential design', in Samuels and Prasad (eds.), *Global Warming*, p. 176.
[137] P. Smith, 'Housing: 2016 and Beyond', paper prepared for 'New Homes for Devon' conference, Exeter, September 1999. New building materials, like Permanent Insulation Formwork systems, allow a flexible shape, short construction times, and very high insulation capacity.
[138] Harvey, *Justice*, p. 435.   [139] Habraken, *Supports*, p. 54.

In terms of sustainability much can be done through the improvement of existing estates through energy saving measures such as introducing solar panels, central heating and extra insulation. In some cases, in cities such as Liverpool and Glasgow, this has made all the difference between the success and failure of large estates, for the reduced costs of alternative energy finally allow the poor to spend money on living, as opposed to existing and struggling simply to meet the bare necessities. The growing appreciation of the need to recycle must also apply to buildings, as it did for earlier generations, so that materials are reused, and usable buildings renovated rather than destroyed. All this, however, hardly amounts to the 'inspired forms of urban design' which Harvey demands.

(II) RECONCILIATION: JUSTICE AND DIFFERENCE

Problems of dwelling, says Harries, 'are above all not architectural but ethical problems'. We need, he says, an architecture responsive to our essential incompleteness, our need for others, for genuine, concrete community.[140] Whilst the need for domestic architecture to respect human integrity, and to allow certain basic standards of privacy, can be overstated, as in 'the Englishman's home is his castle', for most human beings this is still a utopian aspiration. All housing embodies an anthropology and therefore a view of society. The failure of so much nineteenth and twentieth century housing is demonstrably bound up with the ideology it embodied. As we have seen, Bloch and Hundertwasser are amongst those calling for a new humanism in relation to the built environment. Humanism, it should be clear, is not a monoculture. Turner worked with self build groups in four continents successfully. The challenge is to allow a sympathetic, human scale domestic architecture flourish in relation to the huge varieties of human cultures, intimately related to their climates as they are. The principle underlying organic growth, Day notes, is that the physical form grew out of activities, out of the meeting of users and environment.[141] A return to the vernacular would mean as part of the process a recovery of community, re-learning the possibilities implicit in shaping our built environment together.

Another problem is our technocratic conviction that 'anything is possible'. Involved in the new humanism, as Turner implies, must be a fresh recognition of limits. As we have seen, traditional building styles developed by finding solutions to problems that arose through access to

---

[140] Harries, *Function*, p. 363.   [141] Day, *Places*, p. 95.

only a limited range of materials. If we are to rediscover an architecture that is dynamic yet remains authentically traditional, says Simon Fairlie, 'then we can only do so by giving builders free rein to solve fundamental problems with a similarly limited, but updated, range of basic local materials'.[142] The gap which the industrial-technocratic society has introduced into the craft tradition is by no means so great as to be unbridgeable and it is therefore entirely possible that something of the diversity of style which has characterised world vernacular can be maintained or recovered – the opposite of the one house for all human beings which Le Corbusier proposed, and the opposite of the architectural form of McDonaldisation. If the preservation of difference is an important aspect of justice, as Iris Marion Young has argued, then in terms of the built environment this translates as respect for the vernacular.

(III) REDEMPTION: THE IMPORTANCE OF IN-SPIRATION

Ruskin argued for providing housing for working people by 'the building of more, strongly, beautifully and in groups of limited extent, kept in proportion to their streams and walled round, so that there may be no festering and wretched suburb anywhere, but clean and busy streets within and open country without'.[143] Christopher Day represents a continuation of this tradition, in insisting that aesthetics are not irrelevant to the conditions of social justice. Rows of rectangular buildings, he believes, oppress the freedom of the individual and, we can add, depress the spirit. In his own buildings he tries not to make one window the same as another:

The vertebrae of the spine each carry a slightly different load and accept a slightly different movement. They are not identical. Each window likewise has an individual set of requirements to fulfil – unless we are just providing containers for people, albeit elaborate ones. It may be ridiculous to make every window different just for the sake of being different, but it is even more so to make every one the same just for the sake of being the same, or to shape them just to impose an elevational pattern.[144]

Like Morris, Day emphasises the need to cultivate a sense for beauty, a sense suppressed by technocratic cultures. This sense 'used to be so strong that pre-industrial common people could not make a spoon, a cart, a boat, even a house look ugly. To do so would have been a crime

---

[142] Fairlie, *Low Impact Development*, pp. 60–1.   [143] Cited in Mumford, *City*, p. 540.
[144] Day, *Places*, p. 90.

against themselves.' The beauty of ordinary things, he recognises, came from the lived experience of grace:

Everything, from reaping the corn to blessing the meal or carving a chair, was an action giving thanks for God's creation, an artistically satisfying activity. All they made and did was essentially functional: there was no time, energy or space to make anything without a practical purpose; beauty and utility were inseparable. Today we find the reverse. Beauty and utility are widely regarded as separate streams: we all need utility, but beauty is considered to be an indulgence, peripheral to our main concerns in life.[145]

Without this attention to the beauty in diversity of the environment we are left with a culture of dependence, seeking escape in one or other form of addiction. Of course our surroundings must satisfy material functions but 'to carry architecture beyond the threshold of the materially useful, the biologically supportive or the emotionally satisfying, we need to cultivate and bring together both the inspiration which gives moral force to our ideas and the sense of listening to environment which makes those ideas appropriate'.[146] Some maintain that changing technologies and rising standards of living call in question any simple return to the vernacular but, as Simon Fairlie argues, we need to learn to build with a similarly limited, but updated, range of materials.[147] What the new millennium calls for is not the aggressive technocratic imperialism of the twentieth century, but a marriage between new technologies and respect for the past and the regional which will preserve the charm of the world we have inherited.

Building for six or nine billion will not make sense without this recovery of the sacred in the broadest sense. This involves the ability of our senses to tell us what is good or bad for us. Polyurethane coated wood, for example, feels hard, smooth and cold and does not breathe. It looks like wood but it is a lie and is bad food for the human spirit. 'If you want to bring children up to be honest it is not going to help if their environment is full of lies.'[148] Harmony in our surroundings, Day argues, is no mere luxury. Our surroundings are the framework which subtly confine, organise and colour our daily lives. Harmonious surroundings provide support for

---

[145] Ibid., p. 26.

[146] Ibid., p. 29. Jeffrey Cook similarly makes a plea for going beyond architecture which is merely benign. 'In a global environment that is dramatically deteriorating because of accelerated abuses, an architecture that is only neutral cannot heal the wounds and will not restore the equilibrium of the global natural system.' He wants an architecture which extends and enriches the natural landscape. 'Environmentally benign architecture: beyond passive', in Samuels and Prasad (eds.), *Global Warming*, p. 150.

[147] Fairlie, *Low Impact Development*, p. 61.   [148] Day, *Places*, p. 51.

outer social and inner personal harmony. Harmony can be achieved by rules – but rules lack life. Or it can arise as an inevitable but life-filled consequence of listening conversation.[149]

That reference to conversation takes us back to the dialogue both Day and Harries ask for between high and low traditions. In the world of casino capitalism whilst buying an old property is often a status symbol, new palaces are still being created, embodying all the gadgetry of Information Technology. In relation to that we face yet another conundrum. There is no doubt at all that the biblical emphasis is on the stakeholder economy, seeing 'every family under its vine and fig tree'. Furthermore, the demand for participatory building takes us back to Blake's citation of Numbers, 'Would that all the Lord's people were prophets.' Homes for nine billion can only possibly be provided when this is the priority. On the other hand some, though by no means all, of those great houses which we wander around 'guide book in hand' are undeniably beautiful and do express a vision of grace filled life which we cannot but honour. And this, of course, is a standard argument for a class society: the rich function as patrons of the arts and lead the way in architecture. To set against this we have the example of classical Athens, where the entire population lived in extremely modest dwellings, but produced the Parthenon for their communal worship. Perhaps the same might be said for medieval Norwich or even Paris. It is true that 'surplus' is needed to provide the freedom for great architecture to which not all can aspire. In the first chapter I mentioned Karsten Harries' 'ellipse' between domestic and religious building. Have we reached the stage, he asks, where the ellipse becomes a circle, centred on the house and the individual rather than on God or community?[150] Simply to raise the question is to answer it, and to see the point of his remark that the 'pedigreed' tradition takes us out of the everyday and sends us back to it with fresh eyes. Countries where the vernacular is still a cultural dominant, like Norway, show that the vernacular can be insipid, and the pedigreed house can provide excitement and refreshment. But pedigreed buildings which focus the community's values are one thing. Those which simply make status claims for the rich are quite another. What we certainly do not need is a situation where the vast majority – including the world's burgeoning middle class – are condemned to live in soul deadening and unimaginative buildings. Human beings are spiritual creatures. The DIY movement – one of the biggest money spinners in the European economy – is a testimony to the need people feel to shape their own environment. Unfortunately, as our Northern rubbish tips show, this often involves the superimposition of mass produced 'trim'. In building as in every other area in life we get nowhere without education – a process by no means to be identified, of course, with what happens in school and university. All the Lord's people need to be prophets in the shaping of their dwellings from the ground up. We need a new vernacular. But this requires, in turn, education and spiritual discipline if Jane Jacobs' 'great blight of dullness' is to be replaced. And this is an agenda we have scarcely begun to face.

CHAPTER 5

From Eden to Jerusalem: town and country in the economy of redemption

> Then Jesus went about all the cities and villages, teaching in their
> synagogues, and proclaiming the good news of the kingdom . . .
>
> (Matthew 9.35)

'God became human', said Luther, 'that from proud and inhuman gods
he might make real human beings.' Since this refashioning is of flesh
and blood the physical environment in which people live, and which also
shapes them, is part of the story, part of the economy of redemption. In
speaking of the 'economy of redemption' I am alluding to the suggestion
of Irenaeus of Lyons, in the late second century, that rather than think in
a sin–fall–redemption pattern we might rather think of redemption as a
process. Human beings were made in God's image, he argued, but had to
grow into God's likeness, a process in which they were nurtured by God
the Spirit.

> Through obedience and discipline and training human beings, who are con-
> tingent and created, grow into the image and likeness of the eternal God. This
> process the Father approves and commands; the Son carries out the Father's
> plan; the Spirit supports and hastens the process: while humankind gradually
> advances and mounts towards perfection; that is, they approach the eternal.[1]

Note that Irenaeus' account of redemption is Trinitarian. He describes
Christ and the Spirit as the 'two hands of God' through whom the process
of redemption is effected. We only have his work because of the urgent
need to counter the Gnostics, heretical groups who denied the goodness
of the body. By contrast Irenaeus affirms it, above all through his understanding of the incarnation, and the role Christ plays in human history.
In affirming the body Irenaeus affirms the built environment, because
bodies need buildings. People ensoul places, I have argued, in relation
to the house. Better, the Spirit of God in-forms and in-spires the built
environment through people. This is an extension of our existence as

[1] *Adversus Haereses* 4.38.2

soul and body grounded, constituted and maintained by the Spirit of God. Humankind are, in Karl Barth's formula, bodily soul and besouled body. 'Soul would not be soul, if it were not bodily; and body would not be body, if it were not besouled.'[2] The built environment is an extension of this truth. But what form of the built environment? Once humankind moves beyond the hunter gatherer stage, options for living seem to be limited. There are isolated dwellings, hamlets, villages, towns, suburbs and cities. Are all these equally adapted to the purposes of redemption? Does it matter in what kind of physical situation we live? 'We shape our buildings and then our buildings shape us,' said Churchill, famously, of the House of Commons, but the same is true of our larger communities. At least from the time of the emergence of the Greek *polis* in the sixth century BC people have suggested that either the city or the country is the environment best adapted for humanisation. In the West there is a deep seated prejudice which tells us that we are nearer to God in the country than in the town. In this chapter it is this prejudice I want to examine.

THE CONTRAST OF TOWN AND COUNTRY

To begin with we can note a peculiarity of the English language, which distinguishes, in a way other European languages do not, between 'towns' and 'cities'. *'Die Stadt'* in German is any town or city; Assisi is a *'città'* as much as Milan or Rome; Madrid is a *ciudad* as well as Compostella. But in English London, Edinburgh and Chicago are *cities*; Ashburton, Crieff or Desmoynes are *towns*.[3] Much anti urban literature opposes the countryside to the city. There is, however, a worthwhile distinction between towns and cities, which I shall highlight in this chapter, turning to the city proper in the next. Thomas Sharp, for example, a leading town planner in Britain between the 1930s and the 1950s, hated the industrial cities, which he described as 'sordid and ugly', and cursed 'the blind callousness' of the men who created them. He loved the country towns, and envisaged a future of compact towns which preserved their virtues. In this he seems to have been a precursor of compact city theory: 'Surely the ideal town is one which is as compact as the minimum requirements of public health will allow.'[4]

---

[2] K. Barth, *Church Dogmatics* III/2 (Edinburgh: T&T Clark, 1960), p. 350.
[3] Tamil has a similar distinction to English. Villages and towns are *oor*; cities are *naharam*.
[4] T. Sharp, *Town and Countryside* (Oxford: Oxford University Press, 1932), p. 149.

The contrast between town and country emerged quite early. Simon
Schama claims that classical civilisation always defined itself against the
primeval woods, from the epic of Gilgamesh onwards.[5] In Scripture 'the
city was found too problematic to serve as a viable model for human communities. The image of the garden suggested a setting more conducive
to moral conduct and livelihood. The good and godly life was down on
the farm, not in the tumult of the city.'[6] 'The antagonism between town
and country begins with the transition from barbarism to civilization,
from tribe to state, from locality to nation, and runs through the whole
history of civilization to the present day,' wrote Marx.[7] As a matter of
fact it was rather muted in medieval Europe but as the vigour of towns
and cities grew, so it became stronger. It is fundamental to Shakespeare's
comedies, for instance, with their ironic contrasts between court and
shepherd's cot, and was a dominant theme of the early Enlightenment.
Understanding it as a form of class struggle the early Soviet state sought
to abolish the town and country distinction either by locating people in
self contained urban centres, the urbanist solution, or by dispersing the
population throughout the country and producing a townless society, as
the de-urbanists wanted.[8] Neither policy was carried through coherently,
and the distinction remains. There are two major strands to it. One of
these is *aesthetic*. Near the beginning of the automobile era, before car
ownership had become anything like general, Thomas Sharp provided
one of the most splendidly polemical accounts of the relation of town and
country in the twentieth century, like Frank Lloyd Wright anticipating
what the implications of universal car ownership might be but drawing
very different conclusions. 'Tradition has broken down. Taste is utterly
debased,' he wrote. 'There is no enlightened guidance or correction from
authority.'

The town, long since degraded, is now being annihilated by a flabby, shoddy,
romantic nature-worship. That romantic nature-worship is destroying also the
object of its adoration, the countryside. Both are being destroyed. The one age-
long certainty, the antithesis of town and country, is already breaking down.
Two diametrically opposed, dramatically contrasting, inevitable types of beauty
are being displaced by one drab, revolting neutrality. Rural influences neutralize the town. Urban influences neutralize the country. In a few years all will
be neutrality. The strong, masculine virility of the town; the softer beauty, the

5 S. Schama, *Landscape and Memory* (London: Fontana, 1996), p. 82.
6 W. P. Brown and J. T. Carroll, 'The Garden and the Plaza', *Interpretation* 54/1 (January 2000) p. 6.
7 K. Marx,*German Ideology*, in *Collected Works*, vol. v (Moscow: Progress, 1976), p. 64.
8 J. H. Bater, *The Soviet City* (London: Arnold, 1980), p. 23.

richness, the fruitfulness of that mother of men, the countryside, will be debased into one sterile, hermaphroditic beastliness.[9]

Sharp's appeal is both *ad hominem* and aesthetic. 'Surely' it goes without saying that the preservation of the antithesis is desirable in itself. Town and country represent two pure and separate forms, each capable of supreme beauty, each serving two instinctive human desires, each contrasting with, offsetting, and supplementing the other.[10]

Sharp was followed in this approach after the Second World War by Ian Nairn, in a column called 'Outrage' in the *Architectural Review*. He attacked the 'creeping mildew' of urban sprawl and envisaged that by the millennium Britain would consist of isolated oases of preserved monuments in a desert of wire, concrete roads, cosy plots and bungalows, with no distinction between town and country. Today the philosopher Roger Scruton deplores the destruction of both towns and countryside in Britain by planning laws which allow out of town building sites using alien building types.[11]

The major contrast, however, is *moral*. Mumford finds a reaction to the city as early as the 'axial shift' of the sixth century BC when:

To achieve a new life, the holders of the new vision must desert the city: they must either establish themselves in the rural hinterland, in lonely forest or hillside cave, or at least on the outskirts of the city, in gymnasia or in garden colonies . . . If they enter the city, they must form a secret society and go underground, in order to survive.[12]

The contrast of corrupt town versus virtuous countryside became a conventional *topos* of Western thought. It was this, in fact, which inspired Cowper's famous line 'God made the country, and man made the town'.

> The love of Nature and the scenes she draws
> Is nature's dictate . . .
> Lovely indeed the mimic works of art;
> But Nature's works far lovelier . . .
> Beneath the open sky she spreads the feast;
> 'Tis free to all – 'tis every day renewed;
> Who scorns it starves deservedly at home.

[9] Sharp, *Town and Countryside*, p. 11. [10] Ibid., p. 43.
[11] R. Scruton, 'Cold Comfort Towns', *The Times*, 30 January 1999. His account of the charms of nineteenth century Swindon makes an ironic contrast with Ruskin's damning of the very same place on account of its dreadful railway architecture. Nairne too blamed the planners who in his view were responsible for what he called subtopia (suburb + utopia) because of their adherence to a policy of low density dispersal, and he believed this would impact on people's critical faculties to produce 'subtopians'.
[12] L. Mumford, *The City in History* (Harmondsworth: Penguin, 1991), p. 236.

In cities, by contrast,

Rank abundance breeds . . .
    sloth and lust,
And wantoness and gluttoness excess.
In cities vice is hidden with most ease,
Or seen with least reproach; and virtue, taught
By frequent lapse, can hope no triumph there
Beyond the achievement of successful flight.[13]

Flight, of course, might not have been so successful because, as Keith
Thomas notes, in early modern Britain, 'agriculture was the most ruthlessly developed sector of the economy, small husbandmen were declining
in number, wage labour was universal, and the vices of avarice, oppression and hypocrisy were at least as prominent in the countryside as in
the town'.[14]

The idyllisation of country life which we find in Cowper stands in a
long tradition which looks backwards or forwards to a past or a coming
golden age, a process which begins with Theocritus and Greek pastoral in the third century BC.[15] From Horace onwards, writes Raymond
Williams, 'much country pastoral only served to obscure the real nature of relations in the countryside, to promote superficial comparisons
between town and country, and to prevent real ones'.[16] But very often
pastoral had what theologians would call an eschatological dimension.
Thus Virgil dreams of the golden age when the earth will produce its
own fruit, and no creature prey on another:

> Goats shall walk home, their udders taut with milk, and nobody
> Herding them; the ox will have no fear of the lion . . .
> The soil will need no harrowing, the vine no pruning knife . . .
>   (Eclogue IV)

This inevitably recalls the words of Isaiah four hundred years earlier:

> The wolf shall live with the lamb,
> the leopard shall lie down with the kid,
> the calf and the lion and the fatling together,
> and a little child shall lead them.   (Isa. 11.6)

This pastoral eschatology, if we can call it that, fed anti city sentiment.

[13] W. Cowper, *The Sofa, Cowper's Poetical Works* (Edinburgh: Gall & Inglis, 1853), p. 116.
[14] K. Thomas, *Man and the Natural World* (Harmondsworth: Penguin, 1984), p. 246.
[15] Vance points out that words we use to compliment the countryside (arcadian, idyllic) tend to
be Greek and words which insult are Latin derivatives (rustic, villainous, savage, bucolic, rural).
Only 'pastoral' is complimentary. Latin urban references are complimentary (courtly, courteous,
urbane, civilised, citizen). J. E. Vance, Jnr, *The Continuing City* (Baltimore: Johns Hopkins
University Press, 1990), p. 76.
[16] R. Williams, *The Country and the City* (London: Hogarth, 1985), p. 54.

Pastoral takes a new turn in the seventeenth century with the view that in the countryside we are closer to God, and that to live in the country is, as it were, to dwell once more in Eden. A particular form of natural theology encouraged this view, contrasting what was 'man made' with what was 'natural'. Those who are conversant in the fields and woods, said Thomas Jackson in 1625, 'continually contemplate the works of God'.[17] When surrounded by sea or mountains, said Burnet in 1684, '[w]e do naturally upon such occasions think of God and his greatness, and whatsoever hath but shadow and appearance of Infinite, as all things have that are too big for our comprehension, they fill and over-bear the mind with their Excess, and cast it into a pleasing kind of stupor and admiration'.[18]

It is ironic that this view is found amongst Reformed divines, for, Brown and Carroll notwithstanding, it cannot really appeal to Scripture.[19] The Bible begins in a garden but ends in a city. Eden is not so much the site of primitive innocence as of temptation and fall, and the new creation will take the form of a city. Its historical narrative begins with nomadic pastoralists looking for somewhere to settle, and ends in imperial Rome, the world's first truly great city. Much of its focus is on Jerusalem, the centre of the eschatological hopes of the Isaianic community. Suspicion of the town seems to be implied in the gospels, where Jesus prefers the village and tells his disciples that his mission is not to preach in the city. Ched Myers suggests that hostility to Jesus' radical social practice was centred in urban areas, where the symbolic order was concentrated. This may have been the experience of Mark's community, which probably shared the general rural suspicion of Hellenistic urbanisation threatening Palestinian village life.[20] Paul, on the other hand, is one of the best known 'city men' of antiquity, and Christianity in the first two centuries seems to have been largely urban. Attitudes to town and country, then, are rather evenly balanced and, even allowing for Isaiah 11, there is not really a scriptural form of pastoral. Even the Song of Songs is set in a 'city'. The garden of Eden recalls Hesiod's golden age, except that labour seems to have been required even there, but it is open to question whether it is, as Milton described it, 'a happy rural seat of various view'. True, expulsion from the garden is followed by the founding of the city by the first fratricide, Cain, but the urban/rural antithesis is never developed. In truth there is less scriptural warrant for Cowper's line than there is classical.

[17] Cited in Thomas, *Man*, p. 250.   [18] G. Burnet, *Theory of the Earth* (London, 1684), p. 139.
[19] See footnote 6.   [20] C. Myers, *Binding the Strong Man* (Maryknoll: Orbis, 1988), p. 151.

Despite this fact the leading Reformed commentator on the city in the twentieth century, Jacques Ellul, took a profoundly pessimistic view of the town–country relationship. Today, he wrote, 'the country (and soon this will be true of the immense Asian steppe) is only an annex of the city'.[21] The city cannot function except as a parasite. 'What the city produces is for her own use. Notwithstanding tractors, electricity, fertilizer, what the city can produce for the country is absurd and ridiculous compared with what she receives. As for her spiritual worth, her ferment of ideas will be of use nowhere but in the city. On the other hand she spoils peasant values with remarkable virtuosity'.[22] The city was incapable of any other destiny than that of killing the country, 'where God put man to enable him to live his life as best he could'.[23] This idea that God intended human beings to live in the country is, as we have seen, quite new, a product of the cult of nature of the seventeenth and eighteenth centuries.

Keith Thomas traces the origins of the preference for the country at least in part to urban pollution, already a source of complaint in the thirteenth century.[24] The coal which was burned in early modern times had at least twice as much sulphur as that used today, and smoke and soot were accordingly a prominent feature of any large town. Provisions for disposing of sewage were rudimentary and plague intermittent. Hardly surprising that those who could afford to should retreat to the country. The prophet Amos already talks of summer houses and winter houses, and the summer house may have been in the country even then. At any rate, this was the case in twelfth century England and the process of cultural seepage saw it become a fashion by the 1670s in London when Pepys records his hunt for a suitable country retreat, finally opting for a time share in Parson's Green.[25] In addition the gentry had their wealth in the land, and reckoned to spend the summer in their country estates, even if they wintered in the city. The coming of full scale industrialisation completed the process. Wordsworth might praise the view from Westminster Bridge, but what the nineteenth century took from him was the religion of nature:

> And hark! how blithe the throstle sings!
> He, too, is no mean preacher:
> Come forth into the light of things,
> Let Nature be your teacher . . .

---

[21] J. Ellul, *The Meaning of the City* (Grand Rapids: Eerdmans, 1970), p. 147.
[22] Ibid., p. 151.   [23] Ibid., p. 8.   [24] Thomas, *Man*, pp. 244ff.   [25] Ibid., p. 248.

One impulse from a vernal wood
May teach you more of man,
Of moral evil and of good,
Than all the sages can.[26]

Once the working classes had wrested one day a week for leisure the exodus to the 'countryside' was born.[27]

The moral contrast can, of course, be turned on its head, as the word 'civilisation', what the city or the town can do for us, indicates. From roughly the same period in the sixth century there is a contrast, which was to become conventional, between rustic boorishness and urbanity. In Greek the words *asteios* (urban) and *agroikos* (rural) can also be translated as 'witty' and 'boorish', a contrast Richard Sennett derives from the disdain in which the sheer material struggle for existence was held.[28] Sydney Smith expresses this townsman's sneer in his famous description of the country as 'a kind of healthy grave'. It finds expression in authors who had no such disdain. 'The bourgeoisie', said Marx and Engels, in the *Communist Manifesto*, 'has subjected the country to the rule of towns. It has created enormous cities, has greatly increased the urban population as compared with the rural and has thus rescued a considerable part of the population from the idiocy of rural life.' Here is implied a quite other view of redemption. For Cowper and for the pastoral tradition as a whole the only remedy for sin is to flee the city, to take refuge in an *ersatz* monastery, or what Cowper describes as 'the peasant's nest', which he shared with Lady Austen. For this tradition, on the other hand, it is only the town which makes humanisation possible. If we take the Irenaean view, and think of redemption as a history which begins in Eden and ends in the establishment of 'Jerusalem' at the second coming, then towns are a key factor in the process. As the two poles of Irenaean thinking suggest, the process must be understood dialectically.

THE COUNTRY

Thomas Sharp called Cowper's famous verse 'one of the most foolish lines in the whole body of English poetry', and the reason is obvious. Sharp eulogised the English landscape as 'the loveliest, the most

---

[26] W. Wordsworth, 'Expostulation and Reply' (1798), *Complete Works* (London: Macmillan, 1900), p. 85.
[27] Classically expressed in Ewan MacColl's song 'The Manchester Rambler', written to support the mass trespass on Kinder Scout, a hill in Britain's Peak District, in 1932. The 'wage slave' of Mondays to Saturdays is a 'free man' on Sundays, finding his soul in the beauty of the mountains.
[28] R. Sennett, *Flesh and Stone* (London: Faber, 1994), p. 36.

humanized' of all.[29] The eighteenth century enclosers were amongst his heroes, for the landscape they bequeathed to the 1920s – the hedgerows, and rows of poplar, beech and elm. Raymond Williams makes the same point – that 'the country' is as much the result of human labour as the town – whilst drawing attention to the exploitation and inhumanity this involved:

> Even if we exclude the wars and brigandage to which it was commonly subject, the unaccountable thousands who grew crops and reared beasts only to be looted and burned and led away with tied wrists, this economy, even at peace, was an order of exploitation of a most thoroughgoing kind: a property in men as well as in land; a reduction of most men to working animals, tied by forced tribute, forced labour, or 'bought and sold like beasts'; 'protected' by law and custom only as animals and streams are protected, to yield more labour, more food, more blood, an economy directed, in all its working relations, to a physical and economic domination of a significantly total kind.[30]

The point is well taken from both. 'The country' is no more 'natural' than the town. The term 'countryside' was, Raymond Williams tells us, originally a Scots term to describe a specific locality, and applied to rural life as a whole only in the nineteenth century.[31] In a study of the Cumbrian village of Gosforth W. Williams contrasted 'the countryside' not with the town but with the village.[32] The former meant remote farms, where social patterns were quite different to those in the village. By the end of the twentieth century 'the countryside' meant partly a vanishing, if not altogether vanished, way of life, but much more the location for wealthy 'quality of lifers' who could, for the first time in history, easily combine the advantages of both town and country because they could afford to live at a distance from the town and travel to work and places of entertainment. Both town and country need careful definition. 'People have often said "the city" when they have meant capitalism or bureaucracy or centralised power, while "the country" ... has at times meant everything from independence to deprivation ... At every point we need to put these ideas to the historical realities: at times to be confirmed, at times denied.'[33]

[29] Sharp, *Town and Countryside*, pp. 15, 16.   [30] Williams, *Country*, pp. 37–8.
[31] R. Williams, *Keywords* (London: Fontana, 1976), p. 81. Jackson says it originated in France, and came into English in the thirteenth century to indicate the territory of a community speaking the same dialect and engaged in the same kind of farming under the same lord. J. B. Jackson, *Discovering the Vernacular Landscape* (New Haven and London: Yale University Press, 1984), p. 149.
[32] W. Williams, *The Sociology of an English Village: Gosforth* (London: Routledge and Kegan Paul, 1956), chs. 7 and 8.
[33] Williams, *Country*, p. 291.

Complete self sufficiency is possible only where people are content with a very low standard of living. Hunter gatherer societies can only sustain ten people per square mile, and settled agriculture is therefore the prerequisite for the growth of larger communities. The ancient norm of such communities is the village. Hamlets or isolated farms, which tend to predominate in hill country, and also wooded country, or where a shallow well will tap water, all relate to villages or towns to survive. Where deep wells are needed one finds large villages on the streams or where springs break out. Beyond these physical criteria we gather in communities because physically we cannot manage on our own, and because of the desire for fellowship and protection, a major consideration for most of human history.

Most human beings since the dawn of historical time have lived in villages, and it is fair to say, therefore, that the village is mother to the human race: only at the very end of the twentieth century did more people live in cities than in villages. As late as 1871 more than half the population of Britain, at that time the world's most industrialised nation, lived in villages or in towns of less than 20,000, and even today, in the world's two most populous countries, India and China, the majority of the population still do.

The Scott Report into the village community published in Great Britain in 1942 defined a village as any community with a population with less than 1500, whilst the French census still fixes the number at 2000. These figures are, however, arbitrary. As Braudel points out, there are Russian villages much larger than this which still cannot be counted towns, and before 1500 AD the vast majority of towns in the West had fewer than 2000 inhabitants.[34] A. W. Ashby defined a village as 'a collection of houses, larger than a hamlet, in a country district, usually an ancient district, containing a church, with one or more service institutions such as a school or shop, and forming the residential nucleus of the parish'. A hamlet, on the other hand, he calls 'a small group of houses in a country district, containing only a small proportion of the local population, and meagrely supplied, if at all, with service institutions'.[35]

---

[34] F. Braudel, *The Structures of Everyday Life* (Glasgow: Collins, 1981), p. 485.

[35] In an article in *Country Towns in the Future England*, written in 1944. Cited in W. Baker, *The English Village* (London: Oxford University Press, 1953), p. 11. Flora Thompson contrasts village and hamlet in terms of greater social complexity as well as size. 'The village was a little world in itself; the hamlet was but a segment' (*Lark Rise to Candleford* (Oxford: Oxford University Press, 1954), p. 472). According to Vance, 'Villages were a form of rural settlement brought about at least in part by the need for defence at a time when the Pax Romana no longer stretched across the land. These clusters of dwellings had nothing to do with the execution of urban functions, and

Though perhaps adequate for England this would not do for, say, India, where a great many villages lack service institutions, but are too large to be ranked as hamlets.

The Scott Report classified villages according to material structure, layout, plan and economic purpose.[36] There were and are, of course, not simply rural, but a great many fishing, mining, quarrying or mill villages, grouped around one industry. But even rural villages were never completely non industrial, at least before the end of the twentieth century. Blacksmiths and wheelwrights were found in villages, alongside shoemakers, tailors, hedgers, thatchers, sawyers, sadlers, stonemasons, millers, bakers, brewers, mole and rat catchers, quite apart from 'the common labourer' and the women who spun wool and wove it. The coming of mass production and mechanised agriculture destroyed many of these trades. But although size, and the ability of the community to provide for itself to some extent, is an important part of the definition of a village it misses the real heart of it. Thomas Hardy observed in *Tess of the D'Urbervilles* that '[e]very village has its idiosyncrasy, its constitution, often its own code of morality'. Nigel Rapport has glossed this observation at length, in a very postmodern way, challenging the idea that the village is socially and culturally homogenous. He argues that we cannot take analytical categories such as 'rural', 'community', 'kinship', 'class' or 'social structure' for granted. Any one behavioural form can, in specific situations, have a number of different meanings. 'They become instruments of diversity and difference, and yet the conditions of their use remain essentially public, and it is in coordination with significant others and in certain routine and limited ways that these meanings come to be made.'[37] His main informants appeared as 'aggregations of idiosyncracies, whose most vibrant and significant communities were ultimately, perhaps, private to themselves'.[38] This emphasis on difference is doubtless overstated, for if his observations are pushed we cease to be able to talk of local cultures at all, and that seems to be empirically false, but it is a useful caution against over hasty generalisations.

---

the traditional concept of classical geography that the village grows to the town and the town in turn to the city is little supported by either history or logic. Villages remain villages, for the most part, and towns begin as towns' (*Continuing City*, p. 102).

[36] *Report of the Committee on Land Utilization in Rural Areas* (London: HMSO, 1942). By 'layout' it meant whether they were nucleated or scattered, and by plan it meant whether they were formally planned or 'organic'. For this distinction see chapter 8.

[37] N. Rapport, *Diverse World Views in an English Village* (Edinburgh: Edinburgh University Press, 1993), p. 170.

[38] Ibid., p. 192.

What most people in Britain mean by a village is a product of the genre of 'country writing', which begins with Walton's *Compleat Angler*, and includes the work of Richard Jefferies, Flora Thompson, but also Laurie Lee. Lee memorably described the end of the ancient village:

> The last days of my childhood were also the last days of the village. I belonged to that generation which saw, by chance, the end of a thousand years' life . . . Myself, my family, my generation, were born in a world of silence; a world of hard work and necessary patience . . . of villages like ships in the empty landscapes and the long walking distances between them; of white narrow roads, rutted by hooves and cartwheels, innocent of oil or petrol, down which people passed rarely, and almost never for pleasure . . . Time squared itself, and the village shrank, and distances crept nearer . . . The horses had died; few people kept pigs any more but spent their spare time buried in engines. The flutes and cornets, the gramophones with horns, the wind harps were thrown away – now wireless aerials searched the electric sky for the music of the Savoy Orpheans.[39]

The immense success of this book and others in the genre speak of the nostalgia of post industrial human beings for a more stable and more beautiful past.[40] Lee is honest enough about Sladd, but it is as well to remind ourselves what the reality of village life in Britain meant in the decade before the First World War. Recalling a childhood spent in the village in the 1870s the liberal MP E. N. Bennett remembered

> the dull scenery, the slush and mud of the roads, the absolutely mechanical existence of the villagers, who went to bed at eight o'clock to save oil and candles, the careworn faces of the women, the sullen endurance of their husbands, the dreary respectability of the farmers . . . There is so little to refine the mind or cheer the soul in rural England.[41]

The toil has gone, but rural deprivation has not. The widespread failure to recognise it stems from 'the perceived compensations which are a vital construction of rural living. The poor can be disregarded as being "content" with their rural life and the not-so-poor will not be able to reconcile the idea of poverty with the idyll-ised imagined geographies

---

[39] L. Lee, *Cider with Rosie* (Harmondsworth: Penguin, 1962), pp. 216, 230.

[40] Georgina Boyes has demonstrated the way in which an idyllicised countryside was used for propaganda purposes during World War II. '"A country lane", "a cottage small beside a field of grain" were . . . presented as Englishness itself . . . "The Southcountry", its rolling hills and village greens reflecting priorities set by nature rather than current events, offered a timeless and indestructible conceptual retreat to those whose uncertain present was bombing raids, the rubble of destroyed cities, factory production lines and foreign battlefields.' *The Imagined Village* (Manchester: Manchester University Press, 1993), p. 181. The evacuation of inner city children to the countryside, and the emphasis on farming as part of the war effort, brought city and country together for a short time.

[41] E. N. Bennett, *Problems of Village Life* (London: Williams and Norgate, 1914), p. 78.

of the village'. In fact in Britain some 20 per cent or more of rural households live in or close to poverty.[42] If we turn to the Third World, four fifths of those classified by the UN as living in 'absolute poverty' live in villages, and it is this which drives urban migration as it did in many parts of Europe in the eighteenth and nineteenth centuries.

In the late twentieth century, at least in Britain, villages changed again under the impact of 'counter urbanisation', the drift away from the cities back to the countryside made possible by the motor car and increasingly available means of world wide communication. If the nineteenth century was characterised by a tidal wave of people flooding into the cities, in the twentieth century the tide went the other way, in the North at any rate, first into the suburbs and then into the countryside beyond. 'Planned or unplanned, promoted or discouraged, people continue to quit the centre for the suburb, the suburb for the countryside.'[43] In Britain the move away from larger conurbations doubled between 1961 and 1981 and rural areas have had the highest population growth of any category. There have been population increases of one third in towns with as few as 5000 residents. Those who make this move hope to enjoy the advantages of an urban life without its major stresses.[44]

Drawing deeply on the jargon of postmodernity Keith Halfacree explores the ways in which this move can be considered either a postmodern celebration, a piece of reaction, or a realistic and sensible option.[45] He argues that it can be understood either as a reaction against the tyranny of urban rationalism, or a strategy to deny postmodern complexity and to find a world in which 'eternal truths' are created and sustained. Those who return to rural life are seeking guidance from traditional roots and values.

Instead of seeing the desire for openness, quietness, cleanliness, aesthetic quality and nature ... as reflecting a postmodern concern with style or premodern concern with the past we can see it as an attempt to create a 'distance' between the migrant and the rest of the world, as symbolised by the urban population, in order to overcome the dedifferentiating tendencies of postmodernism.[46]

---

[42] P. Cloke and J. Little (eds.), *Contested Countryside Cultures: Otherness, marginalisation and rurality* (London: Routledge, 1997), p. 255.

[43] Ibid., p. 268.

[44] Sandra Wallman, 'Reframing Context', in A. Cohen and K. Fukui (eds.), *Humanising the City? Social Contexts of Urban Life at the Turn of the Millennium* (Edinburgh: Edinburgh University Press, 1993), pp. 52–65.

[45] Keith Halfacree, 'Postmodern Perspective on Counterurbanisation' in Cloke and Little (eds.), *Contested Countryside Cultures*, pp. 70–94.

[46] Ibid., p. 83.

Somewhat implausibly, in my view, the desire for a residential escape, a slower pace of life, a sense of community, safety and familiarity are linked to a need to obtain a sense of belonging in the world as it is today rather than to achieve a return to a past world or to play games of country living. The problem with such a positive reading is that this kind of 'residential escape' is only possible for those with money, and is the reverse side of the rural deprivation already mentioned. 'The countryside' has become a retreat for those who can afford 4×4 vehicles and barn conversions, an updated and extended version of the country house of the seventeenth and eighteenth centuries. What replaces the gamekeepers and the mantraps is political nimbyism, the determination to keep middle class quality of life at all costs, and a savage attack on those who threaten to spoil it, from New Age travellers to gypsies. In effect this is countryside as theme park, a version of the class war, with little regard for the countryside as the place where food for the cities is grown and pastured. In a study of the 'geography of exclusion' David Sibley correctly sees that what is at issue here is the assumption that the countryside belongs to the privileged.[47] When the colonisation of the countryside by urban incomers is added to the impact of industrialised agriculture, with its high tech machinery and huge concrete hangars, then the result is that it is turned into 'a cross between a factory and a drive in museum'.[48] The agonised debate around the countryside in Britain during the Foot and Mouth crisis of 2001 thought of the countryside primarily as a leisure resource, an 'amenity'. Journalists and politicians were united in the view that 'food security' was a dead issue. No longer a factory, then, but a vast park, with farmers as curators. It is, of course, perfectly clear that such views are impossible without the supermarket. The new appropriation of the countryside is defined by the out of town shopping centre.

THE TOWN

As M. O. H. Carver has argued in a brilliant paper, a town is a conversation in matter:

Towns can be flagship of empire, residence of authority, popular theme park, an ideological idol, a shopping machine, a manufacturer's ghetto. These numerous definitions are not the result of failing to find a clear philosophical position to

---

[47] D. Sibley, *Geographies of Exclusion* (London: Routledge, 1995), p. 107. He cites the speech of John Major at the Tory Party Conference in 1992 attacking New Age Travellers, and shows that the rhetoric of the 'countryside' lobby is 'by definition exclusionary'.
[48] S. Fairlie, *Low Impact Development* (Charlbury: Jon Carpenter, 1996), p. xi.

express the entity. *There is no entity.* The idea of the town was never agreed; on the contrary it was a source of permanent contention, a long argument preserved in stone and timber constructions.[49]

Whilst it is true that the idea of the town was never agreed, the claim that 'there is no entity' is probably too strong. In the first place, towns have always existed in relation to their surrounding regions. The town, says Braudel, only exists in relation to a form of life lower than its own.

There are no exceptions to this rule. No privilege serves as a substitute. There is no town, no townlet without its villages, its scrap of rural life attached; no town that does not supply its hinterland with the amenities of the market; the use of its shops, its weights and measures, its moneylenders, its lawyers, even its distractions. It has to dominate an empire, however tiny, in order to exist.[50]

In the Hebrew bible villages are called, delightfully, the 'daughters' of their cities. The relationship between town and village was never one way, however. Before the twentieth century towns had scarcely any excess of births over deaths and so recruitment from surrounding regions was necessary. It has been calculated that in the eleventh century a town of 3000 inhabitants needed the land of ten villages in order to live.[51] Prior to the twentieth century towns could be fed by large scale trade only partially and in rare circumstances, and most towns lived symbiotically with their surrounding countryside. At harvest time artisans and others left their houses and trades behind them and went to work in the fields. This continued in the Scottish city of Dundee, for example, right into the nineteen sixties.[52] Town and countryside 'obeyed the rule of "reciprocity of perspectives": mutual creation, mutual domination, mutual exploitation according to the unchanging rules of co-existence . . . the towns urbanized their countryside, but the countryside "ruralized" the towns too', as urban fortunes were spent on land.[53]

As with villages we can define a town partly in terms of minimum size. Waller suggests 10,000 for a town, 50,000 for a large town and 100,000 for a city.[54] However, the existence of extensive villages which never become a town make this inadequate. Aristotle's *polis* is both city and state, and yet it was certainly smaller than most modern towns.

---

[49] M. O. H. Carver, *Arguments in Stone: Archaeological Research and the European Town in the First Millennium*, (Oxford: Oxbow, 1993), pp. 4–5.

[50] Braudel, *Structures*, p. 481.   [51] This is the calculation of W. Abel, cited in ibid., p. 486.

[52] Until then the school holidays were fixed for the 'tatty picking' (the potato harvest), in which children had to play their part.

[53] Braudel, *Structures*, p. 486.

[54] P. J. Waller, *Town, City and Nation: England 1850–1914* (Oxford: Oxford University Press, 1983), p. 6.

There is also a clear and important distinction between a town and a city. Stoke was designated a city in 1925 but remains a town in popular consciousness, part of the Potteries which are a 'region without a city'.[55] In Britain we have 'county towns', 'market towns' and 'cathedral cities' which resemble each other more than they do the great industrial cities. In America there are the great cities but also 'small town America'. The distinction was made in Rome between the simple *municipium* and the *civitas*, which was a self governing community. The Anglo Saxon burgh, which had its own charter, did not, however, necessarily become a city. Though size is clearly a key part of the definition, the question of diversity of function is more so.

The town has historically provided a centre of trade, recreation, defence, religion and administration. In the town the division of labour is greater than in the village. 'Towns are *hosts to industry* . . . In the medieval town more than a hundred different trades are known from documentary evidence.'[56] Perhaps this is the root meaning of the Hebrew *ir*, city, meaning place of stir. Because of the division of labour people have to obtain their food in the *market*. This means that the town 'generalizes the market into a widespread phenomenon'.[57] It was the development of the market town which meant the end of the feudal manor, its predecessor as a distribution centre. 'Every town, wherever it may be, must primarily be a market. Without a market, a town is inconceivable.'[58] Towns provided *protection*: the Greek word *polis* may come from a root meaning 'to fill', hence a filled in wall serving as a fortress. In most countries until the twentieth century towns might be expected to have gates and walls. Britain was an exception, though even here every ancient town has its echoes of the old gates. Not only that, but the need to organise a larger mass of people meant that a structure of *internal power* was essential, city councils and their agents. Towns also provide *amenities* which are, says Carver, 'among their most robust and enduring properties'.

All towns are shaped by the dominant mode of transport. When the horse was the normal means of traction regular stopping points were needed and the old A roads of England are punctuated by coaching inns at approximately twenty-five miles' distance from each other, the distance a horse could be expected to cover in a day.[59] The importance of the old market town in turn dwindled with changing transportation patterns. Waller instances the ancient town of Wallingford, marooned by the change in line of the London to Gloucester road in the late

---

[55] Ibid., p. 76.   [56] Carver, *Arguments in Stone*, p. 3.   [57] Braudel, *Structures*, p. 481.
[58] Ibid., p. 501.   [59] Ibid., p. 504.

seventeenth century.[60] At the end of the twentieth century, however, the
country town is once again experiencing a revival. It is now perceived to
offer a quality of living able to satisfy a wide range of interests, material
and cultural. 'The overall result is that in the shires of central and southern England there are hundreds of small but expanding villages, towns
and cities, served by a comprehensive system of motorways and inter
city railways, easily accessible to airfields and ferry terminals, developing their own cultural life and together comprising a market of over
18 million people.'[61]

For Braudel, towns are 'so many electric transformers. They increase
tension, accelerate the rhythm of exchange and ceaselessly stir up men's
lives.'[62] This is true of all towns – he reviews Asian, Russian and Muslim
towns in his survey. But the European towns which developed after the
eleventh century differed from others. Alongside the contest between
town and the country, there is also a contest between the city and the
state. Normally the state won. 'The miracle of the first great urban
centuries in Europe was that the city won hands down, at least in Italy,
Flanders and Germany. It was able to try the experiment of leading
a completely separate life for quite a long time. This was a colossal
event.'[63] It meant that these autonomous towns were marked by an
'unparalleled freedom'. They organised taxation, finances, public credit
and customs and excise; invented public loans; organised industry and
the crafts; reinvented long distance trade, bills of exchange, and the first
forms of trading companies and accountancy. They also set in motion
class struggles.[64] Though parasitic on the countryside towns embodied
intelligence, risk, progress and modernity. They were 'the accelerators
of historical time'.

Towns, cities, are turning points, watersheds of human history. When they first
appeared, bringing with them the written word, they opened the door to what
we now call *history*. Their revival in Europe in the eleventh century marked the
beginning of the continent's rise to eminence . . . All major bursts of growth are
expressed by an urban explosion.[65]

Here is as strong an expression as we are likely to find of what I called
earlier the Irenaean idea of redemption. Following Braudel, you might
say, 'No wonder Isaiah, Ezekiel and the author of Revelation all depict
the end time in terms of a city, for it is cities which have been the driving

[60] Waller, *Town*, p. 6.
[61] R. Green, 'Not Compact Cities but Sustainable Regions', in M. Jenks, E. Burton and K. Williams
(eds.), *The Compact City: A Sustainable Urban Form?* (London: Routledge, 1998), p. 146.
[62] Braudel, *Structures*, p. 479.   [63] Ibid., p. 511.   [64] Ibid., p. 512.   [65] Ibid., p. 479.

force of history.' Of course, as soon as it is put like that doubts set in, and the difficulty of ascribing historical causality to social change precludes such a simple explanation. Let us allow their importance, and their indispensable role, but at best, in the whole history of human development, they can only be one factor amongst many. Nevertheless, we have to allow that they do play a very different role in the economy of redemption to villages, and a crucial and creative one at that.

HERMAPHRODITIC LIVING

What Sharp called 'hermaphroditic living' is not an invention of the twentieth century. As we have seen, in earlier ages there was always some osmosis between country and town, and 'innumerable small towns could barely be distinguished from country life'.[66] Rodney Hilton argues that in feudal society the basic conflicts were *within* town and country, not between them. Social and economic links require that they be seen as inseparable parts of the same society. In his view medieval towns should not be regarded as a radically progressive force helping to transform an economically and socially backward countryside.[67] And Raymond Williams adds that, to the contrary, the accumulation of power by the city led to a situation in which the country as a whole was exploited by the city as a whole.[68]

What Sharp opposed, however, was a genuinely new genre which did indeed seek to marry town and country. Sharp's bête noire, the Garden City, represented a reaction to the industrial city, where this relation had broken down. In the famous diagram of *Cities of Tomorrow* Howard outlined a town magnet and a country magnet, the one representing prospects of advancement, social opportunity, and places of amusement, the other beauty, fresh air, and sounds of rippling water. He gave to these a theological gloss, seeing the town as the symbol of society (human work) and the country as the symbol of God's love and care. Neither of these represents 'the full plan and purpose of nature'. 'Human society and the beauty of nature are meant to be enjoyed together. The two magnets must be made one.' His proposal was a new kind of unit, the Garden City, whose organic pattern would in the end spread from the individual model to a whole constellation of similar cities.[69] Mumford

[66] Ibid., p. 487.
[67] R. Hilton, 'Towns in English Medieval Society', in R. Holt and G. Rosser (eds.), *The English Medieval Town: A Reader in English Urban History 1200–1540* (London: Longman, 1990), p. 28.
[68] Williams, *Country*, pp. 51, 54. [69] Mumford, *City*, p. 591.

was an advocate of Garden Cities on the grounds that they sought to re-store human scale to the city, setting natural limits to growth.[70] Howard, he thought, brought the city 'the essential biological criteria of dynamic equilibrium and organic balance: balance as between city and country in a larger ecological pattern, and balance between the varied functions of the city'.[71] What Howard called the 'town cluster', set in a permanent green matrix to form a new ecological and political unit, was in fact 'the embryonic form of a new type of city that would transcend the spatial limitations of the historic city'.[72]

Sharp loathed this vision, reading it as a version of the 'back to Nature' movement.

> Howard does not remember that in marriage the separate married identities remain with their special distinguishing characteristics unaltered: they do not merge into one common form half-way between their two differing forms: nor do the fruits of their marriage display that new form half way between theirs . . . Howard's new hope, new life, new civilization, Town Country, is a hermaphrodite; sterile, imbecile, a monster; abhorrent and loathsome to the Nature which he worships.[73]

Jane Jacobs was another ferocious opponent. Howard's aim, she said, 'was the creation of self sufficient small towns, really very nice towns if you were docile and had no plans of your own and did not mind spending your life among others with no plans of their own. As in all Utopias, the right to have plans of any significance belonged only to the planners in charge.'[74] Tacitly she is echoing Braudel's view of the towns as active and creative. The Garden City, a sleepy dormitory, is 'docile', only fit for people who have no dreams.

The problem with the Garden Cities as they have in fact materialised is that they are neither fish nor fowl; more precisely, they are hard to distinguish from suburbs. This might have been different if Howard's original cooperative dream had been preserved.[75] As might be expected, Sharp disliked the suburbs as much as he did the Garden City, speaking of them as an escape by 'an unorganised band of prisoners breaking gaol, with no very definite plans for what lies before them'.[76] He had in mind the suburbs of mid war Britain, but of course suburbs are as old as cities themselves. The suburbs of Graeco-Roman cities were an integral part

---

[70] Ibid., p. 586.   [71] Ibid., p. 587.   [72] Ibid., p. 595.
[73] Sharp, *Town and Countryside*, p. 143.   [74] Jacobs, *Death and Life*, p. 27.
[75] As Robert Fishman argues. *Urban Utopias in the Twentieth Century* (Cambridge, Mass.: MIT, 1982).
[76] T. Sharp, *Town Planning* (Harmondsworth: Penguin, 1940), p. 40.

of the city, the site of cemeteries, graves, industrial buildings, larger public buildings – stadii, amphitheatre and circuses, characterised by shrines, monuments, gardens and trees.[77] In the medieval city the suburb was the faubourg, in which dwelt small tradesmen, craftsmen and foreigners free from guild or city company restrictions. It was known as a focus of crime, disorder and disease. The modern suburb is quite different from either of these, and is a joint result of the growth of an urban middle class, with its own social ethos, of new modes of transport, and of the reaction to industrialisation. From the start it was residential, and represented an escape from the soot and dirt of the city to a place with gardens and seclusion. The ideology it represented was individualist, but ironically collective transport was essential to its development. The horse drawn omnibus was introduced on the Paddington–City route in 1829. The development of the underground made mass transport from periphery to centre possible, and the suburban development which Sharp so much lamented was driven above all by the Metropolitan and Piccadilly lines, which advertised themselves in terms of an escape to the country.

Despite the original aim of creating *rus in urbe* the modern suburb undeniably lacks both the community of the village and the energy of the town. Suburbs have been the target of fierce social critique, and, although they probably provide the mainstay of the Church's financial support, they are often tacitly despised by the inner city theologians, as places of comfort and affluence without obvious links to Jesus' original discipleship community. We have to remember the basic rule, however, that people ensoul places, and that goes even for the suburbs. Herbert Gans among others argues that the popularity of the suburbs both in the US and in Britain is still growing, and for many represents the continuing ideal of a higher quality of life.[78] We cannot on a priori grounds reject the place where so many people choose to live. The Spirit of God is not absent even there, and they are not as sterile as Sharp imagined. John Hartley argues that the suburbs can be politically blamed for creating an apathetic, reactionary, conservative, conformist petit bourgeois class; being economically unproductive; falling apart socially into atomised units; being sexually the place of women's subjugation; aesthetically being unstylish, twee, naff, genteel, dull, desolate, ugly; spiritually having an awful uniformity; and philosophically violating the binary opposition

[77] E. J. Owens, *The City in the Greek and Roman World* (London: Routledge, 1991), p. 153.
[78] H. Gans, *The Levittowners* (London: Allen Lane, 1967), p. 432, and often; more recently in *People, Plans and Policies. Essays on Poverty, Racism and Other National Urban Problems* (New York: Columbia University Press, 1991).

of town and country.[79] Every item here can be granted, but only on the understanding that these rules are broken in every suburb. The strength of the suburban church is part of the strength of the suburbs as a whole. The suburban church is part of a network of neighbourhood associations which flourish in the suburbs, from gardening, to bowls, to country dancing to amateur drama.[80] Naff and genteel many of these are, and I have chosen my examples deliberately.[81] True, 'community' only too often means dinner parties and barbecues, and the uniformed organisations. But there is also a great deal of energy in the suburbs which is outwardly directed, as any major charity would attest. In the economy of redemption, it is sometimes argued, the suburbs represent the most perfect form of the Deuteronomic vision, 'every family under its vine and fig tree', which history has yet witnessed. The energy of the move to the future is not, perhaps, to be expected from a settled history but it remains, for all that, part of the pattern of redemption.

Whether or not this applies to Joel Garreau's 'Edge Cities' is much more debatable. These are the new developments of offices and housing which have sprung up around the great American cities: they are neither urban nor rural, and they contain more industry than the suburbs. They are, as Paul Barker correctly insists, created by the car, the computer and the fax machine as surely as New York or Liverpool were created by ocean going ships, and Chicago or Manchester by the railway.[82] They are dependent on a network of high speed roads. Garreau describes them as 'the new Frontier', 'a vigorous world of pioneers' responding to the advent of Information Technology. They are therefore generated, he argues, by the construction of five million square feet of leasable office space in an area where people can also live in considerable suburban comfort. He is an enthusiast, but many of those he interviewed were not. People complained that these places were plastic, a hodgepodge, Disneyland, and lacked livability, civilisation, community and a soul.

---

[79] J. Hartley in R. Silverstone (ed.), *Visions of Suburbia* (London: Routledge, 1977), pp. 184–5.

[80] In Exeter, for example, which is largely suburban, and which has a population of 160,000 people, there are more than 600 associations outside the major national organisations. Gans drew attention to the strength of the suburban church, and explained it by the need to belong to the community (*Levittowners*, p. 265). Since his data were collected in the early 1960s such findings may need substantial revision.

[81] It is interesting that in Britain the most politically radical singers of the second half of the twentieth century lived in the suburbs. Ewan MacColl and Peggy Seeger lived in Bromley, and at the time of writing Leon Rosselson still lives in Wembley.

[82] Paul Barker in A. Barnett and R. Scruton (eds.), *Town and Country* (London: Jonathan Cape, 1998), p. 212.

They also used Sharp's word, 'sterile'.[83] It is fair to argue that all cities are chaotic in their origins, but whether these conglomerations will develop the sense of identity to become true cities must be doubtful, just because they are so heavily reliant on the car and Information Technology. Their future seems to be as an extension of the suburb.

Another attempt to marry town and country, or rather, to dissolve the distinction, was Frank Lloyd Wright's 'Broadacre City'.[84] Wright, too, loathed the city, and envisaged people living in homesteads with about one acre of land, growing their own vegetables, travelling everywhere by car, and meeting at 'activity nodes' for cultural or sports activities. It was the architectural descendant of the American frontier dream, only this time, instead of the native population it was the environment which would ultimately suffer. The cities have not disappeared, as he thought they would, and growing potatoes has proved unattractive to those who live in their large mock ranches. Instead there is vast suburban sprawl, and the highest car usage in the world. Meanwhile, 'Broadacre City' might characterise most of rural southern England, with the poor pushed out to 'affordable housing', or blocks of council houses on the edge of villages, and the rich living in the houses of their ancestors and their ancestors' masters, and travelling to 'cultural nodes' in nearby county towns. This development, alongside the growth of highly mechanised and 'rationalised' agriculture, dissolves the distinction of town and country for the wealthy few, but in fact reinforces it by making the countryside a private park, and completing the process of enclosure which began at the end of the fifteenth century.

TOWN AND COUNTRY IN THE ECONOMY OF REDEMPTION

Historically town and country have indeed played very different roles in what I have called the Irenaean process of redemption. Is that variety of roles now over, destroyed by the growth of private transport, of the telephone and the World Wide Web? Even in the North, where counter urbanisation is a significant factor, does the insular village of a century ago any longer exist? Ought we to want it to?

The economy of redemption is that process by which God makes and keeps human life human. Villages, towns and suburbs all contribute distinctively to this process but at the same time all *fail* distinctively. At the

[83] J. Garreau, *Edge City* (New York: Anchor Doubleday, 1988), p. 8.
[84] Garreau believes that 'Edge City' is a realisation of Frank Lloyd Wright's Broadacre City.

heart of the economy of redemption lies the cross. What significance does the cross have for our understanding of settlements in the economy of redemption? Paul talks of 'dying to sin' (Rom. 6.2) and it is this process which each form of human settlement has to undergo in its own distinctive way. 'Sin' is a theological code word for forms of behaviour which diminish or destroy life. To 'die' to sin is to address those life denying sides of our selves and our community, to 'put them to death' so that they do not put our neighbours and the environment to death. As related to our three forms of environment we can say that to be a truly humanising place the village has to die to its class and caste divisions; the city has to die to its factions and its hubristic attitude towards its surrounding villages; the suburb has to die to its atomistic individualism. Only by this process of 'death' can life come to fulfilment in the settlements we create.[85] The seventeenth century Puritan John Owen spoke of the 'death of death'. Christ may have died 'once only, once and once for all' but what flows from that is a process which continues to the kingdom. In all of our settlements we seek the death of death.

When it comes to town and country we can agree that neither God nor human beings made either the country or the town. From the theological point of view, both made both. 'Alongside the act of the creature there is always the act of divine wisdom and omnipotence,' wrote Karl Barth. God 'cooperates with the creature, meaning that as he himself works he allows the creature to work. Just as he himself is active in his freedom, the creature can also be active in freedom.'[86] What the Latin tradition has called 'providence' is in fact the history of grace in which humanisation is accomplished by God in and through human beings, and therefore in and through their settlements. If the urban historians are to be believed we have to ascribe a key role to towns and cities in this process, and it is theologically wrong to do nothing but dream of Eden. On the other hand these towns and cities have to be fed, and this means that, in order to survive, there have to be large rural areas. The idea, mooted in Britain at least, that a country can surrender its agriculture, and maintain itself exclusively by light industry and services, is ludicrous.[87] There is also

---

[85] In similar fashion Kjellberg writes: 'The city has to humble itself in the sense that it can never survive without the countryside, the home of agriculture.' The interconnectedness of rural and urban life can be seen as part of the relationship of 'oneness' with the cosmos itself. S. Kjellberg, *Urban EcoTheology* (Utrecht: International Books, 2000), p. 142.

[86] K. Barth, *Church Dogmatics* III/3 (Edinburgh: T&T Clark, 1961), p. 92.

[87] Churchill said in 1953: '50 million people dwelling in a small island, growing enough food for only, shall we say, 20 million. That is a spectacle of lèse-majesté and insecurity that history has not often seen before.'

the question of human scale, and much advocacy of decentralised living, with small villages and communes as alternatives to large cities, is seeking precisely that. This is above all what the village provided. Mumford talks of the mothering and life promoting environment of the village, its stability and security, rooted in reciprocal human relations and relations with other organisms and communities.[88] To go on to speak of the village as an 'unguarded democracy' in which each member plays their appropriate role at each stage in the life cycle is much too strong for any village in a class society. In peasant societies, when village life is bonded to unremittingly hard manual labour, people move at the pace of the seasons. One can understand the nostalgia for that slower pace of life, especially now the memory of its harsh reality has faded, at least in the West. Given the world's burgeoning population David Harvey may be right that it is the urban which has to move to the centre of our attention 'relative to much of the contemporary preoccupation with wilderness, peripheral peasant movements, preservation of scenic landscapes and the like'.[89] On the other hand the Soviet attempt to abolish the distinction between town and country was not a success and by 1989 those who opted for the 'idiocy of rural life' were often better off than their urban neighbours.[90] There is a strong whiff of hubris about some enthusiasm for the mega city, and about the casual assumption, noted in the third chapter, that 'food security is a thing of the past'. The Network Society still needs to be fed, and this implies agriculture, and agricultural communities. The Worldwatch Institute warns annually about the need to conserve fertile land to feed the numbers which increase day by day, and questions about the wisdom and efficacy of agribusiness continue to rise. Could it be, then, that at the moment of the 'world historical triumph of the city' the need to reinvent or re- discover the town–country distinction may once again be forced upon us?

---

[88] Mumford, *City*, p. 636.

[89] D. Harvey, *Justice, Nature and the Geography of Difference* (Oxford: Blackwell, 1996), p. 186. In *Spaces of Hope* (Edinburgh: Edinburgh University Press, 2000, p. 85) Harvey strongly deplores the nostalgia of many anti urban theorists.

[90] Ian Hamilton, 'Urbanization in Socialist Eastern Europe: The Macro-Environment of Internal City Structure', p. 188; S. L. Sampson, 'Urbanization – Planned and Unplanned: A Case Study of Brasove, Romania', p. 521. Both in R. A. French and F. I. Hamilton (eds.), *The Socialist City* (Chichester: Wiley, 1979).

CHAPTER 6

The meaning of the city

> 'Come, let us make bricks, and bake them thoroughly ... Come, let
> us build ourselves a city, and a tower with its top in the heavens, and
> let us make a name for ourselves; otherwise we shall be scattered
> abroad upon the face of the whole earth.'
>
> (Genesis 11. 3–5)

What is a city? Since everyone knows what a city is the question seems unnecessary, but the answer is not as simple as it might seem at first sight. A
city, for example, is not just a very large town. As we saw in the last chapter, population is sometimes suggested as a marker, ranking anywhere
with more than a hundred thousand inhabitants as a city. But London's
largest borough, Harrow, has a population of more than a million, and it
is certainly not a city. Furthermore, there have been quite small cities –
Periclean Athens and fifteenth century Florence spring to mind – which
have been amongst the greatest cities in human history. What is it, then,
which defines a city? Joel Garreau lists industry, governance, commerce,
safety, culture, companionship, and religion as the function of cities, and
on those grounds argues that Edge Cities are proper cities.[1] All these too,
however, could be found in large boroughs which were not properly cities.
Jane Jacobs wants to define the city in terms of consistent generation of
economic growth from the local economy. In her view any settlement
that becomes good at import-replacing becomes a city.[2] There are many
examples of cities in decline, however, like fifteenth century Rome, or
cities which are off today's world trade map, like Addis Ababa, which
challenge such an economic definition. Kostoff proposes a whole range

---

[1] J. Garreau, *Edge City* (New York: Anchor Doubleday, 1991), p. 26. H. Pirenne (*Medieval Cities: Their
Origins and the Revival of Trade* (Princeton: Princeton University Press, 1948)) suggests that a city
may be defined as 'a locality the population of which, instead of living by working the soil, devotes
itself to commercial activity' (p. 35). Alternatively it may be a community endowed with legal
personality and possessing laws and institutions peculiar to itself (p. 46).
[2] J. Jacobs, *Cities and the Wealth of Nations* (Harmondsworth: Penguin, 1986; first published 1984),
pp. 39, 41.

of criteria: a place where there is an energised crowding of people; a place where there is specialised differentiation of work; places favoured by a source of income; that rely on written records; that have a territory which feeds them; that are distinguished by some kind of monumental definition; which have some kind of physical circumscription to mark them off from the non urban realm; and which are part of an urban system.[3] Clearly, some of these markers would apply equally to villages and towns. More simply Peter Hall describes them as 'places for people who can stand the heat of the kitchen', places full of adrenalin, and for that reason places superbly worth living in.[4] In this respect they are different from small towns or villages. Even here, however, we can instance sleepy or rather dull cities like Bonn which are nevertheless true cities.

Another attempt to define what it is that makes a city, alluded to by Kostoff, begins from the relation of city to region. What decisively marks off a city from a town, according to Geddes and Branford, is that a city 'accumulates and embodies the heritage of a region, and combines in some measure and kind with the cultural heritage of larger units, national, racial, religious, human'. The individuality of the city is for them 'the sign manual of its regional life and record'. 'Regional élan vital fruits in civic life. The city and its region compose into the true social unit.'[5] In a similar way Christian Norberg-Schulz speaks of the *genius loci* of cities as involving the 'gathering' of local and more distant meanings. 'In the town "foreign" meanings meet the local *genius*, and create a more complex system of meanings. The urban genius is never merely local.'[6] Christopher Day puts the relation of city and region in terms of spirituality. When you go from countryside to market town, he argues, you feel this intensified spirit. You feel it even where towns have been swollen and distorted by industry. Paris, Edinburgh or Washington have the spirit of France, Scotland or America as unmistakably as Bristol or Newcastle have the west or the north of England.[7] In the city it is the mood of the region which finds expression in the built environment, which is why Mumford spoke of the region as well as the city as 'a collective work of art'. The invocation of the idea of a resident 'genius' calls

[3] S. Kostoff, *The City Shaped* (London: Thames & Hudson, 1991), pp. 38–40.
[4] P. Hall, *Cities in Civilization* (London: Weidenfeld and Nicolson, 1998), p. 989.
[5] V. Branford and P. Geddes, *The Coming Polity* (London: Williams & Norgate, 1919), p. 158.
[6] C. Norberg-Schulz, *Genius Loci* (New York: Rizzoli, 1980), p. 170.
[7] C. Day, *Places of the Soul* (London: Thorsons, 1999), p. 150. Branford and Geddes express the same view, speaking of cities as 'essentially psychic entities' whilst not forgetting that bread and wine are produced by hand labour. *Polity*, p. 158.

to mind Wink's account of the reality of the Powers, mentioned in the first chapter. Drawing on that idea I want to argue that cities, by virtue of their tradition, or their activity, the way in which they 'gather' their regions, have a degree of *creative spirituality* which other places lack. It is this which constitutes their place in the economy of redemption, and this which the book of Revelation means by the 'angel' of a city, indicated by the fact that they are often addressed as corporate personalities in Scripture.

THE DIALECTIC OF CITIES

To talk of the creative spirituality of cities is to invoke at once millennia of anti city polemic, beginning, perhaps, with the gloomy assessment of cities in the book of Genesis. Looking back to that time of pastoral nomads the author of Hebrews wrote: 'By faith [Abraham] stayed for a time in the land he had been promised, as in a foreign land, living in tents, as did Isaac and Jacob . . . For he looked forward to the city that has foundations, whose architect and builder is God' (Heb. 11.9, 10). This seems to imply that the earthly city has no foundations worth counting. Is it a relativisation of the city, teaching us that our true citizenship is eternal, or could it be construed as an eschatological promise for the cities in which we actually live?

There is certainly a deep ambivalence towards the city in the Christian tradition which is recognised and shared today by many secular theorists.[8] On the one hand the city is understood as a focus of violence and human hubris – this is the significance of the fact that both Cain and Nimrod are said to be the founders of cities. On the other hand the city is the model of what will finally be redeemed, the paradigm of the human home and the focus of human creativity. The city is both Babylon, the place of alienation, exile, estrangement and violence, and Jerusalem, the place where God dwells, sets God's sign, and invites humankind to peace. This twofold imaging of the city calls for a dialectic. Any city is always at any one time both Babylon and Jerusalem, as we are reminded by Jesus' description of Jerusalem, the city of peace, as the one who stones the prophets (Luke 19.41).

The danger with dialectical perceptions is that they tend to fall apart. Thus, on the one hand, doom laden views of the city abound, especially

---

[8] Henri Lefebvre, David Harvey, Lewis Mumford and Peter Hall all express this ambivalence – and especially Mumford.

on the part of those worried about the environmental impact of cities.[9] From the fourth century on there is often a sour hostility to the city amongst Christians. In the city, said John Chrysostom, the devil uses 'lewd sights, base speech, degraded music and songs full of all kinds of wickedness' to lead us on the road to damnation.[10] The most famous Christian account of the city, Augustine's *City of God*, is usually regarded as stressing the negative side of the earthly city. The earthly city, he tells us right at the beginning of his work, is marked by a 'lust for domination' – a fair enough comment on imperial Rome, which is his paradigm earthly city.[11] It lives by self love carried to the point of contempt for God, whilst the *civitas Dei* lives by the love of God marked by contempt for self.[12] 'The one city loves its own strength shown in its powerful leaders; the other says to its God, "I will love you, my Lord, my strength."'[13] Whilst it is on pilgrimage in this world the *civitas Dei* is a collection of resident aliens which 'makes use of the earthly peace and defends and seeks the compromise between human wills in respect of the provisions relevant to the mortal nature of man'.[14] They occupy the same physical city, do the same sort of jobs, live under the same laws, but goal and orientation separate them.[15] What the earthly city prizes is for the most part illusory.[16] True happiness will only be realised in the perfect peace of the eschatological kingdom.[17]

This negative view reappears at the Enlightenment and on to the present. Thomas Jefferson regarded cities as 'pestilential to the morals, the health and liberties of man'.[18] For some contemporary writers the city is parasitic on natural and domesticated environments, since it makes no food, cleans no air, and cleans very little water to the point where it could be re-used. For Mayur cities are 'overgrown monstrosities with gluttonous appetites for material goods and fast declining carrying capacities . . . Only catastrophe awaits such a system of disharmony.'[19]

On the other side we find endorsements of the city from some Christian theologians, obviously reflecting their vastly different situation.

---

[9] Mary Grey cites as examples of such pessimistic assessments Frank Norris' novel *The Pit*, about Chicago, Charles Williams' *Taliessin through Logres*, and Thomas Merton. 'The Shape of the Human Home – A Response to Tim Gorringe', *Political Theology* 3 (November 2000), pp. 95–103.
[10] John Chrysostom, *De Poenitentia* VI.   [11] Augustine, *The City of God*, Bk 1, Preface.
[12] By '*civitas*' Augustine means something like 'community'.   [13] Ibid., Bk 14.28.
[14] Ibid., Bk 19.17.   [15] Ibid., Bk 1.35.   [16] Ibid., Bk 19.4–10.   [17] Ibid., Bk 19.13.
[18] Cited in M. White and L.White, *The Intellectual Versus the City: From Thomas Jefferson to Frank Lloyd Wright* (Oxford, Oxford University Press, 1977), p. 17.
[19] G. Haughton and C. Hunter, *Sustainable Cities* (London: Regional Studies Association, 1994) p. 15. The Finnish biologist Pentti Linkola likewise claims that cities destroy everything valuable for a good life. S. Kjellberg, *Urban EcoTheology* (Utrecht: International Books, 2000), p. 112.

Where Augustine wrote against the background of the still powerful, if senescent, presence of imperial Rome, Isidore of Seville's world in the seventh century needed cities to survive in a turbulent world of barbarian invasions. For this reason '[t]he Church of Isidore's time became a congregation of builders. From the sixth to the tenth century the Christian obligation to provide shelter was put into practice, and a network of cities developed.'[20] The twelfth century and thirteenth century theologians shared in the sense of a new springtime after a greater peace had at last descended on Europe, and trade, law and learning were all at last beginning to pick up, and cities blossoming into new life. No surprise, then, that Abelard, living and working in Paris, could speak of cities as 'convents' for married people, where they could live together in charity.[21] According to Aquinas in the next century the city (again *civitas* – but this time this particular type of settlement) is the most complete of all human communities (as opposed, say, to monasteries or villages). The study of the city is called politics, 'a branch of practical philosophy which excels all others since it deals with the most perfect means of procuring goodness in human affairs through the use of human reason'.[22] It excels all others because theology understands community as essential to human flourishing. For this reason, as we saw in the first chapter, he took from Aristotle detailed plans for the construction of the city, all aimed at the realisation of the good life.

Although the Reformation was an urban phenomenon it did not produce an urban theology. Perhaps this is because it all but coincided with the rise of the cult of nature and a renewed moral critique of the city, as we saw in the last chapter.[23] Nineteenth century theology could hardly affirm the 'cities of dreadful night', but the centrality of cities to God's purposes was newly affirmed by the secular city theology of the 1960s for which the city was the central icon of modern culture. Though this theology was quickly superseded, the liberation theology which followed it, with its emphasis on God's presence on the margins, often seemed to suggest that the inner city was a privileged locus for God's presence, to

[20] R. Sennett, *The Conscience of the Eye* (New York: Norton, 1990), p. 11.
[21] Peter Abelard, *Theologia christiana*, II 43–56, in E. M. Buytaert (ed.), *Petri Abaelardi opera theologica*, II *Corpus Christianorum* XII (Brepols: Turnhout, 1969), pp. 149–155. His own history, of course, seems tragically to deny that.
[22] Aquinas, *Sententia Libri Politicorum, Opera omnia* VIII (Paris, 1891), Prologue A 69–70.
[23] Though 'the cult of nature' had to wait for the eighteenth century, attitudes to nature were already changing in the sixteenth, as we can see from *As You Like It*, in which the natural world, which opposes nothing to human beings but 'winter and rough weather', is opposed to the malice of the human world.

the occlusion of either the comfortable suburb or the countryside. The inner cities and housing estates are alienated from sources of power and influence, writes John Vincent, and as such feel a kinship with Jesus and his friends.

Like the nuclear community of the kingdom of God which Jesus set up in his disciple group, the urban disciple community today represents perhaps a new humanity, a new 'Son of Man', free of race and class and economic and cultural distinction, perhaps because, being nearer the bottom, they know what the basics of human existence are, and what it is that moulds and even secures human beings in mutuality and survival and in the hope of significance – very like the simple basic rules and common life of Jesus and his disciples.[24]

Whilst I agree with the basic thesis of liberation theology of God's 'bias to the poor', a theology which seeks to follow the humanising work of God in history will not, I believe, be able to make such an undialectical assessment.

Most theologies tend to fall on one side or the other of this dialectic. In the twentieth century the most searching theological expression of the ambivalence of the city was provided by Jacques Ellul, as noted briefly in the first chapter. He treated the city as a paradigm of the situation of humankind under sin and grace, calling therefore for a radically dialectical treatment.[25] On the one hand the city is a memorial to human conquest.[26] It is a world 'for which man is not made'. We find no law concerning the city because 'God has cursed, has condemned, the city instead of giving us a law for it.'[27] The city originates in the refusal of Eden, humankind's provided home, and the substitution of one humankind provides for itself.[28] It begins, then, with the rejection of what is freely given, grace. Urban civilisation is warring civilisation.[29] Overlooking much contrary evidence – the campaigns of the early Arab

[24] J. Vincent, 'An Urban Hearing for the Gospel', in C. Rowland and J. Vincent (eds.), *Gospel from the City* (Sheffield: Urban Theology Unit, 1997), p. 112.
[25] Ward misses the ambivalence of Ellul's account, finding only separation here. G. Ward, *Cities of God* (London: Routledge, 2000), pp. 48f.
[26] J. Ellul, *The Meaning of the City* (Grand Rapids: Eerdmans, 1970), p. 16.
[27] Ibid., p. 47.   [28] Ibid., p. 5.
[29] Ibid., p. 13. He derives this from the name Nimrod, the next city builder after Cain, which he translates 'plunderer', and from the name of one of the cities he builds, which means 'cavalry'. Mumford agrees with him here. 'Every part of life became a struggle . . a gladiatorial contest . . . the new myths were mainly expressions of relentless opposition, struggle, aggression . . . Though the more cooperative village practices retained their hold in the workshop and the field, it is precisely in the new functions of the city that the truncheon and the whip – called politely the sceptre – made themselves felt.' L. Mumford, *The City in History* (Harmondsworth: Penguin, 1991), p. 65.

invaders, the German and Scandinavian invaders who formed present day Europe, the Huns and Mongols and more recently Pol Pot – Ellul maintains that there is no such thing as a great agricultural war. 'A rural people is never a ravenous people . . . War is an urban phenomenon.'[30]

The city embodies spiritual power. In fact, for Ellul, it is one of the 'principalities and powers', in a sense more negative than that proposed by Wink.[31] It is not the people in a city who are cursed, but 'the city' as a spiritual entity, as what embodies humankind organised against God.[32] The city is a cursed place by its origin, its structure, its selfish withdrawal and its search for other gods.[33] Sin, 'the world' and the powers of hell are all symbolised in the city. 'In the clear vision of the Lord's Spirit the truth about Rome is the truth about Moscow, about Berlin, about Paris and about Washington.'[34] The life of a powerful city is always a constant succession of revolts against God. This is notwithstanding the fact that the city is the product of good will, 'the engineer's bright eye, the urbanist's broad sweep of mind, the hygienist's idealism'. The results, however, speak for themselves: slavery tolerated and human relations destroyed in the anonymity of the great city. It is a familiar theme: the best virtues of good pagans are nothing but splendid vices. The city is the greatest human work, the attempt to attain autonomy. 'No other of man's works technical or philosophical is equivalent to the city, which is the creation not of an instrument but of the whole world in which man's instruments are conceived and put to work.'[35] Because the city is the great means of separation between human beings and God, the place human beings made to be alone, 'she is the very centre of the world's disorder, and it is therefore useless to speak to her of order'.[36]

Alongside all this negation, however, lies affirmation, as noted briefly in the first chapter. From the oldest period 'there was a tendency to pardon, to accept the city'.[37] Thus Nineveh itself, the bloody city, is saved by Jonah's preaching. But of course mention of Nineveh shows that the city is not necessarily unredeemed. There is the possibility of reconciliation with God in the city (Ps. 87.4). In the cities of refuge the city plays a positive role in the order of preservation which is part of God's plan for the world (Num. 35; Josh. 20).[38] The purpose of these cities is to

---

[30] Ellul *Meaning*, p. 51.
[31] Wink always assumes that the powers are created, fallen and can be redeemed. As it turns out, Ellul shares this view, but in speaking of the city as one of the powers he intends it wholly negatively, as a force aimed against God.
[32] He appeals to Isa. 14.12–15; Ezek 28.1–9 for this reading.
[33] Ellul, *Meaning*, p. 60.   [34] Ibid., p. 50.   [35] Ibid., p. 154.
[36] Ibid., p. 119.   [37] Ibid., p. 72.   [38] Ibid., p. 90.

ensure greater justice.[39] Mumford, too, notes the same function. Even if power was the mainstay of the new city, he says, 'it became increasingly shaped and directed by new institutions of law and order and social comity'.[40] As trade grew the part played by the city as a seat of law and justice, reason and equity also grew, supplementing the part it played as a religious representation of the cosmos. The city, therefore, is both a centre of violence and protection against it.

Ellul goes further than this, however, in finding in Jerusalem an analogy to the incarnation. In the promise to David, God takes possession of Jerusalem and in so doing symbolically takes possession of all cities. Christ had no conciliatory or pardoning words for the cities, but his death and resurrection mean that the city is now a neutral world where human beings can be free again, where there are possibilities for action. There is no question of expecting a new Jerusalem on earth, for the new Jerusalem will be God's creation, absolutely free, unforseeable, and transcendent, but God's act gives human beings room for autonomous action.[41] In particular the person of faith is involved in a battle on a spiritual plane, a battle comparable to Abraham's battle for Sodom, in praying for the good of the city. 'We must ask God to take away this condemnation which we know so well, and herein lies our liberty in relation to the city.'[42]

This dialectic cannot be regarded as a peculiarity of theologians, for it is shared by urban theorists like Mumford. On the one hand the city is 'the most precious collective invention of civilization . . . second only to language itself in the transmission of culture'. It is through the city that labour is sufficiently organised to channel the forces of nature and establish order and justice.[43] On the other hand there is a 'negative symbiosis' resting on war, exploitation, enslavement, and parasitism. Mumford's concern is that the former aspect should not be eclipsed by the latter. David Harvey agrees. The city is both the high point of human achievement, and the site of squalid human failure, 'the lightning rod of the profoundest human discontents, and the arena of social and political conflict. It is a place of mystery, the site of the unexpected, full of agitations and ferments, of multiple liberties, opportunities and alienations; of passions and repressions; of cosmopolitanism and extreme parochialisms; of violence, innovation and reaction.'[44] Henri Lefebvre remarks that the modern city is not thought out because we have not resolved the

---

[39] Ibid., p. 92.   [40] Mumford, *City*, p. 63.   [41] Ellul, *Meaning*, p. 170.
[42] Ibid., p. 75.   [43] Mumford, *City*, p. 67.
[44] D. Harvey, *The Urban Experience* (Oxford: Blackwell, 1989), p. 229.

contradiction between these two traditions but in fact the dialectic is ineluctable.[45] Like all human life cities make manifest the dialectic of sin and grace but it is in what they contribute to the furtherance of life that they play their role in the economy of redemption.

CITIES IN THE ECONOMY OF REDEMPTION

Haddon Willmer puts the question of redemption squarely by asking what sort of humanity is encouraged by different types of city.[46] It is clear that whilst all cities may share certain features in common, some are far more creative, or humanising, than others. In particular we have to ask, as *Faith in the City* did, what cities do for the poor.[47] Much Christian writing about the city is about the struggle of the poor and their triumph over adversity, especially in the genre of 'urban theology'. But if we think about the Indian poor, for example, flooding into the cities from the villages and increasing city populations by tens of thousands every day, we could ask whether it would not be better for them, as Gandhi thought, to remain in the village, where they have the same poverty, but not the same pollution; the same oppression, but not the same pressures of crime and prostitution. Cities, generations of fiction and film have taught us, are characterised by 'mean streets' where only the fittest survive. In the stories of the poor, what is creative about the city *as such*, and what is human hope and courage rising above appalling odds? In enquiring about the redemptive and humanising aspect of cities it is essential to keep that question in view.

   In his history of Western Europe during the first Christian millennium Peter Brown illustrates the way in which cities were, for many centuries, literally life saving. Those in the rural hinterlands retreated behind city walls when raiders came, and the Church played a central part in maintaining them once the old structures of the Roman Empire had disappeared. 'Walls and bishops went together.' The Church helped cope with famine and siege by charitable work and 'the buildings of the church spoke of the day to day determination of cities to survive and

[45] H. Lefebvre, *Writings on Cities*, tr. E. Kofman and E. Lebas (Oxford: Blackwell, 1996), pp. 205–6.
[46] H. Willmer, 'Images of the City and the Shaping of Humanity', in A. Harvey (ed.), *Theology in the City* (London: SPCK, 1989), p. 34.
[47] I take for granted the debate about relative deprivation made famous by Peter Townsend. In speaking of 'the poor' I have in mind both the destitution of the Indian city I know best, Madurai, where some communities live on pavements or by railway tracks, but also the relative poverty encountered everywhere in the North, which excludes many from the goods enjoyed by the majority. In Britain at the turn of the millennium over a million households are officially homeless, and around five million people have an income below the European poverty line.

to be seen to survive'.[48] This function of cities is now over. Artillery began this process and the atom bomb completed it. If anything, security is now associated more with the country than the city, though inner city violence, the possibility of murder and mayhem, has always been part of city life, as the story of Sodom reminds us. Dealing with that violence is part of the construction of urban order, but in thinking of the city's redemptive role we cannot begin there. In considering cities in the economy of redemption we have to give pride of place to what Elias calls '*the civilising process*'.[49] Cities are, by definition, places which 'civilise' us, which teach us the arts of cooperative and creative living. Recalling Luther's account of the purpose of redemption as humanisation, we can compare Mumford's remark in 1961: 'If we are to have cities it is because *they make men*.'[50] Given the literature of the mean streets which goes back at least to Thomas Dekker in the late sixteenth century, and indeed to Genesis, such a claim needs some elaboration.

Mumford's claim goes back to Aristotle who, improbably from our point of view, thinks of cities as *nurseries of the virtues*. The city, he says, originates in the union of a number of villages which come together for the bare needs of life, 'and continue in existence for the sake of a good life'.[51] The good life is directed towards the goals proper to humans, namely to produce human beings who embody courage, temperance, liberality, magnificence, greatness of soul, gentleness, being agreeable in company, wittiness and modesty. This can only be done in a city because such virtues can only be learned through interaction and fellowship and because the urge for community is part of human nature. To live outside community, therefore, is to live an unnatural life, and community, for Aristotle, is the city. The city exists to promote the flourishing of education and excellence,[52] and provides the essential framework for this to happen, for without the justice which the laws of the city imposes human beings are 'the most unholy and the most savage of animals, the most full of lust and gluttony'.[53] To the objection that it is precisely in the city that lust and gluttony are stimulated, he replies that crime and disorder are to be dealt with by moderate possessions and occupation on the part of the citizens, habits of temperance and the study of philosophy.[54] Since the supreme human goal is the exercise of our rationality, this last is the real key. It turns out that the city ultimately exists to make metaphysical contemplation

---

[48] P. Brown, *The Rise of Western Christendom* (Oxford: Blackwell, 1996), p. 61.
[49] N. Elias, *The Civilising Process* (Oxford: Blackwell, 1994).   [50] Mumford, *City*, p. 127 (my italics).
[51] *Politics* 1252b28.   [52] Ibid., 1283a25.   [53] Ibid., 1253a37.   [54] Ibid., 1267a10.

possible for a tiny number of leisured citizens. As Alasdair MacIntyre remarks, 'All Aristotle's conceptual brilliance ... declines at the end to an apology for this extraordinarily parochial form of human existence.'[55] It is also necessary to remind ourselves that the achievements of classical Athens, and the background to Aristotle's philosophising, depended on extremely cruel treatment of slaves.[56]

Aristotle's claims for the city may have been flawed but this does not mean that the idea of the city as a nursery of the virtues is to be rejected, strange as it seems to us after three centuries of experience of the capitalist city. To make sense of it we need to understand the virtues as those things which promote our humanness, which promote the goods of human flourishing. We can then listen to Mumford's judgement that '[t]he final mission of the city is to further man's conscious participation in the cosmic and the historic process'.

> Through its own complex and enduring structure, the city vastly augments man's ability to interpret these processes and take an active, formative part in them, so that every phase of the drama it stages shall have, to the highest degree possible, the illumination of consciousness, the stamp of purpose, the colour of love. That magnification of all the dimensions of life, through emotional communion, rational communication, technological mastery, and above all, dramatic representation, has been the supreme office of the city in history. And it remains the chief reason for the city's continued existence.[57]

The city is the nursery of the virtues in this sense. The city is purposive in a qualitatively different way to the village or town. It represents a corporate attempt to fashion the human future. It is 'larger than life'; the buzz of its diverse trades and conditions stimulates both art and ideas. It provides a stage on which even the poor can act, and that they do so is witnessed by urban theologians. Panache, says Laurie Green, 'is a quality highly valued and applauded in most Urban Priority cultures whether it be expressed as a "Jack the lad" jauntiness or capitalized

[55] A. MacIntyre, *A Short History of Ethics* (London: Routledge, 1967), p. 83.
[56] Thus Oswyn Murray writes: 'The skeletons and evidence of living 300 feet underground in tunnels fed with air through downdrafts created by fires halfway up the shafts, the niche for the guard at the mine entrance, and the fact that the tunnels were so small that the face workers must have crawled and knelt at their work while all porterage was carried out by pre-adolescent children, reveal the truth ... It is an appalling indictment of Athenian indifference that Nicias, whose money was made from child labour of this sort, could widely be regarded as the most moral and religious man of his generation. 'Life and Society in Classical Greece', in J. Boardman, J. Griffin and O. Murray (eds.), *The Oxford History of the Classical World* (Oxford: Oxford University Press, 1986), p. 224.
[57] Mumford, *City*, pp. 655–6.

upon in the street market trader'.[58] The scene which is acted may be tragedy, comedy, tragical-historical, scene individable or poem unlimited, as Hamlet puts it, but in and through it the dimensions of life are magnified and consciousness illumined.

All creativity requires a balance between stability and anarchy, for where there is perfect order there is death. For this reason, Peter Hall argues, creative cities are places in which social relationships, values and views of the world are in the throes of transformation. 'Conservative, stable societies will not prove creative; but neither will societies in which all order, all points of reference, have disappeared. To a remarkable degree, creative cities have been those in which an old established order, a too-long-established order, was being challenged or had just been overthrown.'[59] Practically speaking this means that creative cities are often immigrant cities. 'The creative cities were nearly all cosmopolitan; they drew talent from the four corners of their worlds . . . Probably no city has ever been creative without continual renewal of the creative bloodstream.'[60] Cosmopolitanism, of course, is one of the key distinguishing markers between city and town.

The creativity of cities is manifested above all in the arts, in the economy, and in industry. With regard to the arts the champion of the suburb, Herbert Gans, argues that cities are not necessary for their flourishing. Historically speaking it is simply the fact that they have housed the rich who have supported the creators of culture which gives this impression. Today it is perfectly possible to live in the suburbs without loss of creativity.[61] Whilst many creative people doubtless live in the suburbs, however, there is the question of concentration, the electricity of creativity, the possibility for the innovative to spark each other off, which we find, for example, in Paris at 'the moment of Cubism' or in Periclean Athens, Renaissance Florence, Elizabethan London, and so forth. Putting one's finger on what precisely generates this creativity is, however, no easy matter. Peter Hall, who considers the question in detail in *Cities in Civilization*, admits that 'it becomes increasingly hard to find any single satisfactory explanation'.[62] He does, however, find instability an essential part of the creative mix. Thus he believes that in quattrocento Florence it is rapid accumulation of wealth, and a resultant breakdown

---

[58] L. Green, 'Physicality in the UPA', in P. Sedgwick (ed.), *God in the City: Essays and Reflections from the Archbishop's Urban Theology Group* (London: Mowbray. 1995), p. 109.
[59] Hall, *Cities in Civilization*, p. 286.   [60] Ibid., p. 285.
[61] H. Gans, *The Levittowners* (London: Allen Lane, 1967), p. 424.
[62] Hall, *Cities in Civilization*, p. 282.

of values, which produces the explosion of creative power which gives
us Brunelleschi, Botticelli, Leonardo, Michelangelo and all the rest. But
like Elizabethan London this city was not at all a nice place, Hall points
out, a place of sweetness and light, but a place of murder and mayhem
alongside great spirituality and dynamic commercialism. 'Perhaps the
sense of moral breakdown is the price such a society necessarily pays.'[63]
I shall return to this question shortly.

As well as being centres of artistic creativity, cities are also *nurseries of
industrial innovation and experiment*. Laurie Green senses 'the majesty, energy
and power of God in heavy industry and in that a sense of belonging
with God in a solidarity with God's creativity. . . . a sense of wonder in
industry that we have been given gifts to work with such complexity
and find comradeship, worth and identity in the endeavour'.[64] Hall's
focus is on the processes which make industry possible in the first place,
though it is not clear that the innovation he talks about can always be
ascribed to cities. In the case of Silicon Valley, for example, universities
and the Defence establishment seem to play the key role, along with
Schumpeter's entrepreneurs, whilst in Japan it is 'the state as permanent
innovator'. What are certainly needed, even in the age of Information
Technology, are geographical foci, without which 'synergy', the mutual
sparking off of minds, does not happen. He also finds for the cities he
mentions – Manchester, Glasgow, Berlin and Detroit – a position on
the fringe, but not in outer darkness, a tradition of work in the area
in which innovation came. Marginality meant the absence of well established hierarchies, and therefore an egalitarian ethos was possible.
'There was little sense of deference. Careers were open to talents. The
prevailing ethos, whether inspired by Protestant religion or hedonism or
by shintoism, encouraged achievement in commerce and industry and
the making of money.'[65] Hall seems to put the heroic tradition in first
place, the Schumpeterian entrepreneur beginning in his or her garage
or garret, but all his instances illustrate the importance of networking,
which, in crucial instances, produces 'chains or cascades of innovation'.

The 'career open to talents' is indeed one of the key creative aspects
of the city. Here is one of the classic ways in which the city in itself is
supposed to be able to better the life of the poor. The medieval German
saying that *Stadtluft macht frei nach Jahr und Tag* points to the way in which
it has been possible to escape the social policing of small communities or,

[63] Ibid., p. 71.   [64] L. Green, 'Blowing bubbles: Poplar', in *God in the City*, p. 75.
[65] Hall, *Cities in Civilization*, p. 494.

in the middle ages, feudal obligation, in the more tolerant, or perhaps simply more commercial, atmosphere of the city. But as Mumford points out, what was meant by freedom changed in the transition from medieval to early capitalist city. The medieval city gave freedom from feudal restrictions, whereas the eighteenth century city gave freedom for private investment and profit without reference to the welfare of the community as a whole.

This change is linked to the city's role as market. Without doubt cities have been the mainspring of dynamic economies and it can be argued that they remain today the driving force of the world economy.[66] But then, as Bernard Mandeville pointed out near the beginning of the present, capitalist, phase of the city, in this world public vices are essential for capitalist survival. In the city 'Luxury/Employ'd a Million of the Poor/And odious Pride a million more.'[67] In Ireland Mandeville's book was burned by the hangman because he argued that Christian virtues, conscientiously practised, would lead to commercial failure. Both industrial and finance capitalism have been wedded to a *Realethik* which pours scorn on the Sermon on the Mount.

This takes us back to the dangerous nature of artistically creative cities. Hall's study of the role of the city in civilisation could suggest the Nietzschean thesis that it is Dionysian energy which makes for true humanness, and that Christianity, with its favouring of 'the weak', undermines that. Hall's running together of creativity and injustice could suggest the thesis of Konrad Lorenz that rough and tumble and inequality is necessary to human creativity, or Hayek's vision of human history as a moving column. It is regrettable that those in the rear are trampled on, suffer and die, but it is the price we pay for progress, and it is worth it in the long haul.[68] Were we to achieve social justice would this perhaps mean a dull, safe suburban existence for all which would destroy the exercise of our creativity? To put it bluntly, are Christian virtues humanly counter productive? Artistically we have the disaster of periodic bouts of religious iconoclasm: Savonarola burning piles of great works of art in the market square at Florence because they contravened what he took to be Christian standards of morality. Ought we, then, to redefine the

[66] Finance capital still has relatively few powerful bases: New York, London, Frankfurt, Singapore, Hong Kong, but the position of the great corporations which control the global economy is less clear. They tend to have a host nation, but it is of their essence that they can move freely and at a moment's notice to places where labour is cheapest.
[67] B. Mandeville, *The Fable of the Bees* (Harmondsworth: Penguin, 1914, orig. 1714).
[68] K. Lorenz, *The Waning of Humaneness* (London: Unwin, 1988); F. Hayek, *The Road to Serfdom* (London: ARK, 1986).

virtues, as Nietzsche proposed, and produce a new list, as those things which promote capitalist success?[69] Are Christians eternal Malvolios, protesting against the enjoyment of cakes and ale? How does the gospel respond to the fact that feelings of aggression and sexuality are important survival instincts in the city?[70] Is Mary Whitehouse right, or Nobuyoshi Araki with his claim that 'without obscenity our cities are dreary places and life is bleak?'[71] If, as I have claimed, all creativity ultimately derives from God, is there an *opus alienum* in God, wedded to mayhem and creative destruction, alongside God's *opus proprium* discerned in Christ? To put the question in this way is already to answer it. The gospel can have no truck with social Darwinism of any kind. It is predicated on the assumption that true human flourishing is bound up with the flourishing of all. The tension between stability and anarchy may be necessary for creativity, but this is quite a different thing from injustice and oppression. Following Mumford I spoke of the 'corporate attempt to fashion the future' in the city, but historically this 'corporate' has not included the poor. Their exclusion was not the necessary condition of creativity, I suggest. On the contrary, we have yet to see what creative potential can be unlocked under conditions of justice, precisely the future to which the prophets of Israel, Ambrose, Chrysostom, and all the greatest teachers of the Church have called us. The creativity we have seen is built on an 'in spite of'. What we await is a creativity built on a 'because'.

SUSTAINABLE CITIES?

Will the city continue to play a role in the economy of redemption? With more than half of the world's population now living in cities, and that proportion changing in favour of the city day by day, it is a poor lookout if they do not. Nevertheless the question is serious. One of the key questions is whether the mega city is sustainable, and what we should do about it if it is not. Mumford noted in the nineteen sixties that New York now covered 2,514 square miles and London was 650 times as big as its medieval predecessor. To hold that such cities represent the new scale of settlement to which human beings must adapt their institutions and personal needs was, he said, 'to mask the realities of the human situation and allow seemingly automatic forces to become a substitute for human

---

[69] John Atherton, for example, suggests self interest, efficiency, freedom in competition and the importance of individualism as new virtues compatible with the gospel. *Christianity and the Market* (London: SPCK, 1992).

[70] Green 'Blowing bubbles: Poplar', p. 82.

[71] N. Araki, *Tokyo Lucky Hole* (Cologne: Taschen, 1997).

purposes'.[72] The Population Crisis Committee, reporting in 1990, noted that some cities, such as Tokyo with 30 million, or Mexico City with 20 million, were becoming too big to be efficient.[73] Today Sao Paulo and Shanghai also have populations over twenty million. Schumacher felt half a million was the limit of what was desirable. Above such a size, he said, nothing is added to the virtue of the city whilst enormous problems certainly were created.[74] For Papanek, social chaos ensues above 120,000.[75] Even were we to allow Jane Jacobs' argument that it is city creativity which stimulates regional growth, cities have always been parasitic on their regions in the sense that they cannot produce the food and water they need for their citizens. The advent of mega cities intensifies this to an extreme degree. Not only are cities the main consumers of energy world wide, but they produce vast quantities of waste, demolish forests and lakes and drive the unsustainable rush for cheap food, reflected outside the city in increasing levels of soil degradation. Murray Bookchin argues that such vast conglomerations cannot be adapted to alternative energy. 'To use solar, wind and tidal power effectively, the giant city must be dispersed. A new type of community, carefully tailored to the nature and resources of a region, must replace the sprawling urban belts of today.'[76] It is easy to sympathise with Kirkpatrick Sale's plea for buildings and cities in human scale which can easily be taken in by the human eye, and comfortably walked.[77] He formulates what he calls the Beanstalk

[72] Mumford, *City*, p. 616.

[73] Cited in H. Girardet, *The Gaia Atlas of Cities* (London: Gaia, rev. edn 1996), p. 71.

[74] E. F. Schumacher, *Small is Beautiful* (London: Sphere, 1973), p. 55.

[75] 'With our objective a benign, neighbourly way of life, rich in interconnections and cultural stimuli, we can say that "face to face" communities will consist of 400 to 1000 people (the ideal is around 500), "common neighbourhoods" will accommodate roughly 5000 to 10,000 residents (or 10 to 20 face to face communities), and the "ideal city" will house about 50,000 souls (or 10 to 20 common neighbourhoods). Special functional reasons may decrease city size to 20,000 or increase it to 120,000 – beyond that lies social chaos.' V. Papanek, *The Green Imperative* (London: Thames & Hudson, 1995), p. 112.

[76] M. Bookchin, 'Towards a Liberatory Technology', in *Post Scarcity Anarchism* (London: Wildwood House, 1974), pp. 85–139. Kjellberg found in surveys that approaches to the city could be schematised between cosmological and anthropocentric views. He maps them as follows:

cosmological holism	anthropocentric sustainability
city as organism	city as machine
nature and man together	nature for the benefit of human beings
equitable distribution	economic growth
users' power	elite power
unity of all created	personal freedom

Urban EcoTheology, p. 17. The map points up some of the cultural contradictions of our present situation, and underlines the need for a fundamental cultural and spiritual shift.

[77] K. Sale, *Human Scale* (London: Secker & Warburg, 1980), pp. 38, 59.

principle, that for every animal, object, institution or system there is an optimal limit beyond which it ought not to grow. And its corollary, that beyond this optimal size all other aspects of a system will be affected adversely.[78]

An obvious alternative is to argue for small scale developments based on permaculture. Castells' comment on such proposals is that '[t]he ecological dream of small, quasi-rural communes will be pushed away to counter cultural marginality by the historical tide of megacity development'. 'There will be epidemics and disintegration of social control . . . but megacities will grow in size and dominance because they keep feeding themselves on population, wealth, power and innovators from their extended hinterland. They are nodal points connecting to global networks.'[79]

This proposal, however, seems quite as impossible as the small scale developments he dismisses. Although earlier he has examined Green movements, Castells does not ask at this stage of his work whether this historical tide is either ecologically or socially sustainable. He seems to presuppose the arguments of those economists, like Julian Simon, who maintain that human inventiveness will always come up with something, and then use this as an argument that human beings can do as they please.[80] The record of extinct civilisations ought to warn us of the dangers of such folly.

Radical utopian alternatives are proposed by the Greek thinker Constantin Doxiadis, and the American Paolo Soleri. Doxiadis assumed that the human population would go on expanding up to 22 billion. This, he believed, was the absolute limit of the earth's carrying capacity, and would only be possible if we stopped building on fertile agricultural soil at once (this was in the 1970s). He distinguished four basic spatial areas: one for nature, another for cultivation, another for human living and another for industry. He then broke these up into twelve zones beginning with a zone which was 'as nearly virgin as possible', then one visited by humans but without permanent human installations, up to an industrial area which was the site of 'every possible use for achieving the goal of the best industrialisation'. Looking at the planet he saw a coastline of approximately 261,000 kilometres, and proposed that the area for human settlement should consist of low, medium and high density settlements

---

[78] Victor Papanek agrees. 'My primary conviction as a human being, a designer and an ecologist is *Nothing Big Works – Ever!' Green Imperative*, p. 24.
[79] M. Castells, *The Rise of the Network Society* (Oxford: Blackwell, 1998), pp. 409–10.
[80] cf. J. Simon, *The Ultimate Resource* (Princeton: Princeton University Press, 1981).

. following this coastline, globally.[81] Since Doxiadis' death in 1975 global warming has made a significant impact on world coastlines, leading Paul Ehrlich to suggest that coastal zone development should be limited as far as possible.[82]

Paolo Soleri has proposed housing people in vast structures which are mini cities in themselves. 'Around vertical vectors', he writes, 'megalopoly and suburbia can contract.' As with Le Corbusier the idea is that one can step out from the high rise building into the countryside. His towers are surrounded by greenhouses which both grow food and channel heat into the settlement. Within the settlement transport is eliminated altogether. His image of these vast structures is of great passenger liners, afloat in the global sea, his version of the 'machine for living in'. Like Teilhard de Chardin, his inspiration, he envisages human beings evolving from nature to neonature, partly through the structures of his 'arcology' (architecture plus ecology). High density is central to his thinking. In his view 'death comes when the system uncrowds. No eco thinking can ignore the miracle of crowded living.' The fate of tower blocks seems to be the best commentary on his proposals.[83]

Vance proposed that there has always been an alternative to synoecism (the process by which villages come together to form a city, as proposed by Aristotle), namely what he called diocecism, in which cities dispersed into their rural hinterlands.[84] Some have proposed that Information Technology will reverse the movement of the first industrial revolution. Bill Gates, of Microsoft, believes that there are now 7 million telecommuters in the United States, significantly reducing pressures on traffic. They could, of course, simply lead to what Hall calls 'telesprawl', a further undisciplined spread of suburbia.[85] Counter urbanisation is in part a flight from the mega city, and represents a perception that vast communities are not socially sustainable. This trend, however, is so far only visible in the North, and the cities of the South continue to grow a rate of 20 million a year, so that the planet grows steadily more urban. The push and pull factors which account for this are well known, and include land degradation first and foremost, along with the promise of higher incomes, freedom from the constraints of traditional societies, and greater access to health care and education. As the pressure on the

---

[81] C. Doxiadis, *Ecology and Ekistics* (London: Elek, 1977).
[82] Foreword to R. Samuels and D. Prasad (eds.), *Global Warming and the Built Environment* (London: Spon, 1996) p. xvii.
[83] P. Soleri, *Arcology: The City in the Image of Man* (Boston: MIT Press, 1969).
[84] J. E. Vance, Jnr, *The Continuing City* (Baltimore: Johns Hopkins University Press, 1990), p. 74.
[85] Hall, *Cities in Civilization*, p. 959.

environment grows, however, and as numbers in the shanties, barrios and favellas grow, it is only a matter of time before this tide turns, and a search for more sustainable ways of living in the countryside begins.

If utopian visions and growing suburbanisation seem no solution, others look for specifically city shaped solutions. Many put their faith in the compact city, which will, it is argued, reduce ecological footprints because of more efficient land use and transport.[86] The argument is that they reduce travel distances, save rural land from development, and support local facilities. Hedley Smyth claims that the history of the compact city can be traced back to biblical times when a range of government functions were administered at the city gate, controlling the comings and goings in and out of the city as well as defending it against attack.[87] Thomas Sharp, who, as we have seen, already argued for compact cities in 1932, was inspired by the old English towns, and in a similar way European thinking draws on the model of the densely developed core of the Italian hill city. An example of compact city theory in practice is the fourth report on physical planning in the Netherlands, *On the Road to 2015*. This proposes to concentrate residences, work areas and amenities so as to produce the shortest possible trip distances, most being possible by bicycle and public transport. Work is arranged so that those sites with the most workers are located close to city centre stations; hospitals, research and white collar work are situated near a good station and with good access to motorways; and work which needs high accessibility by car or truck and has relatively few workers is situated close to motorways.[88] This is a reverse of the movement of suburbanisation, where people chose to live as far from the workplace as they conveniently could. In this kind of strategy cities are seen not only as the source of the problem, but also as the means of solving it, and the general objective of achieving sustainability is seen as dependent not on radical utopian schemes but on producing sustainable built environments from the cities and towns already in existence, by steering rather than overnight radical change.[89]

The compact city idea, however, is not without its problems. Some argue that it meets neither energy efficiency nor economic demands, and that it lacks the popular or political support to make it workable.[90]

[86] M. Wackernagel and W. Rees, *Our Ecological Footprint* (Gabriola Island: New Society, 1996), p. 103.

[87] H. Smyth, 'Running the Gauntlet', in M. Jenks, E. Burton and K. Williams (eds.), *The Compact City: A Sustainable Urban Form?* (London: Routledge, 1998), p. 101.

[88] Hall, *Cities in Civilization*, p. 973.

[89] M. Smith, J. Whiteleg and N. Williams, *Greening the Built Environment* (London: Earthscan, 1998) p. 211.

[90] L. Thomas and W. Cousins, 'The Compact City: A Successful, Desirable and Achievable Urban Form?', in Jenks, Burton and Williams (eds.), *Compact City*, pp. 53ff.

Others doubt that it meets the demands of the contemporary workplace and challenge the findings on transport, at the same time pointing out that crowded conditions often do not enhance the quality of life and noisy neighbours are a prominent cause of disputes and even murder![91] Smyth argues that many will come to live in a transition zone because of continuing displacement as a result of urban renewal and gentrification which will then displace lower income groups. This is, in fact, something already well evidenced in London. The result, he argues, will be that this zone will become a doughnut of social disadvantage around the compact city. In the worst analysis this could even be an example of eco fascism.[92] Against those who propose town cramming are those who say that it is vital for urban dwellers to be put back in touch with 'nature' and that we need space for urban farms, orchards and neighbourhood gardens.[93] If sustainability is the new religion, argues Tim Mars, then planners are its priests, and the compact city the new Jerusalem. 'It sounds plausible and seductive but it is a chimera. In environmental terms even compact cities are hardly benign.'[94] If the compact city has a finite capacity then it is not on its own a true, long term, sustainable solution.[95] The case for the compact city, then, 'remains largely unresolved'.[96]

Perhaps this is true, but ongoing suburban sprawl, or megalopolis, is even less benign, and for this reason it is widely accepted that medium sized cities, at least, are not only part of the problem, but also a key part of the solution to the environmental crisis, assuming that there is a solution. Many argue that cities are the most environmentally sustainable way of housing people and providing factories, offices, shops, leisure facilities and many of the other things that society wants.[97] Harley Sherlock even concludes that to prevent pollution in the twenty-first century most of us will have to live in cities.[98] Travel in cities is less energy consuming than in small towns and rural areas, because journey lengths are shorter, so people can walk and cycle more. Some planners hope that well designed and well managed cities can reduce travel

[91] Ibid., pp. 53ff., and K. Williams, E. Burton and M. Jenks, 'Achieving the Compact City through Intensification' in the same volume, p. 90.
[92] Smyth, 'Running the Gauntlet', pp. 103, 107.   [93] Girardet, *Gaia Atlas*, p. 173.
[94] Tim Mars, 'The Life in New Towns', in A. Barnett and R. Scruton (eds.), *Town and Country* (London: Jonathan Cape, 1998), pp. 276–7.
[95] C. Knight, 'Economic and Social Issues', in Jenks, Burton and Williams (eds.), *Compact City*, p. 119.
[96] Editorial comment in ibid., p. 215.
[97] Here T. Burton and L. Matson, 'Urban Footprints: Making Best Use of Land and Resources', in ibid.
[98] H. Sherlock, 'Repairing our Much Abused Cities', in ibid., p. 295.

distances and therefore energy use, though in practice it seems that improved transport facilities promote decentralisation.[99] When these ideas are linked to the importance of obtaining food and energy from the region we are not far from the deep green city and bioregionalism.[100] Far from being utopian some such move from global to local is going to have to be part of any move towards a more sustainable world. A whole raft of practical proposals is available to move in this direction, and have been implemented in various parts of the world. In Stockholm, Stuttgart and Helsinki inner city combined heat and power stations are in use, which greatly reduce damaging emissions and both produce hot water and generate electricity. Recycling and reuse programmes are being introduced in many cities: Stockholm recycles 80 per cent of all aluminium cans, and in Denmark the use of 'one way' plastic bottles is banned; in China human waste has traditionally been used as fertiliser, and ways of using rather than 'disposing' of sewage, let alone dumping it in the sea, need to be found; a new sewage processing system which demands far less water and avoids the use of chlorine has been developed in Australia and is now in use from Japan to Britain. As Herbert Girardet emphasises, cities, which use between two thirds and three quarters of fossil fuels world wide, need to take responsibility for their biocidic processes. In order for the waste gases they produce to be absorbed through photo synthesis cities need to nurture forests as 'symbiotic partners' to ensure climatic stability. Achieving this, as he says, means making commitments on a global scale.[101] As the debate around the Bush administration's attitude to climate change makes clear, culture change underlies the adoption of such practical proposals. To have an ecological city structure we have to have what Kjellberg calls ecological citizenship, based on values which have internalised the ecological question.[102]

---

99 Haughton and Hunter, *Sustainable Cities*, pp. 12–13; G. Barrett, 'The Transport Dimension', in Jenks, Burton and Williams (eds.), *Compact City*, p. 179. A related set of proposals are urban villages linked by light transit systems: already Munich, Freiburg, Stockholm, Vancouver, and Washington DC have such networks. The key aspect of such villages are mixed land use, with commercial and residential properties in together; high density, with everything within walking or cycling distance; extensive landscaping, including roof top gardens; good provision for children and for the community in the form of libraries, child care, centres for the elderly, and perhaps small urban farms, and as high a degree of self sufficiency for the community as possible. P. Newman, 'Urban design, transportation and greenhouse', in Samuels and Prasad (eds.), *Global Warming*, p. 82.
100 E.g. V. Andruss et al., *Home! A Bioregional Reader* (Philadelphia: New Society, 1990); D. Gordon, *Green Cities: Ecologically Sound Approaches to Urban Space* (Montreal: Black Rose, 1990).
101 Girardet, *Gaia Atlas*, p. 166.   102 Kjellberg, *Urban EcoTheology*, p. 46.

THE FUTURE OF THE CITY

In a widely accepted piece of analysis Saskia Sassen speaks of the emergence of global cities. She claims that the combination of spatial dispersal and global integration has created a new strategic role for major cities which function in four new ways: as command points in the organisation of the world economy; as key locations for finance; as sites of production and innovations; and as markets for these. What we have in cities such as New York, London and Tokyo is a new type of city, for which the earth is its hinterland.[103]

The structure of the business and finance centres, the magnitude of them, and the weight in the economies of these cities are what have changed. The power wielded by these cities, Sassen suggests, calls the primacy of the nation state into question. The interactions among them in terms of finance and investment suggest they may be a system. The sharp concentrations of such activities constitute internationalised spaces at the heart of these large, basically domestic, urban areas.[104]

The waning of the power of the state is both a threat and a promise. It is a promise for distinct cultural regions, long dominated by powerful neighbours: Scotland and the Basque country, for example. It is a threat when its disintegration leads to murderous Balkanisation as in Yugoslavia. In this new situation Castells, somewhat surprisingly, puts all the weight on the family. He envisages a situation where people are 'disaffected from the crumbling institutions of civil society' and individualised in their work and lives. In such a situation, in his view, the reconstructed family will be the only security in a dangerous sea. 'Families are more than ever the providers of pyschological security and material wellbeing to people in a world characterized by individuation of work, destructuring of civil society and delegitimation of the state.'[105] But families only exist as elements in larger cultural units, speaking particular languages, cooking in particular ways, forming kinship groups thus and not otherwise. Pentecost is not the obliteration of regional diversity, but the situation where we learn to understand one another, and confess, in our manifold ways, the wonderful giftedness of all things. And in a world of the decline of old nationalisms the region is the site of struggle, not only against the old centres of power, but also against the homogenising cultural power of multi nationals and of the global media. Traditional cultures are under threat all over the world, impacted by the new media

[103] S. Sassen, *The Global City* (Princeton: Princeton University Press, 1991), pp. 3–4.
[104] Ibid., p. 169.   [105] M. Castells, *End of Millennium* (Oxford: Blackwell, 1998), p. 349.

technologies.[106] The family cannot resist such cultural trends. What is needed is a new affirmation of regional power, if not of the nation state as known during the twentieth century.

Braudel argues that the great cities of the medieval and early modern periods 'produced the modern states, an enormous task requiring an enormous effort. They mark a turning point in world history. They produced the national markets, without which the modern state would be a pure fiction.'[107] Perhaps the global city will give birth to a new world order. Alternatively, ecological demands could ensure that cities once again have to find their resources in their immediate regions.[108] Harvey agrees that respecting the diversity of the local environment is a key aspect of the human future. 'The richness of human capacity for complexity and diversity' has to be understood in the context of 'the free exploration of the richness, complexity, and diversity encountered in the rest of nature', and above all in the region.[109] What Geddes, Norberg-Schulz and others argue about the relation of city and region instantiates Aristotle's tenet that respect for limits is a key part of creativity. If this is the case then the emergence of the global city could ultimately be stultifying.

The acid test of the city's role in the economy of redemption is precisely the question of what the city does for the poor qua city. In Engel's city, the city of dreadful night, the poor just disappeared and died, often enough bereft of all support. Examples of this can be found even in the cities of the North, for all their welfare systems, even at the beginning of the twenty-first century. To this extent there is a judgement on the city. It is, however, the urban poor who tell us that this is not the whole story. To concentrate only on judgement is to allow too little place for the

[106] R. Barnet and J. Cavanagh, 'Homogenization of Global Culture', in J. Mander and E. Goldsmith (eds.), *The Case against the Global Economy* (San Francisco: Sierra Club, 1996), pp. 71 ff. Speaking to village activists in Tamil Nadu in 1994 I was told that in the evenings now, rather than telling stories, dancing and singing songs, the whole community sits round and watches western porno videos.

[107] F. Braudel, *The Structures of Everyday Life* (London: Collins, 1981), p. 527.

[108] Folke Günther argues this, for example, believing that cities need to rediscover their dependence on their agricultural hinterland and develop this. *Dense Urban Settlements: Ecological Obstacles and Energy Price Vulnerability* (Stockholm: Department of Systems Ecology, Stockholm University, 1995).

[109] D. Harvey, *Justice, Nature and the Geography of Difference* (Oxford: Blackwell, 1996), p. 202. There is no need to accept unsustainable cities as fate. In particular the present environmental costs of transport mean that it is still essential for cities to respect their regions. Geddes and Mumford argued that it was vital for cities not to turn them into specialised machines for producing a single kind of goods – wheat, trees, coal. To forget the many sided potentialities which a region has as a habitat for organic life is to unsettle and make precarious any economic life at all. Historically we know that some of the greatest ancient cities died because they failed to respect this relationship.

ongoing creativity of the Spirit of God. As with the other forms of the built environment we have to allow that the city too must 'die to sin', to its city pride, to its unsustainable consumption of resources, to its marginalisation of the poor. On the other hand it may be that if we recover and respect our limits the city may remain the focus of human creativity, the place where the Spirit of God is known most intensely, and this is known in the vivacity, warmth and mutual support of many poor urban communities.

To do this it requires focus. Speaking of the new urban developments in the United States, which he calls Edge City, Joel Garreau notes that the shopping mall is the new spiritual centre, and that 'there is apparently no reason for any "ceremonial centres" dedicated to a "life more abundant" to be at the core of Edge City'.[110] This development signifies the loss of the transcendent question about where we are going and what we are for. 'As we collectively produce our cities', writes David Harvey, 'so we collectively produce ourselves. Projects concerning what we want our cities to be are, therefore, projects concerning human possibilities, who we want, or, perhaps even more pertinently, who we do not want to become.'[111] Cities have always been about markets, pleasure, deifying the human project. But the great religious monuments of the past have both challenged this, pointing to a justice to which human societies should aspire, and sublimated it, turning wealth and enterprise into miracles of corporate endeavour.

Lack of transcendent purpose in the city is not an absolutely new phenomenon. If Mumford is right, the Hellenistic city effectively built to celebrate its own achievements, as did imperial Rome. This ought to be a warning to us, for today we wander about in their ruins. For what gave a new lease of life to Rome was Christianity without which, at several points in the past two millennia, it would probably not have survived. Cities necessarily have markets; they are centres of the arts and of innovation. But without a creative spirituality, a sense of transcendent purpose, they die, they cease to be cities in the true sense. Perhaps it was because he wrote in the milieu of the Hellenistic city and of imperial Rome that the author of Hebrews insisted that 'here we have no lasting city, but look for the city that is to come' (Heb. 13.14). With regard to the cities that he knew, he was right, for imperial ambitions, whether

---

[110] Garreau, *Edge City*, p. 65.
[111] D. Harvey, *Spaces of Hope* (Edinburgh: Edinburgh University Press, 2000), p. 159. Cf. Mumford's remark that precisely because cities were part of the humanising process they were formed 'not by necessity but by discipline, desire and design' (*City*, p. 127).

colonial or neo colonial, are no substitute for transcendent purpose. He would be right, too, about Edge City. But here, too, perhaps, we can learn from the past. For it was in those very cities that Paul preached and faith communities took root which, as Peter Brown shows, sustained the city through the dark ages when the city almost died in the West, and after that once more gave it purpose. Socialism, says David Harvey, 'needs must arm itself with concepts and ideas, ideals and imaginaries . . . with foundational beliefs and persuasive arguments if it is to go about its task effectively'.[112] These concepts and ideas, ideals and imaginaries sound pretty much how the author of Hebrews describes the faith which takes us into the future. Such faith stands at the heart of the survival and shaping of the city as a key part of God's economy of redemption.

[112] Harvey, *Justice*, p. 434.

CHAPTER 7

Constructing community

Jerusalem – built as a city that is bound firmly together.
(Psalm 122.3)

If we are dreaming of Eden it is probable that we are dreaming of community. Anthropologists tell us that the group antedates the family and that the human capacity for living in community stems from the fact that only through communal efforts can they survive. Because the hunter gatherer way of life lasted several hundred thousand years, argues René Dubos, it has left an indelible stamp on human behaviour. Since the genetic determinants of human behaviour have evolved in small groups, 'modern man still has a biological need to be part of community'.[1] If there is truth in these claims, it would explain why the search for workable forms of community occupies such a large role in human history. A community is a group of people who have something in common, but what? Throughout history this has included the idea of territory, and territory, I will argue, remains important, even in an age of migration and of identity politics. However, territorially based notions of community are challenged by class, caste, gender, and ethnic divisions because community is also rooted in religion, culture, language, ethnicity, work or ideas. That idea that it is not territory which has primacy but shared interests and values is not an invention of the twentieth century but was alive in first century Galatia, and indeed in Egypt under the Pharaohs. Hardly surprising then that 'alternative' communities go back at least to the Essenes in the first century, and run through Benedict, Bernard of Clairvaux, Francis and Dominic, the Anabaptists, and Robert Owen, to the communes and base communities of the late twentieth century. All of these represent attempts to find the way back to the Garden of harmonious community.

[1] In C. Doxiadis (ed.), *Anthropopolis* (New York: Norton, 1974), pp. 259–60.

Though the quest for community is ancient, it assumed a new intensity in the wake of industrialisation, which has involved, amongst other
things, the dissolution of the small rooted communities which human
beings had lived in for millennia, and their replacement by the anonymous city. These changes were theorised by Frederick Tönnies in 1877 in
terms of the distinction between *Gemeinschaft* – roughly, the community of
the village, based on mutual aid and trust, and centred on family, neighbourhood and friendship – and *Gesellschaft*, the association of the anonymous city, based on individual self interest and contract.[2] He believed
that true community was only possible in the former. Though subjected
to vigorous criticism from the start, not least by Durkheim, his distinction
has proved remarkably resilient. Rather on the lines of the 'God of the
gaps' the Church has often seen its role in the light of this analysis as
providing some glimmer of community where otherwise it is absent. In
many respects the churches achieve a great deal in this way, and I shall
argue that the Christian understanding of community is paradigmatic
for human community as a whole. At the end of the nineteenth century
Christian Trusts, like the Peabody Trust, and priests in slum areas, were
also involved in the attempt to create physical environments conducive
to community. It is this attempt I want to focus on in this chapter.

Already at the beginning of the nineteenth century Robert Owen had
believed that it was possible to fashion community through building,
a belief later shared, ironically, by Margaret Thatcher. Patrick Geddes
believed in 'the vast modificability of life through its surroundings'.[3]
In this process a romanticised vision of *Gemeinschaft* played a key role.
'Romanticism' should not be taken wholly as a term of abuse here. It
emerged as a protest against what industrialisation was doing to the
world, human beings and human community, and many of its products,
like the craft work of William Morris, or the town and estate plans of
Raymond Unwin and Barry Parker in Hampstead, New Earswick and
Letchworth, remain inspirational. Certainly it was immensely superior
to what was produced by the reassertion of the reigning ethos of capitalism, utilitarianism, both in the years between the two world wars and
in the two decades after the second. Whether produced by developers
or by the public sector the emphasis was on cheapness at the expense
of quality, and above all imagination. Public sector estates in particular became 'anonymous and intimidating environments, the dumping

[2] F. Tönnies, *Community and Society*, tr. C. Loomis (New York: Harper & Row, 1963).
[3] Cited in G. Jones, *Social Darwinism and English Thought* (Brighton: Harvester, 1980), p. 71.

ground for those who were found surplus to society's requirements'.[4] In the 1950s Wilmott and Young's famous study of the East End of London found that the intense community produced by slum conditions was lost in the transition to new council estates, a process further intensified by the passion for tower blocks of the 1960s. The failure of many of these schemes kept the demand to 'build community' on the agenda, but by the end of the century visions of *Gemeinschaft* had faded. Against any cosy image of community postmodernism insisted on the priority of difference. Instead of taking the positive value of community for granted, as Unwin and Parker had been able to do, people now talked of the 'myth' of community which pressures those who do not conform to leave or at least know their place.[5] This critique, taken together with a burgeoning individualism in almost every sphere of life, meant that at the end of the century, the 'consensus across disciplines' was that 'community' as an objective had become less relevant in describing societies in the developed world.[6] According to Zygmunt Bauman what took the place of the old *Gemeinschaft* was a neo tribal world, where the tribes are formed by a multitude of individual acts of self identification.

Such agencies as might from time to time emerge to hold the faithful together have limited executive power and little control over co-optation or banishment . . . 'Membership' is relatively easily revocable, and is divorced from long term obligations . . . Tribes 'exist' solely by individual decisions to sport the symbolic traits of tribal allegiance. They vanish once the decisions are revoked or their determination fades out. They persevere thanks only to their continuing seductive capacity. They cannot outlive their power of attraction.[7]

'Community' in this world is a collection of individual consumers, who might change their preference from week to week. If Bauman's analysis is right, this poses a major political problem, for what holds the sub cultures competing for the scarce resource of space together if there is no 'meta narrative' of 'Community' in relation to the myriad different communities which make up society? One of the obvious answers – the nation – was deeply discredited in the course of the twentieth century, and the ethnic cleansing of the closing decade discredited it still further. Life in what Castles and Miller have called 'the age of migration' makes

---

[4] M. Smith, J. Whiteleg and N. Williams, *Greening the Built Environment* (London: Earthscan, 1998), p. 170.

[5] L. Sandercock, *Towards Cosmopolis* (Chichester: John Wiley, 1998), p. 191.

[6] Smith, Whiteleg and Williams, *Greening*, p. 161.

[7] Z. Bauman, *Modernity and Ambivalence* (Cambridge: Polity, 1989), p. 249, summarising the account of 'neo tribalism' of Michel Maffesoli.

it still more difficult, for ethnic and religious loyalties cut right across territorial ones.[8] But what then takes its place? One thing the whole discussion makes clear is that both the meaning of community, and therefore the task of fashioning it, remain an unsolved problem. In turn that leaves a black hole at the bottom of planning theory, in effect filled by the demands of competitive individualism. For unless land is plentiful, as in New Zealand for example, simply proliferating individual houses built at the owners' whim is no option. Some common understanding of community is demanded. By way of seeing what has been, and is, understood by community I shall look at various forms of built environment, before turning to examine what our understanding of Church as community has to contribute to meeting this dilemma.

THE VILLAGE COMMUNITY

'Every state is a community of some kind, and every community is established with a view to some good.' This is how Aristotle begins the *Politics*. He thinks of community in terms of a series of building blocks beginning with the family. The family is the association 'established by nature' for the supply of everyday wants. 'But when several families are united, and the association aims at something more than the supply of daily needs, the first society to be formed is the village.' An association of villages is, as we have already seen, a city.[9]

Aristotle's distinction between family and village corresponds to the pattern W. Williams found in Eskdale as recently as the 1950s. In the village, said Williams, patterns of friendliness and cooperation follow lines of physical proximity; in the countryside (by which he meant remote farms), new neighbours may be bypassed for more distant kin and traditional partners. In the village, community is formed by face to face contact and by gossip whilst the farm wife had to rely on her husband and sons to bring her news of neighbours and kin.[10] On the farm, then, at that stage, community meant the family. Doubtless the advent of car and phone signalled an imminent change even there.

The village, with its 'patterns of friendliness and cooperation', is clearly what Tönnies had in mind by *Gemeinschaft*. One of the most perfect pictures of it in English is Mary Mitford's *Our Village*, a series of sketches published in the *Lady's Magazine* between 1822 and 1827. She writes:

[8] S. Castles and M. Miller, *The Age of Migration* (London: Macmillan, 2nd edn, 1998).
[9] *Politics* 1252.
[10] W. Williams, *The Sociology of an English Village: Gosforth* (London, Routledge and Kegan Paul, 1956), ch. 7.

Of all situations for a constant residence, that which appears to me most delightful is a little village far in the country; a small neighbourhood, not of fine mansions finely peopled, but of cottages and cottage like houses . . . with inhabitants whose faces are as familiar to us as the flowers in our garden; a little world of our own, close packed and insulated like ants in an ant-hill . . . where we know every one, are known to every one, interested in every one, and authorized to hope that every one feels an interest in us.[11]

It could come out of a children's story book, but Three Mile Cross was a real place. Community here is the knowable circle, those we can practically aid, or expect to seek help from. Three Mile Cross had, on Mitford's account, a strong sense of identity, especially fostered by competitive games with neighbouring villages. Here is her account of preparation for the village cricket game (and this was written long before cricket became a national, let alone a middle class or professional, sport):

There is something strangely delightful in the innocent spirit of party. To be one of a numerous body, to be authorized to say *we*, to have a rightful interest in triumph or defeat, is gratifying at once to social feeling and to personal pride. There was not a ten year old urchin, or a septuagenary woman in the parish who did not feel an additional importance, a reflected consequence, in speaking of 'our side'. An election interests in the same way; but that feeling is less pure. Money is there, and hatred, and politics and lies. Oh, to be a voter, or a voter's wife, comes nothing near the genuine and hearty sympathy of belonging to a parish, breathing the same air, looking on the same trees, listening to the same nightingales! Talk of a patriotic elector! Give me a patriotic patriot, a man who loves his parish![12]

What makes Mitford's record significant is that she does not write as one of the gentry, nor as an observer, but as a villager herself who struggled with genteel poverty for most of her life. The villagers of whom she writes are common labourers and the gentry only appear on the margins. But the idyllic picture she paints, we remind ourselves, comes from the period of enclosures, not long before Captain Swing. And Mitford is a contemporary of Jane Austen for whom, as Raymond Williams puts it, the countryside is either weather or a place for a walk and 'neighbours' are the next big house.[13] We have, then, a class society, where amity is preserved so long as people know their place. And seeing that people kept their place was a ruthless priority. 'The use of common land by labourers operates on the mind as a sort of independence,' said a Report on Shropshire, in 1794. For this reason the commons should be enclosed for then 'the labourers will work every day in the year, their children

---

[11] M. Mitford, *Our Village* (London: Harrap, 1947), p. 12.   [12] Ibid., p. 120.
[13] R. Williams, *The Country and the City* (London: Hogarth, 1985), p. 166.

will be put out to labour early . . . and that subordination of the lower orders of Society, which in the present times is so much wanted would be thereby considerably secured'.[14] The class war which was in fact in progress is visible in Mitford only in the shape of deference. It is clearer in the report of the Liberal MP E. N. Bennett, writing eighty years after Mitford, who found that in organising village games, there were always two main obstacles: 'the men are too tired after their long hours of work to indulge in further exercise . . . and they are usually too poor to pay even a small subscription with regularity'.[15] And it was class and deference which, in Bennett's time, effectively stymied the attempt to activate local democracy through the setting up of Parish Meetings and Parish Councils.[16] This attempt was important, however, as recognition of the fact that 'community' does not just happen, is not part of what Aristotle would call 'nature', but needs structures, and is a vital part of the political process of a free society.

Aside from class, the village was also a place where received morality was strictly and even savagely enforced. Alwyn Rees cites a Welsh village in the mid twentieth century, where a middle aged widow was being visited at night by a young lad, and the youth group blamed the widow for enticing him. 'To break up the association they congregated around the house of the widow every time the lad was there, stopping up the chimney and throwing dead vermin and other obnoxious objects in through the door and windows.' In another district a married man having an affair was met by the youth group on his way home, plastered with cowdung and dragged through the river.[17] It is essentially the picture of the Skimmington Ride in Hardy's *Mayor of Casterbridge*. Research in 1994 in two very small Welsh villages found that traditional ideas of domesticity and of 'a woman's place' were very strong. One of the interviewees commented: 'You have to work hard to prove yourself, to feel you belong. There is a lot of pressure, whereas in the city . . . you don't have to make such an effort. You have to conform to expectations or they will gossip about you.'[18]

---

[14] E. N. Bennett, *Problems of Village Life* (London: Williams and Norgate, 1914), p. 28.

[15] Ibid., p. 81.

[16] The Local Government Act which set these up was passed in 1892.

[17] A. Rees, *Life in a Welsh Countryside* (Cardiff: University of Wales Press, 1950), p. 83.

[18] A. Hughes, 'Rurality and Cultures of Womanhood', in P. Cloke and J. Little (eds.), *Contested Countryside Cultures: Otherness, marginalisation and rurality* (London: Routledge, 1977), p. 131. In *Lark Rise to Candleford* Flora Thompson talks of the way a couple involved in adultery were policed by the Skimmington Ride, but otherwise the community she depicts was very accepting of pregnancy out of wedlock and many forms of social difference. It was hardest on snobbery.

Coercion of a different kind is involved in the pseudo villages created here and there in the United States at the end of the twentieth century. In Celebration, Florida, a Disney village of 20,000 people, with weather-boarded houses and white picket fences, there are rules about colour of curtains, the nature of the shrubbery in the front gardens, and what you can work on in the street. As Leonie Sandercock rightly observes, this represents an attempt to turn away from the challenges of the present, and return to an imagined pre industrial golden age of extended families living in small villages which fails to acknowledge the difficulties and injustices of that society.[19]

These facts call in question the common assertion that traditional villages are 'built for community'. This has been argued on the grounds that class and occupation were mixed indiscriminately throughout the village, avoiding the monoculture of housing estates, that the village depended on the active cooperation of all classes, but especially because the vast majority were engaged in activities which were closely related to each other and there was therefore a community of interest.[20] But class mix often fractures rather than unites community.[21] The old community of the village was founded on a deference which was actually a forced acknowledgement of an essentially feudal power.[22] Today, the advance of communication technology, and the depopulation of the countryside as farming has become dominated by agribusiness and lost its demand for labour, has 'reproduced in rural areas an individualized and home centred social life similar to that found in the suburbs'.[23] The same could be said of fishing villages whilst in Britain at least mining villages have virtually ceased to exist. The key change in the disintegration of the old village is not so much a shift in the structure of feeling but the loss of local industry, and therefore of common tasks. Where villages become commuter dormitories, or settlements for the retired, no resemblance to Mitford's village could possibly be expected. In some there are splits

---

[19] Sandercock, *Towards Cosmopolis*, p. 194.

[20] W. P. Baker, *The English Village* (London: Oxford University Press, 1953), pp. 76–7.

[21] This is illustrated in a ludicrous way in Oxford by the notorious 'Cutteslowe wall'. When council houses were built abutting a middle class suburb in North Oxford in the 1930s the residents defended themselves by erecting a wall. In 1999 an attempt at mixed community in North London likewise foundered when the middle class developments found it 'necessary' to gate their flats, causing intense resentment on the part of adjacent council tenants.

[22] In 1999 the son of the Head Gardener to the Duke of Somerset recalled how his father had always referred to his employer as 'Your Grace'. When, as a 13-year-old, he challenged this practice, he was told angrily: 'Keep quiet, boy! You'll lose me my job!' (personal conversation, September 1999)

[23] Smith, Whiteleg and Williams, *Greening*, p. 168.

between 'incomers' and older residents, often accentuated by the construction of estates which break up the fabric of the old village and invite segregation. Where villages are used as dormitories the emphasis is on the family rather than the community. Churches in particular often try to engender a sense of community through events in which as many people as possible are involved, but it is an open question whether sufficiently sustained community of interest can be generated to produce the 'local patriotism' Mary Mitford so enjoyed. The key to this sense seems to be shared weal and woe, shared fate. The recovery of a diversity of trades in the village could lead in this direction, but even then it would be in strong tension with the West's reigning individualism.

THE CITY COMMUNITY

The influence of Tönnies' distinctions is so widespread that when we say 'community' many automatically think 'village'. In the ancient world and in medieval Europe the opposite was the case. According to Aristotle it was the city which was the paradigm community, though his city was, of course, quite small. Plato recommended that a city should contain 5,040 heads of households – about 35,000 to 40,000 people. Aristotle thought the limit was 'the largest number which can be taken in at a single view', which is probably much the same size. The problem of keeping numbers stable was solved by colonisation, the first practical recognition, as Mumford says, of an organic limit to city growth. The Greek city's real strength, he felt, was that it embodied the doctrine of the golden mean and was neither too small nor too big, neither too rich nor poor. Thus 'it kept the human personality from being dwarfed by its own collective products, whilst fully utilizing all the urban agents of cooperation and communion'.[24] Today, it is argued, cities are not communities but 'staging posts, providing leisure facilities, hotels, restaurants, business meetings; and their outer edges act as the setting for home-centred activities. In the electronic age the centuries old rationale for cities is vanishing.'[25] To this every city dweller at once responds that cities are agglomerations of urban villages, and that community remains alive and well in the village. This is not quite true, for the inhabitant of Greenwich village remains a New Yorker, of Camden a Londoner, of Belleville a Parisian. All the same, the sub communities which genuinely make up the city, as

---

[24] L. Mumford, *The City in History* (Harmondsworth: Penguin, 1991), p. 174.
[25] D. M. Hill, *Citizens and Cities* (New York: Harvester Wheatsheaf, 1994), p. 243, summarising a view rather than representing her own.

opposed to its suburbs, do remain in all sorts of ways – for good and for ill. As Harvey points out, much contemporary concern for community is targeted on the affluent whilst leaving the underclass to their fate.[26]

It was early recognised that it was the community, and not the built environment, which makes the city. 'It is not well roofed houses, well built walls, docks and harbours which constitute a city', said Alcaeus, 'but men ready to use their own opportunity.'[27] Amongst the free citizens it is the common pursuit of justice and the good life which constitute the community for Aristotle. In this community all the free citizens could meet to discuss affairs. Accordingly, at the heart of the city was the agora, essentially an open space at the centre of the city's street system which served as the political, religious, social and economic focal point of the community.[28] From this, of course, slaves, women and strangers were all excluded.

The idea that '[t]he city makes one free', mentioned in the previous chapter, represents what the city stood for in the middle ages, when it allowed an escape from the oppression of feudal bonds. Kropotkin argued that in the twelfth century there occurred a 'communalist' revolution in Europe which saved its culture from suppression by theocratic and despotic monarchies. This revolution expressed itself in the local village community and in urban fraternities and guilds. In the later medieval city each section or parish was the province of an individual self governing guild; and the city was the union of these districts, streets, parishes and guilds. These achievements, he argued, were swept away by the centralised state of the sixteenth century.[29]

Mumford depicted the medieval city as 'a collective structure whose main purpose was the living of a Christian life'. Hospitals and almshouses were built to serve the sick and needy, as, later on, were foundling asylums. 'The lay orders, aiming at the practice of a Christian life in the heart of the city without the physical and spiritual withdrawal enjoined by the old monasteries, were part of an organized effort to infuse every aspect of existence with Christian principles.'[30] In this city the monopoly of power and knowledge was renounced and laws and property rights reorganised in the interest of justice. Slavery and compulsory labour were abolished, and gross economic inequalities between class and class eliminated.[31] More plausibly Richard Sennett talks of the way in which the religious

---

[26] D. Harvey, *Spaces of Hope* (Edinburgh: Edinburgh University Press, 2000), p. 170.
[27] Frag 28, quoted in E. J. Owens, *The City in the Greek and Roman World* (London: Routledge, 1991).
[28] Owens, *City*, p. 153.   [29] P. Hall, *Cities of Tomorrow* (Oxford: Blackwell, 1988), p. 144.
[30] Mumford, *City*, p. 345.   [31] Ibid., p. 364.

community in the medieval city served as a point of moral reference. The almshouse, the parish church, and the hospital set standards against which to measure behaviour in other parts of the city. 'It made a city a moral geography. For those under the sway of the new religious values sanctuary was the point of community – a place where compassion bonded strangers.'[32]

Girouard reminds us of much that was oppressive in this idealised city. He focuses on the complex and often chaotic power structure, and the imperative to orthodoxy. That the clergy were exempt from civil law meant that there were thousands of people outside that law. The impression of unity was almost always deceptive and almost all medieval towns were dominated by a lay or ecclesiastical ruler. The middle ages witnessed a slow power struggle which ended in the sixteenth century patriciate.[33] Furthermore, the orthodoxy of the medieval town, like that of the village, was deeply oppressive. There was little room for dissent. It was generally accepted that there were right beliefs and right ways of behaving and any deviation from these was punishable. The city was a hierarchy, divided into ascending levels, and although movement from one level to the other was not impossible it was not encouraged. Those on each level were expected to look and behave in a particular way, and not to act or dress above their stations. An inspection of medieval legal documents shows that they abound with regulations about dress and behaviour. In Florence wedding menus had to be checked in advance; in Siena in 1425 women were forbidden to wear silk clothes or a train or clothes which accentuated their figures. In Nuremberg workmen were fined for parting their hair in a forbidden manner. Even amongst the wealthy ostentation in dress or lifestyle was discouraged and often legally regulated.

The merchants, as much as everyone else . . . accepted an ethos of thrift, sobriety and hard work. Work hours were regulated by bell . . . They ran from sunrise to sunset, with an hour off for midday meal. In Nuremberg the shortest working day was seven hours, the longest thirteen. All towns had a curfew, imposed at dusk, after which it was forbidden to walk about the city except on lawful business.[34]

The coming of industrialisation meant that for the first time cities of millions sprang up. This change of scale was in the first instance a

[32] R. Sennett, *Flesh and Stone* (London: Faber, 1994), p. 159.
[33] M. Girouard, *Cities and People: A Social and Architectural History* (New Haven: Yale University Press, 1985), p. 47.
[34] Ibid., p. 73.

product of early industrial technology, for steam required that the parts of a plant could not be more than a quarter of a mile from the source of power. It was this city that generated the anomie and alienation which Durkheim analysed and which led to a flight from the city into suburbia, or the search for alternatives from Robert Owen's New Lanark onwards. The vision of people like Ebenezer Howard, the founding father of the Garden City, and of Mumford's mentor Patrick Geddes was, writes Peter Hall, 'not merely of an alternative built form, but of an alternative society, neither capitalistic nor bureaucratic-socialistic: a society based on voluntary co-operation among men and women, working and living in small self governing commonwealths'.[35] The great English town planner Raymond Unwin likewise dreamed of voluntary self governing communities. His Garden Cities were vehicles for the progressive reconstruction of capitalist society into a network of cooperative commonwealths.[36] To a certain extent, Peter Hall argues, this vision was realised in the strong city hall politics of many British cities in the twentieth century, though apathy and disillusion with politics, alongside well publicised city hall corruption, has weakened the genuine democratic base. In the United States the Settlement house movement likewise argued that the time had come for 'a great renewal of confidence in the vitality of neighbourhoods as a political and moral unit'.[37] Anticipating Jane Jacobs they recommended the community block as a powerful social force. At the end of the Second World War the Goodmans agreed:

Starting from being neighbours, meeting on the street, and sharing community domestic services (laundry, nursery, school) the residents become conscious of their common interests . . . Where there is a sense of neighbourhood, proposals are initiated for the local good; and this can come to the immensely desirable result of a political unit intermediary between the families and the faceless civic authority . . . Such face-to-face agencies, exerting their influence for schools, zoning, play streets, a sensible solution for problems of transit and traffic, would soon make an end of isolated plans for 'housing'.[38]

A very different option was favoured by Le Corbusier in terms of centralised planning based on class stratification, something which assumed antagonistic communities from the start. In Chandigarh, where he had an opportunity to put his ideas into practice, 'there is a total failure to produce built forms that could aid social organization or social integration; the sections fail to function as neighbourhoods. The city is

---

[35] Hall, *Cities of Tomorrow*, p. 3. [36] Ibid., p. 87. [37] Ibid., p. 123.
[38] P. Goodman and P. Goodman, *Communitas: Means of Livelihood and Ways of Life* (New York: Random House, 1960), p. 55.

heavily segregated by income and civil service rank, different densities for different social groups, resulting in planned class segregation.'[39]

At the opposite end of the scale was Jane Jacobs' prescription for the regeneration of cities, *The Death and Life of the Great American Cities*. What the planners have given us, she argued,

> are low income projects that become worse centres of delinquency, vandalism and general social hopelessness than the slums they were supposed to replace; middle income housing projects which are truly marvels of dullness and regimentation, sealed against any buoyancy or vitality of city life; luxury housing projects that mitigate their inanity ... with a vapid vulgarity; cultural centres that are unable to support a good bookstore; civic centres that are avoided by everyone but bums, who have fewer choices of loitering than others; commercial centres that are lacklustre imitations of standardized suburban chain store shopping; promenades that go from no place to nowhere and have no promenaders; expressways that eviscerate great cities. This is not the rebuilding of cities, this is the sacking of cities.[40]

She wanted instead to keep the inner city neighbourhood more or less as it was before the planners had got their hands on it. As she noted, planning and zoning make it impossible for children to play in a world composed of both men and women. Her remedy to achieve 'exuberant diversity' was mixed functions and land uses, conventional streets on short blocks and a dense concentration of people.[41] A well used city street, she argued famously, is apt to be a safe street where a deserted street is unsafe. Along with many city dwellers she agreed that one of the advantages of the city over the small community were the possibilities for privacy. 'A good city street neighbourhood achieves a marvel of balance between its people's determination to have essential privacy and their simultaneous wishes for differing degrees of contact, enjoyment, or help from people around.'[42] Following her lead, Richard Sennett argued that the square surrounded by townhouses makes human density count socially. Such density permits the expression of personal deviation or idiosyncrasy in a milieu where there are too many people thrown together to discipline everyone to the same norm.[43] Alice Coleman, as we have seen, had many concrete proposals for making neighbourhoods safer and more conducive to genuine community living. Amongst other things this involved largely eliminating the 'shared public space' which

[39] Hall, *Cities of Tomorrow*, p. 214.
[40] J. Jacobs, *The Death and Life of Great American Cities* (Harmondsworth: Penguin, 1994; orig. 1961), p. 14.
[41] Hall, *Cities of Tomorrow*, p. 235.   [42] Jacobs, *Death and Life*, p. 70.
[43] R. Sennett, *The Uses of Disorder* (New York: Norton, 1990), p. 159.

was so fashionable in the sixties and seventies of the twentieth century, and reinstating private gardens, and fences or hedges to lean over and talk to your neighbours.[44]

Jacobs was not a proponent of what Reinhold Niebuhr called 'salvation by bricks'. Like many of the planners she opposed, she too believed that failures with city neighbourhoods are ultimately failures in localised self government 'used in its broadest sense meaning both informal and formal self management of society'.[45] The planning problem was, then, only a planning problem to the extent that it was also a political problem. What is clear is that whilst badly designed built environments can generate crime and vandalism, it is not possible to build people into virtue. Nevertheless, Jacobs' prescriptions quickly became orthodoxy and good neighbourhood design is said to need an identifiable neighbourhood centre and an identifiable edge; a limited breadth to a neighbourhood based on the distance a person can comfortably walk – approximately a quarter of a mile; a mixture of uses and a mixture of different kinds of housing in close proximity to one another; a network of interconnected streets; and appropriate locations for civic buildings – schools, churches, post offices, meeting halls and day care centres. [46]

These proposals all seem based on the facilitating of face to face meeting, but this has been strongly challenged as an ideal for community by Iris Marion Young, who argues that the old *Gemeinschaft* type of community was oppressive and excluded difference. Privileging face to face relations, in her view, has the inevitable consequence that those not in the family, clique, or group are excluded.[47] Cities, on the other hand, instantiate social relations of difference without exclusion. City life is the being together of strangers characterised by the celebration of difference, an ambience in which deviant and minority groups can flourish under the cover of anonymity, diverse activities, 'eroticism' – the enjoyment of the other's difference – and the provision of public space where 'people stand and sit together, interact and mingle, or simply witness one another, without becoming unified in a community of shared final ends'.[48]

Young draws on Richard Sennett's influential *The Uses of Disorder*, which argued that the demand for 'community', purified of all that might convey a feeling of difference, is built on an adolescent fear of the pain of

[44] A. Coleman, *Utopia on Trial: Vision and Reality in Planned Housing* (London: Shipman, 1985), pp. 170ff.
[45] Jacobs, *Death and Life*, p. 220.
[46] P. Langdon, *A Better Place to Live* (Amherst: University of Massachusetts Press, 1994), p. 217.
[47] I. M. Young, *Justice and the Politics of Difference* (Princeton: Princeton University Press, 1990), p. 227.
[48] Ibid., p. 240.

challenge and participation.[49] The family in particular, he argues, acts as a shield from diversity. To grow to adulthood we need to be able to tolerate painful ambiguity and uncertainty, and we therefore need the anarchy the city can provide. 'The great promise of city life is a new kind of confusion possible within its borders, an anarchy that will not destroy men, but make them richer and more mature.'[50] In the healthy city there will be no escape from situations of confrontation and conflict, and this depends on diverse and ineradicably different kinds of people being thrown together and forced to deal with each other for mutual survival.[51] Dense disorderly cities would challenge the capacity of family groups to act as intensive shelters, as shields from diversity, and would create a feeling of need in the individual that he or she had to get involved in situations outside the little routines of their daily life in order to survive with the people around them.[52]

Perhaps the best comment on these arguments is the situation David Harvey discusses, two decades after Sennett was writing, when New York City had to decide which contesting group should control the public space of Tompkins Square Park. The demands of the homeless who slept in the park, the parents who took their children to play in it, the drug pushers who used it for their trade, the skateboarders, the basketball players, the radicals, the punks, the heavy metal bands, chess players and dog walkers were mutually incompatible. In this situation 'openness to unassimilated otherness' breaks apart into open war. New York City's desperate solution was to close the park altogether 'for rehabilitation'. Harvey wittily frames the dilemma:

> What should the policy maker and planner do in the face of these conditions? Give up planning and join one of those burgeoning cultural studies programmes which revel in chaotic scenes of the Tompkins sort while simultaneously disengaging from any commitment to do something about them? Deploy all the critical powers of deconstruction and semiotics to seek new and engaging interpretations of graffiti which say, 'Die, Yuppie scum'? Should we join revolutionary and anarchist groups and fight for the rights of the poor and culturally marginalised to express their rights and if necessary make a home for themselves in the park? Or should we . . . join with the forces of law and order and help impose some authoritarian solution on the problem?[53]

It seems it is not as easy to abandon 'shared final ends' as perhaps Young thinks. Moreover, the face to face has an uncomfortable habit

49 Sennett, *Uses of Disorder*, p. 42.   50 Ibid., p. 108.   51 Ibid., p. 163.   52 Ibid., p. 169.
53 'Social Justice, Postmodernism and the City', in *The Improvement of the Built Environment and Social Integration in Cities* (Luxembourg: Official Publications of the EC, 1992), p. 26.

of reasserting itself, as in Young's description of the city as composed of 'clusters of people with affinities – families, social groups, networks, voluntary associations, neighbourhood networks, a vast array of small "communities"'.[54] These clusters of face to face relations are, on her view, perhaps the source of the difficulties in Tompkins Park.

And in the last decade of the twentieth century cities often developed in quite the opposite direction to 'undifferentiated otherness'. In London's Docklands, for example, a cynical piece of political engineering in the interests of corporate finance eliminated street related activities except for the very rich. This was the opposite of the 'mixed use' formula. The same prioritisation of wealth has led to what Mike Davis called, in relation to Los Angeles, 'the carceral city'. This is the city of omnipresent security cameras, police and private security guards, 'fortress cities' brutally divided between 'fortified cells' of affluent society and 'places of terror' where the police battle the criminalised poor so that the 'Second Civil War' has been institutionalised into the very structure of urban space.[55] In this world 'community' means homogeneity of race, class and home values. The most powerful 'social movement' in contemporary Southern California, Davis remarks ironically, is that of affluent homeowners engaged in defending home values and neighbourhood exclusiveness.[56] The fastest growing type of 'community' in the United States is the gated community. Twenty-eight million Americans now live in such areas. Over 30 per cent of residential development in southern California is now in this form, one example having a wall, moat and drawbridge and a device which shoots a metal cylinder through the bottom of unauthorised cars.[57] We live, says Davis, in a post liberal society, with the gangplanks pulled up and compassion strictly rationed by the Federal deficit.[58] What Garreau writes about Edge City confirms this. The centre of these places are the shopping malls, proud of their crime free record. But they are crime free because they are policed like prisons, and any problem characters are promptly banned. 'It's a question', says Garreau, 'of how much we value safety and comfort. In Edge City there is very little truly "public" space. On purpose.'[59] The elimination of public space is obviously hostile to community, and the great malls

[54] Young, *Justice*, p. 237.
[55] M. Davis, *City of Quartz* (London: Pimlico, 1998) p. 224.   [56] Ibid., p. 153.
[57] Smith, Whiteleg and Williams, *Greening*, p. 146. Harvey notes that between 1987 and 1997 the numbers of Americans living in gated communities rose from one to six million. *Spaces of Hope*, p. 150.
[58] Davis, *City of Quartz*, p. 316.
[59] J. Garreau, *Edge City* (New York: Anchor Doubleday, 1991), p. 52.

are destructive of community in other ways. First, as is well known, their development has devastated many city centres, which become secondary centres 'attracting local customers buying low quality or discount goods'. This starts a downward spiral of degradation which affects every aspect of city life.[60] Secondly, malls are not, like the older style shopping centres, places where people meet and discuss the issues of the day. 'The focus is on consumption, on the pleasure of just being there. The issues that are part of our everyday community are not discussed there, so it doesn't function as a community.'[61]

A related problem in the contemporary city is the complaint that international capital homogenises the city and abolishes difference. This complaint presupposes that local identity is essential to community. It is undeniable that any Western city is now full of the same shops, advertisements and shopping malls. Nevertheless, according to Antony Cohen, people domesticate the city, mark out their own territories, cache resources at strategic points, and invest the city with culture. 'People enculture the city, rather than responding passively to its deterministic power.'[62] This is a version of the claim I have argued for that people ensoul places. As with all 'common culture' arguments, however, the question is whether the politics we see at both local and national level do not belie the claims. We need to give people credit for the ingenuity with which they create social relationships through which they can adapt the spatial and physical environment of the city to their own capacities and resources, says Cohen. But of course this ingenuity can be utilised to marginalise otherness. It is not necessarily used for 'the common good', a phrase which might be disallowed by postmodern critics, but by which I mean that enabling of all citizens which Young and others aim at.

THE SUBURBAN COMMUNITY

Throughout the twentieth century suburbia attracted sharply different views on its merits as a place for community. Though critics like Mumford loathed it the public voted with their feet, and, in the North, suburbia remained the most popular place to live, though this may have been *faute de mieux*. As a locus for community the jury is still out.

Suburbia is nuclear familyland. The arguments in favour of suburbia focus first of all on the benefits for the family, and especially for bringing

---

[60] Smith, Whiteleg and Williams, *Greening*, p. 98.   [61] Langdon, *Better Place*, p. 21.
[62] A. Cohen and K. Fukui (eds.), *Humanising the City? Social Contexts of Urban Life at the Turn of the Millennium* (Edinburgh: Edinburgh University Press, 1993), p. 5.

up children. Questioning people in Levittown Gans found that people spoke first of wanting to get out of the city, and next of bringing up children. Mainly they came for a house, and not a social environment.[63] From the start a strong domestic ideology was expressed in the suburban ideal which quickly established itself as perennial, when it was actually quite new. Until the end of the eighteenth century, as in parts of the Third World today, the gender division of labour was not so marked. Men reaped and women stooked the corn; men wove and women span; men milked and women made butter and cream. In the early industrial revolution men and women worked equally in the factories and mines. It was the growth of the salaried middle class which introduced a new division of labour. The man went out to work and the wife stayed at home. 'The creation of an environment in which this division of middle class male lives between a public world of work contacts and a private world of family life was what the rise of suburbia was all about,' writes F. M. L. Thompson:

The clear separation of work and home, the insistence on social distancing, the treatment of the home as the feminine domain, the importance attached to domestic privacy and the exclusion of the vulgar prying multitude can all be seen as parts of a code of individual responsibility, male economic dominance and female domestic subordination, and family nurtured morality which served to give the bourgeois a social identity and mark them off from the upper class and the lower orders. The separation of work from domestic life was occurring in the late 18th century as a result of changes in production technology and business organization which made the home an unsuitable or impossible place for many kinds of trade and manufacture; the emphasis on personal religious and moral responsibility and behaviour from the Clapham sect, whose message was powerfully reinforced by the French revolution and fears of disorderly, irreligious mobs gave a central role to the family as the main instrument of moral education; and the socially segregated suburb of separate family houses shortly emerged to supply the ideal environment for practising the newly reformed life style incorporating these religious, moral and social aspirations.[64]

These changes gradually spread by cultural seepage, and were generalised in the great suburban estates of the mid twentieth century, which had real advantages. Unlike older industrial housing a garden was available for the children. In the new suburbs, said Mumford, 'the problem of creating an urban environment favourable to the health and nurture of children was solved by the middle classes as it had never been solved

[63] H. Gans, *The Levittowners* (London: Allen Lane, 1967), pp. 36–7.
[64] F. M. L. Thompson, *The rise of Suburbia* (Leicester: Leicester University Press, 1982), p. 9.

before, except in the almost equally open country town or village. The mere opening up of space was an essential part of the solution.'[65] Population density was less than in the city and so there was a greater sense of repose. In the British suburbs at least, before the rise of out of town shopping, shops, schools and post offices were all within easy reach. From the start suburbs tended to attract people of the same social class and Mumford observed that in providing a small face to face community of identifiable people, participating in the common life as equals, it superficially restored the dream of Jeffersonian democracy.[66] Gans argued that whatever the criticism, suburban living, as exemplified by the post Second World War development of Levittown, represented a huge improvement over previous ages:

> By any yardstick one chooses, Levittowners treat their fellow residents more ethically and more democratically than did their parents and grandparents. They also live a 'fuller' and 'richer' life. Their culture may be less subtle and sophisticated than that of the intellectual, their family life less healthy than that advocated by psychiatrists, and their politics less thoughtful and democratic than the political philosophers' – yet all of these are superior to what prevailed among the working and lower middle classes of past generations.[67]

James Richards, who saw an anarchist streak in suburbia, felt that the suburban environment provided an opportunity of individual self expression for people to whom it was otherwise denied. The argument is that creative activity can only be encouraged among the mass of people by building on a foundation of their own existing modes of expression. For this purpose sophisticated standards of taste and criticism can conveniently be forgotten.[68]

For these positives there are, however, vehement negatives. Already in 1913 A. T. Edwards argued that low density housing contravenes humankind's desire for fellowship. Working men, he said, just want a better house and a better street, not a suburb. 'The very word suburban implies something that is second rate, some narrow and pharisaical attitude of mind ... but of all suburbs the most shoddy and depressing is the typical garden suburb. It has neither the crowded interest of the town, nor the quiet charm of the country, it gives us the advantages neither of solitude nor of society.'[69] Philip Langdon argues that it is no coincidence that at the moment when the United States has become a

---

[65] Mumford, *City*, p. 558.   [66] Ibid., p. 569.   [67] Gans, *Levittowners*, p. 419.
[68] J. M. Richards, *Castles on the Ground: The Anatomy of Suburbia* (London: John Murray, 1973), p. 89.
[69] A. Edwards, *The Design of Suburbia* (London: Pembridge, 1981), p. 223.

predominantly suburban nation, the country has suffered a bitter harvest of individual trauma, family distress, and civic decay.[70] In his *Bomb the Suburbs* manifesto William Wimsatt described them as 'an unfortunate geographical location, an unfortunate state of mind. It's the American state of mind, founded on fear, conformity, shallowness of morals and dullness of character.'[71]

The suburbs are lauded as a good place for the family, but the downside of this is neglect of wider aspects of community. Suburbs lack the informal gathering places to be found both in villages and cities – pubs, cafés, coffee shops – and they therefore lack the space for the real formation of community through the invisible filigree of debate and argument. Ironically they have also been attacked for failing to provide enough privacy. 'The group mindedness embodied in the cul de sac seems to be based on a simple "just folks" conviction that no matter who moves into the cul de sac, the little society of neighbours will get along famously. This is a foolishly optimistic assumption.' The option for escape is at least as important as the option for contact, and there are many examples of informal suburban policing of taste quite as strong as anything to be found in a village.[72]

Some deny that the suburbs are a good place to bring up children. 'The traditional street system draws youngsters out, pretty much at their own pace. The world beckons as an interesting place . . . there is no corresponding term for intelligence in modern suburbs . . . youngsters in the cul de sac have a hard time getting to know their community or the communities that lie beyond.'[73] This is partly because suburbia is dependent on the car and the television, both things which isolate people. 'The low density, dispersed city, made possible by the automobile, is a physically and socially fragmented city. Its day to day function causes stress and people retreat to their homes for relaxation and relief.'[74] Mumford pointed out that as soon as the car became common walking distances were destroyed as a normal means of human circulation. Extension of the suburb has made it impossible. 'As a result, Unwin's salutary demonstration, Nothing Gained by Overcrowding, must now be countered with a qualifying admonition: Something Lost by Overspacing.'[75] Overall, Mumford felt that suburbia was based on a flight from reality.

[70] Langdon, *Better Place*, p. 1.
[71] Quoted by Homi Bhabha in R. Silverstone (ed.), *Visions of Suburbia* (London: Routledge, 1997), p. 298.
[72] Langdon, *Better Place*, p. 43. [73] Ibid., p. 49.
[74] Smith, Whiteleg and Williams, *Greening*, p. 166. [75] Mumford, *City*, pp. 575–6.

In the suburbs one might live and die without marring the image of an innocent world ... Here domesticity could flourish, forgetful of the exploitation on which so much of it is based. Here individuality could prosper, oblivious of the pervasive regimentation beyond. This was not merely a child centred environment: it was based on a childish view of the world, in which reality was sacrificed to the pleasure principle.[76]

The suburbs lost the dialectical tensions and struggles which made city life significant.[77] Many authors agree that suburbs bred a flight from civic or political engagement. 'The suburban dream equalled selfishness, a rejection of obligation and commitment to the city where the suburbanite earned his living. A suburban house bred detachment from civic responsibility. It imperilled community spirit by highlighting class distinctions residentially.'[78]

Herbert Gans' field work challenged many of these assumptions. Viewed sociologically suburbs are not simply an aggregation of nuclear families, but a dense network of community groups and organisations which embrace a very high percentage of their occupants. Gans found more than a hundred associations flourishing after only three years. This is perhaps the kind of tribal community of which Bauman speaks, grouped around interests – Gans conceded he found little interest in national affairs there. But even in the village and the city something of the same applies. Gans challenged the existence of the community the critics missed in suburbia. Nostalgic social critics want to 'revive' a sense of community 'that never was save in their imagination, instead of planning for the effective functioning of and improved living conditions in those aggregates to which we give the name "community"'.[79] Two questions in particular pertain to the suburb. First, the ideology which originally led to their formation has broken down, as reflected in the rise to parity of the female workforce. This is a return to the norm of all human societies under the condition of wage labour. Are the suburbs equally suited to this new situation, and in particular the rise in so called one parent families? Secondly, if the kind of social disintegration which Langdon finds in the suburbs is in fact what they produce then they urgently need surgery. He proposes the introduction of pubs, cafés, neighbourhood stores. Gans, on the other hand, finds suburban community in good order, within a roughly lower middle class frame of

[76] Ibid., p. 563.   [77] Ibid.
[78] P. J. Waller, *Town, City and Nation: England 1850–1914* (Oxford: Oxford University Press, 1983), p. 145.
[79] Gans, *Levittowners*, p. 146.

reference. Suburbanites, he says, 'enjoy the house and outdoor living and take pleasure from the large supply of compatible people, without experiencing the boredom or malaise ascribed to suburban homogeneity'.[80] His findings were an accelerated social life, not a diminished one. Colin Ward would agree. Looking at Runcorn New Town, and the network of community associations which Gans found in the United States, he believes that 'there is an automatic community potential, always waiting to trigger its release'.[81]

CHURCH, COMMUNITY AND KINGDOM

'Trinity', as Robert Jenson has taught us, is the Christian name for God.[82] The doctrine is the articulation of three sets of historical experience, but when reflected points us to a God who is not the Unmoved Mover, the Alone with the Alone, but the one who is community in Godself. Nothing was more remarkable in the history of twentieth century theology than the recovery and development of this insight. Though the doctrine is historically given, and not a deduction about the nature of love, it is, of course, also a commentary on the claim that God is love. The recovery of the doctrine has important implications for our understanding of community and the built environment. It seems to privilege face to face community in a way Young and others would find alienating. How should we respond to these claims?

It is true that if we want an illustration of the way in which a community ideology can breed exclusion we need only look at the Christian medieval city, and the growth of the ghetto. On the other hand, if we wanted a phrase to describe the attitude of the figures in the Rublyev icon, 'openness to unassimilated otherness' would do very well. The Trinitarian doctrine of relations has wrestled with this problem, understanding the divine persons as defined by their relations, whilst remaining distinct. Thus the Father is the Father because the Son is the Son, and so on. Who Father, Son and Spirit are is predicated both on real difference (we cannot say 'ontological difference' of course) and on real unity. The doctrine of perichoresis, mutual indwelling, sought to theorise this. If human beings are made in the divine image then it is this form of relationship to which we have to aspire. As is by now very well documented, the doctrine of the Trinity was a dead letter for a millennium and a half

---

[80] Ibid., p. 409.
[81] C. Ward, *New Town, Home Town* (London: Gulbenkian, 1993), p. 62.
[82] R. Jenson, *The Triune Identity* (Philadelphia: Fortress, 1982).

in effectively monarchical societies where power was focused in one ruler. Trinitarian reflection, on the other hand, invites open and mutually defined forms of power. But how to realise that? Young develops her views through a critique of Murray Bookchin, and his 'wildly utopian' communitarian views, which would require the complete re-shaping of the North American city. But as David Harvey observes, her own proposals, like Sandercock's, are quite as wildly utopian and 'naively specified in relation to the actual dynamics of urbanization'.[83] We are committed to assimilation in some shape or form by the very process of living together. This may happen by learning from the other, or by the process by which we internalise our enemies' traits. But the deepest threat to the maintenance of otherness is, as already mentioned, what Gregory Baum calls the power of secondary culture, the global power of the universal image makers which represents, as Marx said of the bourgeoisie, a truly revolutionary force.[84] The limits of this power, which knows no walls or ghettoes, have yet to be discovered.

If we can approach the question of community through the doctrine of God, equally can we through Christology. Human beings are understood in analogy with Jesus of Nazareth, the 'man for others'. This means, as Barth put it, that fellow humanity is fundamental to our being. 'Every supposed humanity which is not radically and from the very first fellow humanity is inhumanity.'[85] I am who I am in encounter. I am created to give and receive help to and from my neighbour, and thus to be human is to be committed to community. From this point of view theologians are bound to be sceptical of the possibilities of the company of strangers. When do we move from being strangers, erotically eyeing up one another, to being neighbours who help one another? A number of well publicised assaults in United States cities where large numbers of people have looked on but not intervened highlight the negative side of Young's heterogeneous, plural and playful public.

Another sceptical question to the critics of community is whether it is not the cultural logic of late capitalism which lurks behind much, if not all, postmodern theory and its respect for difference. Nietzsche is the avowed prophet of postmodernity, but he is also the prophet of the lonely individual, the man of 'azure isolation', at home only with the eagles and the strong winds. This view of humanity is congenial to competitive

[83] D. Harvey *Justice, Nature and the Geography of Difference* (Oxford: Blackwell, 1996), p. 312.
[84] G. Baum, 'Two Question Marks: Inculturation and Multiculturalism, *Concilium* 1994/2, pp. 101–6.
[85] K. Barth,*Church Dogmatics* III/2 (Edinburgh: T&T Clark, 1960), p. 228.

capitalism, which has no time for community save in so far as it keeps people docile. Does 'openness to unassimilated otherness' amount to much more than the individualism of liberal late capitalist society? – a question Young faces but does not, to my mind, answer satisfactorily.

When we speak of 'community' theologically, we speak of the Church. Christ calls into a being a fellowship, a 'body'. True, this is understood as a pilgrim people, leading a marginal existence, but it also has a sacramental significance for humanity as whole. If this were not the case the Church could not be the witness to human salvation and the place where this is sacramentally realised. We can understand this sacramental significance, vis à vis the built environment, in six dimensions, as pointing to what Kjellberg calls an 'emancipatory koinonia'.[86]

To begin with the Church is always first and foremost a *local* community, globally networked. What are or were called in Latin America 'base communities' are the building blocks of the Church. True community begins in the face to face, but looks outward to the entire *oikumene*, the whole inhabited earth. In this respect Church is sacramental for human community at large. No church, not even a cathedral, can be too large, indeed churches have always manifested the self limiting principles of ancient Greek cities, hiving off to form new settlements when they grow too large. Mumford's objections to the 'shapeless giantism' of the great city have a real point. It is essential to begin small, to act local and think global. This is indicated by the fact that industry already seems to be discovering the limits of telecommuting in that it cuts out 'synergy', the creative interaction which happens in face to face meeting. 'There is no substitute', the Goodmans remarked, 'for the spontaneous social conflux whose atoms unite, precisely, as citizens of a city.'[87] At the same time it is at the local level that the alienating structures of the city, bound up with bureaucracy, are dealt with. Writing of the African city Aylward Shorter speaks of the base ecclesial communities as crossing inner frontiers and tending toward anti structure – resisting institutionalisation in the interests of freedom and equality.[88]

The base community or parish principle, what Kirkpatrick Sale calls 'human scale', has long been recognised to have implications for town planning. Thus the American town planner Clarence Perry was already recommending 'neighbourhood units' of 3,000 to 9,000 people in the 1930s. The theory was that a neighbourhood should be small enough

[86] S. Kjellberg, *Urban EcoTheology* (Utrecht: International Books, 2000), p. 84.
[87] Goodman and Goodman, *Communitas*, p. 51.
[88] A. Shorter, *The Church in the African City* (Maryknoll: Orbis, 1991) pp. 106, 108.

for everything to be within walking distance, but large enough to support an elementary school, local stores and services. A contemporary variation of this suggests streets laid out on rectangular grids to provide maximum connectivity, and the slowing down of traffic to enable people of diverse backgrounds to meet frequently, informally and for different purposes.[89] The theory is excellent, but we have yet to learn how to realise it on the ground. Both the post Second World War British New Towns, and Milton Keynes, were built on these principles, and none of them are remarkable for a sense of community. If we ask why, we can of course point to developments which keep people at home – increasing comfort, home 'entertainment', increased mobility, long working hours – but I suspect it is more in terms of the lack of common purpose, a theme to which I shall return. Planted communities like these differ from 'organic' communities which sprang up to meet particular needs, whether of trade, railway building, mining, fishing, or farming. These needs gave people common tasks and purposes which generated intense pride and commitment.[90] The problem of the New Towns is the problem of the suburb – leisure, refuge, escape is the purpose, and this is inadequate to generate community.

Postmodern accounts of cities of difference emphasise the fact that individuals no longer have one single location, but may have several, and that rather than the city being a mosaic of spatially discrete worlds, there are multiple grids within which identity is formed.[91] People live in one place, work in another, and take their leisure in another. This is true, but the micro politics of education, health, transport, and even street design, remains obstinately local.[92] We have, increasingly, to fight for service provision on a local basis. In this respect the importance of the local remains, especially for children, the elderly and their carers, as also for the disabled.

---

[89] Smith, Whiteleg and Williams, *Greening*, p. 173.

[90] The Radio Ballads, put together by Ewan MacColl and Robert Parker, made for the BBC between 1959 and 1970, documenting the lives of people in railways, mining, fishing, road building and other industries, instantiated this.

[91] G. Pratt, 'Grids of Difference', in R. Fincher and J. M. Jacobs (eds.), *Cities of Difference* (New York: Guilford, 1998), p. 27.

[92] Graham Ward argues, in *Cities of God* (London: Routledge, 2000), that the world of Cyberspace renders earlier incarnational and liberation theologies inadequate as a response. He develops a subtle mapping of physical and corporate bodies, all caught up in the body of Christ. He rejects MacIntyre's communitarianism, but puts in its place a 'revised' communitarianism more open to difference. It is difficult to see, however, what this difference would look like in the actual dynamics of community as lived out day by day.

Secondly, Church lives by *memory and tradition*. William Blake, in that great poem of theological geography, *Jerusalem*, calls the cathedral cities of England the 'Friends of Albion': 'Gloucester and Exeter and Salisbury and Bristol, and benevolent Bath' (*Jerusalem* 40:61). What he has in mind by this, I believe, is something like what the Catholic theologian Johannes Metz called a 'dangerous memory'. Like Israel, the Church exists by relating the past to the present. In the eucharist, for example, contemporary Christians find their orientation for living by recalling deeply obscure events which happened in a small, if troublesome, middle eastern city two thousand years ago. In doing this, I would say, they provide a paradigm for society as a whole. Memory loss is a pathology. For Blake the cathedral cities were friends of Albion because they had at their heart a building, an institution, whose function it was to recall the truth of those events 2000 years ago in Palestine and their significance: the priority of peace and justice. But do they? In his day he believed that the friends of Albion were threatened by their dedication to 'druid worship', the addiction to human sacrifice implicit in the Napoleonic wars and in a criminal justice system which constantly sent the poor to the gallows. Today 'druid worship' is still national defence, but still more consumerism. Church exists sacramentally within society to protest against druid worship, but also to instantiate the central significance of memory and tradition in a world where mobility is prized and indeed expected.[93] One of the problems of New Towns is that they have no corporate memory. When a new town was built around the small agricultural community of Stevenage, the community soon divided, the one with one set of memories, the other with memories from elsewhere which could not be simply superimposed on the new place. Memory and tradition depend on rootedness. As Simone Weil argued, early on in the Second World War, human beings do not survive without roots. As we have seen, the average American stays in a place for five years.

Repeated millions of times, the decision to move out robs communities of their memories and their social relationships. It leaves them shallow rooted, ill equipped to provide their residents with sustenance during hard times. Sociologists have discovered that longtime residents make a disproportionately large contribution to a community; they do much to define its character and create a sense of continuity. 'Any human relationship takes time for seasoning, for testing, for the kind of slow, casual knitting that will not break apart under the first signs

---

[93] As in the notorious advice of Norman Fowler to the unemployed under the Thatcher administration: 'On yer bike!'

of strain', John Killinger writes. Rapid mobility . . . 'does not afford the kind of time – years and years of time – that are necessary to become rooted in a place, to really know the neighbours, to truly belong to the community, to celebrate the great milestones of life that can be celebrated in a home church or synagogue, to feel, deeply and responsibly, that there is a bond between ourselves and the land, ourselves and the house, ourselves and the neighbourhood, that nourishes and replenishes our beings'.[94]

Thirdly, Church is the community *where sin is recognised and forgiveness asked for*. It is not an ideal community: Augustine's struggle with Pelagius in the fifth century was precisely over the destructiveness of idealising ways of thought. It is the community of forgiven sinners, but a community on the way to an eschatological goal. Part of the problem with the notion of community has been its idealisation, the power of the image projected by Mary Mitford, effectively without conflict. This is the downside of the romanticism I praised earlier on. In relation to development work Smit argues that 'the notion of a community is always something of a myth. A community implies a consensus. The reality is that communities, more often than not, are made up of an agglomeration of factions and interest groups often locked in competitive relationships'[95] But does community imply consensus? It did not in the earliest church communities we know, in Corinth, Galatia or Rome – far from it. A community which lives by sin and forgiveness is not a community of consensus, but a community which has found a way of coping with conflict and difference. As Laurie Green puts it, God does not despise difference, but creates it.[96] This is similar to the community Young and Sennett want, but unlike Young it seems to me that the network of face to face groups she mentions are the only place such negotiation can happen.

The question of consensus is raised in the sharpest form by the politics of identity. As Andrew Hake has argued, the task of the Church in plural societies is to both support and radically criticise the framework which holds a plural society together, but also to be an active protagonist for minority-group positions. The theological ground for this is the Noachic covenant which embraces all humankind.[97] Without this community degenerates into communalism, in which community is pitted against community.

---

94 Langdon, *Better Place*, p. 76.
95 Quoted in J. Abbott, *Sharing the City* (London, Earthscan, 1996), pp. 119–20.
96 L. Green, *The Impact of the Global* (London: Church House, 2000), p. 45.
97 A. Hake, 'Theological Reflections on "Community"', in A. Harvey (ed.), *Theology in the City* (London: SPCK, 1989) p. 53.

Fourthly, *justice* is essential to community, as the prophets of Israel always maintained. Justice, in their understanding, was what ensured that all Israelites had their rightful share in the land which was gifted to all, and that it was not cornered for the few. Christologically it refers to what is demanded for human beings by the fact that all are sisters and brothers of the Human One. Conditions which degrade some at the expense of others contravene that demand. Pragmatically speaking it is also true that a society which contains within it sharp inequalities in life chances and outcomes will be unstable since the have nots will wish to progress and the haves will protect their advantages.[98] As Moltmann puts it, the protected life of gated communities is pleasant but inhuman whilst the unprotected life of the slums is unpleasant but has more potential for human closeness and community. 'The surrender of the privileges of the rich', he comments, 'is not too high a price to pay for a humane society, with dignity and justice on both sides.'[99] But does not the prioritisation of difference preclude any agreement on justice – the situation Harvey illustrates in relation to Tompkins Park? By way of response Harvey turns to an argument of Engels, to the effect that though it was impossible to achieve philosophical agreement on the notion of the term there was nevertheless a widely accepted meaning which gave it 'political and mobilising power'. Acceptance of this understanding of justice would, he argued, cut through the potentially immobilising insistence on postmodern difference.[100] I believe we are less stymied by disputes about the nature of justice than Harvey allows. At the back of any notion of justice is the idea of human equality: there cannot be 'justice' between the freemen and slaves of Aristotle's Athens, for example. 'Justice' requires equal treatment of equals. The medieval theologians, writing in a profoundly hierarchical society, got round this by distinguishing between distributive and commutative justice, roughly, what is due to every person in virtue of their human needs, and what is due to them in virtue of their social status. Since the eighteenth century this distinction has been re-written in terms of what we have 'earned', what we contribute to society in terms of skill and expertise, and what we deserve by way of the responsibility we exercise. This distinction effectively serves to negate equality, and make it a purely notional matter. At the same time the discourse of rights has put equality at the forefront, constantly underlining the fact that it is deeply paradoxical to expect one person to live in a slum

[98] Smith, Whiteleg and Williams, *Greening*, p. 145.
[99] J. Moltmann, *Experiences in Theology* (London: SCM, 2000), p. 186.
[100] Harvey, *Justice*, p. 35.

or a bleak estate, and another in a gated suburb or mansion. Disputes about justice are often camouflage to obfuscate this paradox. Of course, it is quite unrealistic to expect equal treatment between equals to be honoured in the face of the legacy of ten millennia of inequality, written into the landscape. Since we can only have true community amongst equals this means that community is always going to be an unfinished project in any class divided society. For in relation to the built environment it is not justice but power which shapes the city and, as Harvey observes, finance capital can produce cityscapes from which the mass of the population are alienated in an unrecuperable way.[101] Nevertheless, as a goal to aim for, we need to extend to the built environment and to planning those structures and institutions, treating all alike and embodying serious concern for social justice, which Hake calls for as essential to any community's proper functioning.[102]

Related to this, and embracing the whole, is, fifthly, *common purpose*, the 'shared final ends' Young believes must be dropped from our credo. The Church exists in virtue of a common story and a common hope, but in doing so is it anything more than one shared interest group among many? Should this apply to the city, and if it does, does it oppressively eliminate difference? Kevin Lynch hoped that the city landscape could express the common hopes and pleasures of ordinary people, so that 'the sense of community may be made flesh'. 'Above all, if the environment is visibly organized and sharply identified, then the citizens can inform it with their own meanings and connections, then it will become a *place*, remarkable and unmistakeable.'[103] In practice the articulation of genuinely common hopes and pleasures is essential for the survival of the public places Young celebrates in the city, as the Tompkins Park story illustrates. Can we expect such an articulation in the postmodern city? Adrian Hastings talks of 'a rare moment of *communitas*' in Britain during the Second World War, precisely the time when class divisions were momentarily overcome by the need to resist a common enemy.[104] The community spirit in the former slums was probably generated by the need to help people tackle adverse conditions. Overcoming a common threat is also the key to the success of the village of Husa in Sweden, instanced by the authors of *Greening the Built Environment*. Faced with the collapse of a traditional industry, and a sharply dwindling population, the community took action

---

[101] Harvey, *Justice*, p. 278. Canary Wharf is, of course, a case in point.
[102] Hake, 'Theological Reflections', p. 56.
[103] K. Lynch, *The Image of the City* (Cambridge, Mass.: MIT 1960), pp. 91–2.
[104] A. Hastings, *A History of English Christianity 1920–1985* (London: Collins, 1986), p. 361.

by setting up fifteen cooperative enterprises. The key features of success are community action, participation, inclusiveness and the use of local resources and enterprises.[105] Victor Papanek gives the example of a park in which children never played being turned round, and made the centre of all sorts of community activities, by the simple device of erecting a glass shelter with four used washing machines and a dryer in the centre of it. Parents could then watch over their children and get on with chores at the same time.[106] Colin Ward documents the growth of a genuine spirit of community amongst people building their own houses. A member of the self build group in Lewisham said:

> The one thing that's left me intensely proud is the co-operative spirit on the Brockley site. A wife had a baby the other week. The buntings were out and the balloons ... If someone requires a babysitter ... if someone's working on a car ... or the communal garden ... they get help. They pay a pound a week to a communal fund. They've landscaped the gardens last year. No one tells them to do that. They do it themselves because they have control over where they are living and they contribute.[107]

In the postmodern context, with its 'collapse of meta narratives', is there any chance that huge populations will share a common project except in time of emergency? Were they to do so, what would it be? One answer, which still has great power, is civic pride, as instanced in the re-creation of Birmingham, England, over the past decade. People continue to be proud of their villages, towns and cities, and are increasingly prepared to fight when their integrity is threatened by purely commercial interests. Seppo Kjellberg has sought to promote patterns of dialogue between the various interest groups in Finnish cities, and believes that, at a time when the great meta narratives have been 'criticized to death', religion has a role in enabling people to feel integrated.[108] More globally, very considerable pressure was mobilised over the issue of Third World debt, and it may be that a similar movement will arise on the issue of the environment. In this respect Hans Küng's proposals for a global ethic, based on respect for both people and planet, may be a pointer for the future.[109] To the objection that this is too abstract a thing for people to commit themselves to, the answer is that what we are talking about is the sharing and safeguarding of the basic resources of life, and there is

---

[105] Smith, Whiteleg and Williams, *Greening*, p. 178.
[106] V. Papanek, *The Green Imperative* (London: Thames & Hudson, 1995), p. 194.
[107] C. Ward, *When We Build Again* (London: Pluto, 1985), p. 83.
[108] Kjellberg, *Urban EcoTheology*, p. 24.
[109] H. Küng and H. Schmidt, *A Global Ethic and Global Responsibilities* (London: SCM, 1998).

nothing more concrete than this. This global ethic is, of course, not by
any means identical with the gospel of the kingdom – far from it. But it
has many echoes and analogies in that gospel, and stands in a relation
of creative dialogue with it.

Finally, the Church is *semper reformanda*, always in the process of recreation and re-discovery. Though the Church lives by tradition and
memory it knows no final form, no fixed and forever pattern of ministry, no formulation of doctrine which cannot be revised. In this sense,
most importantly, it is sacramental for the human community at large.
Though we are committed to the attempt to construct community this
will always be fragile, always in need of re-invention. As the texts of
Isaiah, Ezekiel and Revelation all suggest, the full realisation of community will be eschatological. 'Failure' is something we must expect, and
some failures will, perhaps, teach us nothing, but this is not a cause for
cultural pessimism, for theses about the decline of the West, or any other
culture. Because community is an eschatological reality it is founded on
faith and hope, and therefore born afresh in each generation. Looking
at the history of community as articulated in the built environment there
are certainly milieux which make for it, and others which militate against
it. Like the town planners at the beginning of the twentieth century, we
have to seek to learn from these without simply mimicking the past. But
even the worst environments, like the East End slums, can sometimes be
places for supportive and nourishing community. In its story telling and
in its brokenness the Church remains a witness to both the possibility
and the centrality of community to the human journey. It looks forward
to the day Isaiah spoke of when

> They shall build houses and inhabit them:
> they shall plant vineyards and eat their fruit.
> They shall not build and another inhabit;
> they shall not plant and another eat;
> for like the days of a tree shall the days of my people be,
> and my chosen shall long enjoy the work of their hands.
>
> (Isa. 65.21–2)

CHAPTER 8

But is it art?

And in the spirit he carried me away to a great, high mountain and showed me the holy city Jerusalem coming down out of heaven from God. It has the glory of God and a radiance like a very rare jewel, like jasper, clear as crystal.

(Revelation 21.10–11)

The city is a fact in nature, like a cave, a run of mackerel or an ant heap, says Lewis Mumford. 'But it is also a conscious work of art, and it holds within its communal framework many simpler and more personal forms of art.'

Mind *takes form* in the city: and in turn, urban forms condition mind. For space, no less than time, is artfully reorganized in cities: in boundary lines and silhouettes, in the fixing of horizontal planes and vertical peaks, in utilizing or denying the natural site, the city records the attitude of a culture and an epoch to the fundamental facts of its existence. The dome and the spire, the open avenue and the closed court, tell the story, not merely of different physical accommodations, but of essentially different conceptions of man's destiny. The city is both a physical utility for collective living and a symbol of those collective purposes and unanimities that arise under such favouring circumstances. With language itself it remains man's greatest work of art.[1]

Jane Jacobs' great manifesto, *The Death and Life of Great American Cities*, was written to confute most of Mumford's contentions. In cities, she argued, we are dealing with life at its most complex and intense. 'Because this is so, there is a basic aesthetic limitation on what can be done with cities: *a city cannot be a work of art*.' She granted that art was needed in the arrangement of cities, but insisted on a distinction between art and life. When they were confused within cities, she said, you get not art but taxidermy.[2] Nicholas Habraken argues that 'no living town is beautiful

---

[1] L. Mumford, *The Culture of Cities* (London, Secker & Warburg, 1938), p. 5 (my italics).
[2] J. Jacobs, *The Death and Life of Great American Cities* (Harmondsworth: Penguin, 1994), p. 386 (my italics).

193

in the way a work of art is'. The beauty of a town is more like the beauty we find in nature – of plants, rocks, people. 'When we think a town is beautiful we mean something else . . . that we can identify with it, that in the shape we see we can encounter the inhabitants, that we feel a confrontation with daily life.'[3]

Can the built environment be a work of art? Should it be? And does theology have anything to say on the matter? I shall argue that every city – indeed every village and suburb – has its aesthetic, a particular quality to its urban space. In this sense I wish to argue that every settlement can be considered a work of art, which does not preclude there being bad art. As we saw in the second chapter, in the story about public parks in Calcutta, the question of aesthetics is not irrelevant to the question of human liberation, to what promotes fullness of life.

Aesthetics and ethics therefore come together. Settlements as art, however, obviously have certain peculiarities. Like a piece of sculpture, they are embodied art, but they are also, like a play or a symphony, *temporal art*, extended over time – in the case of Jerusalem, Rome or Athens, well over two millennia.[4] In that case they are not the work of one person or even of one community, but the work of many communities, often with different understandings of what it means to be human. At the same time this historical collage embodies corporate memory: the understanding of the human project of past generations continues to speak to us through the buildings that remain and the very layout of the streets. And apart from odd places like Carcassonne or Nablus, which become empty shells, settlements go on changing over time. They are palimpsests. A settlement which stands completely still is dead. To be alive is to write contemporary meanings into our environment. The question is, can we agree what they are?

THEOLOGY, ART AND FORM

Ernst Fischer defined art, using a term with an Aristotelian pedigree, as 'the giving of form.'[5] The architect Christopher Day uses straightforwardly theological categories in describing art as the imbuing of matter with spirit.[6] Fischer and Day's accounts of art correspond to the two different creation stories at the beginning of Genesis. In the beginning,

3 N. Habraken, *Housing Supports: An Alternative to Mass Housing* (London: The Architectural Press, 1972), p. 32.
4 K. Lynch, *The Image of the City* (Cambridge, Mass.: MIT, 1960), p. 1.
5 E. Fischer, *The Necessity of Art* (Harmondsworth: Penguin, 1963), p. 8.
6 C. Day, *Places of the Soul* (London: Thorsons, 1999), p. 25.

according to the first Genesis narrative, God ordered the chaos and darkness. The six days of creation represent the giving of form to 'space' – the void. When we say that a cosmos emerges from chaos we mean that there is now some discernible order, pattern and unity in place of the *tohu ve bohu* – everything random and without meaning. Wim Wenders' *Himmel über Berlin* shows the same process happening to the marshes which originally covered the site of that city, and the same could be said for any human settlement above a refugee camp.

The second Genesis narrative envisages, in Day's words, the imbuing of matter with spirit, and therefore, on that understanding of art, characterises God as the archetypal artist. It would be possible then to argue, as some 'back to nature' theorists and deep ecologists seem to imply, that the less humankind interfere with this work of art the better. Alternatively it can be argued that human beings, in virtue of possessing 'spirit', share in the divine creativity. It is frequently remarked that in the contemporary world art has become a substitute for the transcendent. The valid reason for this (and it is a cultural movement which theology cannot endorse) is that human spirit responds to divine Spirit, and that in art, therefore, people do indeed sense rumours of angels or echoes of transcendence. As artists we do 'imbue matter with spirit' – one only has to look at some of the unfinished Michelangelo sculptures to see that. On a grander scale still some such understanding inspired Abbot Suger, the builder of Chartres, and doubtless countless other unknown medieval builders.

Neither of these understandings of what constitutes art is quite identical with the process which Wolterstorff, probably rightly, identifies as the typical Western understanding of the artist. He traces that back to Augustine's understanding of God as giving free untrammelled expression to his inner self by bringing into existence new realities.[7] But giving form, and imbuing matter with spirit, as I have just described it, are rather more modest activities. At least as far as human creation goes they imply respect for given materials. They are not Promethean.

In describing art as the giving of 'form' I follow what I believe to be Aquinas' meaning as the imparting of significant shape to words, sound or matter. This understanding of form seems to me to avoid the critique of the concept developed by Heidegger.[8] Form, he pointed out, was conventionally contrasted with content, and when applied to art suggested that what really mattered was not the form at all, but the meaning hidden

---

7 N. Wolterstorff, *Art in Action* (Carlisle: Solway, 1997), p. 51.
8 M. Heidegger, *Basic Writings* (London: Routledge, 1978), pp. 151 ff.

in the work of art, as in Hegel's discussion of representation and concept, in which the former is only an inferior prelude to the latter. Heidegger wants to find a way to allow the work of art to speak as a whole, just as it is, and not with the presupposition of a concealed appeal to its meaning, so that the truth of art is just that, and not something it is 'saying'. In the same way, we can say, buildings do not make assertions.[9]

The protest against regarding art as a stepping stone to the 'really real' world of the concept is entirely justified, but it does not make the concept of form any the less inescapable. In his discussion of the Greek temple as a work of art Heidegger talks of the temple 'fitting together', 'gathering around itself a unity of paths and relations', and of the carvings 'entering into their distinctive shapes'. He is talking of form emerging from the givenness of material rather than being mere passive matter for the artist's intentionality. We recall Loos' comment about the peasant house which 'emerges from the hand of God'. This respect for matter does not mean we can eliminate intentionality. On the contrary, intentionality is implied in the very idea of art. What Heidegger's protest can teach us is that in the best art, as in vernacular building, let us say, there is a dialectic between material and intention, so that both in-form the other.

The doctrine of creation from nothing implies a break with Plato, but what Augustine still took from that tradition was his concern for order, proportion, shape and number. In this tradition it was believed that geometrical forms and ratios could lead human beings beyond the world of appearance to the ultimate divine order, and this was part of the inspiration of early Gothic building (though there is also a romanticism about Gothic which goes beyond this).[10] Even more important, and the heart of the Gothic aesthetic according to Otto von Simson, was the belief that all light radiates from some primary source of radiance and glory. This accounts for the glorious windows of Gothic churches. The light of the windows in Chartres, for example, was not just beautiful, but was regarded as a sacrament and analogy for God.[11] We are unlikely to subscribe to this metaphysic, but the moment we think about it we can see that the way in which light is used is a key aspect of the built

---

9 K. Harries, *The Ethical Function of Architecture* (Cambridge, Mass.: MIT, 1998), p. 88, summarising Roger Scruton.
10 The twentieth century architect Le Corbusier shared this view, believing that the proper use of geometry could help bring about human integration. C. Le Corbusier, *Towards a New Architecture* (London: The Architectural Press, 1965), pp. 20ff.
11 O. von Simson, *The Gothic Cathedral* (London: Routledge and Kegan Paul, 1956), pp. 50–5. The source of this kind of thinking was Pseudo Dionysius, 'The Divine Names', ch. 4 in Pseudo Dionysius, *The Complete Works* (New York: Paulist, 1987). Wolterstorff comments on the importance of light in urban spaces. *Art in Action*, p. 181.

environment, on the larger scale as well as in the design of dwellings. What would London be without the winter sunlight on its pale stone, or Delhi without the dawn light? If we think of the beauty of any village we know well, places of deep shade will inevitably play a key part. In the play of light and shade there is an essential movement of activity and repose without which we are not whole.[12]

In the thirteenth century, as the city began to gain in importance over the cathedral, Aristotle took his place alongside Plato, and his idea of the form which actualises substance became central.[13] This actualisation is close to what Heidegger means by the world 'worlding' itself. Form, for St Thomas, was at the heart of ideas of the beautiful. God is beautiful, and all creation shares to some extent in that beauty. There is, therefore, an ontological beauty to created reality to be explained by its origin in God. Created form – say, the form of a village street or a city square – taps into that ontological beauty. In his *Commentary on the Divine Names* Thomas says: 'Beauty is a participation in the first cause, which makes all things beautiful. So that the beauty of creatures is simply a likeness of the divine beauty in which things participate.'[14] The divine beauty is creative because it produces order and harmony, and 'it is always the case that whatever creatures may have in the way of communion and coming together, they have it due to the power of beauty . . . beauty is the effective cause of being and the exemplary cause of the created world'.[15] Compare this with Heidegger's idea that art causes matter 'to come forth for the very first time'.

George Pattison contrasts a natural theology of art, based on humankind's natural endowments and capacities, and as such outside the sphere of grace, with one based on redemption. In the context of the theological framework which I argued for in the first chapter this distinction is impossible, as Pattison himself seems to demonstrate. He rightly denies the dualities of natural form and transcendent truth. What we think, feel, see, say, do or make 'enhances our capacity to affirm

---

[12] Colour is an essential part of the aesthetic of the built environment. Places have their own distinctive hues, depending on the quality of the local stone or brick. 'Paris is grey; San Francisco is white.' In Jerusalem the facing of buildings with Jerusalem stone is law. S. Kostoff, *The City Shaped* (London: Thames & Hudson, 1991), p. 319. The difference it makes to emotional tone can be seen by contrasting the interior of Salisbury Cathedral (Purbeck, cold and blue) with the interior of Norwich (Caen stone, warm and pink).

[13] Cf. Aquinas, in the *Summa Contra Gentiles* (II.54.6): 'In things composed of matter and form, neither the matter nor the form nor even being itself can be termed that which is. Yet the form can be called "that by which it is", inasmuch as it is the principle of being; the whole substance itself, however, is "that which is". And being (*esse*) itself is that by which the substance is called a being (*ens*).'

[14] U. Eco, *The Aesthetics of Thomas Aquinas* (London: Hutchinson, 1988), p. 30.   [15] Ibid., p. 28.

ourselves, our fellow human beings and our world as God's good gift in creation'.

To the extent that we are able to make such affirmations we stand already within the circle of redemption and of the fulfilment of the original judgement on creation: that God saw that it was good. Such movements of aesthetic enhancement of life constitute an awakening to the lure to participate in the divine dance 'from glory to glory advancing' – and this is no less so when the content of such a movement is predominantly sensuous and material.[16]

This is to understand redemption in the Irenaean perspective and, rightly, to see its profound integration with creation.

The views about beauty which Thomas developed from the work of his teachers were, as Henry Adams, von Simson and Panofsky have all argued, instantiated in stone and glass in the medieval cathedrals. A little later, in northern and central Italy, we have the creation of the great city centres which extend the argument into the secular arena. On the Platonic understanding this concern is not 'merely' aesthetic but also ethical. Plato had argued in *The Republic* that beauty, which is measure, form and order, makes an impact on our souls. *The Republic* is essentially an inquiry into how to bring justice and beauty into human life together, and for Plato justice and beauty resemble one another, in that both involve proper order and relation. Justice was a matter of right relations both between the different parts of the community and the different parts of the individual soul. What today we might call integrity or 'being a whole person' was essential, in his view, to the well being of the community: a community of fragmented, disordered selves could not possibly be just. It is precisely the next move which is contentious, or even demonstrably untrue, however. For the implication would appear to be that beautiful architecture and music produces well ordered people, and vice versa, something we know to be false. For though high crime rates are correlated to poor environments, the fault is not with the environment as such, but with the social forces which create and sanction them. And on the other hand, it is quite possible to live in the heart of Venice or Siena, let's say, and be a fascist. No simple relationship between ethics and environment can be established.

Whilst this is indisputable it is also true that the human soul cries out for the nourishment of beauty, and this has implications for the overall vision of a society.[17] Medieval cities, and some Indian and Arab cities, had

---

[16] G. Pattison, *Art, Modernity and Faith* (London: SCM, 1998), p. 135.
[17] A concern for beauty is, says Harries, 'part of all human experience'. *Function*, p. 20.

religion as an artistic unifier. Eric Gill believed this was essential to artistic success. For him the great periods of art were the great periods of religion, and demanded a 'unanimous society with universal acceptance of a final cause outside material life which pervaded, directed and ruled it'.[18] I have already spoken of the ambiguity of religion, and the contemporary world offers plenty of examples of the way in which it can dehumanise us. On the other hand it roots an aesthetic in an appeal to the transcendent, in other words to an overall purpose and meaning. But today, 'marketplace has replaced church as artistic unifier':

The advertising art, the background art, the display art of our commercial establishments, presented to us on radio, on television, in newspapers, on billboards, through loudspeakers, is what today constitutes the art of our tribe as a whole. Where once the spire of the cathedral or the steeple of the church gave the first glimpse of city or village, today it is the Sears and Hancock buildings.[19]

This change in values raises the question of form and function. The dictum that 'form follows function' presupposes that we have a good function in the first place, as the Goodmans argued after the Second World War.[20] 'Is the *function* good? Bona fide? Is it worthwhile? Is it worthy of a man to do that? What are the consequences? Is it compatible with other, basic, human functions? Is it a forthright or at least ingenious part of life? Does it make sense? Is it a beautiful function of a beautiful power?'[21] If the answer to these questions is 'No', as it is if the city is primarily market place, then we will not have beauty but on the contrary something which oppresses human beings, for this vision of the world leaves aside the question of justice and of shared ends. Without question our overall view of the meaning of life determines our built environment, as we can see by looking at medieval, Baroque and industrial cities. The Platonic unity of ethics and aesthetics is a fact of life. More prosaically, we get the architecture we deserve, and today, at worst, we have what Harries

[18] E. Gill, *The Necessity of Belief* (London: Faber & Faber, 1936), p. 337.
[19] Wolterstorff, *Art in Action*, p. 23.
[20] James Vance points out that the idea that form follows function was hardly an invention of the Bauhaus. Most earlier buildings instantiated it. 'In vast periods of human history, building has been predicated entirely on fulfilling a particular function in terms of the best technology then available.' J. E. Vance, Jnr, *The Continuing City* (Baltimore: Johns Hopkins University Press, 1990), p. 19. Papanek claims that the nineteenth century sculptor Horatio Greenough coined the phrase, and that it later became the guiding principle for the Viennese and German art and craft movements and only then for the Bauhaus. V. Papanek, *The Green Imperative* (London: Thames & Hudson, 1995), p. 147.
[21] P. Goodman and P. Goodman, *Communitas: Means of Livelihood and Ways of Life* (New York: Random House, 1960), p. 19.

has called a 'playboy architecture', expressive of our ruling hedonism, or lack of purpose.[22]

If the question of value is at the heart of aesthetics, then education is vital for its recognition. Kevin Lynch talks of the 'legibility' of a cityscape: the ease with which its parts can be recognised and can be organised into a coherent pattern. For him the shape of the city is part of that education in attention which is central to the ethics of Simone Weil and Iris Murdoch:

> In the development of the image, education in seeing will be quite as important as the reshaping of what is seen. Indeed, they together form a circular, or hopefully a spiral, process: visual education impelling the citizen to act upon his visual world, and this action causing him to see even more acutely. A highly developed art of urban design is linked to the creation of a critical and attentive audience. If art and audience grow together, then our cities will be a source of daily enjoyment to millions of their inhabitants.[23]

Here the assumed relation is between the development of critical faculties and political acumen, but it is even more true of our wider spiritual life. Escape from the banality which threatens to envelop us (not least in church) is impossible without such education.

Christopher Day argues that we have become used to the idea that money may be spent to beautify places for recreation and leisure but that places of work or for practical activities should be shaped by utilitarian considerations. 'The implication is that if half one's life is spent as efficiently but inartistically as possible, the other half is free to be artistic and inefficient.'[24] The problem with this is that it is unsatisfying to, and ultimately damages and trivialises, humankind's spiritual nature. We are so accustomed to invert the medieval order, and thus to either ignore or give secondary place to the reality of the spiritual, that it seems almost pietistic to make this point. In this regard the example of Rudolf Bahro, the East German socialist and Green activist, is instructive. Towards the end of his life Bahro, a life long atheist, came to believe that only a new spirituality could deal with the death wish of Western technocracy. Far from being an optional extra he saw that 'spirituality', what is often now called 'the imaginary', is actually what shapes our world. Christopher Day challenges his readers to find an ecologically healthy place which is not also beautiful, by which he means nourishing to the spirit. This definition of the beautiful seems to me more

---

[22] Harries, *Function*, p. 3.   [23] Lynch, *Image*, p. 120.   [24] Day, *Places*, p. 26.

helpful in relation to the built environment than one derived from the tradition of contemplation. We cannot expect to experience the same aesthetic delight in a village or city street that we do when regarding a Botticelli painting, but we certainly know when they are nourishing to the spirit. 'For too long', says Day, 'townscape has been dominated by the accidental consequence of compartmentalized accommodations of material needs.' Can we, he asks, as shapers of the built environment, offer as wide and symbiotic a range of spirit nourishment as can healthy landscapes?[25]

For a proper understanding of how the spiritual shapes our world we need what David Harvey has called a 'utopianism of social process'. The Victorian visionaries like Howard, Geddes or Unwin all believed that the key to social problems was the right social form, in so doing privileging things and spatial forms over social process. What is needed, on the other hand, is a recognition of how the material embeddedness of spatial structures stands in tension with the fluidity of social – and therefore spiritual – processes.[26] We have to seek what Lefebvre calls a 'pedagogy of space'. 'To build a few blocks of flats that are spiral in form by adding a handful of curves to the usual concrete angularities', says Lefebvre, 'is not an entirely negligible achievement – but neither does it amount to very much.'

To take inspiration from Andalusia, and demonstrate a sensual use of curvatures, spirals, arabesques and inflexions of all kinds, so achieving truly voluptuous spaces, would be a different matter altogether. *Neither the plant world nor the mineral world has as yet delivered itself of all the lessons it holds regarding space and the pedagogy of space.*[27]

This is profoundly theologically suggestive, for what the Christian scriptures present us with is an account of the pedagogy of the Spirit. Too often this has been read on a purely intellectual level, but Lefebvre rightly argues that such a pedagogy is at the same time, and necessarily, a pedagogy of space, of the built environment. What do we learn when we look at the environment we actually have? Different forms of settlement – village, town, city, suburb – all have their own aesthetic, but there is also an overlap in aesthetic categories between them. I shall try to understand these on the lines of a theological aesthetic through creation, *nahalah* or stakeholding, power and community.

[25] Ibid., p. 182.
[26] D. Harvey, *Justice, Nature and the Geography of Difference* (Oxford: Blackwell, 1996), pp. 418–19.
[27] H. Lefebvre, *The Production of Space* (Oxford: Blackwell, 1991), p. 397 (my italics).

THE AESTHETICS OF CREATION

Part of the perennial appeal of Gothic is its use of natural form – the tracery of leaves, the lines of trees and branches.[28] Earlier we saw Simon Fairlie's dictum that 'nature abhors a straight line'. The natural world – trees, plants, rivers, coastlines, hills – is sinuous and uneven. As human-kind's primeval environment, it invites imitation, contrasting with the severe lines imposed on buildings and landscapes by human will. Mumford made a fundamental distinction between organic and mechanical forms of growth, which corresponds, to some extent, with romantic and rationalistic approaches to society, and therefore to art.[29] Part of the contrast between organic and planned is the contrast between Gothic and classical aesthetics.[30] Norberg-Schulz distinguishes romantic, cosmic and classical city forms. Gothic is the essence of the former, where space is topological rather than geometrical and the basic configuration is the dense and indeterminate cluster and the free and varied row. Nature is what provides the inspiration. Islamic architecture instantiates the second, shunning sculptural presence and tending to dematerialised forms, whilst Greek architecture with its imageability and articulate order instantiates the last. In practice, he notes, most cities combine all three.[31] In his view, 'all cities ... have to possess something of all these categories of meaning to make urban dwelling possible'.[32]

The principle underlying organic growth, says Christopher Day, is that the physical form grew out of activities, out of the meeting of users and environment.[33] This had two senses. In the first place, Sitte associated the pleasingness of organic design with the *social* use of city form. His

[28] Most obvious in windows, and above all the 'Jesse window', depicting Christ's descent from Jesse in tracery.

[29] In chapter 4 I quoted Adolf Loos' encomium on the peasant house. The passage goes on: 'Ah, what is that? A false note in this harmony. Like an unwelcome scream. In the centre, beneath the peasants' homes which were created not by them but by God, stands a villa. Is it the product of a good or bad architect? I do not know. I only know that peace, tranquillity and beauty are no more ... Why does the architect both good and bad violate the lake? Like almost every town dweller, the architect possesses no culture. He does not have the security of the peasant to whom this culture is innate. The town dweller is an upstart. I call culture that balance of inner and outer man which alone can guarantee rational thought and action. 'Architecture, 1910' in *The Architecture of Adolf Loos*, an Arts Council exhibition (London: Arts Council, 1985), p. 8.

[30] Perhaps the major contrast in understandings of beauty in the built environment is between those for whom 'beautiful' is equivalent to 'broad and straight' (classical) and those for whom it means sinuous, small scale and detailed. Cf. Kostoff's remarks on the differences between fifteenth century Siena and Florence (*City*, p. 70).

[31] C. Norberg-Schulz, *Genius Loci* (New York: Rizzoli, 1980), pp. 68–76. In particular the Gothic cathedral united romantic and cosmic qualities and the Baroque garden palace cosmic and classical.

[32] Ibid., p. 77.   [33] Day, *Places*, p. 95.

preference for public squares, and the right choice and disposition of structures in and around them, rested on the perception that they had to serve a vital purpose for community life. But secondly he also liked the irregularities in old planning because 'they were not conceived on the drafting board but developed gradually *in natura*, allowing for all that the eye notices *in natura* and treating with indifference that which would be apparent only on paper'.[34] 'Nature' also provided the context for the whole.[35] Of course appeals to 'nature' can be a mask for all forms of historical prejudice, but there are good grounds, as Lefebvre also suggests, for once again learning to read what the medieval theologians called the 'book of nature' and making use of those lessons in the built environment.[36] As the outcome of this pedagogy Lefebvre anticipated the creation (or production) of a planet wide space as 'the social foundation of a transformed everyday life open to myriad possibilities'.[37] Hitherto there is little enough evidence for that, but it would be part of the unlearning of that art which has, since at least the seventeenth century, been a manifestation of the *libido dominandi* – a theme I shall return to in the next chapter.

Beginning with the rise of picturesque in the eighteenth century there grew up a theory of 'organic' architecture and planning. Many older towns supposedly followed the tracings of the cows' path, which produced, according to Mumford, a more economical and sensible layout than that of planned towns.[38] 'In organic planning one thing leads to another and what began as a seizure of an accidental advantage may

[34] C. Sitte, *City Planning According to Artistic Principles* (London: Phaidon, 1965; first published Vienna, 1889), p. 50. Sitte argued that city planning should not be merely a technical matter, but 'in the truest and most elevated sense' an artistic enterprise. (pp. 3–4). He meant this in a romantic, anti formal sense. 'To approach everything in a strictly methodical manner', he said, 'and not to waver a hair's breadth from preconceived patterns, until genius has been strangled to death and joie de vivre stifled by the system – that is the sign of our time ... We have at our disposal three major methods of city planning, and several subsidiary types. The major ones are the gridiron system, the radial system and the triangular system ... Artistically speaking, not one of them is of any interest, for in their veins pulses not a single drop of artistic blood' p. 91).
[35] Ibid., p. 16. Sitte's ideas currently enjoy renewed approbation, but Harvey reminds us that Sitte turned to Wagner for spiritual inspiration, and the spaces Sitte championed and created, specifically for the purpose of re-awaking the sense of community, lent themselves to fascism. 'The dramatic spectacles of the sort the Nazis organized certainly brought space alive and managed to appeal to a deep mythology of place, symbolizing "community", but community of a most reactionary sort.' D. Harvey, *The Condition of Postmodernity* (Oxford: Blackwell, 1989), p. 277.
[36] So Harries, *Function*, pp. 114, 133 in an argument which echoes Barth's suspicion of natural theology, but also endorses the medieval view.
[37] Lefebvre, *Production*, p. 397.
[38] L. Mumford, *The City in History* (Harmondsworth: Penguin, 1991), p. 346. It is true that, as he points out, the imposition of straight lines on hilly sites like San Francisco puts 'a constant tax' on human energy (p. 482).

prompt a strong element in a design which an a priori plan could rule out.'[39] The organic approach, then, 'springs out of the total situation', and works cooperatively with the 'materials of others', perhaps guiding them, but first acknowledging their existence and understanding their purpose.[40] In the organic view the city was 'enveloped by sky and earth, at once nurtured and held in check by this primordial frame'.[41] Responding to these principles architects influenced by the picturesque adapted their building to the terrain, as in Bath after 1727, and in Edinburgh after 1767, or introduced deliberate breaks in rectilinearity as in Nash's Regent Street. Sitte's references to the following of nature suggest a natural theology, but we need to use that term with care. It should not suggest the attempt to elaborate a theology independently of revelation. On the contrary, it represents here the attempt to discern and respond to the revelation of God in creation.[42] Had Sitte and Mumford read the evidence correctly, however?

In his great history of form in architecture, *The City Shaped*, Spiro Kostoff calls organic theories into question. Siena, for example, a copybook example of a supposedly 'organic' plan, has 'one of the most highly regimented designs of medieval urbanism'.[43] In most cities, he argues, the organic and the planned are jumbled together. Roman cities in northern Europe, for example, were depopulated after the fifth century AD, and then slowly re-populated, a process which left the original grid scarcely visible. The organic analogy, Kostoff claims, can be traced to the rise of biology as a life science in the seventeenth century, but it is inept. Cities do not repair themselves, but are produced and repaired by human will.[44] What is really meant by 'organic' planning is planning that responds to its site – hill, river, sea front – or to land division prior to settlement, as in Leeds; to the coming together of several villages, as Aristotle proposed, or to the process of piecemeal changes over centuries. The sum of all these processes can produce a built environment dramatically different to

---

[39] Ibid., p. 347.   [40] Ibid., p. 450.   [41] Kostoff, *City*, p. 324.

[42] In *Cities of God* (London: Routledge, 2000) Graham Ward detects a natural theology in Le Corbusier's belief in 'universal laws that govern us and all our actions', and in the famous chapel at Ronchamp (p. 41). To me these seem to be two different things. At Ronchamp Le Corbusier breaks dramatically from his normal mode, finding inspiration in the natural world. This is an 'organic' building. His geometricism is, as already noted, closer to the Neo Platonism of the twelfth and thirteenth centuries. Harries agrees, pointing out that Le Corbusier began as a disciple of Sitte, and at Ronchamp returned to him (*Function*, p. 276). On the other hand, Kostoff (*City*, p. 89) points out the Nazi passion for organic architecture, as instantiated by Reichow. His defence of organic architecture is reminiscent of Heidegger's account of the German farmhouse, and both show the danger of identifying what is 'natural' with the '*volk*', making of it an ideology.

[43] Kostoff, *City*, p. 10.   [44] Ibid., pp. 52–3.

that produced by imperial planners, and this is what Sitte and Mumford appealed to.

So called organic plans instantiate an aesthetic of *surprise*. Mumford cited Alberti: 'Within the heart of the town it will be handsomer not to have the streets straight but winding about several ways, backwards and forwards, like the course of a river.' Note, again, the appeal to a natural feature. Defence was part of this but it also meant that the passenger will 'at every step discover a new structure, and the front and door of every house will directly face the middle of the street' inviting an inspection of the richness of carved detail.[45] Against geometrised blocks Sitte defended 'the small incident, the twisted street, the rounded corner, the little planted oasis unexpectedly come upon'.[46] Wolterstorff notes that the failure to impart dramatic sequence to one's movements through a city, to introduce variety and unity right into the sequence of one's movements, renders it aesthetically poor.[47] The medieval city did this to a superlative degree. It also had the advantage of comparative smallness of scale and absence of traffic, and the whole was a system of limitations and boundaries. As Ruskin argued, in *The Stones of Venice*, attention to detail stretched even to the stones hidden from view. The craftsmen who built the city had, Mumford argued, an incomparable education of the senses in the fields or woods through which they walked to work or took the frequent holidays of medieval society. 'Aesthetic discipline might lack a name . . . but its fruits were everywhere visible.'[48]

The key to their aesthetic was, then, the marriage of town and country. It was this Howard wanted to recapture in his vision for the Garden City, built around a great park, layered with fields, and surrounded by green belt. Jerusalem was to be situated in Eden. Howard's model was not intended to be a suburb, but on the contrary to contain urban sprawl in a purposeful way, but the coming of mass transport changed this. Howard envisaged homes, farms and industry all clustered together, but the possibility of commuting led to zoning, and the Garden Cities effectively becoming dormitories. Their aesthetic qualities were essentially suburban. Geddes argued that the change from coal to electricity would lead to the slums being replaced by Garden Cities. 'Yet the old slum towns have largely passed away to be replaced by endless conurbations of suburbs . . . and the automobile exhaust is more of a menace than the coal smoke.'[49]

[45] Alberti, *The Ten Books of Architecture* (New York: Dover, 1986), p. 75; cf. Mumford, *City*, p. 351.
[46] Kostoff, *City*, p. 84.   [47] Wolterstorff, *Art in Action*, p. 181.   [48] Mumford, *City*, pp. 342–3.
[49] Goodman and Goodman, *Communitas*, p. 8.

The purest example of organic form is probably to be found in the village. These may sometimes be planned,[50] but in most cases they probably represent the sum of a multitude of human decisions, from the original one to settle there, to each decision about the adding of a new house, church, chapel or pub, each decision responding to natural features, the presence of a tree or a stream, and to established patterns of ownership. Can the result be considered art? These decisions were probably rarely consciously aesthetic. The result, however, said Charles Buls, mayor of Brussels at the end of the nineteenth century and a champion of the city's old quarters, is 'a peculiar charm for all who are not insensible to artistic impressions. They may not be called beautiful, but they are attractive; they please by that beautiful disorder that here results not from art but from chance.'[51] In most small villages in Europe the most imposing building is likely to be the church, and it remains important, even in a secular age, as the bearer of 'heritage', as telling the story of those who shaped this settlement before us. But fine buildings are not what make the beauty of a village. In Sladd, Laurie Lee's village, where the church is an unremarkable Victorian building, only the Squire's house really has artistic pretensions. Today, however, this does not stand out as one of the most attractive houses in the village. The beauty of the village, wrote Sharp, lies 'in the *form*, in the ground plan, which the buildings and natural objects together make'.[52] In his view form was the key aspect of the beauty of the built environment, and simplicity of form of the village. Sharp distinguished two types of village, roadside and square. The old roadside village, unlike ribbon development, which he loathed, 'begins definitely and ends definitely'. 'English roadside villages seem somehow to contain their road rather than to be merely a string of buildings pushed aside by it. The road may curve gently away from the straight or it may take a sharp and sudden turn; in either case the village is thereby transformed into a place.'[53] This may have been true in 1932, when it was written, but for many villages motor traffic has changed it for good. Sladd is a roadside village, now situated on a busy B road, with a line of traffic parked to allow the faithful to visit their shrines – school, pub and cottage. Whilst Sharp's comment may have been true when the road was white and rutted, tarmac, and the speed

[50] Milton Abbas, in Dorset, laid out by Capability Brown, is one example. Most British mining villages were built on the cheapest row plan by the mill owners.
[51] Cited in Kostoff, *City*, p. 84.
[52] T. Sharp, 'The English Village', in T. Sharp, F. Gibberd and W. Holford, *Design in Town and Village* (London: HMSO, 1953), p. 1.
[53] Ibid., p. 3.

with which you are forced to pass through it, have now transformed it into a rather straggly ribbon settlement.

The other type of village, which survives motor traffic much better, is built round the square, or the triangle at the junction of three roads. Drewsteignton, in Devon, is an example, with its classic combination of pubs, church and small shops and houses, the remaining houses reaching out like fingers down the hills on which it stands. The rural feeling of the village, Sharp argued, does not depend on any of those things that are popularly associated with it: flowering gardens, irregular, informal and quaint buildings, and so on. 'It seems to depend on much smaller and more subtle things, upon a certain modesty, a certain lack of the smooth, mechanical finish of the town, and above all upon the harmony of the material of its buildings with the countryside.'[54] In other words, he denies that an aesthetic of *charm* is at the heart of it, but rather one of *harmony*. Rapoport does not contradict this in saying that a village environment implies a variety of architecture and a degree of incoherence: different styles, materials of roof pitches, buildings at different angles, interesting and intimate groupings, natural vegetation, mixed age and income and lack of uniformity.[55] Incoherence and lack of uniformity by no means exclude harmony, the fittingness which Wolterstorff finds at the heart of art. Sharp is pointing to the same thing in speaking of the 'simplicity and unity, and dignity of thought' of old villages. Planners, he said, should pay great respect to the traditional features of form and appearance, springing from simplicity of function and smallness of scale. The traditional form of the village is so good for its purpose that even our new villages should be based on it.[56]

Part of the secret of village beauty is the way in which the ordinary buildings respect the environment, and differ according to local conditions and materials. They represent the vernacular writ large. In the Cotswold villages between Burford and Cirencester, in England, for example, what is beautiful is the way the settlements are sunk into their landscape, camouflaged, so that they seem to grow out of the soil rather

---

[54] T. Sharp, *Town and Countryside* (Oxford: Oxford University Press, 1932), p. 67.

[55] A. Rapoport, *The Meaning of the Built Environment* (Tucson: University of Arizona Press, 1990), p. 157.

[56] Cited in W. P. Baker, *The English Village* (London: Oxford University Press, 1953), p. 206. To Sharp's horror this was often threatened by popular taste. He put this question to the young planners he was training at the end of the Second World War: The parish council of an old agricultural village is proposing that the pond at one side of the village green should be made into a model yacht pond with a fountain in the middle, and that concrete paths and flower beds should be laid out round it. Set out your reasoned advice. 'Ninetyfive per cent elaborated their refinements of vulgarity to almost unendurable degrees' (ibid.).

than to be imposed on it. The villages of the Pennines, on the other hand, have the windswept clarity of upland light, the beauty of the moorland which surrounds them. The fishing villages on the east coast of Fife emerge from the rocks which form their small harbours, braced against the onshore winds, whilst the Cornish fishing villages nestle round their coves. In each case, according to Sharp, 'the essence of true village character and good village design is simply simplicity'.[57] In these ways they instantiate an aesthetics of creation, responding sympathetically to the environment, rather than trying to 'tame' it, which would be true, too, for the cities Kostoff discusses under 'organic' forms.

THE AESTHETIC OF *NAHALAH*

In the third chapter I mentioned the concept of *nahalah*, the idea that every family in Israel was a stakeholder, and could expect to settle 'under its vine and fig tree'. In the discussion of the human dwelling I mentioned the view that suburbia was perhaps the most perfect instantiation of this dream ever known. The suburban aesthetic is the most difficult to discuss, whether theologically or otherwise, and I have sought to comprehend it under this category. It draws inspiration from the rediscovery of gothic, and at its best seeks to evoke the village, but it remains essentially the aesthetic of the small owner, the individual marking out his or her plot, doing what they can with modest resources.

As there is no one city form, so there is no one suburban, but there are dominant features. Nash's Park Villages, built on the fringe of Regent's Park in 1824, were, it is generally agreed, a product of the picturesque movement in landscape gardening, and therefore a product of romanticism. They differ from the eighteenth century town house not in having a garden, for gardens had been a normal part of town life at least since medieval times, but in emphasising *difference*. They are self consciously romantic, expressing the ideal of *rus in urbe*. The same cultural turn which produced Walter Scott's novels produced the 1842 pattern book which offered, amongst others, 'burmese', 'egyptian', 'venetian', 'moriso', 'spanish' and Plantagenet Castle styles. Tudor gables were already being offered in the 1830s.[58] Later developments like Unwin's New Earswick were designed to recall village life, and trees and a brook were integrated into the design. As late as 1944 the Dudley report recommended

---

[57] Sharp, 'The English Village', p. 19.
[58] A. Edwards, *The Design of Suburbia* (London: Pembridge, 1981), pp. 13, 15.

sharawaggi, a word derived from a transliteration of the Chinese term for irregular gardening. The basis of sharawaggi was 'to plan irregularly, to disdain formality, to contrive beauties that shall be great and strike the eye, but without any order or disposition of parts as shall be commonly or easily observed, to improve a scene according to the manner suggested by itself, and without regard to symmetrical arrangement'. The report represented, says Edwards, a rediscovery of the principles of Sitte, an application of the landscape architect's preoccupation with 'genius loci'.[59] There are obvious affinities with organic planning. The difference between the organic towns of the middle ages and modern suburbia, says Kostoff, is that in the medieval town rich and poor lived side by side, whilst suburbs were effectively zoned by class.[60]

The problem for suburbia came in its increasing generalisation, and the need to provide mass housing at a relatively low cost. This produced an aesthetic which I will call *debased romanticism*. The rows and rows of Dunroamin's, Coniston's and Bidawee's border on kitsch if they do not actually instantiate it. The need to economise led to the penchant for weatherboarding, for creosoted boards to suggest mock Tudor, and renderings to allow for difference at modest expense. It was universally agreed to be a dull pattern of architecture, for penny pinching is almost inevitably dull in its results.

James Richards, who was a defender of suburbia, understood it as basically anarchic. 'It is typical of the suburban scene', he wrote, 'that it is an accumulation of trivialities; the novelties of this year are always being added to the novelties of last year, and these are always fading into insignificance until they are ready to emerge again in the character of the old and familiar things that we wondered at in childhood.'[61] He felt that this represented an authentic continuation of the picturesque tradition, continued by amateur gardeners, landscapists, decorators and handymen.[62] Twentieth century suburbia was, in his view, a response to a world made unsafe for self sufficiency. Suburban architecture is the attempt to create a kind of oasis in which everything can be accounted for and the unpredictable excluded.[63] The suburb gives to people a sense of belonging to a fairly sympathetic world and an opportunity of making

---

[59] Ibid., p. 156.   [60] Kostoff, *City*, p. 75.
[61] J. M. Richards, *Castles on the Ground: The Anatomy of Suburbia* (London: John Murray, 1973), p. 43. Cf. Hall: 'The suburban house was designed to express individuality; hence the bay window and the corner door, the great variation in very minor detail.' P. Hall, *Cities of Tomorrow* (Oxford: Blackwell, 1988), p. 79.
[62] Richards, *Castles*, p. 67.   [63] Ibid., p. 36.

out of that world something personal to themselves – an outlet for their idealistic and creative instincts.[64]

The early high class suburbs represented a reaction against Georgian design. In the Georgian estate, Edwards comments, the buildings were repetitious, but the scene as a whole possessed variety. In the Victorian villa-suburbia the buildings were varied but the scene as a whole was repetitious. The Victorians failed to see, he says, that the quality of a scene is less a matter of the forms of its buildings than of the scale of its constituents, the nature of its floorscape and the character of its spaces.[65] He identified five problems with suburban aesthetics:

duality of content, which is an inevitable aspect of the suburban ideal except at arcadian densities; its monotony, caused by the need to provide large estates of virtually identical buildings; its weakness of scale, caused by the fact that economy and convenience set a limit of two stories to the height of these dwellings, while the cost of land, the need to avoid overshadowing, and the householder's preference for private, rather than communal gardens, deny suburbia the space for tall forest trees; its restless silhouette and formless spaces, which result from a multiplicity of detached or semi detached houses, and its fragmented floorscape which is caused by man's desire for a garden beside his home, together with the drives and carriageways that are a necessary concomitant of a garage.[66]

It is difficult to deny these problems. There are, of course, exceptions, especially those associated with Unwin and Parker and those inspired by them, but they are mostly upper middle class by virtue of the pressure on land. If we are to make sense of them according to a theological aesthetic it will have to be in terms of what individual creativity makes possible in them.

THE AESTHETICS OF POWER

The underlying theological problem with modern architecture, says John de Gruchy, has been that 'it was too vulnerable to ideological manipulation by those opposed to the common good'.[67] This, however, is not a modern but an ancient problem. It was already obvious in Hellenistic and Roman times, and was typified in Baroque. Twentieth-century tyrannies looked back admiringly to these models. All forms of absolutism have favoured an architecture of power and display – long, straight avenues crowned by a triumphal arch or leading to a majestic building

---

[64] Ibid., pp. 38–9. [65] Edwards, *Design*, p. 20. [66] Ibid., p. 259.
[67] J. de Gruchy, *Christianity, Art and Transformation* (Cambridge: Cambridge University Press, 2001), p. 189.

symbolising the power of the State, the Empire or the Church.[68] As opposed to organicism a completely different approach to the natural world
is implied. Even in the medieval city the skyline was marked with towers and spires, but these spoke of the heavenly city to which the earthly
city aspired.[69] Once technology made skyscrapers possible, the skyline
'described a premeditated human order, one indebted solely to technology and the profit-seeking designs of man', embodying 'an element of
choice and boast'.[70] The city became a monument to human pride.

All these cities have a shadow side, in what happens to those who
are displaced by the planner's T square, in which 'the basis of a whole
tissue of habits and social relations' could be ruthlessly torn down.[71]
Kostoff cites a note from the period of Sixtus V's rebuilding of Rome:
'Those poles placed throughout the city in straight lines across vineyards
and gardens bring fear to the souls of many interested persons who are
not unaware that, in order to make roads without turnings, many a
neck has to be twisted.'[72] The villains of this activity are not just secular
rulers or tyrants, but include many churchmen and popes. The prophetic
critique of the building habits of the rich (Amos 5.11) is here writ large.
Fine streets and squares were built which contributed nothing 'to the
order of the rest of the city, whose population lived at a lower economic
level and was housed . . . in accord with a different principle in which
neither taste nor health nor family life was a consideration'.[73] The values
represented were not common values but those of power and prestige.
The one real contribution to the ordinary citizen, in Mumford's view,
was the generalisation of the great park. Originally aristocratic gardens,
the Baroque, and later imperial, city integrated them within the whole,
thus keeping 'the aristocratic concept of space and verdure as an essential
part of urban life'.[74]

Because power and display were the goal the image of the theatre was
obvious. In Paris, said John Evelyn, the houses were built 'so incompa-
rably fair and *uniform*, that you would imagine your self rather in some
Italian Opera, where the diversity of *Scenes* surprise the beholder, then believe your self to be in a *reall Citie*'.[75] He did not draw the conclusion that

---

[68] Kostoff notes (*City*, p. 217) that it was 'the presumption of absolute power' which explains the
appeal of the Grand Manner to the totalitarian regimes of the Thirties.
[69] Bloch denies this, finding medieval spires likewise an expression of pride. E. Bloch, *The Principle
of Hope*, tr. N. Plaice, S. Plaice and P. Knight (Oxford: Blackwell, 1986), p. 715. But do they not
continue the echoing of the natural we find in the interior of the cathedral, trees straining up to
the light?
[70] Kostoff, *City*, p. 324.   [71] Mumford, *City*, p. 442.   [72] Kostoff, *City*, p. 220.
[73] Mumford, *City*, p. 456.   [74] Ibid., p. 436.   [75] Cited in Kostoff, *City*, p. 224.

the result was rather similar, namely that, unlike the medieval town, a Baroque town can be taken in almost at a glance.[76] This meant that the effect of these plans was the opposite of what was planned. They did of course announce absolute power and limitless money but '[t]hese long avenues serve as a diminishing glass; in the long perspectives of Versailles or St Petersburg, the central human figure, King or Tsar, became ever smaller and soon reached his political vanishing point'.[77]

The arch theoretician of the aesthetic of power in the twentieth century was Le Corbusier. No one has made it clearer how architectural visions rest on a view of the human. Far from presenting us with an architectural natural theology, what he represents is a late version of the Enlightenment religion of reason. Just as for him a house was a machine for living, so a town was a tool. Salvation lay in geometry, which expressed everything that was truly human over against wayward nature.[78] In a famous jibe at organicism he compared a town which followed the lines of the pack donkey with one dictated by reason. 'The pack donkey meanders along, meditates a little in his scatter brained and distracted fashion, he zigzags in order to avoid the larger stones, or to ease the climb . . . he takes the line of least resistance. But man governs his feelings by his reason.'[79] For Le Corbusier the picturesque was boring and sentimental.[80] To be human is to go straight for your goal; a straight line symbolises self mastery.[81] The analogy with the fascist triumph of the will is obvious. The right angle is the essential and sufficient implement of action, because it enables us to determine space with an absolute exactness.[82] Haussmann, who demolished much of medieval Paris, was a special hero.[83]

To his credit Le Corbusier saw that what we now call the destruction of greenfield sites was a problem. The answer was simple: increase the

[76] Mumford, *City*, p. 446.   [77] Ibid., p. 447.

[78] 'Geometry is the means, created by ourselves, whereby we perceive the external world and express the world within us. Geometry is the foundation. It is also the material basis on which we build those symbols which represent to us perfection and the divine.' The layout of the city must be purely geometrical. 'The city of today is a dying thing because it is not geometrical. To build in the open is to replace our present haphazard arrangements . . . by a uniform layout. Unless we do this there is no salvation.' C. Le Corbusier, *The City of Tomorrow and its Planning* (London: The Architectural Press, 1971; first published as *Urbanisme* in 1925), pp. 1, 171. He is looking to the idea of beauty Plato set out in the *Philebus*.

[79] Ibid., p. 210.   [80] Ibid.

[81] Or perhaps just mastery. 'The true message of the skyscraper in America', said Kostoff, 'was the celebration of one man's enterprise' (*City*, p. 327).

[82] Le Corbusier, *City*, p. 19.

[83] Ibid., p. 154. 'It seemed as if Paris would never endure his surgical experiments. And yet today does it not EXIST merely as a consequence of his daring and courage?'

open spaces and diminish the distances to be covered. Construct the city vertically.[84] The basic principles for city planning were de-congestion of the centre, increasing of density, increasing the means for getting about, and increasing parks and open spaces.[85] At the base of the skyscrapers would be a great open space filled with restaurants, cafés and luxury shops. Where Unwin was preaching that 'nothing was gained by over crowding' Le Corbusier sought higher densities. 'We are fond of the crowd and the crush because we are human beings and like to live in groups. In such towns ... with a denser population than that of existing cities, there would be ample provision and opportunity for close human contact.'[86]

There was a side to Le Corbusier which sympathised with the ideals of the Garden City. He recognised that his tower blocks transcended human scale. 'We are still creatures of nature and vast buildings would crush us if there were no common measure between them and ourselves.' His solution was to fill his parks with trees. The tree is 'a sort of caress, a kindly thing in the midst of our severer creations'.[87] Despite this recognition, he still represents high modernism with a vengeance. Glorifying the machine, he took his aesthetic from the air.[88] In that case, as the Goodmans remarked, 'the resources of architecture are helpless'.[89] And as David Harvey observes, we find here 'a subterranean celebration of corporate bureaucratic power and rationality, under the guise of a return to surface worship of the efficient machine as a sufficient myth to embody all human aspirations'.[90]

Stalinist architecture was a version of this form of rationality. During this period an aesthetic emerged, says Gordon Church, 'based in functionalism as symbolizing rationalism and focused on an ethic of design affirming a social commentary'. He talks, apparently without irony, of an 'aesthetic of propaganda'. In Stalinist Bucharest:

---

[84] Ibid., p. 163. [85] Ibid., p. 166. [86] Ibid., p. 240.

[87] Ibid., p. 237. 'How to make people feel at home in skyscraper cities, in cells in buildings 60 storeys high? The answer? We must plant trees ... Why should not the new spirit in architecture ... satisfy the deepest human desires by once more covering with verdure the urban landscape?' (p. 80)

[88] 'Instead of a flattened out and jumbled city such as the airplane reveals to us for the first time, terrifying in its confusion, our city rises vertical to the sky, open to light and air, clear and radiant and sparkling. The soil, of whose surface 70 to 80 per cent has till now been encumbered by closely packed houses, is now built over to the extent of a mere 5 per cent. The remaining 95 per cent is devoted to the main speedways, car parks and open spaces. The avenues of trees are doubled and quadrupled, and the parks at the foot of the skyscrapers do, in fact, make the city itself one vast garden' (ibid., p. 281).

[89] P. Goodman and P. Goodman, *Communitas*, p. 51. [90] Harvey, *Condition*, p. 36.

The orientation of the design lay in the play of mass and movement, making positive social-cum-artistic statements like 'upwardness' or 'forwardness', solidarity of purpose, loyalty to the oppressed and to those that had died in protest, and the links between the worker and peasant. The particular idioms include the clenched fist, the tensed arm, the sober face, and the purposeful human figure . . . the statements are progress, peace, liberation, family, dynamism, and movement.[91]

Monumentality was a key feature, commemorating events and promoting socialist values. The reason the results were so grim was that the whole experiment was based on violence.

From the beginning this manner of building sought to promote 'order'. Roman cities set out a vision of the 'pax Romana' which in fact rested on terror. Not for nothing did Renaissance rulers, princes and popes go back to classical lines. Already in the fifteenth century Ferdinand of Naples was speaking of narrow streets as a 'danger to the State'.[92] It is the result of looking through the other end of the telescope to Alberti's praise of narrow streets as useful for defence. The enemy is now within, the undisciplined mob. Part of Haussmann's intentions in Paris was to prevent another urban uprising such as had happened in 1848. He called the old quarter of Paris, which he demolished, 'the quarter of uprisings and barricades'.[93] Kostoff notes the use of rational planning by both colonial and Fascist governments to eradicate traditional living arrangements and with them loyalties that may be at odds with the State.[94] The Warsaw Ghetto showed again that this could be true. At the end of the twentieth century another variant of the will to order was visible in the emergence of what Mike Davis has called the 'carceral city'. In relation to Los Angeles he speaks of a '*totalitarian semiotics* of ramparts and battlements, reflective glass and elevated pedways' which rebukes any affinity or sympathy between different architectural or human orders.[95] The neo military syntax of contemporary architecture insinuates violence and conjures imaginary dangers.[96] In this view he is joined by Crimp, who finds in postmodern architecture a new authoritarianism which expresses the will of the real-estate developers.[97]

Roman triumphal avenues were laid out for triumphal armies. Baroque avenues were for the carriages of princes. By the eighteenth

[91] G. Church, 'Bucharest: Revolution in the Townscape Art', in R. French and F. Hamilton (eds.), *The Socialist City* (Chichester: Wiley, 1979), pp. 499–500.

[92] Kostoff, *City*, p. 230.   [93] Ibid.   [94] Ibid., p. 258.

[95] M. Davis, *City of Quartz* (London: Pimlico, 1998), p. 231.   [96] Ibid., p. 226.

[97] D. Crimp, 'Art in the 80s: the myth of autonomy', cited in Harvey, *Condition*, p. 114.

century most gentlemen kept a carriage, and by the nineteenth century many of the middle class. The medieval, or organic, city plan did not cater well for this rise in the volume of traffic. The advent of the motor car made the problem still more acute. For Le Corbusier, 'A city made for speed is made for success.'[98] It was another reason for straight streets. 'The curve is ruinous, difficult, dangerous; it is a paralyzing thing.'[99] Since crossroads are an enemy to traffic the number of streets should be diminished by two thirds. The car was the vehicle of aesthetic appreciation. 'A critic said on straight streets he would die of boredom. I was astounded and replied: "You have a car and yet you say that!"'[100] The so called Athens Charter of 1933 believed traffic flow should be the primary determinant of city form.[101] The result has been exactly what Mumford prophesied, namely that public and private space were divorced and the integrity of the city lost. For the Goodmans, urban beauty is a beauty of walking and has no place in the age of automobiles and aeroplanes. In that case, they remark, 'our city crowds are doomed to be lonely crowds, bored crowds, humanly uncultured crowds'.[102]

There is a coda to this architecture of power for, briefly, the industrial revolution ushered in a period in which aesthetics were ruthlessly subordinated to profit. The 'Cities of dreadful night' of the industrial era were thrown up overnight in the need to accommodate the tens of thousands who flocked to them looking for work, and were not planned at all. Haeckel said that the gist of Darwin's theory was that nature evolves new species without design:

It was by following what they presumed to be nature's way that the industrialist and the municipal officer produced the new species of town, a blasted, denatured man-heap adapted, not to the needs of life, but to the mythic 'struggle for existence'; an environment whose very deterioration bore witness to the ruthlessness and intensity of the struggle. There was no room for planning in the layout of these towns. Chaos does not have to be planned.[103]

This was the architectural equivalent of the free market. To make profit the only consideration meant 'the inexorable wiping out of all the natural features that delight and fortify the human soul in its daily rounds. Rivers would be turned into running sewers . . . waterfronts might be made inaccessible to the stroller, ancient trees might be slaughtered and venerable buildings torn down to speed traffic.'[104] The Garden City and the work of

[98] Le Corbusier, *City*, p. 179.   [99] Ibid., p. 16.   [100] Ibid., p. 270.
[101] Kostoff, *City*, p. 154.   [102] Goodman and Goodman, *Communitas*, p. 51.
[103] Mumford, *City*, p. 515.   [104] Ibid., p. 486.

Sitte were a reaction to this, but there is also an architectural equivalent
to the thesis of Veblen about conspicuous consumption. Veblen argued
that whilst the first generation might prioritise capital, the second and
third generations wanted to spend it.[105] The nineteenth century town
halls and museums of Britain are an ample exemplification of this thesis.
That, very often, led back to the 'Grand Manner' which finally disappeared, according to Kostoff after the Second World War. When, in
France, an attempt was made to utilise it in the interests of the working class, all that was achieved was an 'embalmed domesticity' as there
was no public life which they celebrated.[106] This points precisely to the
reclamation of community as the secret of city aesthetic.

THE AESTHETIC OF COMMUNITY

People ensoul not only their houses but the settlements in which they
dwell. At the same time their settlements shape their souls. We can
once again understand this dialectic through theological anthropology.
Human beings, said Barth, are soul and body – *in an order*. 'As a person
is grounded, constituted and maintained by God as soul of their body',
he wrote, 'and thus receives and has the Spirit, there occurs the rule of
the soul and the service of the body.' Human beings are constituted in
this relationship.[107] In terms of the built environment this means that the
primacy is with the community rather than the place.[108] This is the reason
that the most unlikely places may become places of the soul – refugee
camps, slums, prisons, even concentration camps. On the other hand,
there are places which we speak of as 'soulless', places which impoverish
us; and places which have a deep spirituality, in the sense of being places
which nurture the human soul. Following Plato's bringing together of
ethics and aesthetics I want to go on and try to understand the elements
of a creative aesthetic of space. In doing so I am once again using Walter
Wink's account of spirituality.

Most objects we are accustomed to call beautiful, says Kevin Lynch,
such as a painting or a tree, are single purpose things. 'A city is a
multi purpose, shifting organization, a tent for many functions, raised
by many hands with relative speed . . . final meshing is improbable and

[105] T. Veblen, *The Theory of the Leisure Class* (New York: Dover, 1994; orig 1899).
[106] Kostoff, *City*, p. 276.
[107] K. Barth, *Church Dogmatics* III/2 (Edinburgh: T&T Clark, 1960), p. 419 (translation altered).
[108] For Pseudo Dionysius 'beauty is the cause of harmony, of sympathy, of community' (*Complete Works*, p. 77). What I am doing is reversing the claim.

undesirable.'[109] Lynch makes the point that cities, like villages and towns, are the work of many hands, the home of many communities. Many writers suggest that coherence is essential to an aesthetically pleasing urban space. 'Other things being equal', says Nicholas Wolterstorff, 'the more strongly unified the space, the better. When space is allowed to leak out all over, so that the degree of unity is very low, we can scarcely even experience it as shaped space. And other things being equal, the more rich, complex, varied, and contrasting the spaces, the better.'[110] This doctrine of the unity of urban space needs to be treated with great caution for it might be taken to imply that the coherence of the various parts has to be planned. But richness, variety, complexity and contrast spring from 'the works of many hands' inspired by many different visions of the good life.[111] A living city, then, will not have just one aesthetic and its space will rarely be artistically unified. It will, however, as we have seen before, have a *spirituality*, in the sense in which I have defined it, and it is this which provides the aesthetic unity of the city. Form alone does not constitute a beautiful city – the Hellenistic cities or Versailles are instances of that.[112] Leonie Sandercock justly insists that in the post war rush to turn planning into an applied science the city of memory, of desire, and of spirit was lost.[113] She seeks a city aesthetic which has a much more overtly spiritual dimension than that which has emerged under the auspices of centralised planning. If we accept Day's definition of art as the imbuing of matter with spirit then the spirituality of the city is what determines whether we find it aesthetically satisfying or not. Within any great city there will be boring and exciting areas, ugly and beautiful, old and new, but the overall feel, the *image* of the city, as Lynch calls it, will be determined by this spirituality which is bound up with its community life. I want to propose five constituents of the image of the city, those things which make a place 'beautiful'.

First, respect for the natural environment plays its role. Many if not most human settlements group themselves around important natural features, like rivers, harbours, hills. Settlements can effectively deny such features, or they can appeal to them. Rivers can be culverted as a

---

[109] Lynch, *Image*, p. 91.   [110] Wolterstorff, *Art in Action*, p. 180.
[111] Kjellberg argues that a diversity of aesthetic experience is the primary goal of urban aesthetics. S. Kjellberg, *Urban EcoTheology* (Utrecht: International Books, 2000), p. 124.
[112] Thus Mumford speaks of the Hellenistic cities as sanitary, orderly, well organised and aesthetically unified but grossly inferior in their capacity for fostering creative activity to the Greek cities they succeeded. *City*, p. 200.
[113] L. Sandercock, *Towards Cosmopolis* (Chichester: John Wiley, 1998), p. 4.

nuisance, or can have esplanades for walks.[114] They can draw the eye to distant mountains or be buried under dockyard debris. The possibilities of hills for views, for parks, for walks, can be exploited or they can be comprehensively built over and become a nuisance for traffic.[115] Villages and towns can give on to woods and fields which make them open to a different world.[116] In Norberg-Schulz's terms, settlements can 'gather' their regions, as Dundee, Scotland, 'gathers' the highly fertile area of the carse of Gowrie to the west, the rich farmland in Angus, the great mountainous plateau of the Cairngorms to the north, and above all the sea.

Second, beautiful places exude life. Life can be quiet, as in many villages, or it can be teeming, but dead places, no matter how interesting the form, are like old fashioned museums. To use the image of Jane Jacobs, some forms of historical conservation amount to taxidermy. The chaos of an Indian market city, on the other hand, though full of rubbish, dirt, and poor quality buildings, can be profoundly beautiful. Similarly, John Turner found in Latin American favellas and barrios a quite remarkable struggle for beauty and resilience of spirit.[117]

Third, there needs to be respect for the past and for corporate memory. Leonie Sandercock talks of the need to recapture the importance of place and the art of place making; the local knowledges written into the stones and memories of communities.[118] Without such memory we have a corporate version of Alzheimer's disease.[119] Some British cities were damaged in this way more by the post World War II craze for 'modernity' than by the bombs of the war. This is not to say that change is out of the question. Of course, '[t]he idea of somehow dismantling the urban infrastructures of Tokyo-Yokohama or New York city overnight and starting all over again is simply ludicrous'. There is, therefore, a certain sclerosis of the built environment.[120] Since cities never stand still, however, there are always ways in which the aesthetics of place

---

[114] In Idar Oberstein, in Germany, the river which was the heart of the medieval town has been concreted over and turned into a four lane highway, thus destroying the town's integrity.

[115] In Edinburgh, for example, the hills are a vital part of the aesthetic, linking the city to the sea on one side and the mountains on the other.

[116] Heidelberg is a good example.

[117] See, for example, 'Lima's Barriadas and Corralones: suburbs versus slums', *Ekistics* 19 (1965), pp. 152–5.

[118] Sandercock, *Postmetropolis*, p. 4.

[119] As Kostoff puts it, 'The mindless destruction of our old fabrics erases our cultural identity' (*City*, p. 86). He later goes on, 'We cannot bring back the pre-industrial world ... much as we might yearn for it. We should be content with saving as much as we can, to know what we once had – and to add our own pieces sympathetically to this collective artefact, with a feeling and love for the whole' (p. 93).

[120] D. Harvey, *Spaces of Hope* (Edinburgh: Edinburgh University Press, 2000), p. 59.

can be improved or worsened.[121] Decisions about this belong to the community.[122] 'A minority of private interests should not be allowed to dominate the town architecturally any more than it should socially,' Thomas Sharp insisted in relation to Cambridge in 1963.[123]

Relatedly, settlements need community buildings and common space. 'Ancient planners put all their talent into the building of the communal nucleus – inns, churches, city halls,' says Victor Papanek. 'The rest of the settlement then followed by itself. Modern designers are forever concentrating on the rest of the city. But without an organic centre nothing can be held together.'[124] If the contemporary equivalent of inns are McDonald's fast food shops then we are in real trouble, and there are few buildings, in the postmodern world, which genuinely speak for all. Is there a contemporary equivalent to the medieval cathedral, a building of comparable symbolic significance?[125] Amongst public buildings Pevsner offers national monuments, government buildings, theatres, libraries, museums, hospitals, prisons, hotels, warehouses, railway stations, market halls, shops and factories. Ironically the only one of this list which elicits real public affection, at least in Europe, is the one Ruskin most vehemently denied could ever be a source of beauty – the railway station.[126] Even they have today been turned into emporia. If Harries is right, and the church or cathedral can no longer represent transcendent purpose for us, then at the moment, he feels, there is nothing we can do but wait, for 'values . . . cannot be made or invented. They must be discovered.'[127] On the other hand, church is paradigmatic for all human community in the way that it lives in the present out of the past. Symbols change their values, of course, but they do not necessarily die. Pevsner's list makes clear how little there is by way of alternative signals of transcendence.

Harries, like Lefebvre, suggests we should look to spaces for leisure, perhaps a landscape park, but as Harvey has noted with regard to Tompkins Park, these too have their problems.[128] We have to ask what these common buildings, which often sum up the image of a place,

---

[121] Recent examples of improvement in Britain are in Birmingham, carved up by roads in the nineteen sixties, increasingly restored to the pedestrian in the nineties, landscaped with fine urban sculpture; and Dundee, whose medieval heart was bulldozed in the sixties, and replaced by the worst kind of utilitarian building which has now mercifully been replaced with buildings of distinctly better quality. Most cities negotiate this kind of struggle year by year.

[122] Cited in Kostoff, *City*, p. 282.

[123] Failure to heed this advice has done much to damage the skyline of London.

[124] *Green Imperative*, p. 106.   [125] Harries, *Function*, p. 107.

[126] N. Pevsner, *History of Building Types* (Princeton: Princeton University Press, 1976). Ruskin cited in Harries, *Function*, p. 31.

[127] Harries, *Function*, p. 212.   [128] Ibid., p. 367.

actually stand for and say. The great Gothic cathedrals remain life giving because they grew out of passionately life affirming attitudes, faith
in the givenness and goodness of all things, and in the beauty of the
world.[129] The image of the city raises the question of what its corporate
project is, what it is *for*. Harries' suggestion leaves leisure as our common
project, as do sports stadia and other prominent community buildings.
Unfortunately the most prominent buildings in the contemporary city
proclaim clearly enough what they are for. Henry James lamented the
way in which Trinity Church in New York had been humbled and
obscured by office towers, and we can say the same for St Paul's in
London.[130] We do not want the city to speak to us of religious values,
necessarily, but we do not need the brazen triumph of Mammon either.

Lastly there is the question of what a city does with its poor. Almost
every human settlement above the hunter gatherer level has its rich and
poor, but not every settlement condemns the poor to squalid or inhuman
living conditions. How can that be beautiful which fails to respect the
image of God, that image through which we understand the corporate
personality of the city?

To these five elements we need to add a word about traffic. Reversing
the Athens charter, many cities in the West have been opting over the
past twenty years for pedestrianisation, as the experience of thirty years
of increasing car use proved to be increasingly devastating for the use and
enjoyment of cities. Mumford reserves some of his most mordant prose
for the tyranny of the motor car, the superstitious ritual of the worship
of speed and empty space, but Wolterstorff explicitly addresses what the
car does to the city aesthetic. Car passengers, he says, cannot get a sense
of the aesthetic of the city.

What must be added is that since we have insisted that the automobile be allowed
to get within roughly 400 feet of every spot in the city, the car has been positively
destructive of the city's aesthetic quality. We have had to ... compromise both
the unity and the variety, as well of course as the intensity, of the city's spaces.
In addition, the pedestrian who might wish, against the grain, to savour the city
on foot, is surrounded with ribbons of noise and mortal danger.[131]

Only taming the car, he says, will once again allow the city to become a
thing of joy, 'making of God's assurance to us that we will one day dwell
in a new city a beckoning invitation rather than a repulsive horror'.[132]

---

[129] Indian temples, still after fifty years of Independence difficult for Dalits to enter, are more
   questionable, though the exuberance of their vision of life is undeniable. As a commentary on
   the gospel the Vatican is more questionable still.
[130] Kostoff, *City*, p. 282.   [131] Wolterstorff, *Art in Action*, p. 183.   [132] Ibid.

Art is as natural to human beings as is community. As Wolterstorff rightly insists, it has no one definition or purpose. It may represent a response of joy, ecstasy or despair in relation to the natural world; it may be an attempt at sympathetic magic; it may be an attempt to create aesthetic delight; it may be an attempt to intuit the truth of the world, and as such represent a prophetic critique of the society in which we live. The built environment, for the most part, does not operate on the level of high art, though there are obvious monumental exceptions. But because humans are form giving creatures what they make, the shelter they create for themselves, the design of their settlements, always partakes of art, and this may be good or bad. There is an artistic correlate to 'sin' and it is all around us, in our tedious estates, our boring shopping centres, in our tower blocks. Likewise there is an expression of grace in the form of the built environment, wherever forms give pleasure, raise the spirit or proclaim the world home, in suburban gardens, in city streets and parks, in the alleys and narrow lanes of villages. In the creation of such form the work of redemption is forwarded. And for that reason the cultivation of discernment, of the ability to see and to struggle for what is soul nurturing rather than life denying, is one of the key tasks of both theology and Church.

CHAPTER 9

God, nature and the built environment

> The earth lies polluted under its inhabitants;
> for they have transgressed laws, violated the statutes,
> broken the everlasting covenant.
> Therefore a curse devours the earth...
>
> (Isaiah 24.5–6)

A theology of the built environment, I argued in the first chapter, must be a theology of liberation. There is a familiar and ancient division between theologies centred more on creation and those centred more on salvation. Liberation theology belongs more to the latter, we are told: Exodus not Genesis is its paradigm text. This, however, cannot be the case in the present world situation. Writing in 1980 E. P. Thompson characterised the Western mind set as 'exterminism', referring not to nuclear weapons but to the threat posed by the sheer material success of our culture, and arguing that the material volume of the modern economy is incompatible with ecological stability.[1] If that is the case, then the environmental movement, which is fundamentally a challenge to the internal logic of capitalism, must be the first, second and third imperative of a global liberation theology.[2]

THE BUILT ENVIRONMENT AND THE ENVIRONMENTAL CRISIS

There is by now a very substantial literature on the environmental crisis, and I shall not repeat all the arguments and evidence here. The crisis rests on the conjunction of a burgeoning world population (which has grown from 1.6 billion to more than 6 billion since 1900, and nearly doubled since 1961) and the fact that per capita energy and material consumption

[1] E. P. Thompson, *Writing by Candlelight* (London: Verso, 1980).
[2] That liberation theology is not bound to the Exodus motif, but has a vital concern for the environment, is recognised by, amongst others, Leonardo Boff (*Ecology and Liberation: A New Paradigm* (Maryknoll: Orbis, 1995)), and Mary Grey in many of her publications.

have soared faster in the past forty years than human population. The result is that '[a]n irresistible economy seems to be on a collision course with an immoveable ecosphere'.[3]

The crisis has three major dimensions. There are macro problems of global warming and the growth in the hole in the ozone layer; the question of whether resources can keep up with population, especially as regards the availability of water and grain; and problems of environmental degradation and loss of biodiversity.[4] More than two thousand leading scientists issued a joint declaration in 1996 in which they warned that 'many of our current practices put at risk the future that we wish for human society and the plant and the animal kingdoms, and may so alter the living world that it will be unable to sustain life in the manner that we know'.[5] What all this amounts to is that, as Robert Samuels puts it, God may not play dice with the universe, but humans do. In his view: 'In the geological time-frame, humanity could be in the last split second of its existence. Within the lifetime of the generation born today the planet could either be terminally ill, or on a path to sustainable recovery.'[6] This kind of language is obviously apocalyptic, as is much discussion of the nuclear threat and the poverty of the Third World, but this does not mean that we do not have to take it seriously. The impact of much contemporary secular apocalyptic, David Harvey feels, is only 'a general alarmism and sense of catastrophe' from which nothing constructive follows.[7] Jewish and Christian apocalyptic, on the other hand, intends not to evoke horror in the face of the end, but to encourage endurance in resistance to the powers of the world.[8] It is not melancholy interpretation but an urgent call to change. This applies to the built environment as to other areas because it is a significant part, perhaps even the key part, of the environmental problem. When it comes to global warming, for example, Allan Rodger describes the built environment as 'the principal villain' in the story.[9] In Britain the use of buildings accounts

[3] M. Wackernagel and W. Rees, *Our Ecological Footprint* (Gabriola Island: New Society, 1996), p. 13. Although fertility rates show a slight fall off, the base population rate is so large that very extensive increases are inevitable.

[4] Readers not familiar with these details may consult my *Fair Shares: Ethics and the Global Economy* (London: Thames & Hudson, 1999) and the bibliography there.

[5] Union of Concerned Scientists, *World Scientists' Warning to Humanity* (Cambridge, Mass.: MIT, 1996).

[6] R. Samuels in R. Samuels and D. Prasad (eds.), *Global Warming and the Built Environment* (London: Spon, 1996), p. 19.

[7] D. Harvey, *Spaces of Hope* (Edinburgh: Edinburgh University Press, 2000), pp. 216–17.

[8] J. Moltmann, *The Coming of God* (London: SCM, 1996), p. 217.

[9] A. Rodger, 'Sustainable development, energy policy issues and greenhouse', in Samuels and Prasad (eds.), *Global Warming*, p. 96.

for 46 per cent of carbon dioxide emissions and when construction is added it is more than 50 per cent. Energy is consumed in vast quantities at every stage of the process – in the production of bricks, cement, steel, aluminium, glass, plaster; in their transport and assembly, and then heating, cooling and lighting buildings once they are up. The construction industry uses an estimated 3 billion tonnes of raw materials per year – 40 per cent of the total flow into the global economy. Really to understand the part played by the built environment in the environmental crisis, however, we have to ask what the implications are of the fact that half of humankind now live in cities. 'As primary consumers cities use up fossil fuels hundreds of thousands of times faster than they can accumulate in the earth.'[10] The concept of the ecological footprint, developed by William Rees, helps us to chart the impact urbanisation makes. The ecological footprint is the amount of land required to feed a city or region, supply it with timber products and absorb its carbon dioxide emissions. It has been calculated that the ecological footprint of London, with 11 million inhabitants, is 50 million acres, 125 times greater than its actual surface area of 400,000 acres.[11] The OECD nations consume half the world's commercial energy and 40 per cent of this comes from heating, lighting and providing air conditioning for homes and offices.[12] Some of this demand is generated by building which is insensitive to local conditions. Notoriously, Le Corbusier wanted 'one single building for all nations and climates'. Ignoring local climates means installing huge heating and air conditioning systems in offices, factories, homes and hotels around the world.[13] The Sears tower in Chicago uses more energy in 24 hours than an average American city of 150,000 or an Indian city of more than 1 million.[14] New York City uses as much electrical energy as the whole continent of Africa. The richest cities contribute most to world wide environmental degradation because of their dependency on an unsustainable level of resource use.[15] When air conditioning comes into play huge quantities of CFCs are released as well. On these grounds Patrick Troy argues that modern cities are inherently

[10] H. Girardet, *The Gaia Atlas of Cities* (London: Gaia, rev. edn 1996), p. 106.
[11] *Citizen Action to Lighten Britain's Ecological Footprints* (London: International Institute for Environment and Development, 1995).
[12] M. Smith, J. Whiteleg and N. Williams, *Greening the Built Environment* (London: Earthscan, 1998), p. 6.
[13] Ibid., p. 42.
[14] G. Haughton and C. Hunter, *Sustainable Cities* (London: Regional Studies Association, 1994), p. 14.
[15] M. Jenks, E. Burton and K. Williams (eds.), *The Compact City: A Sustainable Urban Form?* (London: Routledge, 1998), p. 4.

ecologically unsustainable because they need to import food, energy and raw materials, produce more waste than they can cope with within their boundaries, and radically change the ecology of their sites. In his view, the larger the concentration of population the less sustainable it is, even if the city's hinterland is included in the equation.[16] For the architect Richard Rogers 'the world's environmental crisis is being driven by our cities . . . the scale, and the rate of increase, of our consumption of resources, and the pollution it inflicts, is catastrophic'.[17] Others point out that cities place a huge burden on the countryside, consuming much fertile agricultural land (at the rate of 2 per cent a decade in Western Europe). The rate of resources consumption per capita increases with city size, especially water, as more is needed for services. In general terms, 'the larger the city, the more dependent the city becomes on external ecosystems', both because consumption rises and because the internal capacity for food and energy is reduced.[18] Cities always had hinterlands, but as we saw in chapter 6 these are now global. Given the amount of food ferried in by air the footprint of any town with a large supermarket expands gigantically. Urban areas are also a centre for air and noise pollution. It is estimated that air pollution in cities may be responsible for as many as a quarter of all deaths of children under five world wide.[19]

Much of this pollution is caused by the use of motor vehicles whose use continues to increase throughout the world at the expense of public transport. In 1987 it was estimated that transport was responsible for 70 per cent of pollution in Moscow, 48 per cent in Warsaw, and 80 per cent in Mexico City. In Britain road transport accounts for 18 per cent of carbon dioxide emissions, 85 per cent of carbon monoxide emissions and 45 per cent of nitrous oxides, most of which are deposited outside the city.[20] A single tank of petrol produces between 120 and 180kg of carbon dioxide and motor vehicle traffic is responsible for about 15 per cent of the world's carbon dioxide output. According to the European Commission's Task Force on the Environment transport is the most important single source of environmental damage but hauliers only pay one eighth of the social and environmental costs.[21] John Adams talks of 'Carmageddon', by which he means that the human scale of settlements is everywhere threatened by the growth of car dependence, and public transport is on the retreat, following a move which happened

[16] P. Troy, 'Environmental Stress and Urban Policy' in ibid., p. 200.
[17] R. Rogers, 'Learning to live with the city', *The Independent*, 13 February 1995.
[18] Haughton and Hunter, *Sustainable Cities*, p. 70.   [19] Ibid., p. 135.
[20] Ibid., pp. 97, 162.   [21] Girardet, *Gaia Atlas*, p. 104.

in the United States in the second and third decades of the twentieth century.[22] In Britain both out of town shopping centres and large hospitals developed in the last twenty years have seen a shift away from locations accessible by bus or on foot towards car-based locations.[23] Suburban, urban fringe and rural developments are car and lorry dependent, and are therefore antithetical to energy efficiency. Fifty years ago in Britain passenger mileage by bus was twice that of the car; now mileage by car is fourteen times that of the bus.[24] The situation is better in some European countries, whilst public transport is still the norm in large parts of Asia. Even here, however, the burgeoning middle class aspire to car ownership, and the seductiveness of the freedom it gives to go anywhere when one wants, without consulting timetables, queuing, waiting for delayed trains or buses, and sharing sometimes very crowded or uncomfortable coaches cannot be underestimated.

In the North, meanwhile, we have constructed a society dependent on the long distance transport of food. Supermarkets are full of fruit, flowers and vegetables flown in from Latin America, Asia and Africa, all of which contribute to the ecological footprint of the communities who buy them. In a famous piece of research Stephanie Boge in 1993 established that one pot of strawberry yoghurt involved 8,000 km of transportation, and the case of more exotic foods would be far greater, much of it involving air travel which poses a serious threat to the ozone layer.[25] In Britain, for example, half of all butter produced is exported, whilst half of all butter used is imported – mainly from New Zealand.

Quite apart from transport and commuting, travel has become an end in itself. World tourism is a major industry, as ever more distant and exotic places have to be found to stimulate jaded appetites, and air travel is the preferential option for business, with ongoing implications for the construction of new airports and continued damage to the ozone layer. The discussion about new airports, constantly in the news, rarely touches the fundamental issue, which is that US style aviation use cannot be generalised without serious damage to the environment. It is aviation, in particular, which 'symbolizes the global rush towards non-sustainability cloaked in a rhetoric of green concerns'.[26]

[22] In A. Barnett and R. Scruton (eds.), *Town and Country* (London: Jonathan Cape, 1998), pp. 217–32.
[23] Smith, Whiteleg and Williams, *Greening*, p. 95.
[24] M. Hillman, 'In Favour of the Compact City', in Jenks, Burton and Williams (eds.), *Compact City*, p. 36.
[25] E. von Weizsacker, A. Lovins and L. Lovins, *Factor Four* (London: Earthscan, 1997), p. 117.
[26] Smith, Whiteleg and Williams, *Greening*, p. 28.

Another form of damage to the environment from the priority we give to transport is that it involves very high land take. Cars need parking space, in Britain 24 square metres per car. Ten thousand parking spaces, as provided at the Merry Hill shopping centre in Dudley, England, use 36 hectares of land and could provide 648 housing units. Local authorities in England alone account for some 24 square kilometres of parking space.[27] As more and more heavy goods traffic is put on the roads, so the implications for land take expand.

Roads designed to take 38 tonne, 15 metre long lorries need more space for their junctions and curves than do roads designed for cars or smaller lorries ... Increases in lorry weight require more substantial structures and road pavements which in their turn demand more of the raw materials of construction ... a lorry requires 0.007 square metres of space per tonne kilometre in comparison to rail which needs 0.0025 square metres. The lorry, therefore, requires almost three times as much space to do the same work as the train.[28]

The rush to roads has received slight checks in Britain, in the form of pedestrianisation, whilst the ecocidal and megalomaniac road building plans of the eighties have been shelved (though not without the destruction of Twyford Down and large areas of Berkshire). Serious steps in terms of fuel tax, however, meet with strong resistance. The authors of *Greening the Built Environment* comment that there is currently little sign of intelligent land use planning in developed countries with the intention of returning space to people and to social interaction rather than vehicles.[29]

Finally, the World Health Organisation estimates that about 250,000 people die every year on the world's roads, more than half of these fatalities being pedestrians and cyclists. Fifty thousand Americans die every year in road accidents, equal to the total number of Americans killed in the Vietnam War.[30]

Over against all these grim negatives can be set the pleasures of travel, and of exploring new places and different situations; the ease with which one can visit friends and family compared with the situation only a generation ago; and the privilege of a fresh and varied diet all year round, which all previous generations could only have dreamed of. But again we have to ask who it is, what proportion of the current world population, that enjoys these things, and at what cost to future generations. All of these goods pose major questions of inter and intra generational equity.

[27] Ibid., p. 106.   [28] Ibid., p. 102.   [29] Ibid., p. 87.   [30] Ibid., p. 127.

QUESTIONING THE CRISIS

In a strongly argued challenge to the assumptions of the kind of thought I have just been outlining David Harvey (in 1996) called 'the very idea that the planet is somehow vulnerable to human action or that we can actually destroy the earth' a repetition in negative form of the hubristic claims of those who aspire to planetary domination.

Against this it is crucial to understand that it is materially impossible for us to destroy the planet earth, that the worst we can do is to engage in material transformations of our environment so as to make life less rather than more comfortable for our own species being, while recognizing that what we do also does have ramifications . . . for other living species.[31]

In his most recent book he is less dismissive of ecological apocalyptic.[32] Harvey concedes that a capitalist political economy involves a triumphalist approach to nature, but he challenges the idea that we have no choice but to live within the limits of the second law of thermodynamics and the inherent sustaining power of ecosystems. The difficulty here is that 'neither principle is helpful at all in explaining the shifting history of human social organization, or even the genesis of life itself'.[33]

He sees little sense in speaking of natural resources as limited for what exists 'in nature' is in a constant state of transformation. Human beings are not outside of nature but part of it.[34] Scarcity is socially produced and 'limits' are a social relation within nature rather than some externally imposed necessity.[35] He suspects that all debate about eco scarcity, natural limits, overpopulation and sustainability is a debate about the preservation of a particular social order rather than a debate about the preservation of nature *per se*, and that control over the resources of others is the real agenda.[36] Apocalyptic rhetoric may lead, not to cooperative and democratic action, but to authoritarian solutions and 'lifeboat ethics' in which the powerful throw the weak overboard.[37]

[31] D. Harvey, *Justice, Nature and the Geography of Difference* (Oxford: Blackwell, 1996), p. 194.
[32] Harvey, *Spaces of Hope*, p. 220.   [33] Harvey, *Justice*, p. 140.
[34] Mary Grey underlines this point, pointing out that the word 'environment' 'does not adequately describe that core of identity, dependence and connection with physical, biotic reality'. 'The Shape of the Human Home – A Response to Tim Gorringe', *Political Theology* 3 (November 2000), p. 96. Can we abandon the term when we speak of building, however?
[35] Harvey, *Justice*, p. 147. The idea that scarcity is *nothing but* a problem of distribution (G. Ward, *Cities of God* (London: Routledge, 2000), p. 246) is extraordinary. One would have thought that Chernobyl was a sufficient warning of the ease with which it could once again become a major problem, to say nothing of developing resistance to the 'all purpose' and 'miracle' weedkiller 'Roundup'.
[36] Harvey, *Justice*, p. 148.   [37] Harvey, *Spaces of Hope*, p. 217.

Of course, Harvey has a point. Green rhetoric has certainly been coopted by those, like the major Transnational Corporations (TNCs), whose principal interest is carving up the world amongst themselves. Or alternatively, deep ecologists can champion the rights of the wilderness over those of local communities. On the other hand to dismiss the possibility of doing irreversible harm to the planet seems far too cavalier. The evidence for global warming is inescapable, as is the determination of the United States to date to do nothing about it. Chaos theory warns us that completely unexpected outcomes are possible. CFCs, vital to refrigeration, air conditioning and the production of foam blown furniture, are a good illustration. Hailed in the 1930s as a breakthrough they turned out, fifty years later, to be one of the main causes of damage to the ozone layer. Systems do not necessarily return to their previous state once stressed and exhaustion can set in. Many climate scientists now believe that the possibility of global warming simply running away is real. Of course scarcity can be socially produced, as Amartya Sen famously showed, but, as in the case of water shortages, there may be natural limits to face as well. For many years now the Worldwatch team have been arguing precisely this in relation to grain production. At the very least, then, we have to recognise that '[w]e face a series of environmental bottlenecks in the twenty first century which have already largely been constructed by past human actions. It is important to take evasive action now to prevent them closing to form solid walls.'[38]

Part of the reason for Harvey's earlier dismissal of apocalyptic thinking seems to rest in a confusion over the term 'nature'. Barry Commoner formulated the laws of ecology as

> everything is connected to everything else;
> everything must go somewhere
> nature knows best
> there is no such thing as a free lunch.[39]

'Nature', in the third proposition, is obviously shorthand for the whole evolutionary process in which, as we know, there is a great deal of wanton destruction, but in which a complex ecological balance is nevertheless maintained. As Schumacher puts it, 'Nature always . . . knows when to stop. Greater even than the mystery of natural growth is the mystery of the natural cessation of growth . . . the system of nature, of which man is part, tends to be self-balancing, self-adjusting, self-cleansing.'[40] 'Nature'

---

[38] Ibid., p. 221. [39] B. Commoner *The Closing Circle* (New York: Knopf, 1971), pp. 33–48.
[40] E. F. Schumacher, *Small is Beautiful* (London: Sphere, 1974), p. 122.

may be red in tooth and claw but it does not destroy itself, although a hail of meteorites could possibly do this by knocking the earth off course, and this might count as a 'natural' process. Harvey agrees with the ecologists that human beings are not external to eco systems but part of them. What has to be added to this is that human rationality makes us not just part of nature in this sense but also transcendent to it. The fact that as a species we are part of nature does not mean that everything we do is 'natural'. On the contrary there are 'cruel and unnatural' punishments, ways of using the imagination which are fiendish. Our 'rationality' gives us both the capacity to enhance our environment, to till and nurture it, as the author of Genesis 2 puts it, but also to destroy it. Harvey insists that we should not think of great cities as 'unnatural'. The answer is – not necessarily. Cities can live sympathetically with their environment, as Chinese cities still do. They can also destroy them. All over the ancient Near East civilisations eliminated themselves by overcropping and overgrazing, and turning their hinterlands into desert. Yes, human beings are part of 'nature' and their settlements extend and modify existing eco systems. But, as Jeffrey Cook puts it, 'Of all the recognized ecological systems it is human urbanism which seems most destructive of its host.'[41] Urban living seems conducive to 'unnatural behaviour' precisely because, where all our needs are met from supermarket shelves, we forget that nature works in closed loops. 'Big city life breaks natural material cycles and provides little sense of our intimate connection with nature.'[42] It fosters a hubristic attitude to the natural world which is in the literal sense potentially lethal.

Again, there are positives to set over against the negatives. As Anthony O'Hear puts it: 'For every oil slick there are a thousand examples of landscape gardening, for every polluted river many acres of reclaimed marshland, for every devastated forest many carefully tended plantations, all cases where human intervention has enhanced nature to great effect.'[43] This is true, but the rain forest still burns, the ice caps are melting, CFCs still released will take more decades to do their work, and the impact of carbon dioxide emissions goes on mounting and at present levels will take at least a century to dissipate. No amount of careful landscape gardening makes up for this.

---

[41] J. Cook, 'Environmentally benign architecture', in Samuels and Prasad (eds.), *Global Warming*, p. 138.
[42] Wackernagel and Rees, *Our Ecological Footprint*, p. 7.
[43] A. O'Hear, 'The Myth of Nature', in Barnett and Scruton (eds.), *Town and Country*, p. 75.

There are, of course, scientists who dispute these claims, but in many cases they work for lobby groups for international capital, which must make their results suspect.[44] The problem is that, as the veteran environmental economist E. J. Mishan put it, someone who throws themselves off a skyscraper is conscious until very near the ground, but by then it is too late to change their mind. We simply do not have enough information to allow us to be cavalier in the face of the environmental problems which already present themselves. Far better to adopt the precautionary principle. This functions to stimulate collective action to safeguard critical life support processes, to try and see that the burden of environmental responsibility is shared, and to promote global citizenship.[45] No one has put this better than Ruskin, writing more than a century ago, when the scale of environmental damage was scarcely guessed at:

God has lent us the earth for our life. It is a great entail. It belongs as much to those who follow us as it does to us, and we have no right by anything we do, or neglect to do, to involve them in unnecessary penalties, or deprive them of the benefit we have it in our power to bequeath.[46]

Harvey feels that to declare a state of eco scarcity is in effect to say that 'we do not have the will, wit or capacity to change our state of knowledge, our social goals, cultural modes, and technological mixes, or our form of economy, and that we are powerless to modify either our material practices or "nature" according to human requirements'.[47] But that is precisely the problem, for there is very little evidence that we have the will to change the destructive aspects of our culture, even if we have the wit and the capacity. As Rudolf Bahro put it: 'We still lack the decisive precondition for salvation, the *will* to turn things round.'[48] We need to go on now to ask why that is the case and what we can do, if anything, to change it.

THE CAUSES OF THE ENVIRONMENTAL CRISIS

In a famous article written in 1967 Lynn White Jnr, a Christian himself, traced the deep roots of the environmental crisis to the Christian attitude to nature. 'What people do about their ecology', he noted, 'depends

[44] See A. Rowell, *Green Backlash* (London: Routledge, 1996), pp. 140ff. for these scientists, and their connection with right wing groups and fossil fuel industries.
[45] Haughton and Hunter, *Sustainable Cities*, p. 220.
[46] Cited by O'Hear, 'The Myth of Nature', p. 79.   [47] Harvey, *Justice*, p. 147.
[48] R. Bahro, *Avoiding Social and Ecological Disaster: The Politics of World Transformation* (Bath: Gateway, 1994), p. 6.

on what they think about themselves in relation to things around them. Human ecology is deeply conditioned by beliefs about our nature and destiny – that is, by religion.' He believed this to be as true in 1967, in the so called 'post Christian West', as it had been in the middle ages. What was it about Christianity, then, which allowed the series of revolutions which have brought on the environmental crisis to happen? In brief, it was the victory over paganism. In destroying pagan animism Christianity made it possible to exploit nature in a mood of indifference to the feelings of natural objects. He suggested a return to the alternative view of St Francis who tried to 'substitute the idea of the equality of all creatures, including man, for the idea of man's limitless rule of creation'.[49] If we extend this argument to include the built environment, we can see that it would tend to favour non urban futures over urban ones.

Carolyn Merchant took this argument further, seeing the emergence of a new synthesis in the sixteenth century between rising capitalism, machine power and Protestantism.

The emphasis on God's will and active power associated with the Reformation tended to legitimate human power and activity in worldly affairs and fostered an interest in technological improvement, empirical observation of God's works in creation, and experimentation to extract and use nature's secrets for human benefit . . . The domination of nature depends equally on man as operator deriving from an emphasis on power and on man as manager deriving from the stress on order and rationality as criteria for progress and development.[50]

Of course this analysis overlooks the extent to which Reformed theology was a theology of grace, and therefore opposed precisely to any 'legitimation of human power'. Tracing intellectual and cultural causality is always tricky, as the century long debate on Weber's thesis shows, and it is an open question whether White and Merchant are right, or whether, rather, Christian theology followed the direction of developing technology and capitalism. Certainly by the later decades of the eighteenth century 'divine nature' was being imaged as a neglected 'fair', abandoned for the cities. This is how Cowper saw it:

> Nature, enchanting Nature, in whose form
> And lineaments divine I trace a hand
> That errs not, and find raptures still renew'd,
> Is free to all men – universal prize.

[49] 'The historical roots of our ecological crisis', *Science* 155/3767 (March 1967), pp. 1203–7. Kjellberg points out the irony that this article appeared only one year after *The Secular City*. S. Kjellberg, *Urban Eco Theology* (Utrecht: International Books, 2000), p. 59.
[50] C. Merchant, *The Death of Nature* (San Francisco: Harper & Row, 1980), p. 234.

Strange that so fair a creature should yet want
Admirers, and be destined to divide
With meaner objects e'en the few she finds!
Stripp'd of her ornaments, her leaves, her flowers,
She loses all her influence. Cities then
Attract us, and neglected Nature pines,
Abandon'd as unworthy of our love.[51]

Cowper already puts cities at the heart of his analysis of what is going wrong. By 1783, when this was written, the industrial revolution was well under way, and Cowper, like Wordsworth and Coleridge a few years later, is responding to it, and to the booming cities it spawned. Harvey points out that the thesis of mastery over nature does not necessarily entail destructiveness, but can just as easily lead to loving, caring and nurturing practices. True enough, but this is not what has actually happened, and there is only too much evidence for the practices of domination which Merchant details. From the mid eighteenth century onwards some have proposed that the remedy for such dominating practices is a new religion of nature. No less a historian than Simon Schama argues that '[t]he cultural habits of humanity have always made room for the sacredness of nature'. To take the ills of the environment seriously 'does not . . . require that we trade in our cultural legacy or its posterity. It asks that we simply see it for what it has truly been: not the repudiation, but the veneration of nature.'[52] What this would amount to in a world where nature has become culture, and nature is reconstructed as an ideal cultural form, is another matter.[53]

The destructive effects of religion have been noted at a number of points in this book already, and Kate Soper properly extends such questioning to the idea of religion coming to the aid of threatened nature. The idea of nature as gift possibly protected nature by encouraging a fear of retribution, she argues, but very divergent views on whether Scripture encourages care, or abuse, of nature are possible and exegesis of the Genesis domination text 'tends to be conducted in the light of the . . . rationalizations to which theology can always be made to lend itself'.[54] She takes an Enlightenment view of the matter, insisting that nature cannot be protected by pretending to forms of belief 'exploded by the march of science and technology'. It is simply a question of taking

[51] W. Cowper, *The Garden* (1783–4), *Cowper's Poetical Works* (Edinburgh: Gall & Inglis, 1853), p. 148.
[52] S. Schama, *Landscape and Memory* (London: Fontana, 1996), p. 18.
[53] M. Castells, *The Rise of the Network Society* (Oxford: Blackwell, 1996), p. 477.
[54] K. Soper, *What is Nature?* (Oxford: Blackwell, 1995), pp. 274, 281.

the rough with the smooth. We have to recognise that damage to the environment is part and parcel of the move which liberated human beings from fear and superstition.[55]

It is fair to criticise religion, but Soper's faith in Enlightenment is surely naive. For the Enlightenment brought with it, as Mumford put it, 'a deep contempt for organic processes that involve maintaining the complex partnership of all organic forms, in an environment favourable to life in all its manifestations'.[56] And if we are inescapably part inheritors of the Enlightenment tradition we are equally inescapably inheritors of the religious tradition as well. The question, then, is what we make of, and do with, both.

'Enlightenment' is bound up with the growth of a world capitalist economy, the move to the city, and the advent of mega cities. It is to this, more plausibly, that we have to look for the causes of the environmental crisis. For at the heart of the capitalist process is a compulsion for growth. Mumford compared Western civilisation to a gigantic motor car moving along a one way road at an ever accelerating speed.

> Unfortunately as now constructed the car lacks both steering wheel and brakes, and the only form of control the driver exercises consists in making the car go faster, though in his fascination with the machine itself and his commitment to achieving the highest speed possible, he has quite forgotten the purpose of the journey. This state of helpless submission to the economic and technological mechanisms modern man has created is curiously disguised as progress, freedom, and the mastery of man over nature. As a result, every permission has become a morbid compulsion. Modern man has mastered every creature above the level of the viruses and bacteria – except himself.[57]

Nowhere is this critique more true than in the commitment of conventional economics to growth which, in becoming an end in itself, completely obscures what Mumford calls 'the purpose of the journey'. For all Western thinkers up to the eighteenth century economics was a sub discipline of ethics. Economics followed from understandings of meaning and purpose. Part of what Karl Polanyi called the 'great transformation' was that this order was inverted: increasingly it came to be the economy, and 'growth', which gave value to human life. The reasons for this are discussed in a huge literature. The efficiencies gained by the division of labour become a treadmill, as increased production demands larger markets in an endless cycle. Machines increase production, but have to

---

55 Ibid., 275.   56 L. Mumford, *The City in History* (Harmondsworth: Penguin, 1991), p. 600.
57 Ibid., p. 636.

turn out more and sell more in order to pay for themselves. Innovations drive old products from the field and call forth yet more innovations. The system of interest is self perpetuating, as my business has to grow to pay back the interest on the money I have borrowed, which requires new loans, and so on. At the most fundamental level capitalism's need to grow to live requires that we all become consumers. As Mumford put it: 'The machine came into our civilization, not to save man from the servitude to ignoble forms of work, but to make more widely possible the servitude to ignoble standards of consumption that had grown up among the military aristocracies.'[58] This is not only bad news for the environment, but extremely bad news for human self understanding. For Aristotle, and for most philosophers and theologians up until the nineteenth century, the good life, and being a whole human being, *essentially involved the acceptance of limits*. St Paul's 'Let your moderation be known to all' was good Aristotelian advice. The doctrine of limits is no obscure piece of ancient scholasticism. On the contrary, any skill requires recognition of limits, and nothing worthwhile is achieved without them. 'Any activity which fails to recognise a self limiting principle is of the devil,' as Schumacher put it.[59]

Limits are vital because huge numbers mean huge impacts. As Daly and Cobb note, 'If "needs" include an automobile for each of a billion Chinese, then sustainable development is impossible. The whole issue of sufficiency can no longer be avoided.'[60] The issue is ethical and political: who decides who can enjoy what, and at what cost? Addressing inequalities in global consumption is essential if ecological damage is to be contained. Thus Wackernagel and Rees have argued that 'if everyone on Earth lived like the average Canadian or American, we would need at least three such planets to live sustainably'.[61] Huge numbers inevitably also put pressure on the basic resources of water and food which, in the view of the Worldwatch team, are under threat. Already in 1992, in a review of the world's water problems Sandra Postel noted that '[i]n many parts of the world, water use is nearing the limits of natural systems' and in some areas they have been surpassed.[62]

The problem with the call for limits is that the quest for more constitutes the spiritual centre of the capitalist world. A meeting of economists

---

[58] L. Mumford, *Technics and Civilization* (London: Routledge, 1946), p. 106.
[59] Schumacher, *Small is Beautiful*, p. 129.
[60] H. Daly and J. Cobb, *For the Common Good* (London: Green Print, 1990), p. 76.
[61] Wackernagel and Rees, *Our Ecological Footprint*, p. 13.
[62] S. Postel, *The Last Oasis* (London: Earthscan, 1992), p. 18.

in 1987 rejected the very idea of limits which could not be taken care of by capital.[63] As David Korten points out this follows because to accept the reality of physical limits is to accept the need to limit greed and acquisition in favour of economic justice and sufficiency.[64] In order to survive, therefore, capitalism is *necessarily*, and not just contingently, committed to inculcating in us the reign of perverse and inordinate desire.

The problem behind the environmental crisis, in other words – and here I agree with Lynn White – is spiritual, in the broadest sense. This growth compulsion is linked to what Mumford called the 'Megamachine', the organisation of power which began in the ancient civilisations of Babylon, Assyria and Egypt, which from the start aimed at the exploitation and manipulation of the bulk of the citizenry.[65] Global capital, with its voracious demand for 'more', is the heart of the contemporary megamachine. It controls not by the whip and the truncheon but by the allurements of the commodity. Since cities and capital go together, this 'more' translates itself into increasing cities as well. Human beings have always been able to destroy their environment, as the ancient Mesopotamian cities, and Easter Island, show. What is new is the scale of the impact, and the level of destruction we can cause. And it is not decisively big business or the military industrial complex which is responsible for this.

It is ultimately with the Mercedes and washing machine detergents that we do the damage, rather than with bombs, nuclear power stations and dioxins . . . A private dwelling full of comforts necessarily confirms the whole worldwide infrastructure – including the need for armaments, because in face of monstrous differences in standards it is a threatened luxury.[66]

Thus there is no simple battle between 'good guys and bad guys' because the power of the Megamachine exists 'within, in the nodal points of research and production, management and business, education and politics, dependent on the psychological power-relations in society'.[67] Indeed, it exists within each consuming self. What Mumford and Bahro are drawing attention to here is what Christianity has spoken of as 'original sin', the human tendency to destroy self, other and creation through idolatry, making created things ultimate.[68]

[63] 15 May 1987; cited in Daly and Cobb, *Common Good*, p. 194.
[64] D. Korten, *When Corporations Rule the World* (West Hartford, Conn.: Kumarian, 1995), p. 81.
[65] L. Mumford, *The Myth of the Machine* (London: Secker & Warburg, 1967), p. 191.
[66] Bahro, *Avoiding*, p. 92.   [67] Ibid., p. 75.
[68] Kjellberg uses the Finnish term *raadollisus* for this, as a way of speaking of the *homo incurvatus in se*, our tendency to make prisoners of ourselves. *Urban EcoTheology*, p. 141.

Much of the dis-ease of twentieth century art was due not just to
the loss of a previously established home, but to an overt nihilism, an
overt absence of meaning, which expressed itself in the death camps
and the nuclear arms race. This nihilism now finds expression in consumerism. 'It should not be a surprise', write the authors of *Greening the
Built Environment*, 'that a materialistic society which takes a short term
view should create and live in a built environment that is being extended and continually recreated at the expense of the earth's capital
resources.'[69] Las Vegas, built in a desert, for the purposes of 'pleasure',
dependent on aquifer resources for its water, needing air conditioning to
make life bearable, illustrates this perfectly but so do greenfield housing
developments and out of town shopping centres. One cannot say, *tout
court*, that it is 'capitalism' which produces these developments, but on
the other hand it both makes them possible and promotes them. The
imperatives of capital – short term profit, market forces and the cultivation of needs – are the driving forces behind them. These forces are
difficult to counter because they have the weight of the multi national
corporations, the banks and finance institutes, but even more our own
pathetically desiring selves behind them, and because the momentum
developed is already so strong.

Because that is the case, breaking the cycle of consumption cannot
begin simply with a challenge to the institutions. Neither can it be a
matter solely of technological fixes, important as these are. It involves,
rather, adopting a new understanding on human nature and destiny, and
a new understanding of the importance of lifestyle options. In overcoming
exterminism, Bahro recognised, 'No order can save us which simply
limits the excesses of our greed. Only spiritual mastery of the greed itself
can help us. It is perhaps only the Prophets and Buddhas, whether or not
their answers were perfect, who have at least put the question radically
enough.'[70] Schumacher already recognised this in *Small is Beautiful*. 'The
cultivation of needs', he wrote, 'is the antithesis of wisdom. It is also
the antithesis of freedom and peace. Every increase of needs tends to
increase one's dependence on outside forces over which one cannot have
control, and therefore increases existential fear.'[71] Schumacher himself
turned to Buddhism for guidance. The question for Christians is whether
there is anything the gospel can contribute to the problems which are
posed us.

[69] Smith, Whiteleg and Williams, *Greening*, p. 210.
[70] Bahro, *Avoiding*, p. 25. [71] Schumacher, *Small is Beautiful*, p. 23.

The word 'liberation' in the phrase 'liberation theology' represents a gloss on an older theology of salvation. Human beings, the Church always said, needed to be saved from 'sin'. Where for centuries this was understood individually and moralistically liberation theology understood it socially and politically, specifying the structures which constituted 'sin'. It is these which Wink understands as the 'Powers', which are created, fallen, and need redemption. The 'power' which underlies the suicidal compulsion to growth is what E. P. Thompson meant by 'exterminism'. The positive side of growth is the recognition of the need to provide the best possible standard of living for all the earth's people. It becomes a fallen Power when it becomes an end in itself, a compulsion. This negative spirituality is what causes the gap between rich and poor to increase all over the globe; what drives the poor increasingly into the shanty towns of the great cities. Above all it is our alienation from the planet, the slow choking of the atmosphere, the predatory approach to resources, which make clear how this form of sin is, in the most literal sense, life denying. It is the refusal to recognise limits which, at the very least, threatens the livelihoods of hundreds of thousands of the world's poorest people through global warming, if it does not actually threaten the planet. If my analysis of the causes of the reckless commitment to growth at any cost is right then, in the contemporary world, savage capitalism is the concrete form of sin.

The fundamental theological opposition to capitalism is the theology of grace, the 'for nothing' of creation and redemption. Those who see the point of gracious living are called, collectively, ec-clesia, which is to say, those not captured by the plausibility structures of capitalism, those who oppose the anti spirituality of profit with the spirituality of thanksgiving, or as the early church said, 'the sacrifice of praise'. Rather than considering all reality from the perspective of profit, they see it from God's point of view, as unconditionally gifted, therefore free, and to be shared and celebrated together. Ec-clesians do not accept determinist views about there being no alternatives, but look for ways of subverting the cunning of exterminism (sometimes called the cunning of reason, or the invisible hand). According to the word of Jesus in Mark 10.43 ('It shall not be so amongst you') ec-clesians are ec-centrics: they have a different centre to others: not the megamachine but what Jesus calls 'the kingdom'.

Being other centred is not being other worldly in the sense of looking for salvation first and foremost beyond this world. On the contrary: where sin makes us strangers, grace calls the world home. Being other centred means challenging global capitalism's claim to be the narrative of the world, replacing it with a narrative of giftedness. Liberation theology seeks practical recognition for that giftedness, for the homeliness of the world. Faith in the God who creates and redeems us *has to work for the world as human home*, or, as Mary Grey has argued, for an environment conducive to human flourishing.[72]

To that assertion Christian critics will immediately respond with, 'Here we have no lasting city.' But the 'kingdom' at the heart of Jesus' gospel cannot be construed as an other worldly agenda. It is about the shaping of the world and Jesus could not fulfil the law and the prophets otherwise. It is true that this world does not exhaust the meaning of 'the kingdom', but without the inclusion of this world the idea makes no sense.

After the apostolic preaching Paul represents the first major commentary on Jesus' programme. He read the opposition between the kingdom and its opponents as an opposition between 'sin' and 'grace', but these were from the start specified quite concretely. In the terms of this book, 'sin' represents our alienation from the world, our reduction of it to nothing but a set of resources for the rich, whilst 'grace' calls the world home, recognises it as gift. A liberation theology of the built environment wants practical recognition for the homeliness of the world. If it concedes that the city is 'a central form of man's co-existence with the rest of Creation' it does so only in recognition of the need for a city healed of its parasitism and voracious consumption.[73]

In a world of manifold alienations liberation theology will, therefore, be a theology of being 'at home'. But there is a problem here manifested by the fact that twentieth century musicians, artists and poets have recorded the dis-ease at not being at home in the world in a way which has no earlier parallel, as far as I can see, and which is bound up with the exponential speed of change since roughly 1800. In a famous image Raymond Williams talked of the 'escalator' of nostalgia, for which the truly homely world is always back over the last hill. Considering the claim that twentieth century changes in rural life meant that 'a whole culture

---

[72] Flourishing, she points out, is an ecological metaphor, rooted in bodily life. '*Flourishing* pushes far beyond the mere fact of survival, to qualitative factors like relationships of mutuality, plentiful provision of nourishment, the giving and receiving of hospitality, just employment, self esteem and esteem of the community . . . [It] can act as an ethical yardstick with more potential than the language of Human Rights, as critique against poor housing, for classroom conditions which in theory pass the basic norm, but in which children cannot flourish, hospitals where the quality of care does not respect the whole person-in-relation, and so on' (Grey, 'Shape', p. 102). The argument is developed more fully in *The Outrageous Pursuit of Hope* (London: Darton, Longman and Todd, 2000). Raimond Gaita, on the other hand, believes that the concept lacks the conceptual resources to deal with the severely afflicted. *A Common Humanity* (London: Routledge, 2000), p. 19.

[73] The phrase is from Kjellberg, *Urban EcoTheology*, p. 71. It neatly expresses Harvey's view of the city as well.

that had preserved its continuity from earliest times had now received its quietus' Raymond Williams traced this sentiment back through to the middle ages, and indeed back to Saxon and Celtic times. Where, he asked, does the escalator of that particular sentiment stop?[74] It is a fair question. The sense of being strangers and pilgrims is not new and seems in particular to have defined early Christian sensibility.

At the same time the threnody of the rural past has a point, for all over the world, in 1900, harvests were in fact gathered by hand and fields ploughed by horse and oxen and that, and all the skills and knowledge which went with it, have in large part disappeared in a matter of decades. Twentieth century pastoral – *Cider with Rosie* is a good illustration – laments the passing not only of these skills but of the sense of being at home which belonged with them. At the end of the twentieth century the historic possibilities of humankind for settlement – hamlet, village, town, city – nowhere remain unaltered. Even in Mongolia the small portable generator introduces colour television to the plains' family's yurt, as it does in the Indian and African village. The millennia humankind has spent in these settlements, however, profoundly shape our sense of the human home. Evolution is not destiny – our past does not imprison us. On the other hand, neither can we accept the hubristic Enlightenment idea that we can begin with a clean slate, and ignore the power of historical memory, allowing ourselves to be guided only by the 'light', or rather the cunning of reason. The problem with this reason is that it is too clever by half and, as Schumacher argued, in pursuing knowledge has forgotten wisdom. Wisdom consists in recognising what has been called the 'second contradiction of capitalism', not just between capital and labour but between the growth compulsion and the determinate ecosphere. The second law of thermodynamics may not explain social organisation or the origin of life, but unless it is allowed to guide our economy then the attempt to ignore entropy is going to bring us up sharp, and sooner rather than later. The key question, then, at the turn of the millennium, is how we preserve the homeliness of the world, a question for the economy and therefore the built environment; a question for the economy, and therefore for our deepest spiritual resources. To this question I turn in the final chapter.

[74] R. Williams, *The Country and the City* (London: Hogarth, 1985), p. 11.

CHAPTER 10

Towards Jerusalem?

> One is calling to me from Seir,
> 'Sentinel, what of the night?
> Sentinel, what of the night?'
>   The sentinel says:
> 'Morning comes, and also the night.
>   If you will inquire, inquire;
>   come back again.'
>
> (Isaiah 21.11–12)

At the end of his three volume analysis of the current world situation, Manuel Castells is upbeat:

> History is just beginning, if by history we understand the moment when, after millennia of a prehistoric battle with Nature, first to survive then to conquer it, our species has reached the level of knowledge and social organization that will allow us to live in a predominantly social world. It is the beginning of a new existence and of a new age.[1]

Peter Hall today seems to share this enthusiasm, but writing in 1988 he was much more cautious:

> The watchman on the height is calling; but his message could spell doom to the city, unless the day rises also on the city of darkness just outside the gate. There is a riddle here, so far unanswerable by the wit of planners, or indeed, of that of any other kind of social engineer; and, as the millennium approaches, it casts a deep pre dawn chill.[2]

This pre dawn chill seems to have evaporated at the turn of the millennium, but worries about the city of darkness just outside the gate – growing poverty, growing numbers, the ability to adequately feed and house them – nevertheless obtrude. Will we, Hall asks in *Cities in Civilization*,

---

[1] M. Castells, *End of Millennium* (Oxford: Blackwell, 1998), p. 478.
[2] P. Hall, *Cities of Tomorrow* (Oxford: Blackwell, 1988), p. 480.

arrive at a world in which there is a total polarisation between the information rich and the information poor? Will there be a true urban golden
age in which the minority enjoy unparalleled affluence, while a majority
are left in dire poverty that is both material and spiritual?[3] The answer
to both questions is that this is already how the world is configured, and
that, as Hall himself has argued in the past, any such contrast between
wealth and poverty precludes there being any kind of golden age, urban
or otherwise. A new, more positive, age – or the growth of the city of
darkness outside the gate? In answering this question Castells represents
an almost entirely unchastened optimism of progress which overlooks the
many periods of retrogression in the past, and we would do well to learn
from these periods.[4] This is especially the case because, at the turn of the
millennium, the balance between the alternatives outlined by Hall can
hardly be said to be even. What we do with the built environment will
have a decisive impact one way or the other, both in terms of our use of
resources, as the last chapter made clear, but also in terms of the building
of settlements which are humanly as well as materially sustaining. What
ought we to do about it? Does the Church have anything to contribute?
Theology, I said in the first chapter, is primarily addressed to the Church.
But today 'Church' is one small interest group amongst countless others.
What is the point of this, or of any, Christian ethical reflection? If Church
structures its reflection around a particular narrative, and one full of
'outdated' ideas at that, as Kate Soper reminds us, what can it contribute
to the common human story? If it is called to be a contrast society can it
reasonably expect to have any impact on the public square? My answer
to these questions is twofold. With the Irenaean tradition of theological
reflection, followed by Geddes and Mumford, I take education to play a
crucial role in human process. Secondly, I have argued throughout this
book that the problems associated with the built environment are not
primarily technical but spiritual, that is to say, they are fundamentally a
question of values, of our understanding of the whole human project.[5]
In that respect Castells' Enlightenment talk of 'conquering' nature may

---

3 P. Hall, *Cities in Civilization* (London: Weidenfeld and Nicolson, 1998), p. 987.
4 We can think of the European 'Dark Ages' evoked by Alasdair MacIntyre at the close of *After Virtue*, or the downturn of expansion at the end of the thirteenth century when Europe 'not only halted but shrank'. J. Le Goff, *Medieval Civilization* (Oxford: Blackwell, 1988), p. 106. One does not have to believe in history repeating itself to be made cautious by these examples.
5 Victor Papanek likewise refers to values as 'introducing the question of the spiritual in design'. The questions he wants to put to the built environment are close to the ones I pose: 'Will the design ... aid ... sustainability? Can it make life easier for ... [the] marginalized? Will it help those who are poor? Will it save energy? Can it save irreplaceable resources?' *The Green Imperative* (London: Thames & Hudson, 1995), p. 54.

be something of a giveaway, for, as feminists and ecologists have been arguing for three decades now, repudiating that attitude is a precondition of our survival.

SPIRITUALITY, EDUCATION AND THE BUILT ENVIRONMENT

Writing in 1948 Paul and Percival Goodman spoke of questioning returning troops about coming home.

> If you ask 'What kind of town do you want to live in? What do you want in your post-war home?' – the answers reveal a banality of ideas that is hair raising, with neither rational thought nor real sentiment, the conceptions of routine and inertia rather than local patriotism or personal desire, of prejudice and advertising rather than practical experience and dream.[6]

Perhaps this is just the educated man's sneer at the culture of the masses but the built environment of the 1950s and 60s at almost every level instantiates their point. This in turn illustrates the way in which the built environment is an expression of our spirituality, in the sense in which I have been using that term throughout this book. Human beings, says the Christian tradition, are body and soul in-formed by Spirit. Their whole constellation, what they are as body–soul unity, manifests their spirituality. As Walter Wink has demonstrated, this goes beyond the individual to the collectivity. The spirituality of a culture expresses itself in, and therefore shapes, ethics, but also art, literature, music, religion, cuisine, and building – the whole of everyday life. 'The making of a society', says Raymond Williams, 'is the finding of common meanings and directions, and its growth is an active debate and amendment under the pressures of experience, contact, and discovery, *writing themselves into the land*.'[7] What Williams calls 'the making of society' issues in what I am calling a spirituality which indeed, for good or ill, writes itself into the land. In world history common meanings and directions have fashioned themselves over centuries, issuing in a host of different cultures and spiritualities, and therefore of vernaculars, building styles, and types of settlement. A spirituality, in this sense, is not something which blooms in a day. All spiritualities have roots which reach back to the emergence of *homo sapiens*, but they are not always and invariably healthy and strong. There are spiritualities which give rise to Cotswold villages, Italian hill

[6] P. Goodman and P. Goodman, *Communitas: Means of Livelihood and Ways of Life* (New York: Random House, 1960), p. 13.
[7] R. Williams, 'Culture is Ordinary', in *Resources of Hope* (London: Verso, 1989), p. 4 (my italics).

towns, compact Indian cities, to the Parthenon, the Dome of the Rock, to Chartres, and the Meenakshi temple, and there are spiritualities which gives rise to the unsustainable cities of Assyria and Babylon, to slums, the enclosing of rivers, Disneyworld, and the carving up of cities by grotesquely misnamed 'freeways'. The depth of a culture's spirituality undeniably waxes and wanes, and shallow periods produce poor, or at least unjust and unstable, environments. Where do we stand at the turn of the millennium? How are we to build dwellings and fashion settlements which are, to use Christopher Day's words, life renewing, soul nurturing, and spirit strengthening? Is there any evidence that we are better placed than the people the Goodmans interviewed?

The problem for the new millennium is to know what happens in the milieu of the global village, which militates against the survival of real difference, and in what seems to many the ruin of long established systems of values.[8] Postmodernism, which represents what Frederick Jameson calls 'the structural logic of late capitalism', represents this confusion both architecturally and ethically. Architecturally it abandons itself to an eclectic quotation of vernaculars world wide, thus proclaiming like the Bauhaus that it has no ideas of its own.[9] Ethically we have been reduced, says Zygmunt Bauman, to excluded vagabonds or rich tourists, moving on, uncommitted, and in danger of losing the ability to be moral.[10] The banality of much postmodern building precisely signifies this loss of direction and, more than that, the covert nihilism which lies behind the rhetoric of the market.

The defenders of postmodernity point out that it emphasises community, locality, place, and regional resistances, social movements and respect for otherness. 'At its best', Harvey remarks, 'it produces trenchant images of possible other worlds, and even begins to shape the actual world.' Unfortunately, at the same time, 'it is hard to stop the slide into parochialism, myopia, and self-referentiality in the face of the universalizing force of capital circulation. At worst it brings us back to narrow and sectarian politics in which respect for others gets mutilated in the fires of competition between the fragments.'[11]

The problem is getting beyond the fragments to the emergence of Williams' *common* meanings. There are, of course, two ways, a positive

---

[8] So K. Harries, *The Ethical Function of Architecture* (Cambridge, Mass.: MIT, 1998), p. 282, and, famously, A. MacIntyre, *After Virtue* (London: Duckworth, 1981).

[9] E. Bloch, *The Principle of Hope*, tr. N. Plaice, S. Plaice and P. Knight (Oxford: Blackwell, 1986), p. 735.

[10] Z. Bauman, *Postmodern Ethics* (Oxford: Blackwell, 1993), p. 248.

[11] D. Harvey, *The Condition of Postmodernity* (Oxford: Blackwell, 1989), p. 351.

and a negative, in which this has already happened. The first is summed up by the notorious remark of the Heinz Chief Executive, Tony Reilly: 'Once people have television, they all want more or less the same thing.' Levis, Coke and McDonald's have formed a global culture of stunning banality, of meanings grouped around the lowest common denominator of a mythicised American youth culture, which spell death to local creativity. One could imagine a kitsch version of Le Corbusier's 'one universal building' as its architectural equivalent and Disneyland as its ideal settlement. If our buildings shape us as much as we shape them we have to ask what the global community is learning from the tower blocks which are to be found in virtually every city world wide.

Common meanings are to some extent generated by threat, as they were by the prospect of 'mutually assured destruction' in the sixties and seventies of the twentieth century. Until March 2001 evidence of global warming seemed to be functioning in the same way, until the fragile results of the three Global Climate conferences were torn up by President Bush, urged on by the corporations. This action calls in question the extent to which the recognition of Earth as a 'lonely planet', which the former director of Greenpeace, Peter Melchett, regards as a defining moment in the growth of environmental consciousness, counters the tribalism of postmodernity.[12] The climate conferences, and their sudden death, are a good illustration of the clash of rationalities, moralities or spiritualities which lie behind global capitalism on the one hand, which believes that the market will solve all problems painlessly, in this case by trading pollution rights with Third World countries, and those who believe that such manoeuvres are cynical and immoral and compromise not only the South but the future. Resistance to such solutions perhaps provides support for Bauman's conclusion that, the tribalism and aestheticism of the postmodern condition notwithstanding, moral responsibility is inalienable, unconditional and infinite. If that is the case, if that faith is justified, it will in due course issue in shared and nurturing spiritualities which draw on and make sense of the past from which we come. They will be shared, because morality is social; they will make sense of the past, because to be historically conditioned is part of what it means to be human; and they will be spiritual, informed by the spirit, which is to say the imagination, the emotion, the creativity of humankind and of each culture. For the Christian, human spirit is not identical with Holy Spirit, but the former does not exist without the latter, and represents both a

---

[12] In a lecture at the University of Exeter, 9 February 2001. He believes satellite photographs of the earth generated this sentiment.

creation of the Spirit and a response to it. This bears on our understanding of the role of the Church. In his review of future possibilities
Castells remarks: 'Religious communes may develop into religious fun-
damentalist movements aimed at re-moralizing society, re-establishing
godly, eternal values, and embracing the whole world, or at least the
nearby neighbourhood, in a community of believers, thus founding a
new society.'[13] The future of religion, in other words, is backward looking versions of identity politics. Bahro too was sceptical of the idea that
the environmental crisis might offer a 'last chance for Christianity'.
'As far as I can see, churches are as little capable of . . . transformation
as states.'[14] But since the past conditions the present in an endless rein-
vention, I cannot be as pessimistic about the Church, as bearer of the
narrative of kingdom, cross and resurrection, as they are. Of course
religions and philosophies can die. We are unlikely to find sustenance
from Marduk and Tiamat,[15] or for that matter from Zoroastrianism.
Perhaps the Christian narrative has had its day, as dwindling congregations around Europe seem to indicate. But perhaps, on the other hand,
the gravediggers have come too early. Religions prove themselves, said
Lessing, in spirit and in power, which is to say to the extent that they prove
able to nurture the human soul. The indictment against Christianity is
severe. All forms of the Church have involved themselves in structures
of deceit and very often systematic coercion. They have been complicit
with the forces of death. 'Can any one say without flinching or without horror', asks Marc Ellis, 'that Christian activity in history has been
in continuity with Jesus?'[16] It is part of the lie in which the churches
are involved that they do indeed affirm this, and of this Christians
can only be deeply ashamed.[17] At the same time, any glance at the
art, music and literature of the twentieth century shows that there are
still extraordinary resources of depth here, that cross and resurrection

[13] M. Castells, *The Power of Identity* (Oxford: Blackwell, 1997), p. 357.
[14] Bahro, *Avoiding*, p. 68.
[15] Though as Wink points out, we may find their myth still instantiated in Pentagon power games. W. Wink, *Engaging the Powers* (Minneapolis: Fortress, 1992), pp. 13ff.
[16] M. Ellis, *Unholy Alliance: Religion and Atrocity in our Time* (London: SCM, 1997), p. 175. Cf. also Gary Wills, *Papal Sin: Structures of Deceit* (London: Darton, Longman and Todd, 2000), which examines, amongst other things, the role of the papacy in relation to the Holocaust, and the continuing failure to apologise for Christian anti Semitism.
[17] Ellis draws attention especially to Pope John Paul's address to Latin American bishops in 1992 in which he spoke of the need for 'the immense wealth of Christian life to flourish' in the hearts of the Latin American people, with no acknowledgement that the Church was complicit in the conquista. He instances, also, his appointment of the chaplain to the military who murdered Oscar Romero as Romero's successor, and his refusal to visit the graves of the six Jesuits who were murdered. *Unholy Alliance*, p. 84.

still refract human reality in hugely complex, profound and interesting ways.[18]

To some extent we can measure what it is Church offers against alternatives. Ernst Bloch remarked: 'Only the beginnings of another society will make genuine architecture possible again.'[19] Recognising this imperative Bahro believed that *integration* was the key to the recovery of spirituality in the face of the megamachine. Only by reunification of our living spirit with its natural roots, he said, and with the wellsprings of culture, was it possible to overcome dead and alienated spirit.[20] An atheist himself, he sought to draw on the resources of Asian religions, but he saw in all the religions an attempt to free us from the narrow socialisation we internalised, through which we were prepared for the exterministic civilisation of consumerism.[21] Mumford believed something similar, describing it as the need for human beings to resume possession of themselves. He thought the city played a key role in the process. 'We must now conceive the city', he wrote, 'not primarily as a place of business or government, but as an essential organ for expressing and actualizing the new human personality – that of "One World Man".'[22] That hope stands in stark contrast to his pessimism in the face of the growth of the mega city. His master, Patrick Geddes, had wanted the city to be the centre for schools of local culture and envisaged a civic version of the medieval cathedral at its centre, bringing together cultural resources, ideals and knowledge.[23] These proposals are reminiscent of the religions of reason of the late eighteenth century and if church history teaches Bahro scepticism surely even greater scepticism is indicated here. In view of its demonstrable creativity, the fruit of the dialectic of cross and resurrection, the facing of pain, evil, nothingness, without bitterness and without despair, why should we not look to the Church? Perhaps it still has its part to play, alongside many other voices, in the creation of those nurturing spiritualities which can teach us to build again. Nurture, in human community, means education.

Presciently anticipating the 'end of work' debate, Mumford saw education as the main function of the city, enabling the change from a power economy to a life economy and thus global political and physical

[18] Think, for example of Chagall's work in the Musée Nationale Biblique, in Nice; of Britten's War Requiem, the poetry of R. S. Thomas or T. S. Eliot, or the prose of Graham Greene.
[19] Cf. Bloch's remark: 'Only the beginnings of another society will make genuine architecture possible again' (*Principle*, p. 737).
[20] Bahro, *Avoiding*, p. 172.   [21] Ibid., p. 201.
[22] L. Mumford, *The City in History* (Harmondsworth: Penguin, 1991), p. 653.
[23] P. Geddes, *Cities in Evolution* (London: Williams and Norgate, 1949 (orig. 1915)), chs. 13 and 14.

transformations. Schumacher believed that a failure of education lay at the root of economic exterminism, the idea that growth will solve all our problems. We are suffering from a metaphysical disease, he said, by which he meant a loss of clarity respecting fundamental convictions, and therefore the cure must be metaphysical. 'Education which fails to clarify our central convictions is mere training or indulgence. For it is our central convictions that are in disorder, and, as long as the present anti-metaphysical temper persists, the disorder will grow worse.'[24] Clarifying central convictions is what Church is about – precisely this is what brought people in fierce contest to Nicaea, Constantinople and Chalcedon. I have argued that in the shaping of the future, in finding ways to house eight or twelve billion not just with dignity but with beauty, community and citizen involvement is essential, but, as Schumacher points out, that could be disastrous in the absence of the emergence of a new, strong and deep spirituality ranked alongside the marginalised, and opposed to the powers of the big battalions. There is an urgent educational task to which Church is called. In the first chapter I spoke of the humanism of Vitruvian man, which, looking to classical sources, inspired a whole new architecture, an architecture of 'man the measure of all things', bold and self confident. That humanism ran into the sand in the machine age, of which the Network Society is but the latest manifestation. A key part of the problem, as we have seen at a number of points, is that technological capacities have suggested that we are free of limits. The reference point of Vitruvian man was the human body; for early twentieth century builders it was the capacities of steel; today the limits are supposedly Cyberspace. In this context John O'Neill calls us to re-think society with our bodies, to reject the alienating vision of robots and cyborgs.[25] He effectively calls us to a new humanism, and, as noted in the first chapter, Christology necessarily has something to say to that. A new architecture springing from a Christologically refracted vision, refracted by cross and resurrection, would be an architecture and planning which recovered human scale, an architecture and planning which were modest and beautiful at the same time. In the educational task of shaping the future Church is but one voice: but it too has a voice.

To understand the task of the Church like this might be the contemporary equivalent of the Isaianic theology of the Servant. The Servant,

[24] E. F. Schumacher, *Small is Beautiful* (London: Sphere, 1974), p. 83.
[25] J. O'Neill, *Five Bodies: The Human Shape of Modern Society* (Ithaca: Cornell University Press, 1985), p. 151.

whether an individual or community, was not called to garner honour for him or herself but to be 'a light to the nations, that my salvation may reach to the end of the earth' (Isa. 49.6). If Church inherits that task, then it is first and foremost called out, imagined community for the sake of the wider human community, and wider human community for the sake of the earth which sustains us. Once again, a positive and negative task are involved. Negatively, because the poor and the planet are so threatened if the perverse logic of capital continues, putting a spoke in its operations is vital, and doing that is part of ec-clesia's *raison d'être*. Positively, the re-imagining of the world involved in 'mission' involves re-imagining our built environment as well. This is but taking up an ancient prophetic task. Jeremiah urged the exiles to build houses in Babylon and seek the good of the city, and both Isaiah and Ezekiel dreamed at length about the new city, the city of peace and justice. None of them dreamed of a city in the next world; on the contrary, they hoped for its realisation here and now. Ernst Bloch traces architectural utopias to these ancient dreams. As he insisted, utopia is not a matter of escapism or daydreaming.[26] Alternative visions are needed to change the world, says David Harvey, providing the grist for shaping powerful political forces for change. 'Utopian dreams . . . are omnipresent as the hidden signifiers of our desires.'[27] Bismarck regarded the Sermon on the Mount as utopian but for the Christian cross and resurrection are the hermeneutic of the Sermon. They announce the realism of utopia. It is in the light of the resurrection that Paul can speak of 'the God of hope' (Rom. 15.13). Hope, Paul already saw, contradicts the hopelessness of the present. 'It is in this contradiction that hope must prove its power.'[28] Hope builds on the possibilities with which the world as it exists is pregnant, 'uncovering real possibilities and alternatives' in a process which Harvey calls 'dialectical utopianism'.[29] In a similar way Moltmann argues that, against the 'realism' of the status quo it is hope alone which is realistic 'because it alone takes seriously the possibilities with which all reality is fraught'.[30] In considering the homes and settlements in which we actually live, the spaces we occupy, the land which is occupied, I have tried to see with what possibilities they might be pregnant, which criteria might guide us toward that more human future, which Isaiah, and the Jewish and Christian traditions after him, have called 'Jerusalem'. This

---

[26] Bloch, *Principle*, pp. 1278ff.
[27] D. Harvey, *Spaces of Hope* (Edinburgh: Edinburgh University Press, 2000), p. 195.
[28] J. Moltmann, *Theology of Hope* (London: SCM, 1967), p. 19.
[29] Harvey, *Spaces of Hope*, p. 206.   [30] Moltmann, *Theology of Hope*, p. 25.

building of a new world is in principle an unfinished task, a 'permanent revolution' to use a phrase of Karl Barth's.[31] This revolution, we have seen, is guided by the criteria of sustainability, justice, empowerment, situatedness, and diversity. To these I want to add, in this final chapter, enchantment. Sustainability I addressed at length in the last chapter and in the discussion of house and city. In returning to these criteria in the context of the journey towards Jerusalem I turn, then, first, to the issue of justice.

I. JUSTICE AND THE BUILT ENVIRONMENT

If the demand for sustainability follows from our theology of creation, the demand for justice follows from our understanding of reconciliation. If all human beings are made in the image of God Christian theology cannot, like liberal political theorists, dismiss the demands of egalitarianism as rhetoric.[32] It has to seek to honour that image practically, in housing as in wage and employment structures. Liberation theology sought to make this practical in terms of the 'priority of the poor' and for fifty years this was thought of as a North–South issue. At the end of the millennium, however, Manuel Castells has argued that the growth of the global economy has changed the global pattern of wealth and poverty, power and powerlessness. The old categories of developed and underdeveloped, First World and Third World, North and South, are no longer analytically useful. Rather, Castells speaks of the rise of a Fourth World, 'made up of multiple black holes of social exclusion throughout the planet'. It comprises much of sub Saharan Africa, Latin America and Asia, but is to be found in the inner cities of the United States and Europe as well. Throughout the world there are 'millions of homeless, incarcerated, prostituted, criminalized, brutalized, stigmatized, sick and illiterate persons' growing in number everywhere, as informational capitalism, and the political breakdown of the welfare state, intensify social exclusion.[33] The gap between rich and poor continues to grow and this inevitably has repercussions in housing. A walkabout of any great city

---

[31] Harvey, *Spaces of Hope*, p. 237, talks of the 'permanent revolution' in spatial forms, echoing a famous article by Paul Lehmann which described Karl Barth as the 'theologian of permanent revolution', taking up a phrase from Barth's commentary on Romans. (*Union Theological Seminary Review* 28/1 (1972)). This happily brings theology and the built environment into the closest working relationship.

[32] As for example John Gray, *Beyond the New Right* (London: Routledge, 1994). Duncan Forrester has now re-stated the Christian case for equality in *On Human Worth* (London: SCM, 2001).

[33] Castells, *End of Millennium*, pp. 164–5.

on earth makes clear that this is one of the areas where injustice is most manifest. Globally the citizens of the Fourth World live in favelas, shanty towns, tent cities, without water or sewage, in tenements or sink estates, with rising damp, poor access, poor schools and high crime rates. Hardly surprising that foremost among the demands of Agenda 21 is the provision of adequate shelter for all.

Social justice is currently an unfashionable issue, and the 'Social Justice' Report prepared for the British Labour Party before the 1997 election eschewed the idea of 'levelling' as harmfully unrealistic (which meant unelectable). Wealth creation not redistribution is the agenda. But when the richest Mexican earns more than the poorest 17 million Mexicans; when, in 1998, three billionaires earned more than all the less developed nations at the United Nations; when half of the world's largest economies are centrally planned for the benefit of less than 1 per cent of the world's people, the suspicion that redistribution might still be on the agenda crosses the mind.[34] In the light of the incarnation, it simply cannot be avoided. The old name for the organised struggle for equity was socialism, in the non dogmatic sense George Orwell affirmed in *The Road to Wigan Pier*: 'We have got to fight for justice and liberty, and Socialism does mean justice and liberty when the nonsense is stripped off it.'[35] The events of 1989 notwithstanding, the need to fashion a sustainable socialist society remains a necessity first because it is demanded by our understanding of what is demanded by the creation of human beings in the image of God, but also because injustice is unsustainable, and wherever you find it you find the attempt to overthrow it. Unjust societies are unstable societies, societies not destined to last. No sustainability without justice, and no justice without sustainability, to paraphrase Rosa Luxemburg.

In spelling out what is meant by 'justice' Iris Marion Young speaks of the 'five faces' of oppression – exploitation, marginalisation, powerlessness, cultural imperialism and violence.[36] It is easy to see how all these dimensions manifest themselves in the built environment: exploitation in

[34] The figures are from United Nations Development Programme Reports. Less than 1% of the world's population own stocks and shares, but fifty of the world's largest economies are transnational corporations, answerable only to their shareholders. Opponents of the idea of social justice, like John Gray or Joseph Raz, maintain that the presence of structural inequality in society does not mean anyone is wronged by it. This could be the case in the world of philosophical debating points, but is not the case anywhere in the real world, where inequalities always go together with vastly different life chances.

[35] G. Orwell, *The Road to Wigan Pier* (Harmondsworth: Penguin, 1962), p. 205.

[36] I. M. Young, *Justice and the Politics of Difference* (Princeton: Princeton University Press, 1990), pp. 42ff.

the rack renting the poor are subject to; marginalisation in the formation of sink estates and 'no go areas'; powerlessness in the lack of consultation and control over their circumstances; cultural imperialism in the destruction of vernacular patterns, violence in the proneness to street crime of poor areas, and the greater risk of car accidents for children. Harvey is sceptical of egalitarian notions of justice because of the conundrum that equal treatment of unequals increases inequality. In a later publication he implicitly recognises that the acceptance of a belief in the equality of persons requires '[f]undamental redefinitions of wealth, well-being, and values . . . in ways that are more conducive to the development of human potentialities of all segments of the population'.[37] We do not have to be starry eyed about building ourselves into paradise to see that all of the dimensions Young highlights not only can be but are often addressed in examples of good practice around the world.[38] 'Concrete utopias' are not just dreamable but attainable. What political will is it, then, which prevents their realisation?

II. EMPOWERMENT

The demand for empowerment follows, I have been arguing, from that text which speaks so powerfully to our present, the demand that all the Lord's people should be prophets. As we have seen there are a wide range of competing, and to some extent contradictory, options about the future of the built environment. Who is to decide between them? Much planning is currently obstructive of people's creativity. At the same time the environmental crisis has underlined the fact that we cannot live without it. How is that contradiction to be resolved? The key point is that *ordinary people, the whole community, have to be part of the process.* This is implicit in the Church's community charter, 1 Corinthians 12, the hierarchy and the power structures of the Church notwithstanding. Where Jesus spoke of 'kingdom' Paul spoke of 'body', a body which itself constituted 'the body of Christ', which was the body of Christ this side of the resurrection. The whole body was 'in-spired', breathed through and empowered by Spirit. The whole body had gifts to offer. And since the source of these gifts was the same in each case it was impossible to value one gift

[37] D. Harvey, *Justice, Nature and the Geography of Difference* (Oxford: Blackwell, 1996), p. 436.
[38] Everyone will be able to offer their own examples of good practice. Dundee, in Scotland, illustrates excellent examples of fine post World War I estates, built on Unwinesque principles, which remain beautiful and well maintained; 1960s estates which are unlettable and vandalised, a sink for drugs and crime; and housing association developments in the late 1990s which try to capitalise on the natural beauty of the city and offer affordable housing which is not just decent but beautiful.

above another. For this reason, though there is a variety of gifts, the whole community contributes to the process of shaping the future.

The need for empowerment was recognised by the founding fathers of town planning, people like Howard, Geddes and Kropotkin, who thought of planning as a popular movement and regarded citizen participation to be the key. For Geddes, every citizen should have an understanding of the possibilities of his or her own city.[39] What the need for democratic planning emphasises is that *place,* and not just shared interest, continues to be constitutive of community. The more power leaches into Castell's 'space of flows' the less genuine democracy, the less real debate about the things that matter in the fabric of our lives, there can be. Place, then, and planning in relation to place, is at the heart of the future of democracy. In 1977 Robert Fishman targeted the loss of common meaning or purpose as the root of the hostility to planning which was so marked a feature of that decade, at the same time observing that the energy crisis might lead to a return to it. The absurdities and disasters of the planning process are well documented, obstructing, as they do, not so much the out of town developers but those seriously concerned for low impact development. John Turner and Colin Ward's plea, which goes back forty years now, for people to have the freedom to express themselves in self build developments is very well taken. At the same time the demands of sustainability make a planning process which can obstruct the rich and powerful, rather than the poor and marginal, an imperative. Voting and shopping patterns, and the behaviour of the house market, show quite clearly that sustainable development has not yet become the new form of the common good, as some have hoped. For this reason, as I have already argued, the process of education to further that end is imperative.[40] Without it devolved decision making will be likely to function to reinforce the power of elite groups, as it tends to be better educated people who get involved in such strategies. 'The talkers nearly always win, and these tend to be the professionals, or those few activists who speak on the community's behalf without necessarily having the community's real backing. So this is a pyrrhic victory.'[41] Citizen

[39] Geddes, *Cities,* ch. 13.
[40] M. Breheny, 'Centrists, Decentrists and Compromisers: Views of the Future of Urban Form', in M. Jenks, E. Burton and K. Williams (eds.), *The Compact City: A Sustainable Urban Form?* (London: Routledge, 1998), p. 20.
[41] T. Gibson, 'The Neighbourhood as a Hidden Resource', in J. Miller and V. Mega (eds.), *The Improvement of the Built Environment and Social Integration in Cities* (Luxembourg: Office for Official Publications of the European Communities 1992), p. 242. The problem was confirmed to me repeatedly at a conference of Liverpool clergy with whom I discussed these ideas. Many of them are involved in administering regeneration budgets, and all confirmed that such money,

participation has been a buzz word since the Habitat Conference of 1976, but the reality is often another form of political manipulation.[42] The fact is that, whilst representative democracy is a great gain over the autocracies which preceded it, we are still in the infant stage when it comes to the effective realisation of democracy. In the age of mass media democracy is often confused with populism, but in fact not only are they not the same, but democracy cannot survive alongside populism. The Press Barons are a greater threat to democracy than were the old dictatorships which, with their crude methods and use of force, generated a counter discourse. The empowerment we need in relation to the built environment is, then, part and parcel of the wider political problem of the realisation of democracy. As Habraken and Turner argue, changes in the way we build could effectively change our understanding of politics. Acknowledging the democratic deficit, liberation theology from the start drew on the work of Paulo Freire and his practice of conscientisation, recognising that the education needed is not simply imparting information, but also cultivating the values which underpin practical politics. As I noted in chapter 7, most neighbourhoods are densely honeycombed with community groups of various sorts, church being one. For much of its history church has avowed a hierarchical and authoritarian structure, and in many of its current manifestations it still does. Where we take Paul's struggles in the first letter to the Corinthians seriously, however, this cannot be the case. Learning to be church involves learning to value the gifts of all, involves a practical egalitarianism, an understanding of shared decision making which is a profound anticipation and training for democracy on a wider stage.

III. SITUATEDNESS

In the discussion of the land, I noted the importance of the theme of rest in Israel's history. 'Rest' is not a purely eschatological promise, as Augustine thought. It has concrete manifestations here and now, as we see clearly

ostensibly premised on empowerment, failed to reach and to benefit the poorest members of the community. Disenchantment with political process was so great in one ward that turnout for local elections was a mere five per cent.

[42] So S. Kjellberg, *Urban EcoTheology* (Utrecht: International Books, 2000), p. 85. The Habitat Conference recommended that communities should be involved in planning, that standards for shelter and services should be based on the felt needs of the population, and that, since public participation is a right for everyone, special efforts should be made to strengthen the role of community organisations. R. J. Skinner and M. J. Rodell (eds.), *People, Poverty and Shelter: Problems of Self-Help Housing in the Third World* (London: Methuen, 1983), p. 13.

from the biblical narratives (Josh. 21.44; 2 Sam. 7.1). What the Deuteronomic writers call 'rest' is what Heidegger speaks of as 'dwelling', and
what I call here situatedness. As we saw in the second chapter, Castells'
analysis is that what he calls the 'Network Society' is fundamentally split
between, on the one hand, the 'space of flows' and its actors, and the
'space of place' in which most human experience and meaning is still
based. Environmental localism challenges the priorities of global capital, driven by an (anti) economic rationality which has no respect for
place. The dominant global elites live in the space of flows and consist
of 'identity-less individuals' while, on the other hand, 'people resisting
economic, cultural, and political disfranchisement tend to be attracted
to communal identity'.[43] The idea that we really live in 'the space of
flows', however, is a day dream of metaphysical idealists. There are, of
course, Bauman's 'tourists', the wealthy for whom the entire world is
a playground, but even they have to educate their children somewhere,
and that implies some degree of permanence. The complete rootlessness
of a playboy existence can never be an option for more than a tiny percentage of people. In fact, the vast majority of human beings seek out
and cultivate the goods of place. Whilst social mobility is exceptionally
high, whether for political, religious, or economic reasons, rootedness remains vital to the human sense of well being and thus, as Castells agrees,
'nimbyism' (not in my back yard) is not necessarily to be despised. It is
one thing when rich communities attack the siting of prisons, asylums
or waste treatment plants in their neighbourhood; it is another when
local communities are fighting multi national capital. This can give rise
to what he calls resistance or project identities.

The communes of resistance defend their space, their places, against the place-
less logic of the space of flows characterizing social domination in the Information Age. They claim their historic memory, and/or affirm the permanence of
their values, against the dissolution of history in timeless time, and the celebration of the ephemeral in the culture of real virtuality.[44]

Territorial identity continues to have an important role to play in this,
even though, in an age of migrations, common memories may often not
go back more than a couple of decades. That the preservation of more
ancient memories is vital is evident in the 'heritage' movement to be
found, in one form or another, all over the world. However undesirable
much of this movement is, and its hijacking either by commercial interests or by the state is certainly to be deplored, it signifies the widespread

---

[43] Castells, *Identity*, p. 356.   [44] Ibid., p. 358.

recognition that memory loss is a pathology which attacks the very roots of our identity. There is a balancing act here, between, on the one hand, idealised versions of the past, and on the other complete loss of the particularity of cultural, economic and physical identity.[45] Church has a long experience in this area, as the discussion of inculturation in mission demonstrates. As Lamin Sanneh argues, it has been part of the genius of the gospel to go into the vernacular in every place, thus stimulating local cultures, renewing them, and sowing seeds of revolution.[46] Following Jeremiah it is essential for it to dwell, which is why, contrary to the desires of missionary bishops, churches have put up buildings everywhere, providing foci and facilities for the meeting and growth of local community.

IV. DIVERSITY

At Pentecost the scattering which takes place at Babel is not reversed, but confirmed as a blessing. All the different languages, the roots of culture, do not blend in some ethereal Esperanto. On the contrary, they become mutually intelligible. The 'oneness' of the Church is, as Moltmann rightly insists, a unity in diversity.[47] There is a promise of reconciliation precisely through the celebration of diversity. The same goes for the built environment. Thomas Sharp was right: a homogenised environment is a poor environment. A world composed primarily of suburbs, or edge cities, or mega cities, or a world which was just 'rurban', would be the poorer. Human beings thrive on difference. Discussions of 'cities of difference' tend to focus on the need to guarantee respect for different lifestyles, on finding space for the legitimacy of all groups. What this respect for difference has actually generated, however, is that postmodern eclecticism in which all true difference disappears. Until the mid twentieth century the difficulty of travel effectively guaranteed the persistence of difference. Ideas of course did travel: the arch went from ancient Greece, to the Muslim Near East, and then back to Europe, but over a period of more than a thousand years. Today, in a city like San Francisco where, as Harvey puts it, the minorities make up the majority, real difference is obscured 'through construction of images

---

[45] G. Haughton and C. Hunter, *Sustainable Cities* (London: Regional Studies Association, 1994), p. 311.

[46] L. Sanneh, *Encountering the West* (London: Marshall Pickering, 1993).

[47] J. Moltmann, *The Church in the Power of the Spirit* (London: SCM, 1977), p. 342.

and reconstructions, costume dramas, staged ethnic festivals, etc.'.[48] In Castells' terms, the coming of the space of flows leads to the generalisation of ahistorical, acultural architecture.[49] 'Irony becomes the preferred mode of expression . . . Because we do not belong any longer to any place, to any culture, the extreme version of postmodernism imposes its codified code-breaking logic anywhere something is built.'[50] This architecture, writes Jeffrey Cook, amounts to the 'international trivialization of human life'.[51] Against that view there are those who argue that ordinary people symbolically mark their localities in inventive ways 'against the new rootless cultural imperialists', but this may underestimate the extent to which our buildings shape us.[52]

In the interests of the homeliness of the world common meanings have to honour the spiritualities, and therefore individualities, of ten millennia. Global meanings need to express themselves through local meanings. Malcolm Wells offers us an evaluation scale for our new buildings, charting their sustainability rating but also asking, finally, whether they are beautiful or destroy beauty.[53] I wish to add the criterion of respect for indigenous cultures. This is not to advocate that we all live in tepees or igloos. It is to argue that the world is a far poorer place if we let the diversity of human exploration be swilled down the drain. Once again, Church experience of inculturation is important here. Though the British empire, in an acute loss of imagination, sought to generalise gothic everywhere as the image of what a church must be, there has never been one image, one heavenly archetype, of what a church building should look like. All local vernaculars have been assimilated to express the gospel. In this respect Church practice ought to provide a model for secular practice.

ENCHANTEDNESS

I argued in the first chapter that the roots of secularisation were to be found in the Hebrew bible. The ancient world was de-divinised. It

[48] Harvey, *Condition*, p. 87.

[49] M. Castells, *The Rise of the Network Society* (Oxford: Blackwell, 1996), p. 418.

[50] Ibid., p. 376.

[51] J. Cook, 'Environmentally benign architecture', in R. Samuels and D. Prasad, *Global Warming and the Built Environment* (London: Spon, 1996), p. 132.

[52] A. Cohen and K. Fukui (eds.), *Humanising the City? Social Contexts of Urban Life at the Turn of the Millennium* (Edinburgh: Edinburgh University Press, 1993), p. 217.

[53] Malcolm Wells, 'Underground Architecture', *Co evolution Quarterly* (Sausalito, California) 11 (Autumn 1976), p. 89.

was not, however, robbed of enchantment, as the psalms and the final chapters of Job show and as the Franciscan tradition in Christianity has especially emphasised. Max Weber famously appropriated a line of Schiller in speaking of the disenchantment of the world. For him this was on the whole a good thing, because it signified our freeing from fate, but good or bad there was no option but to bear it. Today, says Castells, '[s]ocieties are finally and truly disenchanted because all wonders are on-line and can be combined into self-constructed image worlds'.[54] In fact, however, the world remains an enchanted place, as reality has a habit of asserting itself over against virtuality, in both the difficulties and delights of relationships, in the immediacies of every kind of cultural experience, from the pub and café to the theatre and concert hall, and in our encounter with both the natural world and many parts of the built environment. After romanticism the temptation is to think of enchantment as an aspect especially of the natural world, but there are many enchanting villages, towns, and cities, and houses and gardens too can be full of enchantment. By this I mean places which allure us with their beauty, which call us to a halt, which refresh us with their charm and are a positive ease and delight for the spirit. Christopher Day makes the creation of such places the aim of his architectural practice. The world's beauty has not, in fact, disappeared just as space exploration has not dimmed the beauty of the moon. This is not to say that enchantment can be taken for granted, as the recent struggle in Scotland to prevent chairlifts to the centre of the Cairngorm plateau, or the wrecking of Thailand's most beautiful beach in the interests of Hollywood, remind us. Gerard Manley Hopkins' protest that the world 'wears man's smudge and shares man's smell' has more cause now than when it was written, and we are called to be vigilant. But equally, as he goes on to say,

> And for all this, nature is never spent;
> There lives the dearest freshness deep down things;
> And though the last lights off the black West went
> Oh, morning, at the brown brink eastward, springs –
> Because the Holy Ghost over the bent
> World broods with warm breast and with ah! bright wings.[55]

What is important, then, is not to locate enchantment solely in the past, but to seek it in the present, to make it an objective of our building and

[54] Castells, *Network Society*, p. 375.
[55] G. M. Hopkins, 'God's Grandeur', *Poems and Prose of G. M. Hopkins* (Harmondsworth: Penguin, 1953), p. 27.

our town planning. In a world of eight or twelve billion it is also vital that
we retain places where it is possible to be really alone, to be awed, to sense
the sublime, to be surprised. These are the places which in Scripture are
denoted by 'mountain' and 'desert', places of solitude, outside reigning
plausibility structures.

These criteria, and the goals towards which they point us, may all be
very worthy, but how are they to be arrived at, and what have they to
do with Church? Though he was sceptical Bahro thought Church might
have a contribution to make if it began, not with the sin and fall of human
beings, but with the resurrection of Christ.

If it is true that Christ lived and was a man, then we have at least an indication that
the 'anthropological revolution' is possible, as the Catholic liberation theologian
Johann Baptist Metz named it in the context of Marcuse and Christologically
interpreted it. In our reflections about ORDO we should begin, not with the
fall of Adam and Eve, but with the symbol of the resurrected Christ, which the
Holy Ghost gives to all humans.[56]

In his appeal to the resurrection Bahro placed himself unwittingly
alongside the theologians of hope. Christian theology endorses neither the millenarianism of progress, which Castells' *End of the Millennium*
seems finally to propose, nor the apocalyptic threats of doom of the
American Armageddon enthusiasts. It is, as Moltmann puts it, 'a historical theology of struggle and hope'.[57] Christian apocalyptic, guided by
the resurrection, steers a course between facile optimism and melancholy
hopelessness.

In view of the deadly dangers threatening the world, Christian remembrance
makes-present the death of Christ in its apocalyptic dimensions, in order to draw
from his resurrection from the dead hope for 'the life of the world to come', and
from his rebirth to eternal life hope for the rebirth of the cosmos ... Life out
of this hope ... means already acting here and today in accordance with that
world of justice and righteousness and peace, contrary to all appearances, and
contrary to all historical chances of success.[58]

Moltmann might also have mentioned the advice to be as wise as ser-
pents. Harvey calls 'crafty architects bent on insurgency' 'to think strate-
gically and tactically about what to change and where ... how to change
what and with what tools'.[59] Now there's a task for Lent groups ... That
is not just a joke: it is a challenge to re-think Church's task in terms of
its own education and its contribution to the education of society as a

[56] Bahro, *Avoiding*, p. 68.   [57] J. Moltmann, *The Coming of God* (London: SCM, 1996), p. 200.
[58] Ibid., p. 234.   [59] Harvey, *Spaces of Hope*, p. 233.

whole, which proceeds only through the contribution of its participant
groups. It is a question of re-learning that the so-called secular is not
outside our remit, that the High Street is still more of a Christian task
than the repair of the church tower, that, as Bonhoeffer put it, Christ is
'truly Lord of the world'.

Looking at Britain in the early days of the industrial revolution Blake
saw the triumph of a mechanistic and rationalistic world view:

> I turn my eyes to the Schools and Universities of Europe
> And there behold the Loom of Locke, whose Woof rages dire,
> Wash'd by the Water-wheels of Newton: black the cloth
> In heavy wreathes folds over every Nation: cruel Works
> Of many Wheels I view, wheel without wheel, with cogs tyrannic
> Moving by compulsion each other, not as those in Eden, which,
> Wheel within Wheel, in freedom revolve in harmony and peace.
>
> (*Jerusalem* 15.14–20)

Today the loom of Locke has been replaced by the loom of Derrida or
Baudrillard, manufacturing industry by finance and tourism, producing by consuming – but the result is the same: cogs tyrannic moving by
compulsion each other. Blake spoke of the cathedral cities of England as
'friends of Albion', what I have called agents in the economy of redemption. In order to make our cities friends of 'Albion', which is all nations
and all cultures, we have to be determined not to rest from mortal fight
until – let us not say Jerusalem, but at any rate a built environment cor-
respondent to the full realm of human purpose and visions, the good life
not defined by consumerism and the demands of Mammon – is builded
here, in the whole inhabited earth.

Not the end of history, but the beginning, says Castells. Castells bases
his optimism not on the resurrection but on the capacity of reason, but
some will find that faith even more incredible, at the end of two centuries
of 'enlightenment' and market 'rationality', than faith in resurrection.[60]
There can be no underestimating the tasks involved in making the world
home for eight billion. Technical advances like the advent of solar power
will help, but the problem goes far deeper, to the roots of the human
spirit, which need nurturing, watering, fertilising, with stories, dreams,
and visions. The origins of architectural utopias, says Ernst Bloch, are to
be found in the story of the Exodus.[61] Implausible as that sounds it points

---

[60] Harries, for example, notes: 'We must resist . . . that absolutism which makes reason the measure
of reality instead of recognizing the reduction that reality's objectification inevitably entails'
(*Function*, p. 68). I also take for granted Adorno and Horkheimer's *Dialectic of Enlightenment*.
[61] Bloch, *Principle*, p. 732.

to the way in which human dreams of freedom find expression in the environment human beings create for themselves. Such dreams found potent expression, I have argued, not only in medieval cathedrals and cities, but in much vernacular architecture, but we cannot, like much of the nineteenth century, pine after a vanished golden age. In the power of the Spirit, which breathes through all cultures and all generous and humane imaginaries, the human dream of freedom may, and indeed must, find expression in the cities of tomorrow, imaging what Blake calls 'the human form divine' in city streets and the houses of ordinary people. Such a hope implies no false Christian messianism, but a belief in the contribution of faith in the Triune God to the whole human story, faith in the God who identifies with the lowly, who calls slaves out of every Egypt, and who raises the dead from the death of despair to the promise of new life. 'Mortal, can these bones live?' (Ezek. 37.3) A question to the condition of postmodernity, with its social atomism, infinite dispersal, and nihilism. If Spirit truly speaks to spirit, the answer then may be the answer now, finding sinews and flesh in a new common project, a world of beauty and equality which respects the earth. Why not?

Select bibliography

Abbott, J. (1996) *Sharing the City*, London: Earthscan

Abulafia, D. Franklin, M. and Rubin, M. (1992) *Church and City 1000–1500* Cambridge: Cambridge University Press

Alavi, H. (1994) 'The two biraderis: kinship in rural West Punjab', in T. N. Madan (ed.), *Muslim Societies in South Asia*, New Delhi: Vikas

Alberti (1986) *The Ten Books of Architecture*, New York: Dover

Andruss, V. et al., (1990) *Home! A Bioregional Reader*, Philadelphia: New Society

Aquinas (1948) *Selected Political Writings*, ed. A. P. D'Entreves, tr. J. Dawson, Oxford: Blackwell

  Summa Theologiae (1964–81), London: Eyre and Spottiswoode

Archer, J. (1997) 'Colonial Suburbs in South Asia 1700–1850, and the Spaces of Modernity', in R. Silverstone (ed.), *Visions of Suburbia*, London: Routledge, pp. 26–54

Arnold, A. (1880) *Free Land*, London: Kegan Paul

Arts Council (1985) *The Architecture of Adolf Loos*, London

Atherton, J. (1992) *Christianity and the Market*, London: SPCK

Auerbach, E. (1974) *Mimesis*, Princeton: Princeton University Press

Augustine (1865) *Contra Julianum*, Patrologia Cursus Completus, Seria Latina vol. XLIV, ed. J. P. Migne, Paris

  (1972) *The City of God*, tr. H. Bettenson, Harmondsworth: Penguin

Avila, C. (1983) *Ownership: Early Christian Teaching*, Maryknoll: Orbis

Bachelard, G. (1969) *The Poetics of Space*, Boston: Beacon

Bahro, R. (1994) *Avoiding Social and Ecological Disaster: The Politics of World Transformation*, Bath: Gateway

Baker, W. P. (1953) *The English Village*, London: Oxford University Press

Ballinger, J. and Cassell, D. (1994) 'Principles of energy efficient residential design', in R. Samuels and D. Prasad (eds.), *Global Warming and the Built Environment*, London: Spon, pp. 169–87

Balthasar, H. Urs von (1982) 'Liberation Theology in the Light of Salvation History', in J. V. Schall (ed.), *Liberation Theology in Latin America*, San Francisco: Ignatius Press, pp. 132–44

Barnet, R. and Cavanagh, J. (1996) 'Homogenization of Global Culture', in J. Mander and E. Goldsmith (eds.), *The Case against the Global Economy*, San Francisco: Sierra Club, pp. 71–7

Barnett, A. and Scruton, R. (eds.) (1998) *Town and Country*, London: Jonathan Cape

Barrett, G. (1998) 'The Transport Dimension', in M. Jenks, E. Burton and K. Williams (eds.), *The Compact City: A Sustainable Urban Form?*, London, Routledge, pp. 171–80

Barth, K. (1993) *The Epistle to the Romans*, tr. E. Hoskyns, London: Oxford University Press

(1956–75) *Church Dogmatics*, 13 vols., Edinburgh: T&T Clark

(1981) *Letters 1961–1968*, Edinburgh: T&T Clark

Bater, J. H. (1980) *The Soviet City*, London: Arnold

Baum, G. (1994) 'Two Question Marks: Inculturation and Multiculturalism', *Concilium* 1994/2, pp. 101–6

Bauman, Z. (1991) *Modernity and Ambivalence*, Cambridge: Polity

(1993) *Postmodern Ethics*, Oxford: Blackwell

Belloc, H. (1913) *The Catholic Encyclopaedia*, New York: Universal Knowledge Foundation

Benevolo, L. (1993) *The European City*, Oxford: Blackwell

Bennett, E. N. (1914) *Problems of Village Life*, London: Williams and Norgate

Beresford, M. (1967) *New Towns of the Middle Ages: Town Plantation in England, Wales and Gascony*, London: Lutterworth

Bergmann, S. (1995) *Geist, der Natur befreit. Die trintarische Kosmologie Gregors von Nazianz im Horizont einer ökologischen Theologie der Befreiung*, Mainz: Grünewald

Berryman, P. (1996) *Religion in the Megacity*, Maryknoll: Orbis

Birchall, J. (ed.) (1992) *Housing Policy in the 1990s*, London: Routledge

Blake, W. (1969) *Complete Writings*, ed. G. Keynes, Oxford: Oxford University Press

Bloch, E. (1986) *The Principle of Hope*, tr. N. Plaice, S. Plaice and P. Knight, Oxford: Blackwell

Boardman, J., Griffin, J. and Murray, O. (eds.) (1986) *The Oxford History of the Classical World*, Oxford: Oxford University Press

Boff, L. (1979) *Liberating Grace*, Maryknoll: Orbis

(1995), *Ecology and Liberation: A New Paradigm*, Maryknoll: Orbis

Bogucki, P. (1999) *The Origins of Human Society*, Oxford: Blackwell

Bonham Carter, V. (1952) *The English Village*, Harmondsworth: Penguin

Bonhoeffer, D. (1967) *Letters and Papers from Prison*, 3rd edn, London: SCM

Bookchin, M. (1974) *Post Scarcity Anarchism*, London: Wildwood House

Boyes, G. (1993) *The Imagined Village*, Manchester: Manchester University Press

Bradstock, A. (1997): *Faith in the Revolution: The Political Theologies of Muntzer and Winstanley*, London: SPCK

Branford, V. and Geddes, P. (1919) *The Coming Polity*, London: Williams & Norgate

Braudel, F. (1981) *The Structures of Everyday Life*, Glasgow: Collins

Breheny, M. (1998) 'Centrists, Decentrists and Compromisers: Views of the Future of Urban Form', in M. Jenks, E. Burton and K. Williams (eds.), *The Compact City: A Sustainable Urban Form?*, London: Routledge, pp. 13–35

Brook, P. (1972) *The Empty Space*, Harmondsworth: Penguin

Brown, L. (1998) *The State of the World 1998*, London: Earthscan

Brown, P. (1996) *The Rise of Western Christendom*, Oxford: Blackwell

Brown, W. P. and Carroll, J. T. (2000) 'The Garden and the Plaza', *Interpretation* 54/1 (January 2000), pp. 3–11

Brueggemann, W. (1977) *The Land*, Philadelphia: Fortress

Buber, M. (1960) *The Origin and Meaning of Hasidism*, New York: Horizon
(1961) *Between Man and Man*, London: Collins

Burch, E. and Berg, L. E. (eds.) (1994) *Hunter Gatherer Research*, Oxford: Oxford University Press

Burton, T. and Matson, L. (1998) 'Urban Footprints: Making Best Use of Land and Resources', in M. Jenks, E. Burton and K. Williams (eds.), *The Compact City: A Sustainable Urban Form?*, London: Routledge, pp. 298–301

Callander, R. (1998) *How Scotland is Owned*, Edinburgh: Canongate

Carver, M. O. H. (1993) *Arguments in Stone: Archaeological Research and the European Town in the First Millennium*, Oxford: Oxbow

Castells, M. (1996) *The Rise of the Network Society*, Oxford: Blackwell
(1997) *The Power of Identity*, Oxford: Blackwell
(1998) *End of Millennium*, Oxford: Blackwell

Castles, S. and Miller, M. (1998) *The Age of Migration*, London: Macmillan, 2nd edn

Church, G. (1979) 'Bucharest: Revolution in the Townscape Art', in R. French and F. Hamilton (eds.), *The Socialist City*, Chichester: Wiley, pp. 493–506

Clark, P. (ed.) (1976) *The Early Modern Town*, London: Longman

Cloke, P. and Little, J. (eds.) (1997) *Contested Countryside Cultures: Otherness, marginalisation and rurality*, London: Routledge

Cohen, A. and Fukui, K. (eds.) (1993) *Humanising the City? Social Contexts of Urban Life at the Turn of the Millennium*, Edinburgh: Edinburgh University Press

Cole, I. and Furbey, R. (1994) *The Eclipse of Council Housing*, London: Routledge

Coleman, A. (1985) *Utopia on Trial: Vision and Reality in Planned Housing*, London: Shipman

Common Ground (1993) *Local Distinctiveness: Place, Particularity and Identity*, London: 1993

Commoner, B. (1971) *The Closing Circle*, New York: Knopf

Cook, J. (1994) 'Environmentally benign architecture', in R. Samuels and D. Prasad (eds.), *Global Warming and the Built Environment*, London: Spon, pp. 125–51

Corbusier, C. Le (1965) *Towards a New Architecture*, London: The Architectural Press
(1971) *The City of Tomorrow and its Planning*, London: The Architectural Press

Coulanges, F. de (n.d.) *The Ancient City*, New York: Doubleday

Cox, H. (1965) *The Secular City*, Harmondsworth: Penguin

Cox, K. (2000) *Vastu Living: Creating a Home for the Soul*, New York: Marlowe & Co.

Daly, H. (1996) *Beyond Growth*, Boston: Beacon

Daly, H. and Cobb, J. (1990) *For the Common Good*, London: Green Print
Darley, G. (1993) *Local Distinctiveness: Place, Particularity and Identity*, London: Common Ground, pp. 29–36
Davies, J. G. (1972) *Everyday God*, London: SCM
Davies, W. D. (1974) *The Gospel and the Land*, Berkeley: University of California Press
Davis, M. (1998) *City of Quartz*, London: Pimlico
Day, C. (1990) *Places of the Soul*, London: Thorsons (an imprint of Harper Collins)
Denman, D. R. (1958) *Origins of Ownership*, London: Allen & Unwin
Denman, D. R., Roberts, R. A. and Smith, H. J. F. (1967) *Commons and Village Greens*, London: Leonard Hill
Devi, V. (2000) 'A Cry for Justice', *Frontline* 17 / 13 (13 June–7 July)
Dillistone, F. W. (1973) *Traditional Symbols and the Contemporary World*, London: Epworth
Pseudo Dionysius (1987) *The Complete Works*, New York: Paulist
Donnison, D. and Ungerson, C. (1982) *Housing Policy*, Harmondsworth: Penguin
Douthwaite, R. (1992) *The Growth Illusion*, Totnes: Green Books
Doxiadis, C. (1977), *Ecology and Ekistics*, London: Elek
Doxiadis, C. (ed.) (1974) *Anthropopolis*, New York: Norton
Drabble, M. (1979) *A Writer's Britain: Landscape in Literature*, London: Thames & Hudson
Durning, A. T. (1992) *How Much is Enough?*, London: Earthscan
Eco, U. (1988) *The Aesthetics of Thomas Aquinas*, London: Hutchinson
Edwards, A. (1981) *The Design of Suburbia*, London: Pembridge
Eliade, M. (1959) *The Sacred and the Profane*, New York: Harcourt & Brace
Elias, N. (1994) *The Civilising Process*, Oxford: Blackwell
Ellul, J. (1970) *The Meaning of the City*, Grand Rapids: Eerdmans
European Workshop (1992) *The Improvement of the Built Environment and Social Integration in Cities*, Luxembourg: EEC
Fairlie, S. (1996) *Low Impact Development*, Charlbury: Jon Carpenter
Fincher, R. and Jacobs, J. M. (eds.) (1998) *Cities of Difference*, New York: Guilford
Fischer, E. (1963) *The Necessity of Art*, Harmondsworth: Penguin
Fishman, R. (1982) *Urban Utopias in the Twentieth Century*, Cambridge: Mass.: MIT
Forrester, D. (2001) *On Human Worth*, London: SCM
Foucault, M. (1980) *Power / Knowledge*, London: Harvester Wheatsheaf
Frankenberg, R. (1966) *Communities in Britain: Social Life in Town and Country*, Harmondsworth: Penguin
French, R. A. and Hamilton, F. I. (1979) *The Socialist City*, Chichester: Wiley
Froissart (1968) *Chronicles*, ed. G. Brereton, Harmondsworth: Penguin
Gaita, R. (2000) *A Common Humanity*, London: Routledge
Gans, H. (1967) *The Levittowners*, London: Allen Lane
    (1991) *People, Plans and Policies. Essays on Poverty, Racism and Other National Urban Problems*, New York: Columbia University Press
Garreau, J. (1988) *Edge City*, New York: Anchor Doubleday

Gaskell, S. M. (ed.) (1990) *Slums*, Leicester: Leicester University Press

Geddes, P. (1904) *A Study in City Development*, Dunfermline: Park, Gardens and Culture Institutes

(1915) *Cities in Evolution*, London: Williams and Norgate

General Synod of the Church of England (1985) *Faith in the City*, London: Church House

George, H. (1911) *Progress and Poverty*, London: Dent

Giedion, S. (1974) *Space, Time and Architecture*, 5th edn, Cambridge, Mass: Harvard University Press

Gill, E. (1936) *The Necessity of Belief*, London: Faber & Faber

Girardet, H. (1996) *The Gaia Atlas of Cities*, rev. edn, London: Gaia

Girouard, M. (1985) *Cities and People: A Social and Architectural History*, New Haven: Yale University Press

Goff, J. Le (1988) *Medieval Civilization*, Oxford: Blackwell

Goodman, P. and Goodman, P. (1960) *Communitas: Means of Livelihood and Ways of Life*, New York: Random House

Gordon, D. (1990) *Green Cities: Ecologically Sound Approaches to Urban Space*, Montreal: Black Rose

Gorringe, T. J. (1999) *Fair Shares: Ethics and the Global Economy*, London: Thames & Hudson

(1999) *Karl Barth: Against Hegemony*, Oxford: Oxford University Press

Gottwald, N. (1979) *The Tribes of Yahweh*, London: SCM

(1985) *The Hebrew Bible: A Socio-Literary Introduction*, Philadelphia: Fortress

Graham, E. (1996) 'Theology in the City: Ten Years after *Faith in the City*', Bulletin of the John Rylands Library 78.1

Gray, J. (1994) *Beyond the New Right*, London: Routledge

Green, L. (1995) 'Physicality in the UPA', in P. Sedgwick (ed.), *God in the City: Essays and Reflections from the Archbishop's Urban Theology Group*, London: Mowbray, pp. 72–94

(2000) *The Impact of the Global*, London: Church House

Green, R. (1998) 'Not Compact Cities but Sustainable Regions', in M. Jenks, E. Burton and K. Williams (eds.), *The Compact City: A Sustainable Urban Form?*, London: Routledge, pp. 143–54

Grey, M. (2000) *The Outrageous Pursuit of Hope*, London: Darton, Longman and Todd

(2000) 'The Shape of the Human Home – A Response to Tim Gorringe', *Political Theology* 3 (November 2000), pp. 95–103

Gruchy, J. de (2001) *Christianity, Art and Transformation*, Cambridge: Cambridge University Press

Günther, F. (1995) *Dense Urban Settlements: Ecological Obstacles and Energy Price Vulnerability*, Stockholm: Department of Systems Ecology, Stockholm University

Habel, N. (1995) *The Land is Mine: Six Biblical Ideologies*, Minneapolis: Fortress

Habraken, N. (1972) *Housing Supports: An Alternative to Mass Housing*, London: The Architectural Press

Hackwood, P. and Shiner, P. (1998) 'New Role for the Church in Urban Policy?', in M. Northcote (ed.), *Urban Theology, A Reader*, London: Cassell, pp. 72–6

Hake, A. (1989) 'Theological Reflections on "Community"', in A. Harvey (ed.), *Theology in the City*, London: SPCK, pp. 47–67

Halfacree, K. (1997) 'Postmodern Perspective on Counterurbanisation', in P. Cloke and J. Little (eds.), *Contested Countryside Cultures: Otherness, marginalisation and rurality*, London: Routledge, pp. 70–93

Hall, P. (1988) *Cities of Tomorrow*, Oxford: Blackwell
  (1998) *Cities in Civilization*, London: Weidenfeld and Nicolson

Halpern, J. (1967) *The Changing Village Community*, New Jersey: Prentice Hall

Hammond, M. (1972) *The City in the Ancient World*, Cambridge, Mass.: Harvard University Press

Hardy, D. and Ward, C. (1984) *Arcadia for all: The Legacy of a Makeshift Landscape*, London: Mansell

Harms, H. (1982) 'Historical Perspectives on the Practice and Purpose of Self-Help Housing', in P. Ward (ed.), *Self-Help Housing: A Critique*, London: Mansell, pp. 17–53

Harries, K. (1998) *The Ethical Function of Architecture*, Cambridge, Mass.: MIT

Harvey, A. (ed.) (1989) *Theology in the City*, London: SPCK

Harvey, D. (1973) *Social Justice and the City*, London: Arnold
  (1989) *The Condition of Postmodernity*, Oxford: Blackwell
  (1989) *The Urban Experience*, Oxford: Blackwell
  (1992) 'Social Justice, Postmodernism and the City', in *The Improvement of the Built Environment and Social Integration in Cities*, Luxembourg: Official Publications of the European Communities, pp. 21–40
  (1996) *Justice, Nature and the Geography of Difference*, Oxford: Blackwell
  (2000) *Spaces of Hope*, Edinburgh: Edinburgh University Press

Hastings, A. (1986) *A History of English Christianity 1920–1985*, London: Collins

Haughton, G. and Hunter, C. (1994) *Sustainable Cities*, London: Regional Studies Association

Hayden, B. (1994) 'Competition, Labor and Complex Hunter Gatherers', in E. Burch and L. Ellanna Berg (eds.), *Hunter Gatherer Research*, Oxford: Oxford University Press, pp. 223–43

Hayek, F. (1986) *The Road to Serfdom*, London: ARK

Hayward, D. (1975) 'Home as an environmental and psychological concept', *Landscape* 20, pp. 2–9

Hegel, G. W. F. (1967). *Philosophy of Right*, Oxford: Oxford University Press

Heidegger, M. (1966) *Discourse on Thinking*, New York: Harper & Row
  (1971) *Poetry, Language, Thought*, New York: Harper & Row
  (1978) *Basic Writings*, London: Routledge

Hill, D. M. (1994) *Citizens and Cities*, New York: Harvester Wheatsheaf

Hill, H. (1980) *Freedom to Roam*, Ashbourne: Moorland

Hillman, M. (1998) 'In Favour of the Compact City', in M. Jenks, E. Burton and K. Williams (eds.), *The Compact City: A Sustainable Urban Form?*, London: Routledge, pp. 36–44

Hilton, R. (1990) 'Towns in English Medieval Society', in R. Holt and G. Rosser (eds.), *The English Medieval Town: A Reader in English Urban History 1200–1540*, London: Longman, 1990, pp. 19–28

Hinchcliffe, T. (1992) *North Oxford*, New Haven: Yale University Press

Holt, R. and Rosser, G. (1990) *The English Medieval Town: A Reader in English Urban History 1200–1540*, London: Longman

Hough, M. (1990) *Out of Place*, New Haven: Yale University Press

Howard, E. (1985) *Garden Cities of Tomorrow*, Builth Wells: Attic

Hughes, A. (1997) 'Rurality and Cultures of Womanhood', in P. Cloke and J. Little (eds.), *Contested Countryside Cultures: Otherness, marginalisation and rurality*, London: Routledge, pp. 123–37

Huizinga, J. (1965) *The Waning of the Middle Ages*, Harmondsworth: Penguin

Jackson, J. B. (1984) *Discovering the Vernacular Landscape*, New Haven and London: Yale University Press

Jacobs, J. (1986) *Cities and the Wealth of Nations*, Harmondsworth: Penguin
(1994) *The Death and Life of Great American Cities*, Harmondsworth: Penguin

Jacobs, J. M. (1996) *Edge of Empire*, London: Routledge

James, M. R. (tr.) (1923) *The Apocryphal New Testament*, Oxford: Oxford University Press

Jankowski, G. (1998) 'Dieses Land', *Texte und Kontexte* 80 4/98

Jenks, M., Burton, E. and Williams, K. (eds.) (1998) *The Compact City: A Sustainable Urban Form?* London: Routledge

Jenson, R. (1982) *The Triune Identity*, Philadelphia, Fortress

Jones, G. (1980) *Social Darwinism and English Thought*, Brighton: Harvester

Kaviraj, S. (1997) 'Filth and the Public Sphere: Concepts and Practices about Space in Calcutta', *Public Culture* 10/1, pp. 83–113

Kempis, T. à (1959) The Imitation of Christ, London: Burns & Oates

Kjellberg, S. (2000) *Urban EcoTheology*, Utrecht: International Books

Knight, C. (1998) 'Economic and Social Issues', in M. Jenks, E. Burton and K. Williams (eds.), *The Compact City: A Sustainable Urban Form?*, London: Routledge, pp. 114–21

Korten, D. (1995) *When Corporations Rule the World*, West Hartford, Conn.: Kumarian

Kostoff, S. (1991) *The City Shaped*, London: Thames & Hudson

Küng, H. and Schmidt, H. (1998) *A Global Ethic and Global Responsibilities*, London: SCM

Lafferty, W. (1981) *Participation and Democracy in Norway*, Oslo: Oslo University Press

Langdon, P. (1994) *A Better Place to Live*, Amherst: University of Massachusetts Press

Lash, N. (1988) *Easter in Ordinary: Reflections on Human Experience and the Knowledge of God*, London: SCM

Lee, L. (1962) *Cider with Rosie*, Harmondsworth: Penguin

Lefebvre, H. (1991) *The Production of Space*, Oxford: Blackwell
(1996) *Writings on Cities*, ed. E. Kofman and E. Lebas, Oxford: Blackwell

le Gates, R. T. and Stout, F. (1996) *The City Reader*, London: Routledge

Lehmann, K. P. (1998) 'Die Gerechten erben das Land', *Texte und Kontexte* 80 4/98, pp. 15–40.

Longfield, M. (1881) 'Land Tenure in Ireland', in J. W. Probyn (ed.), *Systems of Land Tenure in Various Countries*, London: Cassell, Petter & Galpin, pp. 1–92

Lorenz, K. (1988) *The Waning of Humaneness*, London: Unwin

Lowe, I. (1994) 'The greenhouse effect and future urban development', in R. Samuels and D. Prasad (eds.), *Global Warming and the Built Environment*, London: Spon, pp. 55–66

Lynch, K. (1960) *The Image of the City*, Cambridge, Mass.: MIT
(1996) *City Sense and City Design*, ed. T. Banerjee and M. Southworth, Cambridge, Mass.: MIT

McDowell, L. (ed.) (1997) *Undoing Place?* London: Arnold

MacIntyre, A. (1967) *A Short History of Ethics*, London: Routledge
(1981) *After Virtue*, London: Duckworth

Madan, T. N. (ed.) (1994) *Muslim Societies in South Asia*, New Delhi: Vikas

Mander, J. and Goldsmith, E. (eds.) (1996) *The Case against the Global Economy*, San Francisco: Sierra Club

Mars, T. (1998) 'The Life in New Towns', in A. Barnett and R. Scruton (eds.), *Town and Country*, London: Jonathan Cape, pp. 267–78

Martinussen, W. (1977) *The Distant Democracy*, London: Wiley

Massey, D. (1994) *Space, Place and Gender*, Cambridge: Polity

Marx, K. (1954) *Capital*, Moscow: Progress
(1959) *Economic and Political Manuscripts*, Moscow: Progress
(1973) *Grundrisse*, ed. David McClellan, Harmondsworth: Penguin

Meecham, H. G. (ed. and tr.) (1935) *The Epistle of Diognetus*, Manchester: Manchester University Press

Merchant, C. (1980) *The Death of Nature*, San Francisco: Harper & Row

Methodist Report (1997) *The Cities*, London: NCH Action for Children

Mingay, G. (1990) 'The rural slum', in S. M. Gaskell (ed.), *Slums*, Leicester: Leicester University Press, pp. 92–143

Mitford, M. (1947) *Our Village*, London: Harrap

Moholy-Nagy, S. (1968) *Matrix of Man*, London: Pall Mall

Moltman, J. (1967) *Theology of Hope*, London: SCM
(1977) *The Church in the Power of the Spirit*, London: SCM
(1985) *God in Creation*, tr. M. Kohl, London: SCM
(1996) *The Coming of God*, tr. M. Kohl, London: SCM
(2000) *Experiences in Theology*, London: SCM

Morris, J. and Winn, M. (1990) *Housing and Social Inequality*, London: Shipman

Morris, M. (ed.) (1936) *William Morris: Artist, Writer, Socialist*, Oxford: Blackwell

Morris, W. (1910–15) *The Collected Work of William Morris*, London: Longmans

Mumford, L. (1938) *The Culture of Cities*, London: Secker & Warburg
(1946) *Technics and Civilization*, London: Routledge
(1952) *Art and Techics*, New York: Columbia University Press
(1964) *The Pentagon of Power*, London: Secker & Warburg

(1967) *The Myth of the Machine*, London: Secker & Warburg

(1991) *The City in History*, Harmondsworth: Penguin

Murray, O. (1986) 'Life and Society in Classical Greece', in J. Boardman, J. Griffin and O. Murray (eds.), *The Oxford History of the Classical World*, Oxford: Oxford University Press, pp. 204–33

Myers, C. (1988) *Binding the Strong Man*, Maryknoll: Orbis

(1994) *Who Will Roll Away the Stone?* Maryknoll: Orbis

Nation, M. and Wells, S. (2000) *Faithfulness and Fortitude*, Edinburgh: T&T Clark

Niebuhr, H. R. (1961) *Radical Monotheism and Western Culture*, London: Faber

Norberg-Schulz, C. (1980) *Genius Loci*, New York: Rizzoli

Norman, E. (1979) *Christianity and the World Order*, Oxford: Oxford University Press

Northcotte, M. (1998) *Urban Theology, A Reader*, London: Cassell

Norton-Taylor, R. (1982) *Whose Land is it Anyway?* Wellingborough: Turnstone

Oberman, H. (1992) *The Dawn of the Reformation*, Edinburgh: T&T Clark

O'Hagan, A. (1999) 'Higher Hopes', *Guardian Weekend* (13 March)

O'Hear, A. (1998) 'The Myth of Nature', in A. Barnett and R. Scruton (eds.), *Town and Country*, London: Jonathan Cape, pp. 69–80

O'Neill, J. (1985) *Five Bodies: The Human Shape of Modern Society*, Ithaca: Cornell University Press

Ostwald, M. J. and Moore, R. J. (1998) *Disjecta Membra: The Architect, The Serial Killer, His Victim and Her Medical Examiner*, Sydney: Arcadia Press

Owens, E. J. (1991) *The City in the Greek and Roman World*, London: Routledge

Palladio, A. (1965) *The Four Books of Architecture*, New York: Dover

Panofsky, E. (1957) *Gothic Architecture and Scholasticism*, New York: Meridian

Papanek, V. (1995) *The Green Imperative*, London: Thames & Hudson

Pattison, G. (1998) *Art, Modernity and Faith*, London: SCM

Perlman, J. (1976) *The Myth of Marginality: Urban Poverty and Politics in Rio de Janeiro*, Berkeley: University of California Press

Pevsner, N. (1976) *History of Building Types*, Princeton: Princeton University Press

Pieris, A. (1988) *An Asian Theology of Liberation*, Edinburgh: T&T Clark

Pirenne, H. (1948) *Medieval Cities: Their Origins and the Revival of Trade*, Princeton: Princeton University Press

Postel, S. (1992) *The Last Oasis*, London: Earthscan

Pratt, G. (1998) 'Grids of Difference', in R. Fincher and J. M. Jacobs (eds.), *Cities of Difference*, New York: Guilford, pp. 26–48

Probyn, J. W. (ed.) (1881) *Systems of Land Tenure in Various Countries*, London: Cassell, Petter & Galpin

Quigley, D. (1995) 'Is a theory of caste still possible?', in M. Searle-Chatterjee and U. Sharma (eds.), *Contextualising Caste*, Oxford: Blackwell, pp. 25–48

Raban, J. (1974) *Soft City*, Glasgow: Collins

Rad, G. von (1966) *The Problem of the Hexateuch and other Essays*, Edinburgh: Oliver & Boyd

Rapoport, A. (1969) *House, Form and Culture*, New Jersey: Prentice Hall

(1982) *The Meaning of the Built Environment*, Tucson: University of Arizona Press

Rapport, N. (1993) *Diverse World Views in an English Village*, Edinburgh: Edinburgh University Press

Redfield, R. (1955) *The Little Community*, Chicago: University of Chicago Press (1956) *Peasant Society and Culture*, Chicago: University of Chicago Press

Rees, A. (1950) *Life in a Welsh Countryside*, Cardiff: University of Wales Press

Report of the Committee on Land Utilization in Rural Areas (Scott Report) (1942) London: HMSO

Richards, J. M. (1973) *Castles on the Ground: The Anatomy of Suburbia*, London: John Murray

Roberts, B. (1977) *Rural Settlement in Britain*, Folkestone: Dawson

Robertson, J. (1998) *Transforming Economic Life*, Totnes: Green Books

Rodger, A. (1994) 'Sustainable development, energy policy issues and greenhouse', in R. Samuels and D. Prasad (eds.), *Global Warming and the Built Environment*, London: Spon, pp. 85–111

Rowell, A. (1996) *Green Backlash*, London: Routledge

Rowland, C. and Vincent, J. (eds.) (1997) *Gospel from the City*, Sheffield: Urban Theology Unit

Rybczynski, W. (1988) *Home*, London: Heinemann

Sabine, G. (ed.) (1965) *The Works of Gerrard Winstanley*, New York: Russell & Russell

Sale, K. (1980) *Human Scale*, London: Secker & Warburg

Samuels, R. and Prasad, D. (eds.) (1994) *Global Warming and the Built Environment*, London: Spon

Sandercock, L. (1998) *Towards Cosmopolis*, Chichester: John Wiley

Sanneh, L. (1993) *Encountering the West*, London: Marshall Pickering

Sassen, S. (1991) *The Global City*, Princeton: Princeton University Press

Saunders, P. (1990) *A Nation of Homeowners*, London: Unwin Hyman

Scarry, E. (1985) *The Body in Pain*, Oxford: Oxford University Press

Schall, J. V. (ed.) (1982) *Liberation Theology in Latin America*, San Francisco: Ignatius Press

Schama, S. (1996) *Landscape and Memory*, London: Fontana

Schumacher, E. F. (1973) *Small is Beautiful*, London: Sphere

Schwartz, R. (1958) *The Church Incarnate*, Chicago: Chicago University Press

Scott, T. (1986) *Freiburg and the Breisgau: Town–Country Relations in the Age of the Reformation and Peasants' War*, Oxford: Clarendon Press

Scruton, R. (1999) 'Cold Comfort Towns', *The Times* (30 January)

Seabrook, J. (1971) *City Close-Up*, Harmondsworth: Penguin (1996) *In the Cities of the South*, London: Verso

Searle-Chatterjee, M. and Sharma, U. (1995) *Contextualising Caste*, Oxford: Blackwell

Sedgwick, P. (ed.) (1995) *God in the City: Essays and Reflections from the Archbishop's Urban Theology Group*, London: Mowbray

Sennett, R. (1970) *The Uses of Disorder*, New York: Norton (1990) *The Conscience of the Eye*, New York: Norton (1994) *Flesh and Stone*, London: Faber

Sharp, T. (1932) *Town and Countryside*, Oxford: Oxford University Press
   (1940) *Town Planning*, Harmondsworth: Penguin
   (1953) 'The English Village', in T. Sharp, F. Gibberd and W. Holford, *Design in Town and Village*, London: HMSO, pp. 11–21
Sharp, T., Gibberd, F. and Holford, W. (1953) *Design in Town and Village*, London: HMSO
Sherlock, H. (1998) 'Repairing our Much Abused Cities', in M. Jenks, E. Burton and K. Williams (eds.), *The Compact City: A Sustainable Urban Form?*, London: Routledge, pp. 289–301
Shoard, M. (1997) *This Land is Our Land*, London: Gaia
Short, J. R. (1996) *The Urban Order*, Oxford: Blackwell
Shorter, A. (1991) *The Church in the African City*, Maryknoll: Orbis
Shucksmith, M. (1990) *Housebuilding in Britain's Countryside*, London: Routledge
Sibley, D. (1995) *Geographies of Exclusion*, London: Routledge
Silverstone, R. (ed.) (1997) *Visions of Suburbia*, London: Routledge
Simon, J. (1981) *The Ultimate Resource*, Princeton: Princeton University Press
Simson, O. von (1956) *The Gothic Cathedral*, London: Routledge and Kegan Paul
Sinclair, A. (1992) 'Social Integration and Creation of New Urban Activities', in *The Improvement of the Built Environment and Social Integration in Cities*, Luxembourg: Office for Official Publications of the European Communities, pp. 221–8
Sitte, C. (1965) *City Planning According to Artistic Principles*, London: Phaidon
Skinner, R. J. and Rodell, M. J. (eds.) (1983) *People, Poverty and Shelter: Problems of Self-Help Housing in the Third World*, London: Methuen
Smith, M., Whiteleg, J. and Williams, N. (1998) *Greening the Built Environment*, London: Earthscan
Smyth, H. (1998) 'Running the Gauntlet', in M. Jenks, E. Burton and K. Williams (eds.), *The Compact City: A Sustainable Urban Form?*, London: Routledge, pp. 101–13
Soja, E. (1989) *Postmodern Geographies*, London: Verso
   (1996) *Thirdspace*, Oxford: Blackwell
Soleri, P. (1969) *Arcology: The City in the Image of Man*, Boston, Mass.: MIT Press
Soper, K. (1995) *What is Nature?* Oxford: Blackwell
Spain, D. (1992) *Gendered Spaces*, Chapel Hill: University of North Carolina Press
Sparks, O. B. (2000) 'From Eden to Jerusalem', *Interpretation* 54/1 (January 2000), pp. 45–53
Stretton, H. (1976) *Capitalism, Socialism and the Environment*, Cambridge: Cambridge University Press
Sykes, S. (2000) 'Spirituality and Mental Sickness', in M. Nation and S. Wells (eds.), *Faithfulness and Fortitude*, Edinburgh: T&T Clark, pp. 59–82
Teilhard de Chardin, P. (1967) *Le Milieu Divin*, Glasgow: Collins
Thomas, K. (1984) *Man and the Natural World*, Harmondsworth: Penguin
Thomas, L. and Cousins, W. (1998) 'The Compact City: A Successful, Desirable and Achievable Urban Form?', in M. Jenks, E. Burton and K. Williams (eds.), *The Compact City: A Sustainable Urban Form?*, London: Routledge, pp. 53–65

Thomas, M. M. (1966) *The Christian Response to the Asian* Revolution, London: SCM

Thompson, E. P. (1980) *Writing by Candlelight*, London: Verso

Thompson, F. (1954) *Lark Rise to Candleford*, Oxford: Oxford University Press

Thompson, F. M. L. (1982) *The Rise of Suburbia*, Leicester: Leicester University Press

Thorns, D. (1976) *The Quest for Community*, London: Allen & Unwin

Tillich, P. (1989) *On Art and Architecture*, New York: Crossroad

Tönnies, F. (1963) *Community and Society*, tr. C. Loomis, New York: Harper & Row

Town and Country Planning Association (1944), *Country Towns in the Future England*, London: Faber & Faber

Troy, P. (1998) 'Environmental Stress and Urban Policy', in M. Jenks, E. Burton and K. Williams (eds.), *The Compact City: A Sustainable Urban Form?*, London: Routledge, pp. 200–12

Turner, J. (1965) 'Lima's Barriadas and Corralones: suburbs versus slums', *Ekistics* 19, pp. 152–5

Turner, J. F. C. (1976) *Housing by People*, London: Marion Boyars
    (1982) 'Issues in Self-Help and Self-Managed Housing', in P. Ward (ed.), *Self-Help Housing: A Critique*, London: Mansell, pp. 99–113

Turner, J. F. C. and Fichter, R. (1972) *Freedom to Build: Dweller Control of the Housing Process*, London: Macmillan

Union of Concerned Scientists (1996), *World Scientists' Warning to Humanity*, Cambridge, Mass.: MIT

Vance, J. E., Jnr, (1990) *The Continuing City*, Baltimore: Johns Hopkins University Press

Veblen, T. (1994) *The Theory of the Leisure Class*, New York: Dover

Vincent, J. (1997) 'An Urban Hearing for the Gospel', in C. Rowland and J. Vincent (eds.), *Gospel from the City*, Sheffield: Urban Theology Unit, pp. 105–16

Vitruvius (1914) *The Ten Books of Architecture*, tr. M. Morgan, Cambridge, Mass.: Harvard University Press

Wackernagel, M. and Rees, W. (1996) *Our Ecological Footprint*, Gabriola Island: New Society

Waller, P. J. (1983) *Town, City and Nation: England 1850–1914*, Oxford: Oxford University Press

Wallman, S. (1993) 'Reframing Context', in A. Cohen and K. Fukui (eds.), *Humanising the City? Social Contexts of Urban Life at the Turn of the Millennium*, Edinburgh: Edinburgh University Press, pp. 52–65

Ward, C. (1983) *Housing: An Anarchist Approach*, London: Freedom
    (1985) *When We Build Again*, London: Pluto
    (1993) *New Town, Home Town*, London: Gulbenkian
    (1996) *Talking to Architects*, London: Freedom

Ward, G. (2000) *Cities of God*, London: Routledge

Ward, P. (ed.) (1982) *Self-Help Housing: A Critique*, London: Mansell

Watson, S. and Austerberry, H. (1986) *Housing and Homelessness: A Feminist Perspective*, London: Routledge

Webber, M. M. (1964) *Explorations into Urban Structure*, Pennsylvania: University of Pennsylvania Press

Weber, M. (1960) *The City*, London: Heinemann

Weizsacker, E. von, Lovins, A. and Lovins, L. (1997) *Factor Four*, London: Earthscan

White, L. (1967) 'The historical roots of our ecological crisis', *Science* 155/3767 (March 1967), pp. 1203–7

White, L. M. (1990) *Building God's House in the Roman World: Architectural Adaptation among Pagans, Jews and Christians*, Baltimore: Johns Hopkins University Press

White, M. and White, L. (1977) *The Intellectual Versus the City: From Thomas Jefferson to Frank Lloyd Wright*, Oxford: Oxford University Press

Wightman, A. (1996) *Who Owns Scotland*, Edinburgh: Canongate

Willey, B. (1940) *The Eighteenth Century Background*, London: Chatto & Windus

Williams, R. (1976) *Keywords*, London: Fontana
  (1985) *The Country and the City*, London: Hogarth
  (1989) *Resources of Hope*, London: Verso

Williams, W. (1956) *The Sociology of an English Village: Gosforth*, London: Routledge and Kegan Paul

Willmer, H. (1989) 'Images of the City and the Shaping of Humanity', in A. Harvey (ed.), *Theology in the City*, London: SPCK, pp. 32–46

Wingo, L. (1963) *Cities and Space: The Future Use of Urban Land*, Baltimore: Johns Hopkins University Press

Wink, W. (1984) *Naming the Powers*, Minneapolis: Fortress
  (1986) *Unmasking the Powers*, Minneapolis: Fortress
  (1992) *Engaging the Powers*, Minneapolis: Fortress

Winstanley, G. (1989) *Selected Writings*, London: Aporia

Wolf-Steger, A. (1998) 'Gegen den Ausverkauf des Landes', *Texte und Kontexte*, 80 4/98, pp. 5–14

Wollstonecraft, M. (1889) *Letters written during a Short Residence in Sweden, Norway and Denmark*, London

Wolterstorff, N. (1997) *Art in Action*, Carlisle: Solway

Woods, E. M. (1995) *Democracy against Capitalism: Renewing historical materialism*, Cambridge: Cambridge University Press

Young, I. M. (1990) *Justice and the Politics of Difference*, Princeton: Princeton University Press

Index of names

Abbot, J., 188
Abelard, 142
Adams, John, 225
Alberti, L., 152n., 205, 214
Alcaeus, 171
Anselm, 152n.
Aquinas, Thomas, 1, 6, 18, 20, 41f., 44, 142,
    195
Archer, John, 7
Aristotle, 66, 128, 147, 155, 160, 166, 170,
    171, 197
Ashby, A. W., 123f.
Auerbach, Eric, 12f.
Augustine, 5, 9, 10, 18, 25, 92, 141, 195, 196
Austerberry, H., 81n.
Avila, Charles, 67

Bachelard, Gaston, 85, 86, 89, 100
Bahro, Rudolf, 200, 231, 236, 237, 246,
    259
Baker, W. P., 123, 169n., 207n.
Ball, John, 53
Ballinger, J., 108
Balthasar, Hans Urs von, 2–4
Barker, Paul, 134
Barnet, R., 160
Barrett, G., 158n.
Barth, Karl, 1, 2, 4, 8, 13, 15, 16, 19, 20, 21, 29,
    39, 40, 42, 43, 45f., 115, 136, 216, 250
Basil of Caesarea, 67
Bater, J. H., 116
Baum, Gregory, 184
Bauman, Zygmunt, 165, 182, 244, 245
Belloc, Hilaire, 50
Benevolo, L., 11
Benjamin, Walter, 96
Bennett, E. N. 125, 168
Bergmann, Sigurd, 17
Bewick, Thomas, 61
Bhaba, Homi, 18n.
Blake, William, 7n., 19, 112, 187, 260

Bloch, Ernst, 4n., 93, 105n., 211n., 244, 247,
    249, 260
Boff, Leonardo, 20n., 222n.
Boge, Stephanie, 226
Bogucki, Peter, 51n.
Bonhoeffer, Dietrich, 13, 20
Bookchin, Murray, 153, 184
Boyes, Georgina, 125n.
Bradstock, Andrew, 67
Branford, V., 91n.
Braudel, Fernand, 123, 128, 130, 160
Breheny, M., 53
Brook, Peter, 36
Brown, Peter, 146, 162
Brown, W. P., 116
Brueggemann, Walter, 35, 36, 38, 54, 64, 65,
    69, 73
Buber, Martin, 45
Burton, Elizabeth, 224
Burton, T., 157

Calvin, 1
Campbell, George, 56n.
Carroll, J. T., 116
Cassell, D., 108
Castells, Manuel, 23, 34, 108, 154, 159, 233,
    241, 246, 250, 253, 255–60
Castles, S., 165, 166
Cavanagh, J., 160
Chrysostom, John, 66, 141
Church, G., 213, 214
Churchill, Winston, 115n.
Clarke, P., 126
Cohen, Antony, 178, 257
Cole, I., 99
Coleman, Alice, 78, 98, 100, 174
Commoner, Barry, 229
Cook, J., 92, 111n., 230, 257
Corbusier, C. Le, 32, 99, 101, 110, 155, 173,
    196n., 204n., 212, 213, 215, 224
Cousins, W., 156

275

Index of subjects

accumulation, primitive, *see* primitive
  accumulation
Acts of Thomas, 87
aesthetics, 110, 116, 193ff., 243f.
  city, 211f.
  community, 216
  Gothic, 196
  suburbs, 208ff.
  village, 206f.
apocalyptic, 16, 223, 224, 228, 259
art, 193ff.
attention, 200
autonomous house, *see* house, autonomous

Bauhaus, 93, 244
beauty, 105ff., 197, 198
building, monumental, 95ff.

Calcutta, 30
Catholic Social Teaching, 2
Chandigarh, 173
Christology, 184, 189, 248; *see also* God
Church, 185ff., 248ff., 252ff.
city, 138ff.
  as art, 193ff.
  carceral, 177, 214
  compact, 156
  creativity of, 149
  dialectic of, 140f.
  Edge, 134ff., 161; *see also* Edge Cities
  future of, 159f.
  Garden, 131f., 205
  global, 159
  Hellenistic, 161
  and innovation, 150
  nursery of virtues, 147f.
  secular, 15
  Soviet, 213
  sustainable, 152ff.
  see also aesthetics, city; community and
    city

colour, 197
common ownership, 65
common purpose, 190
Community, 163ff.
  aesthetics of, 216f.
  and church, 185ff.
  and city, 170f.
  fragmentation of, 165
  and suburbs, 178ff.
  and village, 166
  see also aesthetics, community
council housing, 165ff.
counter urbanisation, 126f., 155
country, 121ff.; *see also* theology of countryside;
    nature; pastoral
creation, 5, 14, 18, 48, 107ff., 196f., 202ff.

Deuteronomy, 36, 56
Discernment, 166
Diversity, 256ff.

Edge Cities, 134ff., 138, 161
education, 113, 200, 242, 243ff.
empowerment, 94, 101, 104, 252ff.
enchantedness, 257ff.
environment, 107ff., 158, 217
environmental crisis, 152f., 222ff.,
    231ff.
Epistle to Diognetus, 63, 76
eschatology, 16, 118, 192, 249, 254
ethics, 1ff., 17, 76ff., 191, 222ff., 242ff.
eucharist, 18
existentialism, 12
exterminism, 222

feminism, 32, 73, 81, 83; *see also* space,
    gendered
form, 194ff., 199

Garden Cities, *see* City, Garden
Gemeinschaft, 164, 175

space (*cont.*)
  Trinitarian mapping of, 48ff.
  see also God, spatiality of
Spirit, 114, 161, 201, 243; *see also* God, Trinity
spirituality, 22f., 140, 161, 216, 237,
    243
stakeholder economy, 69; *see also nahalah*
Stevenage, 187
Stockholm, 158
Stoicism, 41
suburbs, 101ff., 149, 178ff., 208f.
sustainability, 107ff., 152f., 156f., 190

taste, 116
telecommuting, 155
theocracy, 6
theology
  and aesthetics, 193
  of city, 138ff.
  of community, 163ff.
  of countryside, 114ff.
  and environmental crisis, 222

of everyday life, 1 ff.
of house, 79ff.
of land, 50ff.
of space, 26ff.
of towns, 114ff.
  see also liberation theology
tower blocks, 99
towns, 114ff.
  and country, 115f.
  function of, 127ff.
  New 186
  and redemption, 130
tradition, 8ff., 187
traffic, 220, 225, 227
transport, 23, 158f.
Trinity, 4ff., 8f., 16f., 24, 43, 47, 48ff., 76ff.,
    114, 183; *see also* God

vernacular, *see* house, vernacular
village, 123ff., 166ff., 206f.

Yagua Indians, 36